Abject Pleasures in the Cinematic

Abject Pleasures in the Cinematic

The Beautiful, Sexual Arousal, and Laughter

Aaron Kerner

EDINBURGH
University Press

Edinburgh University Press is one of the leading university presses in the UK. We publish academic books and journals in our selected subject areas across the humanities and social sciences, combining cutting-edge scholarship with high editorial and production values to produce academic works of lasting importance. For more information visit our website: edinburghuniversitypress.com

© Aaron Kerner, 2023, 2024

Edinburgh University Press Ltd
13 Infirmary Street
Edinburgh EH1 1LT

First published in hardback by Edinburgh University Press 2023

Typeset in 12 on 14pt Arno Pro and Myriad Pro
by Cheshire Typesetting Ltd, Cuddington, Cheshire

A CIP record for this book is available from the British Library

ISBN 978 1 3995 0110 1 (hardback)
ISBN 978 1 3995 0111 8 (paperback)
ISBN 978 1 3995 0112 5 (webready PDF)
ISBN 978 1 3995 0113 2 (epub)

The right of Aaron Kerner to be identified as author of this work has been asserted in accordance with the Copyright, Designs and Patents Act 1988 and the Copyright and Related Rights Regulations 2003 (SI No. 2498).

Contents

List of Figures vi
Acknowledgments vii
Preface ix

1 Abject Pleasures in the Cinematic: A Taxonomy of Cinematic Strategies for Eliciting Pleasure 1

PART 1
2 On the Beautiful 39
3 Neo-Giallo: "It's beautiful, it's beautiful, it's beautiful," the Affective Experience in *Suspiria* 57
4 Musicality: Poetic Ruptures in Spike Lee's *25th Hour*, and Chris Cunningham/Björk's Music Video "All Is Full of Love" 76

PART 2
5 On Sexual Arousal 107
6 Pornography: Erotic Disavowal, Regressive Content, and the Chikan (Sub-)Genre 130
7 Romance: *The Handmaiden* and its Arousing Spectacles 160

PART 3
8 On Laughter 189
9 Body Humor: Dick Pics in Cringe Comedy and the Carnivalesque Grotesque Body 205
10 Conclusion: The Limitation of Theories of Affect 235

Bibliography 260
Media-ography 276
Index 280

Figures

3.1	*Suspiria*, Luca Guadagnino, 2018	68
4.1	*25th Hour*, Spike Lee, 2002; *Assassination Nation*, Sam Levinson, 2018; *Do the Right Thing*, Spike Lee, 1989	85
4.2	*Björk: All Is Full of Love*, Chris Cunningham, 1999; *The Handmaiden*, Chan-wook Park, 2016	97
5.1	*Björk: All Is Full of Love*, Chris Cunningham, 1999; *The Wayward Cloud*, Ming-liang Tsai, 2005	124
6.1	*Married Teacher Molester Train*, Kanie, 2015	143
7.1	*Salò, or the 120 Days of Sodom*, Pier Paolo Pasolini, 1975; *The Handmaiden*, Chan-wook Park, 2016	165
7.2	*The Hunger*, Tony Scott, 1983; *The Handmaiden*, Chan-wook Park, 2016	170
7.3	*The Hunger*, Tony Scott, 1983; *The Handmaiden*, Chan-wook Park, 2016	172
7.4	*The Handmaiden*, Chan-wook Park, 2016	178
9.1	*What if men harassed women IRL like they do online?* Miranda King, 2016	209
9.2	"Ricky Berwick," John Elerick and James Patton, *Tosh.0*, Comedy Central, Season 9, Episode 11, June 6, 2017	226
9.3	"Ricky Berwick," John Elerick and James Patton, *Tosh.0*, Comedy Central, Season 9, Episode 11, June 6, 2017	226
10.1	Kerner Sense Survey	247
10.2	Kerner Sense Survey responses to a screening of Chan-wook Park's 2013 *Stoker* (Spring 2019)	249
10.3	Kerner Sense Survey responses to a screening of Chan-wook Park's 2013 *Stoker* (Spring 2019)	252
10.4	Kerner Sense Survey responses to a screening of Chan-wook Park's 2013 *Stoker* (Spring 2019)	254

Acknowledgements

Many people have helped with the present book, whether indirectly with emotional support or materially by directly contributing to the ideas presented herein, not least of which my family—Aki, Axl, and Anders. Assuredly I have unintentionally overlooked some, but to be sure there are many named and unnamed that have helped in some fashion.

Brent Malin, at the University of Pittsburgh, formerly a colleague of mine at San Francisco State University, assisted in my efforts to work out the affective elements related to music, specifically Thom Yorke's score for *Suspiria*. I am hopelessly ill-equipped when it comes to music theory, or notation, and any vague intelligence related to my discussions of music likely stems from Malin. Any errors are mine.

Katie Morrissey, a former (and much missed) colleague, offered many insights on the romance genre and generously humored my naïve and lengthy emails.

My colleague Rosa Park took the time to read an earlier draft of my chapters on the beautiful and musicality. I want to thank her for her encouragement—we have affinities with one another in our shared interest in the affecting power of sound.

There were a handful of people that were willing to share their work with me. Maria Belodubrovskaya kindly shared her article, "The Cine-Fist: Eisenstein's Attractions, Mirror Neurons, and Contemporary Action Cinema." Similarly, Alexia Kannas graciously shared her article, "All the colours of the dark: Film genre and the Italian *giallo*." David Church, a former student, and now prolific writer and the go-to-guy on all things related to cult cinema and fan-cultures, kindly shared his book *Disposable Passions: Vintage Pornography and the Material Legacies of Adult Cinema*. Malcolm Turvey, also very kindly shared his article, "Mirror Neurons and Film Studies: A Cautionary Tale from a Serious Pessimist," and subsequently indulged me in an exchange of ideas via email (even though we have different opinions).

I want to thank my Fall 2020 CINE720 Critical Paradigms and the Cinematic graduate seminar that read early drafts of my chapters. This was a valuable exercise, from which I learned a great deal, and their insights contributed to the final shape of the present volume. Specific ideas attributed to some of my students are referenced in the book.

Our graduate student-led reading group, "Losing Atari," named for a YouTube closed captioning error for "Deleuze and Guattari," has been incredibly inspirational. I learned so much in this group. Graduate students selected texts to read, and we would meet once a week. It was a rugged group of true masochists—the first book we tackled was *A Thousand Plateaus*, and it only got worse (or better?) from there. A motto soon emerged from certain factions within the group, and I'll echo it here, "FUCK Deleuze."

As part of the Losing Atari group (or part of a class) we interviewed a number of individual scholars, and I want to thank them for their generosity: Martine Beugnet, Vittorio Gallese, Julian Hanich, Alexia Kannas, John Lechte, Susanna Paasonen, and Celine Parreñas Shimizu.

Particular thanks go to David Mai, one of my former MFA students. He is a contributing author to the conclusion of the present volume. He was also instrumental in helping me design and visualize my "Sense Survey" (discussed in the conclusion of this volume).

I want to express profound thanks to my tireless research assistant Birdy Wei-Ting Hung. She is also a contributing author to my concluding chapter, and is referenced at many points in the book, as I couldn't rightly claim some of the ideas as my own. I would still be writing the book to this very day if it were not for her. She was an amazing interlocutor, the inspiration for many ideas, and incredibly generous with her time and support.

Preface

Donald Trump intensified my compulsion to write this book. He singularly generated so much negativity—so much so that I was sickened by his voice and could not bear to listen to the news. I felt compelled to locate pleasure in the world, wherever it might be found. It's so easy to dwell on the negative, to find fault, or to wag the finger of discontent at the politically regressive. And no doubt, there's some of that in the present volume. It's in our disciplinary DNA to do that.

Although we, in the field of cinema and media studies, emphasize the visual, and we presume that the field of vision is the site of the aesthetic experience, more often than not, what's really responsible for eliciting pleasurable affects is the audio design, and specifically, music. We tend to take music and audio design for granted and ascribe the affective experience to the visual imagery. I wouldn't go so far as to say that the visual field is unimportant, most certainly it is. However, because of audio's lektonic basis, its physical properties (sound waves touch us), it wields the most potential to elicit an affective response.

Alas, I am completely ignorant of music. I never learned to play a musical instrument (though I always wanted to). I have no capacity to read sheet music, or identify notes, or any other such thing. And this handicapped my ability to do the very thing that I set out to do (at least at certain points in the volume). I'm hopelessly ill-equipped. I have, nevertheless, been especially interested in music and sensitive to its affective power. As a youngster (I got my first record when I was 10 years old—an album that I still own and play to this day), a brooding teen, and a twenty-something goth kid I could—and very often did—listen to the same track over and over. Nearly all of my discretionary money went to buying CDs, or going to live shows—Ice-T pointed his finger at me and said, "Stand up motherfucker!" at the first Lollapalooza; at the same show Siouxsie Sioux singled me out, and gave me a hug that I will never forget (maybe she pitied me after the Ice-T incident?); my friends and I got an autograph from Robert Smith;

Johnny Lydon pulled a tampon out of his ass and threw it at us; and at a show on Halloween in 1991 I rushed the stage to hug Morrissey. (Just this year, I discovered that the Morrissey concert was filmed, and is available on YouTube. And reviewing the video, it was less a hug—which is how I recalled it—and more of a football tackle. Sorry SPM.[1]) I am certainly not alone in this, but music has been an important part of my life. While I could never verbalize, in technical terms, music had (and still has) the capacity to move me. Although I didn't have the capacity to point to anything specific, I would "know it when I heard it," to riff off Justice Potter Stewart's acknowledged inability to precisely define what is obscene. And this squarely hits upon the affective experience, how it is so difficult to name, and often is experienced as inexplicable and ephemeral. While I might play music to suit my mood (my emotional state), at the same time music has the capacity to produce a reflexive physiological affect—namely, goosebumps, tears. In some cases, I have sought assistance with how to grapple with the music and audio design.

I acknowledge that I am writing from a position of privilege. Privilege that comes in many guises and facets. Not least of which is my position as a tenured full professor. And thus, I am afforded some leeway in my choice of subjects, examples to examine, tone, and diction. In some of my discussions about the present volume, and when I have sought suggestions of cinematic material to consider, some (with the best intentions) have offered the usual suspects from the annals of cinematic history. But often what I have found is that the suggestions that have been offered speak to the mind, not to the body. I am explicitly interested in the visceral, how our body responds to cinematic material, and more often than not the cinematic "greats" address the mind. Of course, this is not always the case, there are some "classic" films that elicit a truly visceral response. And please do not take this to mean that I am dismissing cinematic history and the great filmmakers that our discipline elects to celebrate. The present volume is not concerned with what we might call "intellectually beautiful," what Kant would characterize as "agreeable," which is different from the beautiful. That is not my focus here. I suppose I am "puritanical" in my scope: What gives us goosebumps, what gives us a hard-on or makes us wet, what bends us over with laughter? This is the focus of the present volume—without apology, and in celebration of cinematic pleasures no matter where they are found!

Note

1 "Morrissey – Live At The Shoreline Amphitheatre (31st October, 1991)," Morrissey posted to YouTube, May 22, 2020, accessed January 20, 2022. https://youtu.be/5WM28fb0248?t=1891.

1

Abject Pleasures in the Cinematic
A Taxonomy of Cinematic Strategies for Eliciting Pleasure

Introduction: Affect and Emotion

This book strives to locate pleasurable affects stemming from abject content, with a particular focus on the cinematic strategies that—even despite the content—wields the capacity to elicit strong pleasurable feelings. In short, how does the cinema make us feel good even when that content is resolutely crass, politically problematic, or deeply unethical? The affective experience is frequently disavowed or figured as a distraction from the "true value" of the cinematic—its meaning. Our disciplinary DNA compels us to analyze the cinematic to locate meanings, and thus, to reveal the "message" that it harbors. That is to say its cultural significance, its ideological message, or disentangling plot complexities to reveal what the narrative "really means." And this is not to suggest that (narrative) meaning and affect are in opposition to one another necessarily—often an affective experience is intended to enhance narrative meanings—nevertheless, they are different forms of stimulus, processed in their own way, and thus require different paradigms of assessment.

And there most certainly are political ramifications for overlooking the affecting experience, as the human experience is not governed by rationality alone, rather we are perhaps just as likely to make determinations based on a feeling. As we might say in colloquial terms, "It was a gut decision."[1] While there is a knee-jerk progressive proclivity within our discipline, affect pledges no allegiance to any particular political inclination. Neither progressives nor progressive content hold a monopoly on affect. The beautiful—which is different from the agreeable, or the pleasant—has no inherent bond to the good (that is, the morally good, or that with cultural merit), rather it is an affective experience, and it might come to us in the most unlikely and unsavory places. While porn studies often champions "alternative" pornographic productions, what Tristan Taormino dubs "organic, [or] fair-trade porn,"[2] porn with the most regressive content nevertheless wields the possibility to be sexually arousing even despite our own ethical objections. While well-intended academics routinely claim that watching people get hurt is not funny, and we might appreciate the gesture to cultivate our better angels, such assertions do not always align with reality. Moreover, we laugh for many reasons, including as a defensive gesture to ward off disgust, or the abject.

To be abundantly clear, what I am interested in is the power of the cinematic to elicit visceral experiences—a sudden flush of goosebumps or tears (as prompted by the beautiful), reflexive sexual arousal, and laughter. How does the cinematic stimulate the body and its senses? And this should not be confused with the emotional appeal of the cinematic. Where emotion relates to nameable feelings—such as happiness, enjoyment, sadness, frustration—affect, on the other hand, pertains to the ineffable visceral sensate experience. Emotions are the product of cinematic meanings, or in other words, the narrative. The thrill of witnessing the coupling of characters after the narrative ruble has been cleared to make room for that long-delayed kiss. Or the sadness prompted by the dashing of all hope that our couple will ever come back together again. Either way, emotions stem from our comprehension of the cinematic narrative. Affect is altogether different, because it is frequently born from cinematic form, often manifesting in style, and potentially elicits those inexplicable viscerally felt experiences. There are no affective narratives as such, no affective films, rather affect strikes like lightning—sudden, instantaneous, a fleeting moment, and just as suddenly gone. Where emotions are prompted by an encounter with a narrative, affect, on the other hand, is potentially divorced from meanings, from narrative content, and rather is symptomatic of how that narrative is presented. In other words, cinematic form. And to be clear, I use the term "cinematic" to refer to moving audio-visual material across mediums—from theatrically released films to videogames. That is to say material that utilizes the various audio-visual strategies associated with the cinematic arts—from diegetic and non-diegetic sound design to all the various techniques employed in cinematography, through to the vast array of post-production techniques that can be applied to audio-visual content.

Some might imagine that my parsing of affect and emotions is too stringent, that these might be too hard to cleave apart. And that would be true if I took affect and emotion at face value, applying these terms according to their colloquial conception. But I follow Brian Massumi's lead here; he too observes that affect is often too loosely used "as a synonym for emotion." Rather, for Massumi, affects "follow different logics and pertain to different orders." While affect and emotion relate to the subject's feelings, emotion, as stated previously, relates to a namable experience. As Massumi says, emotions refer to a fixed sociolinguistic experience—a culturally shared understanding of a feeling. "Emotion is qualified intensity," Massumi argues, "the conventional, consensual point of insertion of intensity into semantically and semiotically formed progressions, into narrativizable action-reaction circuits, into function and meaning." In other words, a namable feeling. "It is intensity owned and recognized." Massumi finally adds, "It is crucial to theorize the difference between affect and emotion." This, in part, is the implicit objective of the present volume. And this is not to suggest that there is always some hard and fast division between affect and emotion, because clearly there are instances when emotions are coupled with a strong visceral charge. And it is possible to conceive affect as something like a "pre-emotional" experience, where an affective experience might be retrospectively framed as a coded emotion, where, for example, "reflexive" sexual arousal might be cognized as amorous feelings for a lover. Nonetheless, each of these experiences is distinct enough, each demands concentrated attention. More often than not though, affect has gotten the short end of the stick precisely because it is an ephemeral subjective experience. Affect is in a sense "reflexive," a paroxysm beyond our cognition, it is something that we might say happens to us, as opposed to belonging to us, or as Massumi says, affect "is not ownable or recognizable and is thus resistant to critique."[3]

Sara Ahmed argues against this position, noting that in our lived-experience affect and emotion for all intents and purposes are synonymous. Ahmed contends that the sensorial body is an overdetermined site where stimulus is apprehended by a multiplicity of processing systems. "It is through the recognition or interpretation of sensations, which are responses to the impressions of objects and others, that bodily surfaces take shape." Ahmed urges, in this instance echoing Massumi's main contention, "that emotions are [not] the same thing as sensations," Ahmed however qualifies this by arguing that "the very intensity of perception often means a slide from one to another, as a slide that does follow as a sequence in time. Hence whilst sensation and emotion are irreducible, they cannot simply be separated at the level of lived experience."[4] In effect, no sooner are we affected, than we begin to narrativize, contextualize, attribute meanings. I am not totally predisposed to dismissing this position, indeed, in our day-to-day experience we often attribute meanings to the sensate experience—this gentle caress which elicits goosebumps means she loves me, this laughter means this character has committed some social *faux pas*. At the same time, it does not automatically follow that we should surrender to the apparent indistinguishability between affect and emotion. And perhaps—exactly because of this presumption regarding the homogeneity of affect and emotion—it stresses the need for a careful parsing of emotion and affect. Furthermore, even in our day-to-day experience, we very well might encounter affective experiences that are "orphaned," where we might not be capable of contextualizing or attributing meanings or an emotion to a visceral sensation.

Eric Shouse adds further that "it is important not to confuse affect with feelings and emotions." Citing Massumi's definition of affect/affection in his translator's introduction to Deleuze and Guattari's *A Thousand Plateaus*, Massumi states that neither affect or affection "denotes a personal feeling."[5] That is not to suggest that affects are not personally felt, but we do not own the affective experience. We might, for example, say "I am sad." This is to own the feeling of sadness as a commonly understood emotion. But we do not say, "I am goosebumps." "Feelings are personal and biographical, emotions are social, and affects are prepersonal," Shouse adds.[6]

Furthermore, emotion is durational. We can speak of a "happy movie," or a "sad movie," and such a characterization identifies a particular lasting emotional quality. But in colloquial speech we might also conflate affect and emotion. We might for example characterize a film as a "beautiful movie," but what is often meant by this is that it was an agreeable, pleasing, or good film. We can also speak of a "funny movie," but what we usually mean by this is that it provided multiple instances of laughter. The same might be said of a "steamy movie," where there are localized instances that are affecting, as opposed to a generalized enduring mood. In the context of the present book though, I am often referring to these localized and isolated moments within the cinematic. Affect—per our interest in the present volume (the beautiful, sexual arousal, laughter)—unlike emotion, is an instant, a single moment, ephemeral. Trying to identify specific affecting moments is like sand running through one's fingers. Emotion, on the other hand, builds as a response to a narrative situation, often leading to a final instance—a final mood, or an overall generalized feeling, a lingering impression.

Additionally, the affective experience is inherently subjective, making it a particularly challenging subject of analysis. And on a related matter, here are the various criticisms that will predictably be levied against the present volume: (1) affect is too subjective to submit to a genuinely rigorous scholarly analysis, (2) what is the body here? (3) whose body? (4) who is the implied spectator? and (5) an exclusive focus on affect surrenders all ethical obligations.[7] Regarding the latter, it is essential to recognize that no ideological perspective has a monopoly on affect. As a felt bodily experience, an experience that is independent of cognitive processes, it stands outside ethical regimes. As Gregory J. Seigworth and Melissa Greg observe, "As much as we sometimes might want to believe that affect is highly invested in us and with somehow magically providing for a better tomorrow, as if affect were always already sutured into a progressive or liberatory politics or at least the marrow of our best angels, as if affect were somehow producing always better states of being and belonging—affect instead bears an intense and thoroughly immanent neutrality."[8] Regarding my conception of the body, whose body, and the like, frankly, I take a naïve approach to the conception of the body, a body that is equally affected by a cold winter morning, or an amazing live-performance of an aria—either of which might give us goosebumps. While a chilly morning is an innate biological response, an aesthetic experience (in response to an aria for instance) is an inherently subjective biological experience; it is not unique or individual, though the visceral experience of the flesh and blood body is a commonly shared experience. The human species continues to make beautiful or affecting music precisely because it feels good. Does it always elicit intense bodily responses such as welling up with tears, or running flush with goosebumps? No. Of course not. Will it be experienced in the same way by others? Assuredly not. Does the pornographic elicit a strong affective charge? Quite probably (if we are honest with ourselves). Does it affect everyone in exactly the same way? Of course not. While some might become aroused, others might laugh, gag or avert their gaze in disgust, or even shrug with ennui. When we witness some epic fail that involves some grievous bodily injury, will all spectators reflexively laugh? No. Of course not. Are these commonly shared experiences? Yes, indeed they are. What then are the shared traits of the cinematic material that speak to this commonly shared affective experience? That is what I am pursuing here.

Our discipline fetishizes cinematic meanings and tends to disavow the affective experience. General filmgoers, on the other hand, are not always intent upon locating meanings, as the financially successful Hollywood tentpole films appear to indicate—think for instance of the *Transformers* franchise, or the Marvel universe. Based on box-office success, in fact, the general filmgoer is not looking for (profound) narrative meanings, rather by this measure it seems that spectators are far more invested in the "untamed attractions" that appeal to the visceral experience. And let us not forget that one of the most trafficked forms of cinematic material over the Internet is pornography. The pornographic genre is generally consumed for its potential to elicit an affective response; and, in fact, narrative ostensibly frustrates the affective intent of the genre.[9] "If porn has an aesthetic dimension," Brian McNair posits (and his use of "aesthetic" is significant—aesthetic meaning the stimulation of the senses), "it lies in the extent to which a text succeeds in its erotic ambitions—a quality largely independent of such elements as plot, script, character development, or production design."[10] Susanna Paasonen adds to this, "Good pornography is whatever turns on its viewers, gives rise to carnal resonance, and moves the bodies of those watching."[11] In 2019, 42 billion people visited the Pornhub site (a popular online distribution platform for pornographic content). Summarizing Pornhub statistics in a *Forbes* article, this amounts "to 115 million [visits] per day . . . In data storage terms, that's 723,041 GB transferred per hour. Every minute on Pornhub saw 80,032 visits, 77,861 searches . . . and 219,985 video views."[12] And to place this in further perspective, this traffic only accounts for visits to the Pornhub site and does not account for other similar video sharing sites, Google searches, or other online distribution networks. (Throughout the present volume I reference a number of porn scholars, from Linda Williams to the afore mentioned Paasonen and contributors to Celine Parreñas Shimizu's co-edited volume *The Feminist Porn Book*, as well as a host of others from outside the discipline of media studies.)

Nonetheless, cinematic and media scholars, as if governed by some unspoken imperative to locate meanings within the cinematic "text," intend to "save" a film by, as Carl Plantinga says, "lifting it up," and to recontextualize it within "some kind of brief philosophical treatise, and take the implication of that treatise as the purpose of the film, or at least as the locus of its true worth." And even in the field of porn studies, where the very objective of the subject of analysis is the affective experience, there often is an emphasis on locating cultural or political meanings (discussed further in the Arousal Section of this volume). Some film scholars, such as Vivian Sobchack and Steven Shaviro, though, as Susanna Paasonen notes in her examination of online porn, have been critical of the disciplinary resistance to the affective experience and "take seriously the visceral aspects of the media they have studied. As the embodied, sensory, and affective have been downplayed or even rendered invisible, cinema has been conceptualized in terms of language, narrative, and representation."[13] But something is robbed from the cinematic experience in that insistent bid to attribute meanings, because, as Plantinga notes, "this way of thinking about film diminishes the art form by reducing it to a bare bones propositional message."[14] The sensate encounter with the cinematic is ignored or overlooked at best, disavowed at the worst, in favor of some sort of meaning.

The prejudice against affect and emotion is deep-seated. The Western imagination has had a long-held suspicion of the body—the well-worn, and quite tired mind-body split. Christianity assimilated Platonic ideals and located sin within the body. The body and its senses are not to be trusted, something that must be "contained" by rational discourse (or religious/societal mandate). And this dovetails with our ingrained iconophobia, which is endemic to Western values. And thus, as Rosalind Galt identifies in her excellent book, *Pretty: Film and the Decorative Image*, our discipline privileges the gritty, unembellished, anti-pretty image as it harbors "true value," while "the pretty, by contrast, connotes the vacant, the unserious, and the false."[15] And this distrust has a long history. "When Plato turns to the question of beauty," Galt recounts, "he has harsh words for those he calls sight-lovers (*philotheamones*), consumers of culture who privilege images, colors, and fine things over philosophical knowledge." The Platonic situates the image, the visual field, as "closely related to the superficial and ungrounded, the sensual and trivial, and is opposed to the abstract truths of linguistic reason. In this model of the image, Plato lays the foundations for an iconoclasm that grounds much modern image theory." The affective experience is painted with a similar brush, as it bypasses the organ of reason and goes straight to the nervous system.[16]

Some though have questioned our Platonic inheritance. Contrary to the Platonic, the sensible is not an inferior form of knowledge Emmanuel Levinas argues, "Sensibility is enjoyment." We come to understand the external world (including the cinematic experience) not only through cognitive processes, but through our senses. Maurice Merleau-Ponty insists that our physical bodies are integral to our perception of the world. "In short, my body is not merely one object among all others, not a complex of sensible qualities among others." Rather, Merleau-Ponty adds that the body "is an object sensitive to all others, which resonates for all sounds, vibrates for all colors, and that provides words with their primordial signification through the manner in which it receives them.[17] We "feel" for our characters onscreen, and it is through the sensate (along with our cognitive faculties) that we "understand." We need to throw off the yoke of our Platonic distrust of the image and the sensate experience. Plantinga, similarly, surmises that there are a handful of reasons why cinematic and media studies have routinely ignored, or disavowed the affective experience: neo-Brechtian film theorists viewed material intended to elicit emotions with suspicion; sexism within the discipline devalued "emotions as feminine"; there has been an insistence on locating the "real" meanings of films in their (often hidden) ideological messages; and the "emotional experience as necessarily subjective and idiosyncratic" has been dismissed.[18]

Affect, the visceral, occupies a privileged position within this volume, not because I think it is necessarily more important than anything else (for example, the meaning of any given narrative, revealing the ideological message of a film), but rather because it is so often given short shrift. Moreover, it is not that affect is set in opposition to cognition, but a different kind of perception of the world, what Alfred North Whitehead has called "prehension." "We respond to things in the first place by feeling them," Steven Shaviro points out, summarizing Alfred North Whitehead's position, "it is only afterward that we identify, and cognize, what it is that we are feeling."[19] Whitehead privileges affect ("feeling" in his parlance) over cognition. "The 'affective tone' that suffuses every experience of perception both determines and exceeds cognition. We do not first perceive what is before us, and then respond emotionally to these perceptions," Shaviro relates. Rather, for Whitehead it is the reverse. "For 'the direct information to be derived from sense-perception wholly concerns the functionings of the animal body.' Perception is first of all a matter of being affected bodily." We experience the external world, and not simply through our cognitive faculties, but through the whole array of our sensorial systems. "Every perception or prehension thus provokes the body into 'adversion or aversion'—and this is already the 'subjective form' of the prehension."[20]

As I will discuss throughout the volume, the body can and does in fact betray us when it comes to the affective experience. The body is not governed by ethical regimes; intellectually we might think, "Oh, this is so wrong!" and at the same time laugh our asses off. Something similar very well might happen with the pornographic, where we might vocalize what we are "supposed to say," "The objectification of bodies is problematic here!" all the while eliciting biological reactions within our loins. Furthermore, readers expecting the present volume to level socio-political criticisms will likely be disappointed. This is not the intention of the volume. My unapologetic focus is on the visceral experience of the cinematic. This is not to suggest that socio-political interventions are unimportant. Rather, affect is often overlooked, because it is either conflated with emotion, or because it is disavowed or ignored altogether, and thus my intention is to place the visceral experience front and center. There have been numerous efforts to engage with the affective experience. The following section surveys some of the approaches to the affective potential in the cinematic.

Theories of Affect

The turn to affect is nothing new. Early film theorists discussed this very thing. Even our earliest accounts of the cinema suggest an affective experience: audiences leaping out of the way of an approaching train.

Sergei Eisenstein, as a film theorist and filmmaker, was very much interested in the visceral in what he termed "the montage of attractions." Tom Gunning, in turn, takes his cue from Eisenstein when he termed "the cinema of attractions" films that—prior to formal codification of cinematic narrativization—emphasized spectacles and outwardly addressed the audience. Maria Belodubrovskaya insists, however, that while there are some similarities between Eisenstein's and Gunning's conceptions of the attraction there were also significant differences. While the latter positions attractions as antithetical to narratives (or as "tamed attractions" that disrupt narrative progression), Eisenstein views the attraction as integral to the narrative, and the visceral response as the point of the narrative (to incite political action).[21]

In opposition to Dziga Vertov's kino-eye (or cine-eye), Eisenstein instead advanced the "cine-fist," in his 1925 article, "The Problem of the Materialist Approach to Form."[22] Eisenstein considered an attraction to be "any aggressive moment in theater, i.e., any element of it that subjects the audience to emotional [or sensual] and psychological influence, verified by experience and mathematically calculated to produce specific emotional shocks in the spectator in their proper order within the whole."[23] As Belodubrovskaya recounts, among "Eisenstein's examples of attractions was the set of techniques used at the Grand Guignol Theater, where, he wrote, 'eyes are gouged out or arms and legs are amputated on stage.'"[24] Thus, Belodubrovskaya discerns that, "An attraction [for Eisenstein] was any stimulus capable of producing a universally powerful reaction, whether consciously experienced or involuntary."[25]

While Eisenstein moved away from "basic visceral attractions," Belodubrovskaya observes, "attractions continue to be a useful concept," as these might be understood from a neurological perspective. "Looking at attractions through the neurological framework puts in sharper relief what Eisenstein was after: identifying the spectators' involuntary, primal imitative response systems as a basis for aesthetic experience." (Belodubrovskaya is referencing the operation of mirror neurons, which will be a subject of discussion later in this chapter and in the arousal section of this book.) Eisenstein's conceptualization of the attraction, well beyond Eisenstein's own work, "helps explain why for hundreds of years audiences have paid to watch not only engaging characters and stories, but also slapstick, stunts, action, chases, races, and sports. A neurological cine-fist" Belodubrovskaya concludes "is impossible to resist."[26] Eisenstein though was not, by any means, the only figure in early film theory (and filmmaking) that recognized the affective potential in the cinematic.

Nearly ten years prior in 1916, Hugo Münsterberg published *The Photoplay*, where he argues that our initial ocular encounter with the cinematic comes "to our eye [and] at first awaken[s] only sensations, and a sensation is not an emotion." This visual stimulus, though, is then processed cognitively, and "our consciousness of the emotion itself is shaped and marked by the sensations which arise from our bodily organs." Encountering some cinematic embellishment, by Münsterberg's estimation, can solicit a response from the sensate body, which then might be channeled into a recognizable emotion.[27] Interestingly too, Münsterberg emphasizes in particular the form of the moving image, not simply the content. Münsterberg predicted that as the cinema matured with developments in technology and artistry, the "photoplay," as it was termed, would increasingly wield the capacity to affect and emotionally move the spectator. "The value of these formal changes for the expression of the emotions may become remarkable," Münsterberg anticipates. "The characteristic features of many an attitude and feeling which cannot be expressed without words today will then be aroused in the mind of the spectator through the subtle art of the camera."[28] The present volume is very much invested in the very thing that Münsterberg predicts—the audio-visual embellishments that elicit physical sensations in the spectator.

As Siegfried Kracauer notes, "Different kinds of pictures call forth different reactions"; "some address themselves directly to the intellect, some function merely as symbols or such." While some films, according to Kracauer, appeal to our minds, inviting us to contemplate narrative meanings, there are however other kinds of films that "affect primarily the spectator's senses," eliciting a physiological response in the viewer prior to intellectual cognition.[29] Although the affective experience was not necessarily a central concern for these early film theorists, there was nevertheless, an acknowledgement of it. And if only implicit, there was even a suggestion of a difference between the visceral appeal of the cinema and its appeal to our intellect (or even to emotion—interpreting a narrative as sad, good, or enjoyable).

Later generations of film theorists, especially in the turn to structuralism (in the late 1960s and early 1970s), largely turned a blind eye to affect. And this was not out of neglect or hostility to the affective experience necessarily, but rather with every methodological approach there are certain things that slip into a methodological blind spot. Structuralism offered a set of tools (namely, semiology and linguistics) to analyze narrative meanings, and inherent to the structuralist methodology is the intent to "decode" the narrative, to treat cinematic content as a text to decipher, and from a stoic, "objective," or nearly scientific perspective.

Set apart from this stoic approach, the phenomenological approach, largely spearheaded by Vivian Sobchack's work, is perhaps the most prominent affect-orientated methodological strategy in our discipline. Sobchack's landmark, *The Address of the Eye: A Phenomenology of Film Experience*, published in 1992, emphasizes embodied viewing and how the cinematic can potentially engage with our "sense memory"—how, for instance, Christopher Doyle's lavishly shot dumplings might elicit a personal recollection of eating something similar, even causing us to actually salivate.[30] Others have taken up the phenomenological torch—prominent examples being Laura Marks and Jennifer M. Barker. Julian Hanich as well—most notably in his superb 2018 book *The Audience Affect*—applies a phenomenological approach to the collective experience of, among other things, laughter.

Sobchack is largely interested in "synaesthesia," which Marks succinctly describes as the translation of sensual information. And in this movement between different sensate experiences, she notes that one of the tasks of the critic is to "translate something about their audiovisual, sensuous materiality into words."[31] Sobchack specifically is interested in what she terms the "cinesthetic subject." Sobchack characterizes the cinesthetic subject as one that can feel or taste cinema, drawing from psychoneurologist Richard Cytowic's definition of synaesthesia. Sobchack positions the cinesthetic subject contiguous with the experience of synaesthesia, which is an "involuntary experience in which the stimulation of one sense cause[s] a perception in another."[32] Clinically, a true synaesthetic is an individual who can, for example, taste color, see sound as certain shapes, and so on. Sobchack has no intention of diagnosing the cinematic spectator as synaesthetic, but rather her interest resides in the transmutation of sensual information, how do our "dominant senses of vision and hearing," which are central to the cinematic experience, "speak comprehensibly to our other senses?"[33] I personally find the phenomenological methodology the hardest to mobilize, because it relies so heavily on analogy ("it is as if I am touched") and the unique eloquence of any given author to offer a vivid "translation" of the cinematic encounter into words. Phenomenologists tend to be fantastic patients, vividly capable of describing particular affects, but often leave aside the root causes of affective symptoms. This is not to suggest that a phenomenological approach has nothing to say about the affective experience of the cinema, but that as a methodological tool I find it hard to use. Nevertheless, phenomenological discourses lurk in the background of the present volume. And if not the methodology itself, then, at the very least a kinship with a shared objective to discuss how the cinematic elicits a hedonic response.

Cognitivist theorists have also been concerned with the affecting potential of the cinema—Noël Carroll being one of the chief proponents of this approach. Affect for Carroll is in sum a primitive form of emotion. Carroll is wary of the catchall term "emotion," observing that the colloquial conception of "emotion" "can be exceedingly broad and elastic, sometimes ranging so widely as to encompass hard-wired reflex reactions (like the startle response), kinesthetic turbulence, moods, sexual arousal, pleasures and desires, as well as occurrent mental states like anger, fear and sorrow."[34] Emotions, properly speaking, for Carroll are those things that "at least involve both cognitions and feeling states where the two are linked inasmuch as the former cause the latter." Affect, on the other hand, for Carroll, are those instances that stand outside cognitive processes—bodily paroxysms such as stomach churning as a response to a roller coaster or, for example, as he offers, "watching the car chases in *Bullitt*." Affects, then, are raw "unprocessed" feelings, emotions properly speaking "require a cognitive component."[35] With Carroll's framing of emotion and affect, the latter tends to get overshadowed as an "unthought," or "primitive" form of emotion. Nevertheless, affect as "yet-to-be-emotions"—even if only implicitly—runs the risk of conflating the two.

Carl Plantinga, a cognitivist as well, gives considerable attention to the subtle differences between emotion and affect—notably, in his book *Moving Viewers: American Film and the Spectator's Experience*. He also conflates these types of feelings, but nonetheless he does make some effort to differentiate them. "In all of the academic talk about film interpretations, meanings, negotiated readings, comprehension, and so on," Plantinga bemoans, "what is often forgotten is that for the vast majority of film spectators, movie viewing is first and foremost a pleasurable experience, suffused with affect."[36] He adds that, "Film and media scholars sometimes use the tired literary metaphor of 'a reading' to describe the viewer's encounter with a film."[37] What this reveals is the intrinsic prejudice in cinematic and media studies (as well as popular film criticism), which again and again directs our attention to (narrative) meanings, often at the expense of the affective experience.

One of the most common iterations of affect theory in our discipline comes via Gilles Deleuze. His work on the cinematic, artistic practice, and philosophical explorations has also inspired a good deal of scholarship. Largely premised on Deleuze's theorization of the subject, the work has an emphasis on a decentralized poststructuralist approach. From the body without organs, to the rhizomatic, to deterritorialization, to abstract machines—along with his sometime-collaborator, Félix Guattari—Deleuze argues against an ego-centric model of the subject, as found in the psychoanalytic model, and in favor of a subject set within an interwoven fabric of networked relations. In one of the more lucid examples of this, which comes early in the co-authored volume *A Thousand Plateaus*, the writing duo references the symbiotic relationship between some species of orchids and wasps. The orchid *Drakaea glyptodon*, for example, is singularly pollinated by the male Thynnid wasp. The orchid simulates the female sex pheromones of the wasp, thus inviting the wasp to "mate." "After landing on the labellum male wasps may briefly attempt copulation before attempting to fly off with it," the botanist Rod Peakall explains. In its effort to mate with the orchid, which resembles the flightless female wasp, the male wasp functions as a pollinator.[38] Deleuze and Guattari view this as an instructive example of the process of deterritorialization where the wasp and the orchid are "always connected, caught up in one another." In this symbiotic relation the wasp becomes "a piece in the orchid's reproductive apparatus." While it is possible to view these as individuated entities, as "reterritorialized," Deleuze and Guattari see these two species as so deeply imbricated that it becomes impossible to cleave them apart. "Wasp and orchid, as heterogeneous elements, form a rhizome. It could be said that the orchid imitates the wasp, reproducing its image in a signifying fashion (mimesis, mimicry, lure, etc.)."[39] (Mimicry and lure will have important implications later in my discussion of allure in the chapter on arousal.) In this deeply imbricated rhizomatic relation, there is "a veritable becoming, a becoming-wasp of the orchid and a becoming-orchid of the wasp." And with each of these becomings, there is a deterritorialization of each individuated entity, and "the two becomings interlink and form relays in a circulation of intensities pushing the deterritorialization ever further."[40] In this rhizomatic network, where the boundary between wasp and orchid dissolves, is where the affective experience potentially lies. The affective experience takes place in the encounter between deterritorialized entities, if only for an instant, open to the other. (There are some interesting parallels to be drawn with Mikhail Bakhtin's conception of grotesque realism, which is discussed in Part 3 of the present volume.)

Deleuze addresses the subject of sensations most explicitly in his book on the English painter Francis Bacon, its subtitle *"the Logic of Sensation"*. While Deleuze aligns narrative with figuration (or the figure—lower case "f"), he positions the Figure (capital "F") with the sensate experience. Deleuze asks us to consider, for example, El Greco's *The Burial of the Count of Orgaz* (1586–8). There is a graphic horizontal break in the painting dividing the top and lower parts of the painting: "upper and lower, celestial and terrestrial. In the lower half, there is indeed a figuration or narration that represents the burial of the count, although all the coefficients of bodily deformation, and notably elongation, are already at work." But in the celestial portion of the painting, Deleuze observes, "where the count is received by Christ, there is a wild liberation, a total emancipation: the Figures are lifted up and elongated, refined without measure, outside all constraint."[41] There are clear affinities with the cinematic here. The El Greco painting serves as an analogy for the cinematic. Where the narrative takes place in the lower part of the El Greco painting, the upper part of the painting is akin to some narrative rupture. The upper part of the painting might be viewed as something like a dream-sequence or cutaway, where embellishments of the cinematic craft might be applied to affectively amplify the material set apart from the main diegetic narrative. What we are often considering are fleeting instances—where the narrative is ruptured with cinematic embellishments that harbor the potential to elicit the sensate experience. As we will find throughout the present volume, the potential for affect lies in cinematic form, rather than narrative meanings as such—it is how the content is presented to us, not necessarily what is presented to us. The nature and qualities of the referent are almost negligible. As Shaviro observes of Whitehead, what is at stake "is not what something is, but how it is—or, more precisely, how it affects, and how it is affected by, other things."[42]

Susanna Paasonen similarly observes that, "In *Anti-Oedipus*, Gilles Deleuze and Félix Guattari criticize the focus on meaning and suggest a shift from the question 'What does it mean?' to 'How does it work?'" Further, in thinking about this paradigmatic shift, Paasonen notes that the project of locating the "inner essence" through the reading of texts is for Fredric Jameson an allegorical exercise intended to "master" the subject of examination.[43] And in so doing, the scholar rises above their subject of analysis. And an allegory works nicely in this respect as an allegory is a sustained metaphor, one text that effectively hovers in parallel above another (never to intersect or touch one another). The scholar in inscribing this parallel text then might locate the "inner essence," while remaining "untouched," or "above the subject," and thus remaining unaffected by the material that they are examining. Moving from "What does it mean?" to "How does it work?" necessitates a closer degree of proximity, to acknowledge that a scholar, including myself, is moved, touched, affected.

The work that I have found the most promising is the work that takes a more eclectic approach. And some might take my specific eclectic approach as a Frankenstein's monster—an assembly of theoretical and methodological approaches that at times are even antagonistic toward each other. There is no singular established "affect theory" as such, hence my endeavor to cobble one together to accomplish the established objective here. Others have taken an eclectic approach too, though, generally aligned with the Deleuzian perspective. One of the most prominent figures in film and media studies that does this is Steven Shaviro. In addition to Shaviro, Martine Beugnet also takes an eclectic approach. Her 2007 book *Cinema of Sensation: French Film and the Art of Transgression*, I have found particularly inspirational. Like Shaviro, Beugnet effectively calls for a paradigmatic shift in cinematic analysis to account for the sensate experience (indeed much of my recent work has striven to answer this call too). There are certain ruptures in the cinematic that are not invested in "meanings" as such, and rather intend to explore a particular mood, or feeling. These instances, however, are not well-suited to the dominant modes of analysis in the field of cinema and media studies. Beugnet surveying our disciplinary landscape notes that our discipline has a "predilection for 'scientific' rigour," and that there are effectively three to four disciplinary camps: "the study of narrative and genre systems; semiotics and the study of cinema according to the linguistic paradigm or as ideological system of representation and enunciation; and, since the 1970s, psychoanalysis." And lastly, Beugnet groups the various politically-oriented approaches—from post-colonial theory to cultural studies inflected analysis—under the larger heading of "sociologically oriented methods," which strive to contextualize the cinematic text within a socio-cultural milieu.[44] It is not that these general analytic approaches somehow arrive at erroneous conclusions, and in fact they are well-suited to engage with (narrative) meanings. These narrative-focused modes of analysis, however, are not well-equipped to deal with the affective experience. They are analogous to attempting to use a hammer to drive in a screw. While a hammer might get the job done—through brute force, but without any grace—the tool best suited for the job clearly is a Black and Decker cordless power-screwdriver. And thus, the imperative is to come equipped with the analytic approach that is best suited to address the affective experience.

As I have already suggested, the challenge with affect is its relation to the body, to the sensate experience, to an experience that operates outside the jurisdiction of cognition—and this introduces a methodological problem. The affective experience is inherently subjective (as already stated), and it requires a degree of vulnerability from the affect theorist. One cannot simply survey the affective landscape from "above," because conventional scholarly detachment, as Paasonen reflects, "blocks from view both the power of those materials and phenomena to move oneself, as well as the ways in which this motion affects acts of interpretation." Invariably, working within the paradigm of affect theory necessitates making oneself vulnerable.[45] The conventional paradigms of critical assessment in media studies (in most of its variants) privilege narrative and meaning, and dismiss, castigate, or simply ignore the sensate experience. Or, and this is perhaps worse, they imagine that it is negotiating affect, when in fact it is only attentive to emotions. Disciplinary imperatives dictate that we—even when dealing with "low brow culture"—apply "high-minded" thinking, to wave the banner of progressive values, and above all to appropriate the veneer (and let us be frank it is only a veneer) of scientific aloofness, unmoved by the object of analysis.[46] Nonetheless, behind the veneer of rigorous critical inquiries, there lurks the somatic potency of the cinematic, and its eternal promise to elicit an affective experience for the spectator.

Beugnet points to the cinematic form as the site/sight of affective potential—typically occurring at moments where there is a breakdown of form—of content, of clear boundaries, of clearly definable objects. She identifies a number of formal cinematic strategies that harbor the potential to elicit affect: "Blurring or overload of photographic precision, extreme close-ups, superimpositions, under-exposure or over-exposure, variation in sound pitch and intensities." With these cinematic strategies there is the introduction "of mutating sounds and images that often ebb and flow between the figurative and the abstract, and where the human form, at least as a unified entity, easily loses its function as the main point of reference." Beugnet concludes (with a discernible Deleuzian resonance) that, "One way or another, the cinema of sensation is always drawn towards the formless ('*l'informe*'): where background and foreground merge and the subjective body appears to melt into matter."[47]

Beugnet's work coincides with the emergence of what was dubbed by the curmudgeonly art critic James Quandt "New French Extremity." At the turn of the millennium a string of hyper-violent and sexually explicit films from France were released, many of which in their content and their stylization elicited strong emotional and affective responses. Many critics, though, latched onto the extreme content and overlooked the significance of the cinematic form (this is one of the things that I tried to call attention to in my co-authored book *Extreme Cinema*).[48] This tendency toward extreme content and experimentation with cinematic form became something of an international movement, not exclusive to France. That all said, Beugnet's work, because of its focus on transgressive French films, tends to focus on the abject elements. The findings in Beugnet's work however are not limited to "negative" sensations, but to the affecting experience in general—as many of the mechanics of affect are capable of eliciting the whole spectrum of hedonic experiences. Furthermore, even the most horrific encounters have the potential to move beyond disgust; as Julia Kristeva writes, "The abject is edged with the sublime."[49] This, I argue, is what takes place in Luca Guadagnino's 2018 film *Suspiria* (discussed in Chapter 3), and in the "fuck you" soliloquy in Spike Lee's 2002 film *25th Hour* (discussed in Chapter 4).

Drawing from Marks, Beugnet locates the affectively charged instance where the cinematic "plays on the material qualities of the medium to construct a space that encourages a relation of intimacy or proximity with the object of the gaze, privileging primary identification with the film as event, rather than identification with characters caught in plot developments." (And this intimacy or proximity will also be significant when we discuss embodied simulation—especially as it relates to the arousal spawned by erotic content.) Relenting to the cinematic medium, foregoing the imperative to ascertain meaning, "the spectator may surrender, at least partly, a sense of visual control for the possibility of a sensuous encounter with the film—where the subject affectively yields into its object." Beugnet specifically cites the horror genre here, where compositional strategies such as the use of close-ups (or more often than not, extreme close-ups) are employed, which invites an encounter with an image that is effectively rendered formless, the (extreme) close-up tearing the object from the moorings of intelligible representation. There is the possibility that the spectator may be gripped by terror, pulled into "the void and the systematic dismantling of conventional notions of subjecthood that the passage from figuration to indifferentiation or formlessness can affect," Beugnet observes.[50]

Affect appears to stem from the non-object, the non-linguistic, or as some have framed it, the "pre-linguistic." Kristeva most notably offers a number of theoretical approaches that address the non-object or non-/pre-linguistic: the semiotic, abjection, and melancholia. Culture, the Symbolic, which is nothing more than coded breath, this renders the animalistic body intelligible, properly communicative. In Kristevan terms, the "naked expressions" are the instances where the semiotic is made most evident. Early in Kristeva's work, in her fundamental volume *Revolution in Poetic Language*, she notes that her mobilization of the term "semiotic," draws on the Greek etymology as a "distinctive mark, trace, index, precursory sign, proof, engraved or written sign, imprint, trace, figuration."[51] It is the body, and its drives, that leave their semiotic "mark" on the Symbolic. The semiotic is not a language, but lays the foundation for it, and leaves behind traces of the body. And thus, as I have already established above, in order to locate the source of affecting material we must examine the form of the cinematic content.

Similarly, Beugnet observes that an encounter with a stylized cinematic moment has the capacity to elicit an affective experience, and it is not the object as such (the thing represented, the narrative content), but rather in the form of the object. And this aligns with the conception of the beautiful and allure discussed in the sections on arousal and the beautiful. The hedonic experience is made possible when the cinematic attempts to connect "us, even fleetingly," as Beugnet observes, "with those pre-objective sensations and affects that operate before desires and drives are inscribed (defined, encoded, fixed) in the linguistic or discursive planes of organisation."[52]

As previously stated, the present volume aims to identify the cinematic strategies that elicit an affective experience—with a particular focus on pleasurable hedonic experiences even when the content is abject. The intention is not to dismiss the work that has come before, but rather to assimilate, or synthesize my predecessors' research in conjunction with my observations and theorization of the affective experience. In many cases, we are attempting to address the same thing, but from different methodological approaches. It is less about who is "right," and more about locating the best critical tools to assess the affective experience.

When approaching cinematic affect, one must address how the audio-visual referent is presented to the viewing body. The default mode of cinematic analysis, though, squarely focuses on what is presented to the spectator. But this is not to suggest that affect is utterly devoid of meaning, but it stands as meaning of a different order—sensual "meaning." In fact, we come to understand the experience of characters through the sensate experience. To "get" the (Bakhtinian) grotesque body is to laugh. To "understand" the "meaning" of pornography is to cum. To "understand" a character's encounter with the beautiful is to run flush with goosebumps, or to well-up with tears.

In short, the affective experience often rests in the stylistic treatment of the cinematic. The etymology of the word "style" comes from the Latin "stilus" referring to "a stake or pale, pointed instrument for writing, [to a] style of speaking or writing."[53] Thus "style" refers not to what is communicated (what is written), but the manner in which it is transcribed. Echoing what I have already said here, and elsewhere, Vittorio Gallese and Michele Guerra note that "content has to do with 'what,' style has to do with 'how.'" Gallese and Guerra add, drawing from Nelson Goodman, "that it is often thought that style starts when the facts are finished and feeling takes over, as if style were related exclusively to affective forms of expression rather than to the logical and cognitive elements of a work of art." While Gallese and Guerra appear to be suspicious of style's special relationship with the affective experience, they add, "In purely pragmatic terms, it can be said that style is everything we can't talk about unless we have actually seen the movie."[54] "What we call a style," as Graham Harman notes, paraphrasing José Ortega y Gasset, "is nothing other than a specific mode of de-creating images and recreating them as feeling-things."[55] In short, the affective experience is often located in the stylistic elements of the cinematic.

Affect is determined by any myriad number of imbricated factors—from historical and cultural context to individual taste informed by individual dispositions. Scientific research has grappled with this issue as well. In Avram Goldstein's seminal study, "Thrills in response to music and other stimuli," he acknowledges that only half of his study participants "experience thrills as so commonplace an accompaniment of strong emotion that they presume them to be universal." Goldstein goes on to note that for others though "the phenomenon is entirely unknown, so that its very existence is regarded with skepticism."[56] It would come as no surprise, given the nature of the present volume, that I count myself among the former group. And while some are unmoved, in effect anesthetized to external stimuli, what is clear is that many do in fact experience frisson. Originating in the French, "frisson" here means "aesthetic chills or emotion-centered shudders from music, art, and ideas."[57]

Thus, I contend that it is still within our grasp to locate patterns, motifs, and various cinematic strategies that harbor the potential to elicit a shared affective experience. And to this end, I will on certain occasions venture outside our disciplinary boundaries. I have no pretension to locating any universal cinematic experience, but rather to locate instances of commonality. To understand how the audio-visual referent plays upon the body and its senses will necessitate some tentative explorations into the sciences—something that cinema and media studies have long loathed to do. Specifically, I make use of the neurologist Vittorio Gallese's work. Gallese was among a group of researchers, known as the Parma group, that discovered mirror neurons in the brains of macaque monkeys in the early 1990s, "and the subsequent discovery of mirroring mechanisms in the human brain," where the witnessing of an action, for example, grabbing an object will activate tactile centers in the observer's brain. And this speaks to the "role of the body in social cognition."[58] Among Gallese's lengthy list of published works, is his book *The Empathic Screen: Cinema and Neuroscience*, co-authored with Michele Guerra.

This latter work in particular has been criticized by David Bordwell and Malcolm Turvey—balking at the introduction of the sciences, neurology, and specifically mirror neurons into the discipline of film and media studies. In general, the argument goes: (1) the sciences cannot assess the quality and value of the cinematic arts; (2) the science is not settled (specifically as related to mirror neurons); (3) the sciences cannot address the historical or cultural value of the cinematic arts; and (4) the sciences cannot determine the quality of a narrative.[59] And I would actually wholeheartedly agree with these critiques. Posted to David Bordwell's blog, the famous narratologist hosted a debate between himself, Malcolm Turvey, and the authors of *The Empathic Screen*. Turvey's ideas presented in the debate were published as a stand-alone article, "Mirror Neurons and Film Studies: A Cautionary Tale from a Serious Pessimist," in the journal *Projections*. Bordwell and Turvey skewer Gallese and Guerra, rehearsing the criticisms cited above. Fellow cognitivist, Noël Carroll, though, is less skeptical. Drawing on the findings of mirror neurons, Carroll employs the idea of "mirror reflexes," noting how the onscreen body invites an involuntary mimicry from the spectator.[60] For Carroll affects are in essence "pre-emotional," a reflexive response that is yet cognizable, or as he says, "not full scale emotional states," and "mirror reflexes are undoubtedly affective states and they are contagious."[61]

And as inferred previously, when it comes to assessing the narrative and the historical/industrial significance of any cinematic work, the sciences are poorly equipped. This, however, is not the objective of the present volume. Rather the issue at hand is the affective experience, which is not necessarily related to the concerns raised by Bordwell and Turvey. "It would be good," Bordwell ruminates, if Gallese and Guerra, or presumably anyone else for that matter, "would spell out how ES [embodied simulation] is preferable to its philosophical rival."[62] First, I do not believe that Gallese, or anyone else is suggesting that a neurological approach is going to supplant any of our established methodological approaches to cinema. Gallese, at numerous times, respectfully acknowledges the value of the humanities. Rather as Gallese himself suggests, neurology might supplement (not replace) our modes of analysis. Second, neurology, in fact, can assess how the body responds to external stimuli, including cinematic material. Each methodology is a tool, designed to do a specific job. Neurology can offer some insights into how the body perceives audio-visual stimulus.

As Bordwell himself acknowledges, phenomenology is one of the approaches to the affective experience, but "all too often [phenomenology] proffers lyrical description rather than concrete explanation."[63] I share Bordwell's view. While I would not place myself in the phenomenological camp, coupling a phenomenological account with embodied simulation has the potential to yield some very promising results—to in effect lend further evidence to the phenomenological account. That all said, my application of embodied simulation is far more modest. I do not endeavor to ascertain the (cultural/artistic) value of the cinematic material discussed within this volume. Rather embodied simulation is deployed as a tool to appreciate how a spectator might respond to specific instances in the cinematic—an exhibition of caressing, touching, movement. Embodied simulation is employed here not as the singular tool, but as one in a suite of tools. In effect, what I am aiming to do is to assemble a tool kit capable of addressing the affective experience.

Linda Williams, in her article "Film Bodies: Gender, Genre and Excess", outlines what she calls the body genres—horror, melodrama, and pornography. With each of these genres, a female character is presented as "out of control"—she screams in terror in horror, she sobs in melodrama, or is lost in ecstasy in pornography. And central to the body genres, as Williams observes, is that they invite the spectator to mimic the sensations exhibited onscreen. Embodied simulation reinforces Williams's conceptualization of body genres. Let us consider pornography for a moment, just because it offers such a stark example. Pornography is not regarded for its narrative involvement, we are not invited to engage with the characters as such, rather we are generally invited to engage with the pornographic through a fetishistic gaze. In pornography the characters—their desires, their motivations, their psychological states—are not the primary concern.

And it is here, for example, where embodied simulation might have something to offer in our understanding of how we respond to the exhibition of sensual touching. Gallese and Guerra observe that external stimuli are multimodal, that is to say that visual stimuli are not only "understood" through ocular and cognitive processes, but that we process external stimuli through other neural processes as well, including those associated with touch. As a brief illustrative aside, consider the case of Daniel Kish, who, as a toddler developed ocular cancer (retinoblastoma) and his eyes were removed. Kish taught himself to echolocate (analogous to how bats use echolocation), and in MRI imaging, when Kish echolocates the visual areas of his brain light up. In a sense, Kish "sees" via his aural neural network.[64] In short, as Gallese has already established, multiple neural processes intercept external stimuli. The authors of *The Empathic Screen* deduce that "it is highly probable that embodied simulation gives us the possibility to map the bodily experiences of other people by reusing our own somatosensory representations in bodily format." The implications for the body genres are clear, and most especially with respect to the pornographic genre. "By exploiting the same neural circuits as those recruited for subjective bodily experiences, it is possible to establish a direct intersubjective link between ourselves and others, and so we are able to have an experiential understanding of their tactile experiences." The authors submit, "that this mechanism plays an important role in determining the tactile quality of moving images on the cinema screen."[65] We "understand" the pornographic genre, not through narrative meanings or character development, but rather through these "direct intersubjective" links through tactile processes.

Turvey counters that embodied simulation offers "an impoverished conception of [a] 'deep understanding'" of another person or character. Turvey insists that, "This is a good example of how a scientific theory can distort our understanding of artistic practice, in this case our notion of what 'comprehending a character' consists of."[66] And Turvey is absolutely correct, when assessing character motivations, to understand the emotional appeal of a narrative, or when examining the overall "meaning" of a narrative, embodied simulation is not equipped to negotiate these "higher" levels of cognitive perception. However, as suggested with the stark example of pornography, our "understanding" of the character is not premised on our "comprehension" of their desires, their emotions, or their goals (other than cumming), rather our relationship with the characters onscreen is tactile. What is at stake in the present volume are the "small" events (that might be nested in a larger narrative context), those instances where lightning strikes and our body inexplicably goes flush with goosebumps, when our body reflexively responds to pornographic content with sexual arousal, or whatever the case might be. My mobilization of embodied simulation, in this sense, is limited in scope—it is supplementary. I hold no illusions that embodied simulation might "explain" a narrative, to level artistic or cultural valuations, the only thing that "[n]eurons ... 'know' about" Gallese observes are "ions passing through their membranes."[67] I agree with Bordwell and Turvey that embodied simulation is limited in its capacity to tell us what any particular story might mean, however, embodied simulation is highly instructive in how specific moments in the cinema might affect us—how the cinematic might "touch" us.

Film theory and criticism has largely emphasized some form of narrative analysis (invested in locating "meanings"), nevertheless, the affective experience or (bodily) sensations remain a lingering specter, haunting our discipline. There have been many efforts to engage with the affecting experience in the cinema, none of which, to my mind, has been completely satisfactory. All told, what this very brief survey reveals is that there is a need to synthesize affect theories and to encourage a general paradigmatic shift in our discipline. This is the subject of the following section.

A Disciplinary Paradigm Shift

Our discipline clings, for instance, to various forms of content analysis, as viewed through various political lenses (for example, postcolonialism, feminism), and even to psychoanalytic theories, which in the end—especially in the adaptations of Freudian and Lacanian psychoanalysis—is yet one more mode of narrative analysis, an effort to locate "deeper" meanings. And in the waning of psychoanalytic approaches to the discipline, there are a host of other methodological approaches that gained favor, by and large these are geared toward locating if not narrative meaning, then, cultural meanings.

This is not to suggest that narratives and meanings are unimportant. Eugenie Brinkema is highly skeptical of the turn toward affect. She suggests that media studies, when confronted with some novel turn in the cinematic experience, tends to form "curious connections" to where novel cinematic strategies "are said principally to appeal to skin and body to agitate the corpus in new and exclusive ways. Each time a turning toward affect has taken place, it has demonstrated one thing above all: the intellectual seductions of this very call." The turn to affect, Brinkema argues, is merely a knee-jerk response, because "affectivity figures the very notion of 'affect' as a placeholder for the unthought of this (or of any) discipline."[68] In fact, in more terse terms, Brinkema continues this line of thinking in a note, observing that at the "Affect as Rhetorical Strategy" panel, at the 2011 Society for Cinema and Media Studies conference, panelists "repeatedly insisted that affect needed to be attended to in the discipline of film studies," as though affect had not been attended to in the past. "Rather," Brinkema continues in even decidedly more pointed terms, "their renewed call for attention to affect just shows how seductive the term 'affect' is an empty heralding of the unsaid."[69] To Brinkema's mind the turn towards affect is a vacuous gesture that insists upon "the humanities [to] direct new and urgent attention to the previously ignored concept of _____."[70] As stated previously, affect is not new to our discipline (as I have already surveyed above), nor is the turn toward affect intended to displace other modes of analysis.

Brinkema in effect stands in contradistinction to my efforts to offer a taxonomy of affect. I personally want to know. I am genuinely interested in exploring the power of the cinematic to elicit an affective experience, and as an educator—encountering emerging filmmakers and scholars—I want my students to be thinking about specific cinematic strategies that are potentially affecting. For filmmakers looking to manipulate their audience (and I mean this in the best sense—all films manipulate), I want to offer the critical skills and demonstrate a self-awareness of how the cinematic plays on spectators. It is not so much a playbook, or a color-by-numbers directive, but a conceptual understanding of how the cinematic form potentially affects us. At its core, what the present volume strives to do is to outline the cinematic strategies that wield the potential to viscerally affect the viewing body.

Again, Brinkema for her part skirts the issue: How does one go about assessing affect? Focusing specifically on disgust in this particular case, Brinkema refrains from naming the "unnamable," insisting that "definition-giving (in the sense of coming into focus or line-drawing) is precisely what disgust conceptually compels, theory should resist the urge to align so squarely with the affect's insistence of an iconography of its own." She continues, "If one falls for this lure, disgust becomes but a set of itemized disgusting things. Every critic has his or her own privileged ones."[71] I concur that we should make concerted efforts to be rigorous, to acknowledge personal biases and preferences, but working towards a taxonomy of cinematic affect, need not fall prey to diarist-thinking, or a list of objects. There is no question that Brinkema's contribution to the field serves an important function, however, her commitment to philosophical rigor lets disciplinary perfection (or is it purification—disavowing affect?) get in the way of practical applications. The fact is that the cinematic is a cultural product, and thus inherently contains audio-visual referents that will affectively resonate across a segment of the population. This is not to suggest that every instance of body-humor will land with a laugh, that a specifically constructed fetishistic image will elicit arousal with all viewers, or that a particular harmonic sound will prompt goosebumps with every spectator, rather I point to specific cinematic strategies that wield the potential for affect.

Where our paths re-converge is an insistence on form, as opposed to content, or to specific things. Here Brinkema and I are in complete agreement. Brinkema insists that disgust cannot be ascribed to any singular object. And every time a scholar or critic formulates an itemized list of disgusting things they effectively claim "that the worst has been reached, identified, and corralled and that no worse will come into play. Naming the objects of disgust each time puts the cleanliness of the word into the mouth and thus annihilates the other oral activities the affect might compel."[72] This, I think, is Barbara Creed's error in her landmark book *The Monstrous-Feminine*—she names (this object, that thing), as opposed to focusing on how those things/objects are presented. As Kristeva observes, "The corpse, seen without God and outside of science, is the utmost of abjection."[73] It is how the corpse is presented, not the corpse itself necessarily. When the corpse is presented within religious rituals, it is approachable—abjection is kept at bay. When the corpse is contextualized in a scientific setting (for example, hospital, mortuary, forensic investigation), it is likewise approachable. I have deep affection for *The Monstrous-Feminine*, it is instrumental in the introduction of challenging ideas, nonetheless, Creed directs our attention to a taxonomy of objects. Our knee-jerk response is to ask, "What is affecting?" when we really should be asking, "How is this affecting?" And although she never explicitly says as much, Brinkema appears to be inviting us to consider the how.[74]

In fact, Brinkema speaks to the ghettoized study of horror within the larger discipline of film studies, noting of Noël Carrol and Julia Kristeva that, "Despite their differences, both . . . have engendered critical offspring that emphasize the disgusting in place of disgust due to an overinvestment in objectified offensive things."[75] Brinkema urges us to locate meanings in textual form, to return to the reading of cinema, as opposed to feeling the cinematic. To simply limit our approach to pornography through the lens of "reading the text," would fail to consider the very intention of the pornographic genre: to elicit bodily sensations. My endeavor then—in the widest of terms—is to catalog audio-visual strategies that elicit "positive" affects. (Though, I stake no claim to being exhaustive.) From cinematography to editing, from the use of audio design or music, from the mobilization of color to compositional framing (particularly in the treatment of the human form), any of these and more wield the potential to elicit sensations. It is not necessarily what the cinematic presents to us, but how it does it.

In Troy Bordun's review of my earlier co-authored book, *Extreme Cinema: Affective Strategies in Transnational Media*, he notes that its subtitle really should have been *Disgust in Transnational Media*.[76] On this specific matter, I concede Bordun's point. However, what Bordun chooses to ignore altogether was *Extreme Cinema*'s objective, which was, to a large extent, to create a taxonomy of affective strategies employed in the post-millennial trend of extreme cinema. For example, Bordun took issue with our approach to David Wnendt's 2013 film *Wetlands*. Bordun observes that we "walk the reader through the film's narrative and observe the moments where eroticism and disgust overlap in relation to taste and scent." In our emphasis on the affective experience embedded in the cinematic narrative, we neglected a scene where Bordun admits to feeling "arousal without disgust," namely "the sequence of a middle-aged black man, complete with headlamp, shaving the teenaged protagonist's pubic region—a sequence ripe for race and age analysis."[77] I invite Bordun, or anyone else for that matter, to do exactly this! Bordun is absolutely correct that this scene in *Wetlands* is ripe for a sociopolitical analysis. However, that is not what *Extreme Cinema* strove to do.

Furthermore, what Bordun overlooks is that it is not only narrative content that we call attention to (in *Extreme Cinema* and the present volume), but rather how that content is presented. What Bordun takes issue with, without explicitly acknowledging it, is the paradigm of assessment. No single paradigm of assessment is a "catch all." And paradigms of assessment generally dictate the scope and focus of any analysis. Moreover, what *Extreme Cinema* and the present volume strive to do is to engage with material regardless of its moral stance. The pornographic, for example, is rife with politically regressive content, and yet it still wields the potential to elicit pleasure. I have no intention to "resolve" this tension, or to somehow justify the politically regressive, but rather to demonstrate how the cinematic elicits an affective response. From Spike Lee's *25th Hour*, featuring a vitriolic xenophobic diatribe (which still elicits the beautiful), to regressive porn (which despite the criminal behavior elicits sexual excitation), to the exhibition of suffering on the *Tosh.0* program (which despite the pitiful situation elicits laughter)—the point is to identify the aesthetic strategies that elicit an affective experience. I view the present volume as something of a follow-up to *Extreme Cinema*, albeit with the express intent of pursuing pleasurable affects. And readers expecting value judgements, political posturing, or the unearthing of narrative "meanings," will be unquestionably disappointed. I make no apologies for the fact that the present volume is concerned with the sensate experience as elicited by the cinematic.

That is not to suggest that a study of affect is divorced from political perspectives altogether. Academia fetishizes "the role of reason and rationality" in the formulation of cultural values, as Ruth Leys observes, noting that the rationalist approach offers an unnuanced and "disembodied . . . account of the ways in which people actually form their political opinions and judgments." Human beings are not automatons or Vulcans—responding to the world in purely rational terms. Rather "we human beings are corporeal creatures imbued with subliminal affective intensities and resonances that so decisively influence or condition our political and other beliefs that we ignore those affective intensities and resonances at our peril."[78] While the affective experience is emphasized in the present volume, this is not to mean that what is presented here is apolitical. Think for instance of Stephen Colbert's coining of the term "truthiness," for something that is false, but feels true.[79] (A prophetic vision of Trump's reckless disregard for the truth, and the emergence of the era of "alternative facts" that "feel right" —at least to some.) Turning our attention to affect is in itself a political gesture.

The affective experience is inherently subjective. And what I have attempted to do here, and elsewhere, is to point to particular cinematic strategies that have the potential to elicit an affective experience (X cinematic strategies have the potential to produce Y physiological affects). The compulsion to focus on the "negative" is generally speaking a safer exercise, as stated earlier, because it often massages our own progressive egos, offering a tacit assurance that we are in the "club." Speaking honestly about pleasurable affects potentially opens us (okay, that pronoun was a coy deflection, let's be frank, me) to accusations of fetishism, to an objectifying and sadistic gaze, to an exoticizing gaze, to acknowledging some guilty pleasure, to inviting some rebuke ("Wait, what, you like that?"), and finally potential expulsion from the "club."

Furthermore, there is a general suspicion built into film theory and criticism. Despite the fact that the cinematic by its very nature is an audiovisual medium, there is a long-held wariness of representations, and most specifically visual representations. In Galt's book, *Pretty*, cited previously, she charts this prejudice in our discipline. "In citing the seduction and shallowness of the aesthetic image, we locate film theory within a philosophical history that dates from Plato's separation of idea from image. For many readers of Plato," Galt relates, "the word or idea is primary, with the image at best a copy incapable of articulating philosophical reason and at worst a deceptive and dangerous cosmetic." Galt asserts that the history of Western aesthetics is "logocentric," and "the image . . . [is] secondary, irrational, and bound to the inadequate plane of the surface."[80] Galt adds, citing Jean-Luc Nancy, "The image is degraded as secondary, as imitative and therefore as inessential, as derivative and lifeless, as deceitful and weak: nothing could be more familiar to us than this motif." Nancy adds that there is a "deep suspicion regarding 'appearances' or 'the spectacle.'"[81] The tools that our discipline has adopted only cement the privileging of the logocentric perspective—from the appropriation of linguistics and semiology to Marxist, feminist, and psychoanalytic theories the image is either framed as a form of "false consciousness," or dangerously deceitful and designed to hide some deleterious ideological agenda. And this is especially true of the attractive or "pretty" image, which should not be trusted precisely because it is seductively bewitching, often framed as feminine, and/or foreign (for example, the arabesque). As a consequence, as Dudley Andrew observes, some of the chief iconoclasts of our era are Marxists and feminists—located in their passionate diatribes.[82] Galt wonders, "So how do we reconcile a medium based on images with this intellectual inheritance of iconoclasm, the tearing down of images?"[83] There are affinities with the present volume and Galt's *Pretty*, though while Galt endeavors to locate (political) meanings in the pretty image (and to expose the prejudices endemic to our discipline), my objectives are more circumscribed, simply acknowledging the pleasures that we might derive from the cinematic experience, even when those pleasures might go unacknowledged, ignored, disavowed, or perhaps in less malicious terms "unseen," blinded by disciplinary strictures.

There is, however, something particularly challenging when attempting to critically assess the affective experience (which *Extreme Cinema* also strove to do): media studies (in all its variants) appears to be largely allergic to pleasurable affects, instinctively we typically turn our attention to the "negative." Of course, there are many examples of "progressive" readings of the cinematic, championing the agency of a particular character coming from outside the dominant culture for example, or potentially reading something against the grain and highlighting some progressive rupture in mainstream culture. In the broadest of brushstrokes, we academic scholars tend to fall into one of two camps: lovers or haters. Nonetheless, and wherever on the lover-hater spectrum one stands, it is in the DNA of our discipline to be critical, which is often conflated with issuing a rebuke, to locate fault, to castigate the politically regressive, to point to the abject—and this emphasis on the "negative" discloses an underlying anxiety in addressing the pleasurable. No matter how much one veils their own subjective experiences, their own preferences and prejudices—behind the façade of academic rigor, which is a mere fig leaf—the author always reveals something of their own disposition when assessing the affective experience. Moreover, most of this is about what a narrative means, not how it feels. And whether acknowledged or not, this tricky business of acknowledging how the cinematic stimulates our senses, might well place limits on discussions of the pleasurable, especially as it relates to sexual arousal.[84]

In the classroom too, discussing (pleasurable) affect can be terribly fraught, and even potentially dangerous (especially for untenured faculty). It is far easier, and frankly safer to focus on "negative" affects, such as disgust. I am not placing myself at much risk when I review and outline the qualities of *2 Girls 1 Cup*. This was actually a trailer to a full-length pornographic coprophagia film (*Hungry Bitches*, Marco Antonio Florito, 2007). Shortly after its release it "went viral," and was widely shared online, and also popularized "reaction videos," where individuals would video themselves or others as they watched the trailer—often inducing gagging, reflexive defensive gestures, and laughter. To proclaim that *2 Girls 1 Cup* is disgusting merely reaffirms that, at least in this case, my own disposition corresponds to standard social mores. But to reveal that something elicits pleasurable feelings potentially invites rebuke: I found this beautiful (although it is saccharine and/or kitsch), I found this sexually arousing (despite its regressive content), I laughed uncontrollably (even though it is ethically problematic). We can hide behind disciplinary rigor and advertise our progressive credentials all we want, to paraphrase Shaviro, but there is something potentially disingenuous here when the affecting experience is disavowed.[85] In fact, precisely because politically regressive content can elicit pleasure appears to demand engagement. And whether the cinematic material is regressive or progressive, I see no need to sweep the hedonic experience under the rug. There is absolutely nothing to be gained by pretending that the cinematic does not affect us, but there is a great deal to lose.

In our paradigmatic shift toward affect theory this necessitates moving past "good" or "bad" media, and what this turn affords us is the ability to be honest brokers in negotiating the affecting experience. This is not to discount any political or narrative critiques that might be mobilized in the assessment of the cinematic—there is a place for such interventions—the scope of the present volume, however, demands that our attention be placed on the affective experience. The point, then, is not to level moral value statements, nor whether the cinematic object merits our cultural esteem, or even personal ethics (be it to appease our progressive egos or engage in a self-congratulatory exercise of wagging the finger of discontent), but rather to honestly evaluate how the cinematic elicits an affective response.

Contours of the Book

In the end, different affective experiences require their own set of theoretical and/or methodological approaches. While it would be a lot easier if I could locate some grand unifying theory to explain all kinds of pleasurable affects, alas, there is no singular theoretical model or methodological approach that can accommodate the full spectrum of hedonic experiences. And hence, my commitment to an agnostic, or eclectic approach. I am like a mechanic under the car calling out to an assistant: "wrench," "lube," "screwdriver." Whatever tool is best suited to the job is called upon.

I intend to build off existing research on the emerging area of affect theory in cinema and media studies, as referenced above. The current volume, however, has a narrow focus—I will concentrate my attention on "positive" affective experiences often located within problematic or crass content, and the cinematic tropes that tend to elicit such affects. I make no claim that the present volume will be exhaustive—either in the affective experiences explored, or in the selection of cinematic examples that I will draw upon. The films, and other media that I will be addressing are merely examples—and in no way do I mean to suggest that these are "the" instances of affective experience. Furthermore, without a doubt, some of the examples that I will call attention to will not resonate with all readers. Affect, as already suggested, is contextual and subjective.

While some scholarly approaches to affect are overly invested in demonstrating theoretical prowess, others are too idiosyncratic and diaristic. Neither approach is particularly productive: the former is so abstract that it fails to connect with the lived cinematic experience and the latter is too personal to function as generalized principles that might be applied by others. My objective is to locate a middle ground. And this gets to the structure of the present volume, the respective sections—On the Beautiful, On Sexual Arousal, and On Laughter—begin with an introduction to the theoretical methodology applied to the respective topic. This is then followed with a series of examples, modeling how affect theories might be applied to the cinematic experience.

While each section can be taken on its own, there is something of a "progression" of ideas as they relate to the development of a quiver of theoretical approaches to affect (which is one of the implicit objectives of the present volume). The beautiful in particular, as it is viewed through the Kantian lens, theorizes how the subject "prehends" external stimuli. The concept of the beautiful, in turn has affinities with the conception of sexual arousal (fueled by the economies of allure and fetishism). Though I survey the three most common theoretical approaches to comedy and laughter—superiority, incongruity, and relief—as it turns out we laugh for many reasons, and it might have nothing at all to do with what we find humorous. Rather laughter potentially figures as a defensive gesture to ward off disgust, an encounter with grotesque realism (Bakhtin), and what is inopportune.

Chapter 2, "On the Beautiful," surveys the Kantian conception of the beautiful. The beautiful is not a thing or object, rather it is a subjective experience—a disguised expression of pleasure. The following chapter continues to explore the beautiful examining neo-giallo films as an example, with a particular focus on Luca Guadagnino's 2018 film *Suspiria*, what one of the lead actresses, Tilda Swinton, refers to as a "cover" (as in a "cover song") of Dario Argento's 1977 cult classic.[86] Though populated with instances of abject horror, through the composition and cinematography and Thom Yorke's scoring Guadagnino's *Suspiria* invites an encounter with the beautiful. The play with film speed, editing, and composition (particularly when paired with Yorke) musicalizes the image, amplifying its affective potential. This is the subject of the following chapter, Chapter 4 "Musicality: Poetic Ruptures in Spike Lee's *25th Hour*, and Chris

Cunningham/Björk's Music Video 'All Is Full of Love,'" which explores how musicalization potentially summons an experience of the beautiful. Where our primary character, Monty, in his hate-filled diatribe in *25th Hour* slips from abjection to the beautiful, Cunningham's music videos and particularly Björk's "All Is Full of Love," move from the monstrous and/or machinic to the beautiful.

Like the beautiful, sexual arousal is obviously a subjective experience. Arousal is not governed by any transcendental object(s), but rather individually and historically, and is culturally contingent. Chapter 5 "On Sexual Arousal" theorizes the economies of allure and fetishism. While the latter are the objects that populate external stimuli and our own internal predilections, allure is the force that brings these external and internal fetishistic objects together—similar to what is found in molecular cohesion where two like molecules cohere. And to be clear, I position fetishism adjacent to the psychoanalytic model, which associates it with castration and lack, and rather mobilize it as an overvalued object. Reinforcing the allure-fetishism economy are the operations of mirror neurons. Identified by the Italian neurologist Vittorio Gallese and his colleagues, their neurological studies indicate that subjects witnessing some action—whether in the flesh or represented, and whether auditory or visual (including reading)—will activate tactile neural networks associated with the witnessed act. The implications for pornography are self-evident and reinforce other cinematic theories, from Linda Williams's body genres, which anticipates "mimicry," to Susanna Paasonen's conception of "resonance." The succeeding chapter, "Pornography: Erotic Disavowal, Regressive Content, and the Chikan (Sub-)Genre," further explores sexual arousal. It is no secret that the pornographic genre is littered with politically regressive content, nevertheless, and even despite our own moral qualms with such resolutely bankrupt content, it wields the potential to elicit arousal. As an example of this, I examine the Japanese (sub-)genre of chikan (groper), which along with other variants, typically features a female character that is groped on a bus or train, leading to a sexual encounter. The seventh chapter, "Romance: *The Handmaiden* and Its Arousing Spectacles," harmonizes the emotional and affective experience through the tropes of the (lesbian) romance genre. It focuses on Chan-wook Park's 2016 film *The Handmaiden*, which also negotiates female fantasies and sadistic situations, explicitly trading in fetishistic imagery to invite our erotic interest.

Chapter 8 "On Laughter" explores the experience of laughter. Despite our assumptions that laughter is spawned by the comedic, behavioral scientists and other scholars observe that we humans laugh for a whole host of reasons that have nothing to do with humor. And while many scholars address our better angels, assuming that the ethically crass—for example, watching someone get severely injured, even die—cannot, or should not elicit laughter, nonetheless, in truth such things very well might induce laughter. And this might not necessarily be because it is funny necessarily, but as a way to negotiate disgust, the abject, and so on. This aligns with Mikhail Bakhtin's conception of grotesque realism, where unlike the modern conception of the human subject as a unified whole set outside or above the natural world, instead the body is conceived as open, porous, less an individuated entity and more a node in a rhizomatic system. Encountering this slippage in individuated boundaries—in consumption/excrement, life/death, fecundity/putrescence—invites abject laughter. Exploring these ideas further, the subsequent chapter, "Body Humors: Dick Pics in Cringe Comedy and the Carnivalesque Grotesque Body," examines the materialization of dicks and the crippled body that potentially elicit laughter. Whether in dick pics (both in the economies of social media, including sexting, and in the cinematic), or Ricky Berwick (who has Beals-Hecht syndrome) on his YouTube channel or his appearance on *Tosh.0*, laughter manifests relative to the right/wrong time and place.

Notes

1 Ruth Leys, "The Turn to Affect: A critique," *Critical Inquiry* vol. 37, no. 3 (2011): 436. See Nigel Thrift, "Intensities of Feeling: Towards a Spatial Politics of Affect," *Geografiska Annaler* vol. 86, no. 1 (2004): 64; and Lee Spinks, "Thinking the Post-Human: Literature, Affect, and the Politics of Style," *Textual Practice* vol. 15, no. 1 (2001): 23.
2 Tristan Taormino, "Calling the Shots: Feminist Porn in Theory and Practice," *The Feminist Porn Book: The Politics of Producing Pleasure*, eds Tristan Taormino et al. (New York: The Feminist Press at CUNY, 2013), 261.
3 Brian Massumi, *Parables for the Virtual: Movement, Affect, Sensation* (Durham, NC: Duke University Press, 2002), 28.
4 Sara Ahmed, *The Cultural Politics of Emotion* (New York: Routledge, 2013), 25. Also see Sara Ahmed, "Creating Disturbance: Feminism, Happiness and Affective Differences," in *Working with Affect in Feminist Readings: Disturbing Differences*, eds Marianne Liljeström and Susanna Paasonen (London: Routledge, 2010), 32.
5 Brian Massumi, "Notes on the Translation and Acknowledgements," in Gilles Deleuze and Felix Guattari, *A Thousand Plateaus: Capitalism and Schizophrenia*, trans. Brian Massumi (Minneapolis: University of Minnesota Press, 2005), xvi.
6 Eric Shouse, "Feeling, Emotion, Affect," *M/C Journal* vol. 8, no. 6 (2005): no pagination. https://doi.org/10.5204/mcj.2443.
7 These, in fact, were some of the issues raised in the Reader Reports at the proposal stage of the present volume.

8 Gregory J. Seigworth and Melissa Gregg, "An Inventory of Shimmers," in *The Affect Theory Reader*, eds Melissa Gregg, Gregory J. Seigworth, and Sara Ahmed (Durham, NC: Duke University Press, 2010), 10.
9 Susanna Paasonen notes that stories in pornography were never emphasized, and this is especially true after the introduction of video. Paasonen even takes Linda Williams to task for her lamentations for the "golden age" of 1970s porn. See Susanna Paasonen, *Carnal Resonance: Affect and Online Pornography* (Cambridge, MA: MIT Press, 2011), 183; 184–185. Paasonen references Linda Williams, *Hard Core: Power, Pleasure, and the "Frenzy of the Visible"* (Berkeley: University of California Press, 1989), 48–9.
10 Brian McNair, *Striptease Culture: Sex, Media and the Democratization of Desire* (London: Routledge, 2002), 41.
11 Paasonen, 185.
12 Curtis Silver, "Pornhub 2019 Year In Review Report: More Porn, More Often," *Forbes*, December 11, 2019, https://www.forbes.com/sites/curtissilver/2019/12/11/pornhub-2019-year-in-review-report-more-porn-more-often/#1aa7270f4671.
13 Paasonen, 15.
14 Carl R. Plantinga, *Moving Viewers: American Film and the Spectator's Experience* (Berkeley: University of California Press, 2009), 3.
15 Rosalind Galt, *Pretty: Film and the Decorative Image* (New York: Columbia University Press, 2011), 51.
16 Ibid., 181. Galt cites Plato, *Republic*, V, 745c–e, 714–15.
17 Maurice Merleau-Ponty, *Phenomenology of Perception*, trans. Donald A. Landes (New York: Routledge, 2012), 245.
18 Plantinga, 4–5.
19 Steven Shaviro, *Without Criteria: Kant, Whitehead, Deleuze, and Aesthetics* (Cambridge, MA: MIT Press, 2009), 57.
20 Ibid., 56. Shaviro cites Alfred North Whitehead, *Process and Reality* (New York: The Free Press, 1978), 176; 215; and 184.
21 Maria Belodubrovskaya, "The Cine-Fist: Eisenstein's Attractions, Mirror Neurons, and Contemporary Action Cinema," *Projections* vol. 12, no. 1 (Summer 2018): 5.
22 Ibid., 4.
23 Sergei Eisenstein cited in Belodubrovskaya, 5. Interestingly, Belodubrovskaya in an endnote observes that the word, "In the original Russian," is given as "emotional," but "Eisenstein uses the word chuvstvennyi, which could also be translated as 'sensual' or 'feelingful.'" Belodubrovskaya, 15 n6. See Sergei Eisenstein, "The Montage of Attractions," in Richard Taylor, ed., *The Eisenstein Reader* (London: BFI, 1998), 30.
24 Belodubrovskaya, 5; Eisenstein, "The Montage of Attractions," 30.
25 Belodubrovskaya, 5.
26 Ibid., 14.
27 Hugo Münsterberg, *Hugo Münsterberg on Film: The Photoplay: A Psychological Study and Other Writings*, ed. Allan Langdale (New York: Routledge, 2001), 107–8.
28 Ibid., 108.
29 Siegfried Kracauer, *Theory of Film: The Redemption of Physical Reality* (Princeton: Princeton University Press, 1997), 158.
30 Here I am thinking of Fruit Chan's 2004 film *Dumplings*.

31 Laura U. Marks, *Touch: Sensuous Theory and Multisensory Media* (Minneapolis: University of Minnesota Press, 2002), ix. Elsewhere Marks writes: "My challenge is to suggest how film and video, which are audiovisual media, can represent nonaudiovisual sense experiences." Laura U. Marks, *The Skin of Film: Intercultural Cinema, Embodiment, and the Senses* (Durham, NC: Duke University Press, 1999), 2.

32 Richard Cytowic cited in Vivian Sobchack, *Carnal Thoughts: Embodiment and Moving Image Culture* (Berkeley: University of California Press, 2004), 67.

33 Sobchack, 67.

34 Noël Carroll, "Film, Emotion, and Genre," in *Philosophy of Film and Motion Pictures: An Anthology*, eds Noël Carroll and Jinhee Choi (Hoboken: Wiley, 2009), 217.

35 Ibid., 220. Elsewhere Carroll articulates a degree of frustration with terms like "emotion" and their varied application:

> As occurs with people's usage of other emotion-vocabularies, speakers and writers, including experts, employ the relevant terminology in diverse, often conflicting, incommensurate, and/or mutually canceling ways. For example, even what are called emotions can vary appreciably. Some count reflexes and phobias to be emotions, while other categorize moods as emotions—for example, what some psychologists call "mood-induction" procedures might be more accurately be called "emotion-induction" procedures, since what they elicit are short-lived, episodic states rather than more enduring ones.

Noël Carroll, "On some affective relations between audiences and the characters in popular fictions," in *Empathy: Philosophical and psychological perspectives*, eds Amy Coplan and Peter Goldie (New York: Oxford University Press, 2011), 163. Also see Paasonen's summary of the "unmediated" stimulus and its capacity to elicit sensations in her *Carnal Resonance: Affect and Online Pornography* (Cambridge, MA: MIT Press, 2011), 194.

36 Plantinga, 2.

37 Ibid. Paasonen also comments on "reading" images:

> Acknowledging the status of images as nonlinguistic entities that operate in a different register of meaning and experience than texts bound to specific structures, it is fair to say that reading is not the best term for investigating them ... But although one may not be able to read an image, it is certainly possible to write about it. If porn tries to show how carnal sensations feel, then interpretation involves textual translation of the interactions taking place. Much is necessarily lost in acts of translation from one sensory regime and modality to another. When writing about porn, words often seem to fail to grasp what grabs: descriptions pin down scenarios and scenes while also translating them into something literal and fixed, knowable and certain.

Paasonen, 200.

38 Rod Peakall, "Responses of male *Zaspilothynnus trilobatus* Turner wasps to females and the sexually deceptive orchid it pollinates," *Functional Ecology* (1990): 160.

39 Gilles Deleuze and Félix Guattari, *A Thousand Plateaus: Capitalism and Schizophrenia*, trans. Brian Massumi (Minneapolis: University of Minnesota Press, 2005), 10.

40 Ibid.

41 Gilles Deleuze, *Francis Bacon: The Logic of Sensation*, trans. Daniel W. Smith (New York: Continuum, 2003), 9.

42 Shaviro, *Without Criteria*, 55.
43 Paasonen, 132. See Gilles Deleuze and Félix Guattari, *Anti-Oedipus: Capitalism and Schizophrenia*, trans Robert Hurley, Mark Seem, and Helen R. Lane (New York: Penguin Books, 2009), 109. Also see Fredric Jameson, *The Political Unconscious: Narrative as a Socially Symbolic Act* (New York: Routledge, 2002), 7–8; 13.
44 Martine Beugnet, *Cinema of Sensation: French Film and the Art of Transgression* (Carbondale: Southern Illinois University Press, 2007), 28.
45 Paasonen, 23.
46 Steven Shaviro, *The Cinematic Body* (Minneapolis: University of Minnesota Press, 1993), 14–15.
47 Beugnet, 65.
48 See Aaron Kerner and Jonathan Knapp, *Extreme Cinema: Affective Strategies in Transnational Media* (Edinburgh: Edinburgh University Press, 2016).
49 Julia Kristeva, *Powers of Horror: An Essay on Abjection*, trans. Leon S. Roudiez (New York: Columbia University Press, 1982), 11.
50 Beugnet, 68.
51 Julia Kristeva, *Revolution in Poetic Language*, trans. Leon S. Roudiez (New York: Columbia University Press, 1984), 25. The *Oxford English Dictionary* gives the etymology for "semiotic" as, "significant; also, concerned with the interpretation of symptoms." And "symptoms" is perhaps a helpful way of understanding the Kristevan semiotic.
52 Beugnet, 128.
53 "Style," s.v. OED.
54 Vittorio Gallese and Michele Guerra, *The Empathic Screen: Cinema and Neuroscience*, trans. Frances Anderson (Oxford: Oxford University Press, 2020), 85.
55 Graham Harman, *Guerrilla Metaphysics: Phenomenology and the Carpentry of Things* (Chicago: Open Court, 2005), 110.
56 Avram Goldstein, "Thrills in response to music and other stimuli," *Physiological Psychology* vol. 8, no. 1 (1980): 128.
57 Kristin Neidlinger et al., "AWElectric: that gave me goosebumps, did you feel it too?" in *Proceedings of the Eleventh International Conference on Tangible, Embedded, and Embodied Interaction* (2017): 317.
58 Vittorio Gallese and Hannah Wojciehowski, "How stories make us feel: Toward an embodied narratology," *California Italian Studies* vol. 2, no. 1 (2011): no pagination. https://doi.org/10.5070/C321008974.
59 See Malcolm Turvey, "Mirror Neurons and Film Studies A Cautionary Tale from a Serious Pessimist," *Projections* vol. 14, no. 3 (Winter 2020): 21–46.
60 Carroll, "On some affective relations between audiences and the characters in popular fictions," 177–80.
61 Ibid., 179.
62 David Bordwell, "Brains, bodies, and movies: Ways of thinking about the psychology of cinema," *Observations on film art* (blog), *David Bordwell's website on cinema*, April 29, 2020, http://www.davidbordwell.net/blog/2020/04/29/brains-bodies-and-movies-ways-of-thinking-about-the-psychology-of-cinema/.
63 Ibid.
64 In a study—where Daniel Kish is cited as a consultant, and a contributing author—for an experiment on human echolocation, the researchers found that: "Functional MRI

revealed reliable blood oxygen-level dependent (BOLD) activity in auditory cortex as well as in the calcarine sulcus and surrounding regions of 'visual' cortex in EB and LB when they listened to recordings of their echolocation clicks and echoes, as compared to silence." Lore Thaler et al., "Neural correlates of motion processing through echolocation, source hearing, and vision in blind echolocation experts and sighted echolocation novices," *Journal of Neurophysiology* vol. 111, no. 1 (2014): 3. Also see Sarah Cooper, Paúl M. Velazco, and Hunter Schantz, "Navigating in Darkness: Human Echolocation with Comments on Bat Echolocation," *HAPS Educator* vol. 24, no. 2 (2020): 38–9. For a great podcast feature on Kish see: "How to Become Batman," in *Invisibilia*, NPR, January 23, 2015, https://www.npr.org/programs/invisibilia/378577902/how-to-become-batman.

65 Gallese and Guerra, 163.
66 Turvey, 35.
67 Vittorio Gallese, "Mirror neurons and the neural exploitation hypothesis: From embodied simulation to social cognition," in *Mirror Neuron Systems: The Role of Mirroring Processes in Social Cognition*, ed. Jaime A. Pineda (New York: Humana Press, 2009), 165.
68 Eugenie Brinkema, *The Forms of the Affects* (Durham, NC: Duke University Press, 2014), 26–7.
69 Ibid., 271.
70 Ibid., 26–7. The blank space is included in the original text.
71 Ibid., 130.
72 Ibid., 130–1.
73 Kristeva, *Powers of Horror*, 4.
74 Brinkema also laments the application of Kristeva's work: "Her analysis in *Powers of Horror: An Essay on Abjection* gives shape to abjection, but in the critical tradition that followed, her version of disgust was misread and inappropriately objectified." Brinkema, 137.
75 Brinkema, 134.
76 Troy Michael Bordun, "The End of Extreme Cinema Studies," *Canadian Review of Comparative Literature* vol. 44, no. 1 (March 2017): 124.
77 Ibid., 126–7.
78 Leys, 436.
79 *The Colbert Report*, "Stone Phillips," Comedy Central, season 1, episode 1, October 17, 2005, http://www.cc.com/video-clips/63ite2/the-colbert-report-the-word---truthiness.
80 Galt, 2.
81 Jean-Luc Nancy, *The Ground of the Image*, trans. Jeff Fort (New York: Fordham University Press, 2005), 31–2. Galt cites this passage—see *Pretty*, 2–3.
82 Dudley Andrew cited in Galt, 2–3. See Dudley Andrew, "A Preface to Disputation," in *The Image in Dispute: Art and Cinema in the Age of Photography*, ed. Dudley Andrew (Austin: University of Texas Press, 1997), viii.
83 Galt, 2–3.
84 See Paasonen, 192–3.
85 Shaviro, *The Cinematic Body*, 14–15.
86 "Tilda Swinton Exclusive Interview – SUSPIRIA (2018)," *JoBlo Celebrity Interviews*, YouTube video, November 1, 2018, https://youtu.be/Up_3ogsBKNo.

PART 1

2

On the Beautiful

Introduction: "It's so beautiful..."

The beautiful has been "out of fashion" for quite some time. As Steven Shaviro observed (and this is still probably true more than two decades later since this was first written): "It has become quite fashionable to talk about the Sublime, as it is presented in Kant's *Critique of Judgement,* in relation to postmodernism. But it is rare to find anyone who similarly considers Kant's presentation of the Beautiful."[1] The sublime has the potential to appeal to our more "negative" inclinations—the overwhelming dread or awe popularized in dystopian (sci-fi) narratives (zombie narratives, apocalyptic narratives, cataclysmic [climate] narratives—perhaps even the Marvel universe?). "The Sublime seems more appropriate to contemporary taste," Shaviro observes, "because it is an aesthetic of immensity, excess, and disproportion. Whereas the Beautiful is one of harmony and proportion. It is as if Beauty were somehow old-fashioned, whereas the Sublime is considered more radical."[2] But frankly—in the Trump era, coupled with a global pandemic (only previously envisioned by those very same sublime dystopian narratives mentioned above)—I have had enough. It is time that we reclaim the beautiful and other pleasurable affects.

Pleasurable affects are synonymous with the Kantian conception of the beautiful. Immanuel Kant argues that the beautiful is a subjective experience that is representative of the subject's feelings and reveals nothing innate about the referent which is characterized as "beautiful." To say that the interstitial moments in Terrence Malick's 2011 film *The Tree of Life* are beautiful, actually says very little. The cosmos set to the soaring operatic score of Zbigniew Preisner's "Lacrimosa," again, reveals very little about the audio-visual referent, instead it reveals something about the subject making the utterance—namely, these moments in *The Tree of Life* elicited from me intense pleasure (goosebumps). Expressing that something is "beautiful," then, is little more than a veiled expression of pleasure, and reveals nothing about the innate characteristics of the cinematic material, or whatever the affecting referent might be. Lurking within Kant's *Critique of Judgement*, and specifically his "theory of the beautiful," as Shaviro observes, "is really a theory of affect and of singularity; and it implies an entirely new form of judgment."[3] The aesthetic is a subjective position, it reveals more about the subject than it does about the nature of the referent that is recognized as pleasurable. But this exposes a paradox, because the aesthetic experience is singular (that is, subjective), and "[t]here is no concept to determine it. On the other hand," Shaviro observes, "we see such a judgement as universal, and we demand assent from others regarding it."[4] This formulation of the aesthetic judgement expects concurrence from others, and I will return to this later.

We should pause a moment and think about what this term "aesthetic" actually means. At the root of this discussion of (pleasurable) affects is the visceral experience. The "genuine" aesthetic experience, as Kant deems it, becomes more self-evident when we consider the antonym of "aesthetic," "anesthetic"—that which is supposed to "dull the senses." "Aesthetics," then, in contrast is an experience that "stimulates the senses."[5] Kant uses the "beautiful" as his primary example of the aesthetic experience; he argues that the "beautiful" is a subjective experience that is representative of the subject's feelings and reveals nothing innate about the referent which is characterized as "beautiful." Objects in themselves are not innately beautiful or ugly.

Between 1781 and 1790 Kant published his three Critiques. We can read them as a successive attempt to address the process of judgement, each critique refining the argument further, or if not refining it, teasing out various nuances. Kant's first critique, the *Critique of Pure Reason*, was published in 1781, and largely addresses his ideas on rationality and empiricism. *Critique of Practical Reason* follows this several years later in 1788, focusing on his moral philosophy. In the first two Critiques, as David Shier notes, "Kant examines theoretical and practical judgments—judgments that do not involve determinate concepts. The revelation of the third critique [*Critique of Judgement*] is the existence of an altogether different type of judgment," one that is not based on empirical or intellectual concepts, but a judgement based on sensations.[6] Thus, we have a divide between the first two critiques and the third: the first two focus on cognitive reasoning, while the third focuses on extra-cognitive processes, or, for a lack of a better word, on feelings, on affect. Kant is then speaking of two wholly different types of logic, two separate paradigms of judgement—one that is determined by logic and reason, and another that is determined by feelings, sensations—a theorization of the aesthetic, of affect. "The *Critique of Judgement* might seem to play merely a marginal role in Kant's system," Shaviro observes. "But when Alfred North Whitehead says that philosophy should begin with a 'critique of pure feeling,' instead of reason, this amounts to putting the Third Critique first. For Whitehead, affect precedes cognition, and has a much wider scope than cognition."[7] The present volume, as stated in the previous chapter, has no intention of arguing for the supremacy of affect, rather I simply wish to bring it front and center, bring it out from the shadows and margins where it is generally relegated.

An aesthetic judgement stands outside our cognitive faculties, but it is not without order, or some governing system, "the power of judgement, which in the order of our cognitive faculties forms a middle term between understanding and reason." There is, in a sense, an embodied intelligence (to borrow a phrase from Vivian Sobchack).[8] Kant then wonders what the principles guiding this aesthetic perception of the world are. And the guiding principles of the aesthetic "give a rule *a priori* to the feeling of pleasure and displeasure, as the middle term between the faculties of cognition and desire, just as understanding prescribes laws *a priori* for the former and reason for the latter?" To this rhetorical question, Kant responds, "This is the topic to which the present critique [*Critique of Judgement*] is devoted."[9] In very general terms, then, we might say that Kant attempts to reveal how the subject in the realm of feelings—not logic, the intellect—makes judgements.

If we consider that Kant is merely attempting to redress the deficit of his earlier attempts at theorizing judgement, then his discussion of beauty is one only of expository convenience; he is not interested in beauty necessarily, but the subject's capacity to make judgements in the realm of the senses. "Hegel and Kant," Theodor Adorno notes, "were the last who, to put it bluntly, were able to write major aesthetics [treatises] without understanding anything about art."[10] Beauty is merely a vehicle for Kant to discuss aesthetic judgement, that is, to make judgements even within the domain of feelings, as opposed to the domain of logic and reason. We might say that the framing of beauty for Kant is little more than a philosophical exercise. For Kant, the judgement of taste is the capacity to perceive and make judgements regarding sensations. Kant's philosophical intervention with *Critique of Judgement*, as Michel Foucault suggests, was to articulate a "metaphysical discourse and reflection on the limits of our reason."[11] To discern feelings (taste), or to reflect upon the limits of reason, as with the Kantian beautiful, invites us to think about the affective experience in wider terms.

The Beautiful: A Logic of Sensation

The beautiful is a concept without an object. Kant insists that, "If we wish to discern whether anything is beautiful or not, we do not refer the representation of it to the object by means of understanding with a view to cognition." Rather to determine whether anything is beautiful "we refer the representation to the subject and its feeling of pleasure or displeasure." The aesthetic appeals to us "not [as] a cognitive judgement, and so not logical, but is aesthetic—which means that it is one whose determining ground *cannot be other than subjective*."[12] Theories of affect in cinema and media studies often dovetail with this understanding of the aesthetic experience. This, indeed, has been my guiding principle in attempting to theorize the affective experience. And this has been one of the reasons that I have made efforts (as others have) to delineate the difference between emotion and affect. The aesthetic experience—be it the beautiful, or something else (for instance, the ugly, the abject)—does not assist in our assessment of an object or concept; as Kant states, it "contributes nothing to knowledge," but rather draws from a different regime of judgement.[13] The emotional operates within the realm of cognition, the perceived meaning, and narrative context.

This is not to suggest that the beautiful, or the aesthetic experience in general, has no communicative capacity as such. Rather, as in Jean-François Lyotard, summarizing the position of Kant (and Theodor Adorno), the referent eliciting the aesthetic experience "is not a thinking of non-communication but of non-conceptual communication."[14] It communicates pleasure. Perhaps in this sense the beautiful is like love, where even the most gifted lyricist will fail to communicate the experience in words. To say, "this is beautiful," is to a certain extent to admit a failure, to bow to an inability to express exactly what elicits the feeling of pleasure. Consider briefly, the soliloquy in Spike Lee's 2002 film *25th Hour* (discussed in more detail in the following chapter). I can say that the rant made me feel uncomfortable because of its xenophobic diatribe. I can say that I was exhilarated by its articulation of rage against, as Monty says, "Michael Douglas Gordon Gekko wannabe motherfuckers figuring out new ways to rob hardworking people blind!" These are emotions—discomfort, exhilaration, rage—that are directed to specific objects, to concepts. The beautiful does not refer to specific emotions (within the subject), or to any concept (outside the subject), rather the beautiful is elicited in the poetic or musical form of the discourse. It is not the content, or specifically what Monty says that elicits affect, but the form of the content.

Similarly, when Sarah Jane, in Douglas Sirk's 1959 film *Imitation of Life*, tearfully flings herself across her mother's coffin, proclaiming, "Mama, mama, I didn't mean it. I didn't mean it. Mama, do you hear me?" This is a profoundly sad moment (only those with stone-hearts would fail to cry at the sight). While there is a physiological response, in the form of tears, it is prompted by the emotion of sadness. The melodramatic logic of "too late" is on full-display here, and it is the knowledge that Sarah Jane will never have the opportunity to tell her mother that she did—despite her earlier disavowal—love her. Too late. Tears in this instance are brought on by the perceived meaning, and narrative context—in short, through our cognitive faculties. This is an emotional moment, not necessarily an affective one.

Affect, on the other hand, works by a different "logic." And the beautiful, as outlined by Kant works by this "different logic"—to borrow a phrase from Deleuze, the "logic of sensation." We might take a moment to review the moments immediately prior to Sarah Jane's arrival in *Imitation of Life*. Mahalia Jackson, a renowned American Gospel singer, gives a chilling performance of her 1959 spiritual, "Trouble of the World." Her rich deep voice is backed by a choir singing a harmony—just some variation on "ahhh." While the lyrics befit the narrative moment, and certainly amplify the emotional charge of the scene, it is how Jackson delivers the lyrics that elicit the affective experience. "I'm going home to live with God / No more weepin' and wailin' / No more weepin' and wailin' / No more weepin' and wailin' / Going home to live with my Lord." But it is not simply the communicative value that the spiritual delivers (Sarah Jane's mother is with the Lord now), but rather Jackson's long-drawn-out utterance that comes from the diaphragm—deep within the body. This is the well-spring of affect. While the "message" serves the emotional tenor of the narrative, Jackson's incredible voice (harmonizing with the lektonic utterances of the choir) has the capacity to send chills down the spectator's body. The beautiful lies not in the message, but in the elements that are "empty" of meaning.

Kant agrees, music such as "fantasias (without a theme), and, indeed, all music that is not set to words" has the potential to elicit the beautiful.[15] Just as a momentary thought-experiment: imagine if I were to sing, or just read Jackson's lyrics aloud. How might you respond to such a recitation? My guess is that the experience would either fall flat, or perhaps even come off as grating. I am a terrible singer, and interestingly, if my singing caused a "negative" affective experience, it would be rooted in the dissonant character of my delivery—in a word, form! Now listen, or perhaps better yet watch Jackson sing, "Trouble of the World," in *Imitation of Life*, preferably with a good sound system (form matters, and tinny computer speakers will not quite match the experience of hearing it with high quality speakers). While the content in my little thought experiment is identical (that is, the lyrics and the implied narrative are the same), it is the form that changes, and thus pointing us toward the formal qualities of the cinematic.[16]

This in fact is where affect might intersect with politics—where rousing speeches might elicit an affective charge. And this is something that politicians of every political stripe use. Whereas speech (that is, spoken, or even written discourse) anticipates and prioritizes communication, music—or the musicalization of the voice—is lent far greater latitude to embellish utterances with texture, tone, intonation, rhythm, the truncation or elongation of an enunciation. And this is one of the "secrets" to great oration—whether it is Martin Luther King, Barack Obama, Michelle Obama, Maya Angelou. Is it any wonder that those that I have listed also have connections to black American spirituals, to rousing gospels—drawing on the very aesthetic strategies illustrated in Jackson's performance? Interestingly, in Questlove's 2021 documentary, *The Summer of Soul (. . . Or, When the Revolution Could Not Be Televised)*, Reverend Al Sharpton explains, "Gospel was therapy for the stress and pressure of being Black in America." He adds, "We didn't go to a psychiatrist. We didn't go lay on a couch. We didn't know anything about therapists. But we knew Mahalia Jackson."[17] To slightly reconfigure Kristeva's phrase, "art is a substitute for prayer," and analogously we might say, music has the ability to serve as a substitute for the analyst's couch.[18] Music resonates with the soul. And it achieves this not just in what is communicated, but in how the message is delivered and where it nearly tumbles into musicality—particularly with rhyme schemes, poetic turns of phrase, and strategic pauses that establish rhythmic beats. It is in this musicality of the voice that affect lies. Recall how Martin Luther King's "I Have a Dream" speech soars upward: "And I've seen the Promised Land," King proclaims stressing and elongating the word "seen." Followed by a flatter delivery with, "I may not get there with you." And the "flatness" of the previous line almost serves as a launching pad for the following lines that rise in intensity and volume, "But I want you to know tonight, that we, as a people, will get to the promised land!" There is an emotional appeal in the message that King delivers, but it is laced with affect as well in its poetic or musicalization of the voice.[19]

The capacity to levy judgement in the realm of the sensate is what Kant refers to as "taste." Kant posits that "the judgement of taste is simply contemplative, i.e. it is a judgement which is indifferent as to the existence of an object, and only decides how its character stands with the feeling of pleasure and displeasure." Kant adds to this, though, emphasizing that this contemplative state is not "directed to concepts; for the judgement of taste is not a cognitive judgement (neither a theoretical one nor a practical), and hence, also, is not grounded on concepts, nor yet intentionally directed to them."[20] Exercising the capacity to make a judgement in the sensate experience is to demonstrate taste. "Taste is the faculty of judging an object or a mode of representation by means of a delight or aversion apart from any interest," Kant conceives. "The object of such a delight is called beautiful."[21] (The term "interest" is significant, and it is something that I will return to shortly.)

Subjective Universality, Disinterestedness, and Taste

Implicit in the judgement of taste is a presupposed "ought." To stake a claim that, for example, Mizoguchi's highly stylized encounter with the Golden Pavilion in Paul Schrader's 1985 film *Mishima: A Life in Four Chapters* is beautiful—that moment when the Golden Pavilion splits apart and towers over Mizoguchi in all of its golden glow coupled with Philip Glass's score—is to implicitly state, "you ought to feel the same." Clearly, though, we understand that in fact there will not be unanimous agreement here by any means, nonetheless we might appreciate how this might be a commonly shared experience. Kant insists that judgement of taste presupposes pleasure (or displeasure) from everyone, and thus the individual that states "this is beautiful," "has reason for expecting a similar delight from everyone." Although a judgement of taste—to make a judgement in the realm of the aesthetic experience—is not based in logic, it might nonetheless be conceived as though it were. And thus, the individual might "speak of the beautiful as if beauty were a feature of the object and the judgement were logical (forming a cognition of the object by concepts of it)." An aesthetic judgement "bears this resemblance to the logical judgement, that it may be presupposed to be valid for everyone. But this universality cannot spring from concepts." The beautiful, or the aesthetic experience, has nothing to do with concepts, concepts do not yield "the feeling of pleasure or displeasure (save in the case of pure practical laws, which, however, carry an interest with them; and such an interest does not attach to the pure judgement of taste)." Exercising the (pure) judgement of taste, "with its attendant consciousness of detachment from all interest, must involve a claim to validity for everyone, and must do so apart from a universality directed to objects, that is, there must be coupled with it a claim to subjective universality."[22] And it is in this subjective universality where the "ought" might be resolved. While we might not all experience the same thing, a specific referent that might elicit pleasure (or displeasure) in one might leave another feeling nothing, the judgement of taste is itself a universal human faculty.

Kant adds further that we do not say, "This is beautiful for me." If it needs to be qualified "for me," then, it is not a purely aesthetic judgement. In the presence of company, we might blame others "if they judge differently" from us, and exclaim that any dissenters have no taste, or in a diplomatic gesture we might say, "Everyone has ... [their] own taste." Kant, though, is not interested in diplomatic gestures and insists that saying everyone has their own taste is "equivalent to saying that there is no such thing at all as taste, i.e. no aesthetic judgement capable of making a rightful claim upon the assent of everyone."[23] This is yet one more reason why the object is not beautiful, the beautiful has nothing to do with any external referent, but rather the beautiful only refers to the feeling of pleasure, and thus is universal insofar as it is a universal human experience.

Kant invites us to consider form by calling our attention to disinterestedness, or purposelessness. The aesthetic experience is "disinterested" Kant declares, in other words, the experience is aroused by something that has no function, no communicative value necessarily. In fact, this component of aesthetic judgement "is of the utmost importance," a "pure" aesthetic judgement is disinterested, and any "judgement of taste with that which is allied to an interest," is not properly speaking an aesthetic judgement.[24] Kant concedes that "[t]here can be no objective rule of taste by which what is beautiful may be defined by means of concepts." Every judgement of taste has as its determining ground "the feeling of the subject, and not any concept of an object." Kant implores us not to waste our time looking "for a principle of taste that affords a universal criterion of the beautiful by determinate concepts." In other words, there is no logic as such to determine what an aesthetic object might be. The beautiful cannot be reduced to a formula so to speak, "because what is sought is something impossible and inherently contradictory." While it is impossible to name beautiful objects, the capacity to make judgements of taste stems "from a deep-seated ground, one shared alike by all human beings, underlying their agreement in judging the forms under which objects are given to them."[25] Is the present venture then nothing but a fool's errand? Of course, I respond in the negative, as evident in the premise established at the outset of this volume: I stake no claim to creating a taxonomy of things, or objects that might elicit the beautiful (or pleasurable affects in general), rather I stress forms, style, or the manner in which content is treated. If it is possible at all to create anything approaching a taxonomy of the beautiful, it is going to be found in the audio-visual strategies that affect how we perceive it—it is not the object in itself, but how it is presented and apprehended, and subsequently subjected to a judgement of taste.[26] And this returns us to Eugenie Brinkema's insistence, discussed in the previous chapter, that developing a taxonomical list of items that are disgusting, that is to identify specific objects as abject, is to miss the point.[27]

I also should emphasize that the how is critical, how the external referent is presented to us. And this applies to the directly lived-experience, or in some representational form. Thus, a landscape at noontime, when the sun is directly overhead, might for example appear to us as mundane and unmoving. As opposed to the early morning hours, for example, where that very same landscape might be dramatically lit by the sun low in the horizon cutting through trees and mist, the stillness felt in the chilly air, and the soundscape filled with birdsong. Nothing changes, the object remains the same, it is how that object is perceived that changes, and it is in this how the aesthetic experience potentially resides. As for representational forms, let us take Godfrey Reggio's 2002 film *Naqoyqatsi* as an example. In the opening moments of the film, which linger over Michigan Central Station in Detroit, closed in 1988 and abandoned, the building might have an "agreeableness" to it, but that is premised on concepts. It is agreeable in its neoclassical style and ruined state, the latter inviting comparisons to the Romantic tradition (for instance, Caspar David Friedrich's 1809–10 painting, *Abbey in the Oak Forest*). In this cognitive apprehension of the content, there is the potential for pleasure, but this is not an aesthetic judgement—it is not beautiful. If, though, at the same time we find aesthetic pleasure in this sequence, it stems from Reggio's embellishments. It comes in the form of color, tone, lighting, camera movement, and most significantly the Phillip Glass soundtrack. It is not Michigan Central Station itself that is deemed beautiful, but in how it is treated, and our subsequent aesthetic perception of it. In fact, were we to replace the audio-design with some Eli Roth inspired soundtrack—dripping water, low bassy drone, dissonant stringed instruments, grinding rusty metal—this very same material with its muted palette and ruined state might well elicit the abject.

The experience of the beautiful, or the aesthetic experience in all its possible forms, is what sets humans apart from the animal kingdom. Kant identifies three types of pleasurable feelings: "[t]he agreeable, the beautiful, and the good." However, these forms of pleasure spawn from different kinds of judgement. While the agreeable gratifies us, and thus has a function, and is even evident "with animals devoid of reason." The good, on the other hand, "is good for every rational being in general," and is the product of a moral law. The beautiful, though, is on a different order and "simply pleases us." The aesthetic experience lends evidence to something like a "spirit," or "soul" in Kant's view: "beauty has purport and significance only for human beings, i.e. for beings at once animal and rational (but not merely for them as rational beings—as spirits, for example—but only for them as both animal and rational)."[28] And from this view, it is little wonder why so many religious practices might intend to elicit an aesthetic experience in an effort to "touch" or to "move" the soul: songs, incantations, recitations, chanting, ornate regalia, rituals, processions, architecture intended to elicit awe. The religious narratives might vary—be they Hindu, Buddhist, Islamic, Jewish, Christian, or some other organized spiritual belief—but they all mobilize the aesthetic experience in some fashion to aesthetically "touch" their devotees.

Julia Kristeva makes a similar observation regarding the abject: "The various means of purifying the abject—the various catharses—make up the history of religions, and end up with that catharsis par excellence called art, both on the far and near side of religion. Seen from that standpoint," Kristeva continues, "the artistic experience, which is rooted in the abject it utters and by the same token purifies, appears as the essential component of religiosity. That is perhaps why it is destined to survive the collapse of the historical forms of religions."[29] Religious and artistic practices have developed strategies to elicit and capitalize on the aesthetic experience.

The beautiful, which stems from Kantian disinterestedness, insists upon a different mode of "thinking," if we can even call it that. Rather than "thinking" or even "perception," Shaviro directs our attention to Alfred North Whitehead's conceptualization of "prehension." "To avoid the anthropomorphic—or at least cognitive and rationalistic—connotations of words like 'mentality' and 'perception,' Whitehead uses the term prehension for the act by which one actual occasion takes up and responds to another." As it is conceived prehension is not human-centered, but an innate condition of all entities, as Shaviro explains, "the earth prehends the sun that gives it energy; the stone prehends the earth to which it falls."[30] To prehend is to be affected by another entity, often unconsciously—and it need not be a "thing" as such. A judgement of taste is a type of prehension, which is disinterested. (Interestingly, the term "prehend" means to "grasp," or to "seize," and finds affinities with Susanna Paasonen's conceptualization of "resonance" or "grabbing"—where pornography relies less on "identification," and more on being "grabbed." Paasonen is discussed further in the Arousal Section.[31]) By contrast, where interest relates to what the referent might be—its characteristics, its conceptualization (its meaning), its place in the regime of categories—the aesthetic experience is less an object and instead stands, as Melissa McMahon observes, as "more a 'sign,' a trigger.

The attribute of beauty attaches not to the object but to the 'event' of the beautiful."[32] To imagine the beautiful as an experiential event, as opposed to a thing in the world is highly productive.

Shaviro positions the Kantian beautiful in exactly these terms. An encounter with the beautiful is indicative of "being lured, allured, seduced, repulsed, incited, or dissuaded." Shaviro suggests that "[b]eauty is therefore an event, a process." An external referent, be it a flower, or the "Lacrimosa" sequence in *The Tree of Life*, "is not beautiful in itself," as I discuss above, but elicits the sensation of pleasure. "Beauty is fleeting," Shaviro adds, "and it is always imbued with otherness . . . I can only find beauty when the object solicits me, or arouses my sense of beauty, in a certain way."[33] And thus, as I stated in the introductory chapter of the present volume, we cannot really speak of "beautiful movies" as such, only instances of the beautiful in our encounter with the cinematic. It is a fleeting encounter that is ephemeral and subjective.

The aesthetic experience is solely in the realm of the visceral—the body and its senses. We could take classical music as an example of how "disinterestedness" functions, because beauty is located not in what the music "communicates"—if it communicates anything at all—but in the "raw" musicality itself; the beautiful is that inexplicable moment when Johann Sebastian Bach's "Saint Matthew Passion," or some other work, causes your hair to stand on end, when you get a shiver, when you are moved to tears by harmony, melody, tone, and so on. Analogous to the discussion above regarding *Imitation of Life*, it is not the content of the music (for example, the lyrics, or in this example the Passion), but the form that potentially triggers the aesthetic experience. Sung in German, and in the classical sacred music tradition, this in fact would preclude many listeners from perceiving the "meaning" of the audio referent. And yet I would wager that for many it would be moving. Think too of the wildly popular 2017 pop-song "Despacito," by Luis Fonsi and Daddy Yankee, which broke into non-Spanish speaking markets. The success of the song at least in part owes to its affective appeal, rather than any cognitive judgement.[34] As Michael Caine's character in *Youth* (Paolo Sorrentino, 2015) explains, "Music is all I understand, because you don't need words and experience to understand it. It just is." Caine's character is renowned for his collection of "Simple Songs," and indeed, the compositions are lyrically simple—no different than any pop song. But despite the simplicity of the words (downright cliché in fact) Sumi Jo, a professional singer, plays herself, and if there is affect in it is in her soaring delivery in "Simple Song Number 3" (which was actually nominated for the 2016 Academy Award for best song).

As previously established, there is an implicit "ought," in the declaration that something is beautiful. "The judgement of taste," Kant states, "expects agreement from everyone; and a person who describes something as beautiful insists that everyone ought to give the object in question . . . [their] approval and follow suit in describing it as beautiful." And in this presumed "ought in aesthetic judgements," even though it fulfills the prerequisite for a pure judgement of taste, "is still only pronounced conditionally."[35] Again, it is not that everyone will share the same experience necessarily, but that the aesthetic experience is in itself universal, and it is in the latter that there should be agreement. And yet we still might not tolerate divergent views when "we describe anything as beautiful," and this is despite the fact that "we do not rest our judgement upon concepts, but only on our feeling. Accordingly," Kant states, "we introduce this underlying feeling not as a private feeling, but as a common one." A pure judgement of taste, however, cannot be subsumed under the principle of "common sense," as it is premised on some conception of an ideal, as Kant says, "common sense is a mere ideal norm."[36] Nevertheless, as Samantha Matherne concludes, this notion of an aesthetic common sense indicates that taste can be acquired "through effort and education."[37] Pierre Bourdieu likewise suggests that far from being an innate experience, what might be characterized as common sense is a product of exposure and the cultivation of a disposition. "The 'eye,'" the ability to prehend the beautiful, to have taste, Bourdieu argues, "is a product of history reproduced by education."[38] The common sense of an ideal aesthetic norm is not strictly speaking a "pure" aesthetic judgement, but it stands as a template, a model, a map charting a path toward the experience of the beautiful. And this is, at its heart, my objective in the present volume.

The *Critique of Pure Reason* enquires about the nature of judgement, and Kant determines that judgement is the ability to submit something to a set of rules: "the power of judgment is the faculty of subsuming under rules, i.e., of determining whether something stands under a given rule (*casus datae legis* [case of the given law]) or not."[39] So, for example, if object X has a fur coat, four legs, pointed snout, and barks it must be a dog. This conclusion that object X must be a dog is the order of judging, because these qualities satisfy the criteria for "dog-ness." But this brings forth an immediate question: what happens when we encounter something that defies practical judgement? In other words, what happens when we encounter something that does not conform to any rules, to perceptible categorization, or to concepts? The beautiful is nothing but an example for Kant in his effort to isolate how we make judgements in the face of a non-object, a perception that does not conform to any category, rule, or concept. Kant suggests that the capacity to make judgements is innate to the human condition, or that there is an archaic form of human judgement, and Kant hopes to unearth the nature and power of this supposed innate, or archaic capacity to make judgements. And analogous to the earlier division between Kant's critiques, he decides to introduce "a distinction between determinant and reflective judgments."[40] While determinant judgements might be made in the domain of cognition, "aesthetic judgments are a variety of reflective judgment."[41] Thus, my earlier example, where X must be a dog, would be a determinant judgement; whether the dog was beautiful or ugly, that would be a reflective judgement.

In addition to our individual subjectivity, historical and cultural context are critical in determining taste—in other words, the capacity or openness to discern hedonic experiences. We often perceive taste as an indicator of cultural elitism, at least this is how taste is often framed colloquially, but rather taste might be imagined as a historical and cultural lens through which the subject interacts with the world. Bourdieu similarly speaks of taste as an acquired disposition, associated with class and education.[42] For Bourdieu it is not predetermined or predestined, but rather an individual steeped in a particular cultural milieu might be more receptive to certain experiences.[43] Because it is a stark example, let us return to music once again. Musical traditions vary from culture to culture. While Western music is premised on halftones, other traditions, for example Persian music, are premised on quartertones. As a result, to a Western ear, some Persian music might sound dissonant as it might be perceived as "in-between" notes (see for example the Sigah scale). Similarly, those unfamiliar with the traditions of minimalist music, take for instance Philip Glass's "In the Upper Room: Dance No. 8" (1987), which to uninitiated ears might come off as annoyingly repetitive, others familiar with Glass, or minimalist scoring generally, might be swept away by its repeated circular melody. (This circular motif will reappear in my discussion of Thom Yorke's scoring of Guadagnino's 2018 film *Suspiria*.) Thus cultural, historical, and personal context plays a part in a subject's disposition, their taste, their capacity to be moved by a particular referent. This would also account for differences in human attraction—in what is conceived as beautiful in a particular historical and cultural context.

Conclusion: The Common Aesthetic Experience

The beautiful, then, operates according to the principle of subjective universalism. While the operation of the beautiful itself is universal to the human condition, the specific external referent that might "trigger" (using McMahon's terminology) the beautiful is subjective. And this might suggest that the present discussion of the beautiful is essentially futile. "The beautiful is composed of examples that nevertheless cannot be reduced to rules," Shaviro notes. "Instances of the beautiful are examples in themselves, but not examples of anything." Shaviro adds, "You can point to them as examples; but you cannot point to that of which they are examples. Each is a singularity [that is, subjective]: an instance that can be emulated, but not imitated."[44] However, what is abundantly clear is that humanity endeavors to make beautiful things, in an effort to elicit the aesthetic experience. While everyone might not experience goosebumps upon encountering Sumi Jo's performance in *Youth*, the moment when Mizoguchi stands before the Golden Pavilion in *Mishima*, the interlude in *The Tree of Life* set to "Lacrimosa," Jackson's performance in *The Imitation of Life*, or Michigan Central Station in *Naqoyqatsi*, these represent examples of the commonly shared aesthetic experience. It is my task here to identify what appear to be the typical cinematic strategies that might elicit this commonly shared aesthetic experience.[45]

It certainly would be a lot easier if there were a universal human experience—to point to an innate biological response. Or if there were specific things or objects that elicited an aesthetic experience. The human experience, alas, is far more complex than any deterministic model would be capable of apprehending. Historical and cultural context matters too—not to mention formative individual experiences. Thus, my ambition here is to identify an aesthetic common sense (as referenced above), not to itemize beautiful things as such (which would not even qualify as a pure disinterested judgement), but to discern representational strategies that harbor the potential to elicit an aesthetic experience. And it is not things or objects that necessarily elicit the beautiful, but the form, or the style in which objects are presented. Thus, the beautiful is often a response to an encounter with those more ineffable "things"—the lektonic elements such as color, composition, and sound design. And it is the compositional, chromatic, and auditory strategies that are mobilized in neo-giallo films that elicit the aesthetic experience. This is the subject of the following chapter.

Notes

1 Steven Shaviro, "Beauty Lies in the Eye," *Symplokē* vol. 6, no. 1/2 (1998): 96.
2 Ibid.

3 Steven Shaviro, *Without Criteria: Kant, Whitehead, Deleuze, and Aesthetics* (Cambridge, MA: MIT Press, 2009), 1.
4 Shaviro, "Beauty Lies in the Eye," 100.
5 Susan Buck-Morss discusses this in her essay, "Aesthetics and Anaesthetics: Walter Benjamin's artwork essay reconsidered," *October* vol. 62 (1992): 3–41.
6 David Shier, "Why Kant Finds Nothing Ugly," *The British Journal of Aesthetics* vol. 38, no. 4 (October, 1998): 413.
7 Shaviro, *Without Criteria*, 14. Shaviro earlier notes:

> Kant's aesthetics is just one part of his system. He insists that aesthetic judgments are noncognitive, in order to differentiate them from judgments of understanding (which concern matters of empirical fact) and from moral judgments (which are categorical obligations or commands). This attempt to distinguish different sorts of judgment, and to circumscribe the powers and limits of each, remains crucial today. For it warns us against the totalitarianism of reason, or (to express the point more modestly) against the endeavor of scientists, philosophers, political despots, and religious fanatics to impose a unified field of assessment, in which the same fundamental critical standards would apply across all disciplines. Such an imposition could only have catastrophic consequences, for it would mean the end of any sort of novelty, creativity, or invention. Needless to say, this dream of totalizing reason is as incapable of realization as it is undesirable in principle. But it is also a dream that never goes away, since it is what Kant calls a "transcendental illusion," a self-deception built into the very nature of reason. Since we are always being lured by this illusion, like moths to a flame, we always need Kant to warn us against it. In the end, of course, the mania for reason, truth, foundations, and universally valid criteria is as singular, as gratuitous, and as intractable as any other passion. As Whitehead says, "the primary function of theories is as a lure for feeling"; and we cannot do without such theories and such lures.

Shaviro, *Without Criteria*, 13–14. See Alfred North Whitehead, *Process and Reality* (New York: The Free Press, 1978), 184.
8 Vivian Sobchack, *Carnal Thoughts: Embodiment and Moving Image Culture* (Berkeley: University of California Press, 2004), 84.
9 Immanuel Kant, *Critique of Judgement*, trans. James Creed Meredith (New York: Oxford University Press, 2007), 4.
10 Theodor Adorno, *Aesthetic Theory*, trans. Robert Hullot-Kentor, eds Gretel Adorno and Rolf Tiedemann (Minneapolis: University of Minnesota Press, 1999), 334.
11 Michel Foucault, *Aesthetics, Method, and Epistemology: Essential Works of Foucault* Vol. 2., trans. Robert Hurley et al., ed. James Faubion (New York: The New Press, 1998), 76.
12 Kant, 35. Emphasis in original.
13 Ibid., 36.
14 Jean-François Lyotard, *The Inhuman: Reflections on Time*, trans. Geoffrey Bennington and Rachel Bowlby (Stanford: Stanford University Press, 1991), 109.
15 Kant, 60.
16 Graham Harman makes an analogous observation regarding poetry:

> This explains the unsatisfying, even annoying effect that occurs when people quote poems and song lyrics for content, as though they were translatable into statements of prosaic wisdom. In fact, poets have less in common with oracles than with the voluptuous sorcery of drummers or chefs, and are just as difficult to quote out of context as cymbals or wine. In any case, the animating style of the artwork makes it analogous to

the human body, so central to Merleau-Ponty's thought: each of these is 'a nexus of living meanings, not the law for a certain number of covariant terms.

Graham Harman, *Guerrilla Metaphysics: Phenomenology and the Carpentry of Things* (Chicago: Open Court, 2005), 56. Harman cites Merleau-Ponty, *Phenomenology of Perception*, trans. Colin Smith (London: Routledge, 2002), 208.

17 Reverend Al Sharpton in *The Summer of Soul (. . . Or, When the Revolution Could Not Be Televised)*, Questlove, 2021.
18 Kristeva actually says in *Black Sun*, "Painting as a substitute for prayer? Contemplating the painting might perhaps replace prayer at the critical place of its appearance—where the nonmeaning becomes significant, while death seems visible and livable." Julia Kristeva, *Black Sun: Depression and Melancholia*, trans. Leon S. Roudiez (New York: Columbia University Press, 1989), 138. In one of the few instances where Kristeva actually discusses the cinema, she suggests that the "cinema would be nothing else but a new Church." Julia Kristeva, *Intimate Revolt: The Powers and Limits of Psychoanalysis*, trans. Jeanine Herman (New York: Columbia University Press, 2002), 80.
19 Perhaps at the other end of the spectrum, see, for example, Nina Simone's performance of "Stars / Feelings" (Live at Montreux, 1976). There are long pauses between lyrics, and these long pauses are viscerally painful, adding emotional/affective force to the utterances of "feelings." And furthermore, the actual delivery of the lyrics is almost flat (or even slightly dissonant), but the long pauses introduce visceral feeling into phrases like: "I will always have my feelings / Nothing can destroy them / Cause I know that that is all that there is at the base for you." This is available on YouTube: https://youtu.be/Mf_5l1yTKNY. Interestingly, Ja'Tovia M. Gary, in her 2019 experimental documentary *The Giverny Document (Single Channel)*, appropriated the Simone material, and inserted various animated sequences and other footage, to musicalize the image. See more about this in the "musicality" chapter. I wish to acknowledge my research assistant Birdy Wei-Ting Hung for calling my attention to this material.
20 Kant, 41.
21 Ibid., 42.
22 Ibid., 43.
23 Ibid., 44.
24 Ibid., 37.
25 Ibid., 62.
26 Kant suggests that it might be possible to create a taxonomy of the beautiful, but with some caveats. See Kant, 63.
27 Eugenie Brinkema, *The Forms of the Affects* (Durham, NC: Duke University Press, 2014), 130–1.
28 Kant, 41.
29 Julia Kristeva, *Powers of Horror: An Essay on Abjection*, trans. Leon S. Roudiez (New York: Columbia University Press, 1982), 17.
30 Shaviro, *Without Criteria*, 27–8.
31 "Prehend," s.v., OED. See Susanna Paasonen, *Carnal Resonance: Affect and Online Pornography* (Cambridge, MA: MIT Press, 2011), 16. My research assistant, Birdy Wei-Ting Hung, made this connection between prehension and grabbing.

32 Melissa McMahon, "Beauty: Machinic repetition in the age of art," in *A Shock to Thought: Expression after Deleuze and Guattari*, ed. Brian Massumi (New York: Routledge, 2002), 46. McMahon references Immanuel Kant, *Critique of Judgement*, trans. Werner S. Pluhar (Indianapolis: Hackett, 1987), 30.
33 Shaviro, *Without Criteria*, 3.
34 As Marisa Arbona-Ruiz reports the song "made history as only the third Spanish-language song to reach No. 1 on the *Billboard* Hot 100." Marisa Arbona-Ruiz, "From 'La Bamba' To 'Despacito': What Comes After A Huge Spanish-Language Hit," *Alt.Latino*, NPR, November 20, 2017, https://www.npr.org/sections/altlatino/2017/11/13/563920922/from-la-bamba-to-despacito-what-comes-after-a-huge-spanish-language-hit.
35 Kant, 68.
36 Ibid., 70.
37 Samantha Matherne, "Kant on Aesthetic Autonomy and Common Sense," *Philosopher's Imprint* vol. 19, no 24 (June 2019): 20.
38 Pierre Bourdieu, *Distinction: A social critique of the judgement of taste*, trans. Richard Nice (Cambridge, MA: Harvard University Press, 1984), 3. Earlier in the same text, Bourdieu wrote,

> Whereas the ideology of charisma regards taste in legitimate culture as a gift of nature, scientific observation shows that cultural needs are the product of upbringing and education: surveys establish that all cultural practices (museum visits, concert-going, reading etc.), and preferences in literature, painting or music, are closely linked to educational level (measured by qualifications or length of schooling) and secondarily to social origin. The relative weight of home background and of formal education (the effectiveness and duration of which are closely dependent on social origin) varies according to the extent to which the different cultural practices are recognized and taught by the educational system, and the influence of social origin is strongest—other things being equal—in "extra-curricular" and avant-garde culture. To the socially recognized hierarchy of the arts, and within each of them, of genres, schools or periods, corresponds a social hierarchy of the consumers. This predisposes tastes to function as markers of class.

Pierre Bourdieu, *Distinction*, 1.
39 Kant, 268.
40 Salim Kemal, *Kant's Aesthetic Theory: An Introduction* (London: Macmillan, 1992), 28.
41 Ibid.
42 Pierre Bourdieu, *Distinction*, 466.
43 See the section entitled, "An Anti-Kantian 'Aesthetic,'" in Pierre Bourdieu, *Distinction*, 41–4. Bourdieu writes,

> If formal explorations, in avant-garde theatre or non-figurative painting, or simply classical music, are disconcerting to working-class people, this is partly because they feel incapable of understanding what these things must signify, insofar as they are signs. Hence the uninitiated may experience as inadequate and unworthy a satisfaction that cannot be grounded in a meaning transcendent to the object. Not knowing what the "intention" is, they feel incapable of distinguishing a tour de force from clumsiness, telling a "sincere" formal device from cynical imposture.

Pierre Bourdieu, *Distinction*, 43.
44 Shaviro, "Beauty Lies in the Eye," 100.

45 Some research suggests, however, "that up to 40% of the population does not experience the phenomenon of awe." Kristin Neidlinger et al., "AWElectric: that gave me goosebumps, did you feel it too?" in *Proceedings of the Eleventh International Conference on Tangible, Embedded, and Embodied Interaction* (2017): 315.

3

Neo-Giallo
"It's beautiful, it's beautiful, it's beautiful," the Affective Experience in *Suspiria*

Introduction: (Neo-)Giallo and Affect

Before discussing Luca Guadagnino's 2018 film *Suspiria*, which is the primary focus of this chapter, I will first address the renewed interest in the giallo film.[1] Giallo, meaning yellow in Italian, referred to pulp fiction novels (with yellow covers) that featured stories such as murder mysteries, police procedurals, and stalk and slash narratives to which the American slasher film owes a deep debt. Drawing from the literary model, giallo films were, as Lindsay Hallam recounts, "made in high numbers throughout the 1960s and 1970s, gaining popularity within Italy while also garnering screenings and fans abroad."[2] The giallo, indeed, reached audiences far and wide—take for example, screening practices in Taiwan. Under the rule of the Kuomintang party, which established martial law from 1949 until 1987, the regime implemented strict censorship ordinances. To skirt regulations theater owners would insert illicit material—often smuggled from abroad, including giallo films—and splice them into sanctioned films. Theater owners established an array of mechanisms to alert the projection booth when government inspectors would arrive, allowing the theater to switch back to certified material. Seasoned audience members played right along with the whole routine, and even anticipated a disjunctive viewing experience. Edwige Fenech, one of the "sex goddesses" associated with giallo films, was a major draw for Taiwanese audiences. Newspaper advertisements merely needed to mention her name (which served as a nod and wink) to bring in audiences, who reveled at the prospects of seeing some sexually charged spectacle featuring Fenech, or other well-known starlets of the genre.[3] In the American context, giallo films gained traction with videocassette distribution, and prior to that, as Raidford Guins observes, "were exhibited in limited release, or found on the midnight movie circuit, or at paracinema festivals, or at drive-in cinemas after their post-War glamour period had run its course."[4] Regardless, the point here is that spectators did not attend these screenings for coherent narratives as such, but rather were lured to the theater with the promise of seeing some sort of rousing spectacle.

While the hallmark of the giallo rested upon its promise to deliver audio-visual spectacles, the exact parameters of the genre are subject to some debate. Giallo films, as Hallam notes, "are a melding of Agatha Christie style murder mysteries, with victims dispatched one by one, and Edgar Allan Poe inspired horror expressed through an air of paranoia and a tinge of the Gothic, often seen in an expressionistic and stylized set design suggesting psychological disturbance and mental fracturing." Hallam then surmises that, "the design aesthetic of these films plays a significant role in creating a sense of fear, unease, and disorientation, as much as, perhaps even more, than the plot itself, again highlighting the emphasis on affect rather than narrative."[5] No matter how threadbare the plot, or how outlandish the killing numbers were, giallo films were often dismissed by respectable critics, but loved by audiences because of their indulgences that privileged style over substance (read: narrative). It should be noted, though, that giallo films (and filmmakers such as Argento and Mario Bava) garnered some cultural cache as "cult-art" films.[6]

Dario Argento's mobilization of embellished colors, and the highly orchestrated and spectacular killing numbers, as well as bold scoring make *Suspiria* a touchstone in the giallo tradition. The narrative of Argento's *Suspiria* is fairly thin (Guadagnino's film differs significantly in this respect, which will be discussed later). "The narrative of the giallo, which was never a strong element, is thrown aside in order to emphasise the giallo's power to provide a sensory experience," as Hallam recounts. "Things never really made sense in a giallo, events were often implausible, psychological motivations were sketchy and trite, and resolutions usually arbitrary and unsatisfying." Rather the giallo delivered on the promise to offer "sex and violence not as events to progress the narrative but as visceral experiences which attracted audience attention precisely because they were cinematic events that audiences could feel, without having to follow the story."[7] There has been a renewed interest in giallo aesthetics: from the husband-wife filmmaking duo Hélène Cattet and Bruno Forzani—having made *Amer* (2009), *The Strange Color of Your Body's Tears* (2013), and *Let the Corpses Tan* (2017)—to Peter Strickland's 2012 film *Berberian Sound Studio* and his 2018 film *In Fabric*. *Amer*, in particular, is invested in the giallo tradition that treats the cinematic experience as a theme park attraction—an untamed cinematic attraction—unyielding to narrative imperatives and instead, like a roller coaster, invites the spectator on an audio-visual thrill ride.[8]

What these neo-giallo films share in common with original giallo films is their pretension toward affectively charged sexual and/or violent numbers. The narratives in the original giallo were secondary to the spectacles, which were designed to elicit a strong visceral response from the spectator. Neo-giallo films, drawing on the genre's emphasis on affectively charged spectacles, retain their "power to create strong affects, rather than (and often at the expense of) telling a coherent story." Neo-giallo films emphasize big bold spectacles, embellished with strong color palettes, occasional heavy-handed cinematography (extreme close-ups especially focusing on eyes, zooms), and sound design, intended to reach the spectator "at a sensory level, not a narrative level. There is a conscious intertextual engagement with previous giallo films, in a way that emphasizes their fundamental affective qualities."[9]

Guadagnino's film is far more invested in narrative than Argento's original, and the giallo tradition generally. Nonetheless, Guadagnino's *Suspiria* emphasizes the affective charge at particular narrative moments. While (neo-)gialli films in general lean into dread, or the horrific—in short, what we might call "negative affect"—Guadagnino emphasizes the beautiful. Make no mistake though, Guadagnino does not turn away from "negative affects"—the dread and the exhibition of gore are both there—but there is also beauty in the horror. Just briefly—because again the whole objective here is to locate the beautiful—but when the coven kills the wayward dancer Olga in Guadagnino's film, it is executed in the most brutal fashion. Madame Blanc appears to harness Susie's movements to Olga, through some witch's spell turning Olga into a helpless marionette. As Susie dances, Olga is violently thrown up against walls and the floor, her limbs dislocate and contort in the most unnatural position (including her jaw), she drools and urinates, and in the end lays in a disfigured monstrosity. The audio design as well amplifies the dread associated with this sequence—the crunchy sounds of bones and sinews snapping, the unintelligibility of Olga's crying and screams of agony. All this—possession, leaking, unnatural contortion, the lektonic utterances of agony—is what potentially elicits the abject. Nonetheless, there are other instances, perhaps even co-present with the abject, where Guadagnino elicits a strong positive affective response.

Beauty in the Horror

Luca Guadagnino's 2018 film *Suspiria* is not quite a remake of Dario Argento's 1977 cult classic film of the same name, though there are some similarities. Tilda Swinton, who plays Madame Blanc (and surreptitiously two other roles) in Guadagnino's film, refers to it as a "cover" (as in a "cover song").[10] In whatever way we wish to characterize it—re-imagining, cover, homage, inspired by—there are still some clear affinities in the plot: Susie (Suzy in Argento's film) an aspiring American dancer joins a German dance company, which just so happens to be run by a coven of witches. In this way the films are similar, though Guadagnino diverges from Argento's narrative in some significant ways (which I will discuss later). In terms of style, there might be some slight similarities as well, specifically with the use of color. Guadagnino's film remains largely "naturalistic," though notably cool and muted in its earthy palette, while Argento is well known for his use of bold contrasting colors. Guadagnino, though, especially in the climactic moment of the film, applies a crimson filter, which harkens back to Argento. Both films also utilize striking scores: while Argento makes fantastic use of the proto-goth band Goblin, Guadagnino commissioned Thom Yorke (of Radiohead fame) to compose a haunting soundtrack that greatly amplifies the affective charge of his film.

In both cases, the narrative is adapted from Thomas De Quincey's 1854 collection of fantastical essays, "Suspiria de profoundis," meaning "sighs from the depths." These collected reflections were conceived as a continuation of his earlier 1821 publication *Confessions of an English Opium-Eater*. Fueled by opium, dreamwork, and impassioned language—De Quincey wrote in poetic prose—the source text for *Suspiria* is laden with the sensate experience—its title "sighs from the depth" already suggests this. De Quincey lyrically explores themes such as loss and mourning. In actual fact, in terms of narrative content, there is very little to go by in De Quincey's original text that would even vaguely suggest the plots found in either film. Argento and his then-wife, Daria Nicolodi, wrote the screenplay. Apparently, Nicolodi's grandmother attended a musical academy that also taught Black Magic, and this also served as inspiration.[11] For his part, De Quincey gives us the broadest of brushstrokes, a cast of characters that haunted his opium-fueled dreams, recounting that while a boarding student at Oxford he often "saw Levana in my dreams. I knew her by her Roman symbols."[12] The Roman goddess, Levana, was present at childbirth, and "her name [came] from the Latin verb (as still it is the Italian verb) levare, to raise aloft," and thus, at birth the child would be held up (raised aloft), the umbilical cord cut, and the paternal figure assumed paternity. Levana oversees the "raising" of the child, of education, in effect escorting the infant through the passage of the pre-linguistic into the Symbolic.[13] No stranger to melancholia, De Quincey views Levana through the loss of his sister, which from a very early age, and apparently throughout his life, acquainted him with intense sadness. De

Quincey associates the child's severance with grief, noting that children who are separated from their mothers frequently die. "I speak of what I know," De Quincey decries. "The complaint is not entered by the registrar as grief; but that it is. Grief of that sort, and at that age, has killed more than ever have been counted amongst its martyrs."[14]

In De Quincey's dreams Levana, in her familiarity with grief, consorts with Our Ladies of Sorrow, the three sisters: Mater Lachrymarum, Our Lady of Tears; Mater Suspiriorum, Our Lady of Sighs; and Mater Tenebrarum, Our Lady of Darkness. "I know them thoroughly, and have walked in all their kingdoms," De Quincey relates. "Three sisters they are, of one mysterious household; and their paths are wide apart; but of their dominion there is no end. Them I saw often conversing with Levana, and sometimes about myself."[15] While the poetic prose elicits a degree of musicality (which is more pronounced in other passages not cited here), the content of the narrative often points to religious rituals, prayer, hymns, and incantations. De Quincey rhetorically asks of the three sisters, "Do they talk, then? O, no! Mighty phantoms like these disdain the infirmities of language." De Quincey seems to suggest that Our Ladies of Sorrow "communicate" through extra-Symbolic means, through the logic of sensations(?), "amongst themselves is no voice nor sound; eternal silence reigns in their kingdoms. They spoke not, as they talked with Levana; they whispered not; they sang not." While De Quincey characterizes the realm of the Ladies as silent, nevertheless, "they might have sung: for I upon earth had heard their mysteries oftentimes deciphered by harp and timbrel, by dulcimer and organ."[16] Our Ladies of Sorrow, then, are channeled through (deciphered by) musical instruments—through lektonic means. And without recourse to their "silent language" De Quincey is left to "read the signals. They conspired together; and on the mirrors of darkness my eye traced the plots. Theirs were the symbols; mine are the words."[17] While De Quincey does not explicitly situate Levana and Our Ladies of Sorrow with the affective experience, in form and content—from the poetic prose to the references to music and prayer—the English essayist appears to point toward the affective realm, or something adjacent to it (intense passion, inflamed emotion). Laced throughout the original text is the affective experience, and this—just as much as Our Ladies of Sorrow—is assimilated into the cinematic adaptations.

And to circle back just for a moment, one of the striking elements of Goblin's scoring is the use of the dulcimer-like sound, other instruments, and lektonic vocals. Though *Suspiria* comes prior, and giallo inspires many of the motifs found in the American slasher, we might nevertheless consider—because it is so widely known—the *Friday the 13th* franchise, which is exemplary of the American slasher, and how it mobilizes the sound design to signal a malevolent presence. We know that Jason (or Mrs. Voorhees in the first installment) is present through the point-of-view cinematography and the stylized "breathing" of, "tsu, tsu, ha, ha, tsu, tsu, ha, ha," delivered in a reverberant tone.[18] The repeated motif, at a narrative and emotional level, invites a degree of dread-filled anticipation. Similarly, Goblin's scoring likewise suggests that the witch/witches, or her/their power is present. Goblin's keyboardist and founding member, Claudio Simonetti, notes that, "We used things like the bouzouki [a Greek stringed instrument] and the tabla [an Indian drum]. I used a big Moog synthesizer."[19] The synthesizer, which plays both low and high-end registers, laces the soundtrack with tinkling music-box sounds, and at the same time floods the track with fat drones so characteristic of early synthesizers. The bouzouki, following the contours of the tinkling music-box sounds, is reminiscent of the dulcimer. The thundering drumming (which sounds almost like a Japanese taiko drumming troupe) assaults the spectator with its relentless beat. At the same time, the lektonic vocal utterances—near cackles, bellowing moans, sounds that are drawn out in long exhalations, wispy—are periodically, and quite sharply, punctuated with "witch!" The soundtrack greatly enhances the emotional intensity of the various killing numbers (for instance, the killing of Sara and Daniel), and possibly carries with it an affective potential, especially with the lektonic vocal elements which might be grating or dissonant and elicit some degree of dread. Moreover, what the soundtrack begins to do is to slip between diegetic and non-diegetic audio designs. The bouzouki (which again is reminiscent of the dulcimer) and the other instrumentation and lektonic utterances in effect "translate" the non-linguistic expressions of the witches as described by De Quincey. The killing numbers are choreographed to elicit a strong emotional and affective response.

While Argento's film is more in keeping with the giallo, emphasizing the spectacular killing numbers, Guadagnino is more invested in narrative while still being especially attuned to the affective experience. Nathan Williams notes in his profile that, "No filmmaker engages all five senses quite like Italian director Luca Guadagnino." Williams surveys Guadagnino's cinematic work—specifically citing his 2013 film *A Bigger Splash*, and his critically acclaimed 2017 film *Call Me By Your Name*—as "cinematic psychostimulants, an exceptional kind of sensory overload." Tearing a page out of Vivian Sobchack's phenomenological playbook, Williams recounts how Guadagnino's films invite the experience of coenesthesia, where "sight and sound, taste, smell and touch become the means of his film's transformative narratives—for example, the downward yank of Primo Reggiani's briefs in *Melissa P.* (2005) or Tilda Swinton's orgasmic bite of a prawn in *I Am Love* (2009)." Williams adds, "*The New Yorker* said watching Swinton was 'the best sex you will get all year.'"[20] Keenly attuned to the affective experience, Guadagnino—from his cinematography, mise-en-scène, and use of music and audio design—is well positioned to bring the affective spirit of De Quincey's "sighs from the depths" to the screen.

Argento positions his female lead akin to the American horror cinematic motif of the final girl. While Suzy's fellow cast of characters meets a mysterious and gruesome demise, in the end it is Suzy that confronts and kills the head witch—Helena Markos. Diverging significantly from Argento's narrative, Susie in Guadagnino's film actually comes to realize that she is not haunted by the witches, but rather that she is a witch. And not just any witch, but an incarnation of Mother Suspiriorum. There is some ambiguity in Guadagnino's narrative: when does Susie realize this? Or perhaps she has always known? There is a very short flashback to Susie's childhood, where during a Mennonite homeschool geography lesson, she draws long lines "pouring" down like blood from her home state of Ohio on the word, "BERLIN," scribbled out in pencil. Susie's mother seems to think that her daughter is evil. Whatever the case might be, the moment of revelation for the spectator (and perhaps for Susie herself too) invites an affective experience. We do not learn that Susie is Mother Suspiriorum until the climactic moment of the film, we do nevertheless come to realize that she is a witch (a particularly powerful witch) in one specific moment, which unfolds in a montage.

Following a recital, which ended abruptly when another dancer, Sara (re-)breaks her leg—a brutal compound fracture of the tibia. Madame Blanc comes to counsel Susie in her dorm room but is startled when Susie "speaks to" her telepathically—the "silent language" of Levana and Our Ladies of Sorrow. Susie is coming into her power, and Madame Blanc wants to help her come to terms with it, to control it, to understand her presumed role in the coven. Susie's arrival though comes at a moment of transition, where within the coven a rift has emerged. And viewed retrospectively (after one knows the truth of Susie's character), one comes to realize that Susie's arrival at this particular moment was not a mere coincidence, but rather that she is the source of that internal strife. That all said, earlier in the film a vote is held to determine who will be the head witch: Madame Blanc, or the long-reigning Helena Markos. The latter emerges with the most votes. Furthermore, Markos is incredibly old, perhaps hundreds of years old, and needs a new host body. Previous attempts to locate a suitable young woman have failed. Susie is supposedly being groomed for this role, which is what Madame Blanc believes is happening.

And whether Susie fully comprehends who she is remains unclear. But nonetheless in the transition between Susie and Madame Blanc's exchange and the montage that visualizes Susie's own revelation, she is effectively "re-born"—or perhaps like a caterpillar emerging from a cocoon she is born anew. A title card, "Act Six—Suspiriorum," partitions the exchange between the two characters, and Susie's blossoming montage, which is illustrative of the act of becoming. In the dance studio, Susie contorts her body in the choreography of modern ballet (the film is self-consciously set in 1977, and the tenor of the dance reflects the period). The dance is mildly erotic, Susie writhes on the ground. Her legs are splayed open at one point, almost suggestive of birthing, or perhaps sex. From this a montage sequence is introduced: beginning with a near extreme close-up of Susie's eyes in low-key lighting the camera slowly pulls back, after which comes a series of shots of Susie's unclothed body as it ungulates in a black void—shoulder blades peak out nearly ready to tear through the taut skin, individual vertebrae dot her back, the nape of the neck exposed. Through camera angles, the absence of perspectival markers, and superimposition of shots, the exact geography of the body is somewhat obscured. The various shots, unfolding in slow-motion, traces of the images remaining from frame-to-frame—blur.

The clarity of the pictorial image in contemporary cinema is privileged in most mainstream narrative films. When the image blurs, or the spectator is assaulted with lightning-fast edits (which is the complaint leveled against the likes of Michael Bay[21]), this is both a stylistic and aesthetic choice, and there is often a conscious effort to elicit a sensorial response from the spectator.[22] Even as new technologies promise "unprecedented heights of iconic fidelity," Erika Balsom notes, "filmmakers are once again turning against the automatic production of exact likeness, in search of blurrier, smudgier ways of seeing."[23] French Impressionist filmmakers of the 1920s, for example, also experimented with soft-focus, superimposition, editing, and compositions to emphasize the emotional drama playing out in the narrative—the form, in effect, doing the emotional work of the narrative. D. N. Rodowick also points to Deleuze, regarding the blurred image as found in Francis Bacon's paintings. "An intense movement flows through the whole body," Deleuze writes, "a deformed and deforming movement that at every moment transfers the real image onto the body in order to constitute the Figure."[24] It leads Rodowick to suggest that the "sensation flows not from a unique form or figure, but rather from the multiplicity of compositional elements and traces of actions—lines, curves, random or accidental marks, blurs and erasures—that populate the picture plane as lines of becoming."[25] And this is precisely how Susie's body is treated in *Suspiria* in her becoming a witch, becoming Mother Suspiriorum, becoming the sighs from the depths.

What also emerges is the animalistic, lurking within the sinews of the body, the meat-flesh. In a telling moment of dialogue, Madame Blanc quizzes Susie, this promising new dancer, "When you were dancing, what did it feel like, inside your body?" Susie responds, "It felt like what I think it must feel like to fuck." Madame Blanc asks for clarification, "You mean to fuck a man?" "No, I," Susie pauses for a beat, and says, "was thinking of an animal." Animality is there, in the content of the narrative, and in the cinematic rendering of the body. Returning to the instance where Susie is in a state of becoming, becoming Mother Suspiriorum, the sequence is highly stylized, overwhelmed by the cinema of sensations. It is akin to Gilles Deleuze's meditation on the work of Francis Bacon, where the figure (lower case "f") is constitutive of representation, of narrative, and the Figure (upper case "F") often manifests in abstraction, the *informe*. "Cézanne gave a simple name to this way of the Figure: sensation." Deleuze posits that, "The Figure is a sensible form related to a sensation." Where the figure (narrative, representational form) is processed via cognitive processes, the Figure "acts immediately upon the nervous system, which is of the flesh, whereas the abstract form is addressed to the head and acts through the intermediary of the brain, which is closer to the bone."[26] Abstracted (think of the origins of the term—to be dragged out, to be pulled out) from the narrative and perspectival space, the meat-flesh is rendered "bare"—as Figure.

Here is the moment, in the breakdown of form—of content, of clear boundaries, of clearly definable objects—where the affective potentially emerges. As noted in the introductory chapter, Martine Beugnet has made a similar observation that the cinematic strategies that loosen their grip on the imperative to be clearly representative are pregnant with the sensate experience. From the blurring of the image to the use of extreme close-ups where spatial markers are torn from their anchors, where figurative forms are made indistinct, or abstract, these are the visual strategies that often wield the potential to elicit an affective response—from abjection to the beautiful. Audio design, not to be underestimated, also plays an important role. And analogous to the visual form the use of audio design might be difficult to locate between diegetic and non-diegetic sound, and where there is typically an emphasis on lektonic audio referents.[27] This is precisely what happens in Guadagnino's *Suspiria* montage.

While the visual field does a lot of the affective work here, what is actually doing the lion's share of it is Thom Yorke's scoring, which greatly enhances the affective charge of the sequence. Specifically, Yorke's "The Inevitable Pull," and "Open Again." While "The Inevitable Pull" is moody and sets the emotional tone for the exchange between Susie and Madame Blanc, "Open Again" spirals around and around with its melodic guitar riff, and in its circularity echoes the main score of "Suspirium."

Before continuing with the scoring, let me take a moment to also survey the audio design of this sequence. As Susie and Madame Blanc speak—sometimes telepathically, sometimes aloud, sometimes in English, sometimes in French—Madame Blanc clutches and massages Susie's hands. What is emphasized is the sound of skin upon skin. It is not overplayed and does not disrupt the "naturalistic" veneer, it is nonetheless slightly amplified to emphasize the tactile qualities of skin touching skin. This caressing gesture is illustrative of how the cinematic potentially touches us. And not in the way that Laura Marks might situate it—"it is as if I am touched," though such an argument could be made—rather the audio design amplifies tactility and the affective charge of the sequence. (Interestingly, neurological studies suggest that, "When we see other people being touched, we simulate this experience activating parts of those cerebral areas that we normally activate when we ourselves are touched in the same places."[28] These ideas are explored further in the chapter on pornography.)

When the image loses control over the fixed position of the body—as with blurring or superimposition in the cinema—when the cinema is liberated from the imperative to represent, then, as Deleuze says, "the eye becomes virtually the polyvalent indeterminate organ that sees the body without organs (the Figure) as a pure presence." Though Deleuze is discussing the medium of painting, the cinematic, as Hallam insists below, "gives us eyes all over: in the ear, in the stomach, in the lungs (the painting breathes . . .)."[29] We conceive ears and eyes as our means of processing the cinematic, however, our whole bodies are receptive organs to it. "The act of looking is not just a physiological process, it produces sensations and affects felt throughout our bodies," Hallam observes. Evoking the phenomenological approach, Hallam argues that looking enlists "other senses, particularly that of touch." The cinematic experience invites, for Hallam, "an immediate moment of engaging with the image in a physical sense that envelopes us." Hallam adds, "We are touched by these images in a provocative interplay of seduction and violence."[30]

The tactility of hands, or skin generally, is also emphasized in Hélène Cattet and Bruno Forzani's neo-giallo film *Amer* from the wrenching back of a finger stiffen from rigor mortis to a packed tram with patrons pressing sweaty flesh up against one another, to the protagonist Ana pulling her bare thigh away from a sunbaked leather car-seat to the crinkling of leather gloves. Hallam makes a similar observation, "The close-ups also serve to heighten the emphasis on textures, which is further enhanced by the accompanying sound—the squeaking of the leather gloves, the razor scraping against skin, and most effectively and affectively, that sound of the razor grating along Ana's teeth."[31] The cinematography, in some cases with shots in extreme close-up (or tight close-up) to accentuate the sense of touching the audio design, like in Guadagnino's *Suspiria*, emphasizes the tactility and the potential to elicit an affective response. With *Amer*, however, there is often dread associated with the sensory experience.

Immediately before Madame Blanc enters Susie's dorm room, an iridescent cloud shimmers in the corner of her room, the translucent spectral mist accompanied by a chorus of wailing or screaming female voices. The voices are modulated, heard as if off in the distance, and unintelligible. The spectral presence appears to be channeling female suffering throughout the ages, and perhaps at the same time the female life force from which the witches draw their power. There is a tradition where the vital force of the martyred witch then shares her power with woman-kind. Eiichi Yamamoto's 1973 erotic animated feature *Belladonna of Sadness* (which has enjoyed renewed niche interest, apparently having influenced *Amer*), concludes with the burning of the primary female character on a cross. Amongst the onlookers at the execution is a group of women that take on her likeness as she turns to ash. Similarly, Lars von Trier's 2009 *Antichrist* concludes with the primary male character killing his wife (who has studied witchcraft) and burning her body. Following this, throngs of women emerge from the forest—an embodiment of the spirit of women across history. There is then a shared motif that runs through these witch narratives. In the climactic moment of *Suspiria* too—even in the summoning of death and the killing of Helena Markos and her followers—Susie as Mother Suspiriorum assimilates the collective power of the women. A gaping vaginal wound splits down the middle of Susie's chest—linking both death and birth. (Though it is impossible to know this, just from seeing the film, the actress that plays Susie's mother, Malgorzata Bela, also plays Death—a paratextual gesture that also links death and birth.) The expression on Susie's face is that of ecstasy. The audio designed associated with the splitting wound might elicit a degree of disgust with its sloppy wet sound and gloppy gush of expulsive blood, but more significantly what returns is that chorus of wailing or screaming female voices (heard earlier in Susie's room), though more pronounced. In addition, the myriad of female voices quickly oscillates between speakers, to give a sense that the women's spirits are wildly moving through the

68 Abject Pleasures in the Cinematic

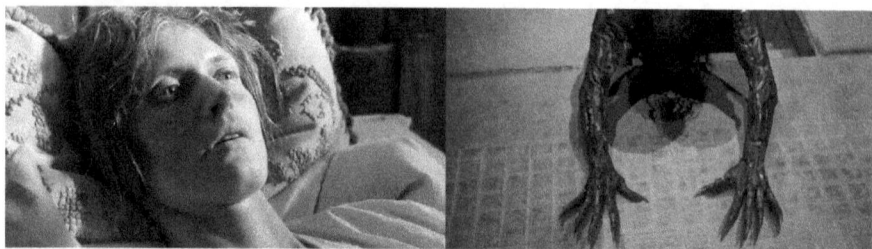

Figure 3.1 *Suspiria* (Luca Guadagnino, 2018)

space—perhaps dancing. The women's feral howls are piercing, maybe even grating, which very well might elicit a degree of unease.

At the same time though, once again, this scene of gruesome violence—where for instance, Death with a single gesture of the hand causes Markos supporters' heads to explode—is accompanied by Yorke's score, "Unmade." Having assumed control of the Black Mass, Susie as Mother Suspiriorum pronounces, "Yes, dance. Dance. Keep dancing. It's beautiful. It's beautiful. It's beautiful." And indeed, even despite the copious amounts of blood spilled, entrails littering the floor, and decapitated bodies, it is beautiful. As the killing has come to an end, as if a Darvish, dancers spin around and around Mother Suspiriorum (the motion slowed slightly), the crimson filter suffusing the screen, and a strobing effect applied to the image. Even in the scoring, Yorke noted that he was obsessed with "trying to use the cinema space, the surround-sound thing—really use it. Like, put one part of the melody in one speaker, another part delayed in another speaker, to give the cumulative effect of a melody scattering around the space."[32] And this movement between different speakers encircles the spectator, wrapping them into the narrative and the sensational experience. And this circular audio motion and the repeated musical motifs are suggestive of the serpentine line.

Serpentine Gestures: Different Approaches to the Beautiful

Although I take Kant's general conceptualization of the beautiful as central to the underlying theorization of the affective experience here, there have been numerous efforts to identify the characteristics of the beautiful. William Hogarth's *Analysis of Beauty*, for example, emphasizes the serpentine line. Miranda Stanyon observes that De Quincey mobilizes Hogarth's serpentine line, both in his narrative content, and in the form of his circuitous meanderings. "Serpentine lines appear at the very beginning of *Suspiria*,"

Stanyon observes, "in the image of a 'caduceus wreathed about with meandering ornaments.' The 'true object' of De Quincey's opium confessions, he maintains, was not the 'naked physiological theme' of the deadly drug, but," citing De Quincey's text, "those parasitical thoughts, feelings, digressions, which climb up with bells and blossoms round about the arid stock; ramble away from it . . . with perhaps too rank a luxuriance; but at the same time, by the eternal interest attached to . . . these digressions . . . spread a glory over incidents that for themselves would be—less than nothing."[33] Stanyon continues to note that the symbol associated with Hermes, the caduceus, "is a staff wreathed around by curving serpents." Adopted by the medical profession, the caduceus obviously evokes the serpentine line with the intertwining snakes wrapped around the staff. But, again, Stanyon invites us to consider that "*Suspiria*'s digressions are Hogarthian serpentine lines, 'waving and winding at the same time different ways.' . . . The text . . . claims to be structured by ornaments, by ornamental curling lines.'"[34]

The serpentine is plainly evident in Argento's *Suspiria*—from the gilded banister at the dance academy, to the Aubrey Beardsley-inspired imagery in Olga's apartment, Madame Blanc's office, and Helena Markos's quarters. The serpentine line is less obvious in Guadagnino's *Suspiria*, at least in the visual field, however, it manifests in Thom Yorke's scoring. A number of the pieces composed for Guadagnino's film spiral around and around with repeated refrains (as I have already mentioned with respect to "Open Again"). Certain phrases might wander astray, but then circle back. While the serpentine might well have certain pleasing qualities to it, I remain skeptical if it wields the power to be affecting. Nevertheless, the work of adaptation is not merely in narrative content, but also in the form of De Quincey's original text. And this spirit of the serpentine line is found in Yorke's scoring.

The title track, "Suspirium," like the caduceus, circles around and around. And many of the other pieces that Yorke composed for *Suspiria* echo this basic structure. "Suspirium" is structured on a three-note triad that repeats. There are moments where the repeated motif "rambles away" especially in its "rank luxuriance" of Yorke's airy falsetto crooning. The three-note motif, isolated by itself and heard only once (not in its repeated caduceus form), would be less than nothing. But the rambling luxuriance is spellbinding—bewitching. "I think the hypnotic thing is extremely important," Yorke acknowledges, "because what you're trying to do is lull people into some sort of odd, false sense of security, and then not let them go . . . The repetition would be like, 'Come here, come here, come here. *Now you can't leave.*'"[35] (Yorke's three-time repeated, "come here," is perhaps another nod to the three-note motif.) Noah Yoo's review of "Suspirium," while not evoking the serpentine, similarly identifies the circularity of the repeated motif. "A single flute enters while the baroque chords carry on underneath, hinting at a glimmer of hope with each rotation but never finding resolution." Yoo adds, "'Suspirium' is perfectly creepy because it feels unnaturally neutral, like a quavering meditation induced as the darkness fully takes hold."[36]

The scoring and the background diegetic sound elements, specifically the rustling of leaves in a gentle wind, seamlessly blend with the subtle electronic drone that lies beneath the repeated circular motif that leads the hypnotic rhythm. Woven into the lattice work of the repeated three-note triad, which effectively holds everything up, is the vague airy drone, the harmonics of the accompanying instrumentation (synthesizer, violins, and cello), and Yorke's piercing voice. The tendrils of all these other aural elements weave their way through the rigid melody. The natural (diegetic elements)—the human voices (Dr. Lutz Ebersdorf's descendants(?)—or the new owners of his East German cottage) and the rustling of leaves—in short, those things associated with organic life, appear to give root to the underlying drone which precedes the introduction of the repeated three-note triad. And this underlying drone corresponds to the body and souls of the witches—to Levana, and the three Ladies of Sorrow and their non-linguistic expressions channeled in the lektonic qualities of the music. Similar to "Open Again," discussed earlier, there is a sense that the body and souls of the witches—their wailing, their collective suffering, their ecstasy, their breath—are intoned. In his approach to scoring the film, Yorke observes that Guadagnino's script is pervaded by a "sense of melancholy," and that it is something "like a study in ritual, or collective female energy, or dance."[37] That sense of "female energy" is evoked in that airy drone, while once again the circular melody conjures dance. This is reinforced in the lyrics. "The full-bodied arrangement of 'Suspirium,'" Simon Vozick-Levinson observes in his review, "feels like a breath of cold night air by contrast. 'All is well, as long as we keep spinning,' he promises, or warns. It's peak Yorke, and scary good."[38] In addition to "female energy" and dancing, Yorke also cites the ritualistic qualities of *Suspiria*, and this once again also brings us back to De Quincey.

Conclusion: Touching the Beautiful

For all its dark atmospherics, its grim muted color palette, and the imperatives of the horror genre, Luca Guadagnino's 2018 film *Suspiria* nevertheless offers encounters with the beautiful. And true to the Kantian beautiful, these instances are not located in specific objects as such, but rather in the form—not in the content of what we see and hear necessarily (for example, characters, architectural features, non-diegetic score), but in how those elements are presented to us. Recall, for example, Susie's transformation into Mother Suspiriorum (at the beginning of "Act Six"), the beautiful manifests not in the narrative content, but in the audio-visual design of this plotpoint: the compositional treatment of Susie's face, mostly in shadow, the fluid cinematography that pulls back from Susie's pensive upward glance; the cut to Susie's nude undulating body, mixed with superimpositions, and soft-focus or even blurred beyond recognition, and where flesh dissolves into the darkness of shadows; the cutaways to empty spaces dramatically lit and that same fluid cinematography (recalling Godfrey Reggio's treatment of the Michigan Central Station in his 2002 film *Naqoyqatsi* discussed in the previous chapter); and, oh dear God, Yorke's "Open Again," which circles around and around, mixed with Yorke's soul piercing voice and the wispy airy drone that blows in and out, coupled with—subtly and barely registered—the non-communicative expressions of female sexual excitation (or is it dancing, or both?). These elements taken together invite the experience of the beautiful.

Interestingly, many of these elements in some fashion approach the sensation of touch, and specifically the touch associated with love: from Madame Blanc's caressing of Susie's hands (discussed above) where the sound of skin touching skin is emphasized, to Susie's self-caressing of her upper torso before she opens up her vulva-chest-heart (coupled with the expression of ecstasy on her face), to the violent but tender dispatching of women in the climactic moments of the Black Mass—Susie as Mother Suspiriorum asking the sacrificial women, "What do you want?" each responding, "To die." As Mother Suspiriorum, Susie gently caresses the women's faces and with a gentle kiss each woman falls to the ground. Furthermore, Yorke's circular melodies in effect encircle us, and in fact as cited above, Yorke consciously mixed that climactic scene to take advantage of theatrical surround sound to emphasize the experience of being encircled. Even Susie's repeated line of dialogue, "It's beautiful, it's beautiful, it's beautiful . . ." in the triplet echoes Yorke's encircling three-note triad on which the melody rests. In all these ways *Suspiria* evokes caressing—being wrapped up, going around and around, touching, holding, hugging.[39]

And if only adjacent, to be touched is not that far removed from the beautiful. To be touched is a sensual experience. And recall that the aesthetic experience is a matter of viscerality—the body and its senses. Think of how a gentle caress, the stroking of hair, a gentle hand that might run along the nape of the neck down the bare skin of the back—these instances of intimate touching have the capacity to elicit goosebumps. And let us not forget that sound is in fact a physical force—soundwaves actually touch us. And this is not just a theoretical abstraction, Anne Fernald echoes this in a *Radiolab* episode, "Sound as Touch," observing that, "We're used to thinking of sounds as being about something. Speech is always about something. But it feels to me more like touch. Touch isn't about something." This finds affinities with my theorization of affect, which is not necessarily "about something," but rather a "raw" uncoded sensation. "And I think," Fernald concludes, "actually sound is kind of touch at a distance."[40] *Suspiria* in its encircling gestures manages to touch us at a distance and invites an encounter with the beautiful.

As noted above, most of the affective work done here stems from Yorke's scoring. The lyrics for "Open Again," are of little or no consequence when it comes to eliciting the beautiful; the content or the "meaning" of the song might contribute to the emotional force, but the affective experience is elicited from the non-communicative aural stimulus: the hypnotic repeated melody that shares certain affinities with Philip Glass's minimalist compositions, and the harmonic delivery of the lyrics—"Just singing / Just say the magic words / Open again / We live again"—emphasized in both the application of reverberation and the elongation of the utterances. The "meanings," or the words are nearly negligible, the affective instead emerges from an encounter with musicality (with its ability to easily slip into the lektonic), rhythm, and harmonics. This is the subject of the following chapter.

Notes

1 Lindsay Hallam argues that Dario Argento's 1977 film *Suspiria* is not, properly speaking, a giallo film, and her reasoning would apply to Guadagnino's film as well. Alexia Kannas notes that, "[Peter] Bondanella's chapter on gialli defines them as 'mystery, detective, or thriller films' and draws a definitive line that excludes gialli featuring supernatural agents of cause and effect." Kannas, however, argues that the conceptualization of genre itself is problematic, and "Recent scholarship on the giallo film—and the Italian horror more broadly—has emphasized the use of the Italian term *filone*, instead of 'genre,' to describe this group of films. Meaning 'vein,' 'streamlet' or 'tradition,' but also—as in Christopher Wagstaff's explications—'formula,' the term *filone* helps to describe the particular production and reception contexts of Italian genre films in the post-war period." Kannas continues citing Koven, who discusses *filone*, and "the connotations it carries in Italian phrases like 'sullo stesso filone' ('in the tradition of') or 'seguire il filone' ('to follow in the tradition of')." Kannas views *filone* as a productive umbrella term that can accommodate the cross-pollination of genres that happens in what we broadly

call giallo films. Alexia Kannas, "All the colours of the dark: Film genre and the Italian giallo," *Journal of Italian Cinema & Media Studies* vol. 5, no. 2 (2017): 175; 177. See Peter Bondanella, *A History of Italian Cinema* (New York: Continuum, 2009), 374. See Mikel J. Koven, *La Dolce Morte: Vernacular Cinema and the Italian Giallo Film* (Lanham, MD: Scarecrow Press, 2006), 5. Also see Lindsay Hallam, "Touching the Colour and Sound of Your Body's Tears: Affect and Homage in the Neo-Giallo," *Filmtidsskrft* vol. 16, no. 9 (October 22, 2017): no pagination. http://www.16-9.dk/2017/10/touching-the-colour/.

2 Hallam.
3 I wish to acknowledge my research assistant Birdy Wei-Ting Hung here, who called my attention to the circulation of giallo films in Taiwan. Hung cites Hsuan-En Chan's MA thesis, "Analysis of Erotic Film Viewing (1968–1988): From Social, Cultural and Gender Perspective," Master's Program of the Institute of Gender Studies, Kaohsiung Medical University (2019): 1–184.
4 Raiford Guins, "Blood and black gloves on shiny discs: new media, old tastes, and the remediation of Italian horror films in the US," *Horror International* (2003): 16.
5 Hallam.
6 David Andrews, *Theorizing Art Cinemas: Foreign, Cult, Avant-Garde, and Beyond* (Austin: University of Texas Press, 2013), 112. For a discussion of the "high-low" debate as it relates to the giallo, see: Alexandra Heller-Nicholas's *The Giallo Canvas: Art, Excess and Horror Cinema* (Jefferson, NC: McFarland and Company, 2021).
7 Hallam.
8 See Aaron Kerner and Julian Hoxter, *Theorizing Stupid Media: De-Naturalizing Story Structures in the Cinematic, Televisual, and Videogames* (Cham: Switzerland: Palgrave Macmillan, 2019).
9 Hallam.
10 "Tilda Swinton Exclusive Interview – SUSPIRIA (2018)," *JoBlo Celebrity Interviews*, YouTube video, November 1, 2018, https://youtu.be/Up_3ogsBKNo.
11 Daria Nicolodi explains in the 25th anniversary DVD release of *Suspiria*,

> When I was a little girl, I loved listening to fairy tales, like all kids, and my grandmother, who was a great French pianist, Yvonne Loebb, used to tell me this story that really happened to her. When she was very young, she had gone to take a piano course in this Academy, which I don't want to mention by name because it still exists and it could be very dangerous, as they profess to teach biological agriculture, dance, piano, music. But in reality, they teach Black Magic. She got very scared and ran away.

Suspiria 25th Anniversary, directed by Gary Hertz (Blue Underground, 2011), DVD.
12 Thomas De Quincey, *Suspiria De Profundis* (Blackmask Online, 2001), 29. http://public-library.uk/ebooks/28/2.pdf
13 Joel D. Black, "Levana: Levitation in Jean Paul and Thomas De Quincey," *Comparative Literature* vol. 32, no. 1 (1980): 46.
14 De Quincey.
15 Ibid.
16 Ibid.
17 Ibid.
18 Apparently, the composer of the *Friday the 13th* score, Harry Manfredini, explains that he was inspired by Mrs. Voorhees's line of dialogue, parroting Jason's demand, "Kill her

mommy!" And thus, Manfredini drew from this and recorded, "kil, kil, ma, ma." See "Friday the 13th: the Game — Interview with Harry Manfredini and Wes Keltner," Gun posted to *YouTube*, October 29, 2015, accessed March 21, 2022. https://www.youtube.com/watch?v=dJG_ZiuAoJo.
19 Matthew Whitehouse, "How *Suspiria* Became One of the Best Horror Movie Soundtracks of All Time," *i-D Vice*, August 10, 2018, https://i-d.vice.com/en_us/article/kzyxgz/how-suspiria-became-one-of-the-best-horror-movie-soundtracks-of-all-time.
20 Nathan Williams, *The Eye: How the World's Most Influential Creative Directors Develop Their Vision* (New York: Artisan, 2018), 388.
21 See Aaron Kerner and Julian Hoxter's chapter, "The Stupid in the Contemporary Hollywood Vernacular: Spectacularly Stupid *Transformers*," in their book, *Theorizing Stupid Media*, 31–70.
22 See Martine Beugnet, "Introduction," to *Indefinite Visions: Cinema and the Attractions of Uncertainty*, eds Martine Beugnet, Allan Cameron, and Arild Fetveit (Edinburgh: Edinburgh University Press, 2017), 6.
23 Erika Balsom, "One Hundred Years of Low Definition," in *Indefinite Visions: Cinema and the Attractions of Uncertainty*, eds Martine Beugnet, Allan Cameron, and Arild Fetveit (Edinburgh: Edinburgh University Press, 2017), 87.
24 Gilles Deleuze, *Francis Bacon: The Logic of Sensation*, trans. Daniel W. Smith (Minneapolis: University of Minnesota Press, 2003), 18.
25 D. N. Rodowick, "The Forces of Small Gestures," in *Indefinite Visions: Cinema and the Attractions of Uncertainty*, eds Martine Beugnet, Allan Cameron, and Arild Fetveit (Edinburgh: Edinburgh University Press, 2017), 218.
26 Deleuze, 31.
27 Martine Beugnet, *Cinema of Sensation: French Film and the Art of Transgression* (Carbondale: Southern Illinois University Press, 2007), 65.
28 Vittorio Gallese and Michele Guerra, *The Empathic Screen: Cinema and Neuroscience*, trans. Frances Anderson (Oxford: Oxford University Press, 2020), 161.
29 Deleuze, 45.
30 Hallam.
31 Ibid.
32 Thom Yorke interviewed by Tim Greiving, "Thom Yorke on Scoring The New *Suspiria*," NPR, November 3, 2018, https://www.npr.org/2018/11/03/663408956/radiohead-thom-yorke-suspiria-score.
33 Miranda Stanyon, "Serpentine Sighs: De Quincey's *Suspiria De Profundis* and the Serpentine Line," *Studies in Romanticism* vol. 53, no. 1 (2014): 38. There is one passage in Kant's *Critique of Judgement* that hints at this conception of the beautiful:

> To deem something good, I must always know what sort of a thing the object is intended to be, i.e. I must have a concept of it. That is not necessary to enable me to see beauty in something. Flowers, free patterns, lines aimlessly intertwining—technically termed foliage,—have no signification, depend upon no determinate concept, and yet please. Delight in the beautiful must depend upon the reflection on an object leading towards some concept or other (whatever it may be). It is thus also differentiated from the agreeable, which rests entirely upon sensation.

And then elsewhere, Kant says, "So designs *à la grecque* [in a Greek manner], foliage for framework or on wall-papers, etc., have no intrinsic meaning; they represent

nothing—no object under a determinate concept—and are free beauties." Immanuel Kant, *Critique of Judgement*, trans. James Creed Meredith (New York: Oxford University Press, 2007), 39; 60.
34 Stanyon, 38–9. Stanyon cites William Hogarth, *The Analysis of Beauty*, ed. Roland Paulson (New Haven: Yale University Press, 1997), 42.
35 Yorke interviewed by Greiving. Emphasis in original.
36 Noah Yoo, "Thom Yorke: 'Suspirium,'" *Pitchfork*, September 4, 2018, https://pitchfork.com/reviews/tracks/thom-yorke-suspirium/.
37 Yorke interviewed by Greiving.
38 Simon Vozick-Levinson, "Song You Need to Know: Thom Yorke, 'Suspirium' First taste of the Radiohead singer's horror-flick score is a chilly, gorgeous treat," *Rolling Stone*, September 6, 2018, https://www.rollingstone.com/music/music-features/thom-yorke-suspirium-suspiria-score-717706/.
39 These ideas emerged from a discussion with my research assistant Birdy Wei-Ting Hung.
40 Anne Fernald interview, "Sound as Touch," *Radiolab*, NPR, September 24, 2007, https://www.wnycstudios.org/podcasts/radiolab/segments/91514-sound-as-touch. Also see the *Science Friday* episode, "Could Ordinary Household Objects Be Used To Spy On You?" which explores the ability to visually record ordinary objects—such as a house plant, or bag of potato chips—and by measuring the slight vibrations registered in those objects an audio signal can be generated. See Jon Callas, Kevin Fu, and Hae Young Noh interview, "Could Ordinary Household Objects Be Used to Spy On You?" in *Science Friday*, NPR, October 29, 2021, https://www.sciencefriday.com/segments/side-channel-surveillance/.

4

Musicality

Poetic Ruptures in Spike Lee's *25th Hour*, and Chris Cunningham/Björk's Music Video "All Is Full of Love"

Introduction: Beyond the Communicative

As discussed in the previous chapters, music, perhaps more than anything else, wields the capacity to elicit frisson. Whether it is something dissonant that causes us to wince, or something beautiful inducing tears or goosebumps—music, or something approaching music, such as the musicalization of the voice in poetry, or the musicalization of the image, is nearly magical in its ability to affect us. Is it any wonder then that so many ritualistic or religious services incorporate music? Eric Shouse agrees, observing that, "Music provides perhaps the clearest example of how the intensity of the impingement of sensations on the body can 'mean' more to people than meaning itself." Music (or any aural stimulus for that matter) does not always serve a "communicative" function. Though one could say that "raw" rhythmic beats or harmonic tone is still "communicative." That all said, and the point being that music has no imperative to convey "meanings" as such, and more than this we perceive music not only through aural perception, rather it touches us. The ontological nature of sound is that physical waves are transmitted through the air and strike our bodies (not just our ears). And perhaps this is why music (in particular) has the capacity to move us, because it is by its very nature a sensual experience. Shouse observes further that, "the pleasure that individuals derive from music has less to do with the communication of meaning, and far more to do with the way that a particular piece of music 'moves' them." Shouse admonishes though, that "it would be wrong to say that meanings do not matter, it would be just as foolish to ignore the role of biology as we try to grasp the cultural effects of music." Shouse also notes that music does not have a monopoly on the affective experience, clearly, and that many other things elicit sensations from the body is evidenced throughout this volume.[1] All told though, music and those things approaching music are especially attuned to eliciting sensations from the body.

What follows are instances where the voice and/or the image is musicalized. In our first example, I will discuss Spike Lee's *25th Hour*, precisely because it is so blatantly abject, and yet has the capacity to elicit the beautiful. Our primary protagonist's hate-filled direct-address diatribe is musicalized in its rhythmic delivery and somehow tumbles over into the beautiful. In our second example, I will illustrate how Chris Cunningham's music videos musicalize the image, especially through his adroit editing, lighting, and cinematography—and how his musicalization wields the capacity to elicit sensations. I give particular attention to Cunningham's music video for Björk's "All Is Full of Love."

"My great rival, music": Beautiful Hate in Spike Lee's *25th Hour*

> "In the beginning was emotion ...," Céline often repeated in his writings and interviews. Reading him, one has the impression that in the beginning was discomfort. Suffering as the place of the subject. Where it emerges, where it is differentiated from chaos. An incandescent, unbearable limit between inside and outside, ego and other. The initial, fleeting grasp: "suffering," "fear," ultimate words sighting the crest where sense topples over into the senses, the "intimate" into "nerves." Being as ill-being.[2]
>
> — Julia Kristeva *Powers of Horror*

One of Spike Lee's trademark tropes is his use of direct address to the camera, and this is used to great effect in his 2002 film *25th Hour*. The protagonist, Monty Brogan, is a drug dealer, and the film largely focuses on Monty's last day of freedom prior to serving a seven-year sentence in prison. The film was the first feature film to be shot in the wake of the 9/11 terrorist attack in New York City, and much of the narrative is inflected with the immediate post-9/11 angst, as well as plot elements that directly reference the terrorist attack, and the ruined World Trade Center site. And indeed, Lee levies some poignant political commentary in this relatively underappreciated film, and at some point, I would like to return to this topic, but that is beyond the scope of the present volume.

In Lee's signature direct to camera address comes one of the most moving instances of cinematic poetry, and it is just that: beautiful poetry! It is truly chilling as the recitation builds to its climax. We can find a similar diatribe in Lee's 1989 film *Do the Right Thing*, where characters spew vile racist slurs and stereotypes. While remarkably similar in content, with some of the most vile and hateful language (trafficking in some of the same stereotypes), what sets the *25th Hour* rant apart is the form of its delivery. And perhaps even despite its content, this instance of cinematic poetry has the power to elicit the beautiful. This example emphasizes that the aesthetic experience (and this might apply to sexual arousal and laughter as well) is divorced from ethical and moral considerations. Steven Shaviro, reflecting on the Kantian beautiful, notes that beauty "is as free from any notion of goodness or perfection as it is from any notion of utility." And this is how the beautiful is often imagined in colloquial terms—as a manifestation of "Goodness." But the aesthetic experience is divorced from all meanings as such, including morality. Kant, as Shaviro notes, does make some room for the "good," but "[a] sensitivity toward the beautiful may . . . indicate a disposition toward the good. But that is as far as Kant is willing to go. The aesthetic taste itself may not be subordinated to any pre-existing criterion of morality."[3] As discussed in Chapter 2, the agreeable and the good are set apart from pure aesthetic judgements, which is what the beautiful is.

I cite a sizable part of the monologue to illustrate the repetition, but also know that there are other lines of dialogue that pepper the audio background, as well as Terence Blanchard's affecting score. Monty, at his father's bar, stands before the bathroom mirror with the phrase, "fuck you," scrawled across the bottom right corner of the mirror. Around the edges of the mirror firefighter stickers, and a 9/11 inspired sticker with an image of the twin towers backed by the stars and stripes. Monty in response to the graffiti, mumbles to himself, "Oh yeah, fuck you too." This initiates the characteristic Lee direct-to-camera address, though spoken via Monty's reflection in the mirror. Monty's reflection begins his hate-filled tirade rhetorically asking, "Fuck me?" Immediately initiating the direct address:

> Fuck you.
>
> Fuck you and this whole city and everyone in it.
>
> Fuck the panhandlers grubbing for money, smiling at me behind my back. Fuck the squeegee-men dirtying up the clean windshield of my car. Get a fucking job.
>
> Fuck the Sikhs and the Pakistanis bombing down the avenues in decrepit cabs, curry steaming out their pores, stinking up my day. Terrorists in fucking training. Slow the fuck down!

Fuck the Chelsea Boys with their waxed chests and pumped-up biceps, going down on each other in my parks and on my piers; jiggling their dicks on my Channel 35!

Fuck the Korean grocers with their pyramids of overpriced fruit and their tulips and roses wrapped in plastic. "Ten years in the country, still no speakee English."

Fuck the Russians in Brighton Beach. Mobster thugs sitting in cafes, sipping tea in little glasses, sugar cubes between their teeth, wheelin' and dealin' and schemin'. Go back where you fucking came from.

Fuck the black-hatted Hasidim strolling up and down 47th Street in their dirty gabardine with their dandruff, selling South African apartheid diamonds.

Fuck the Wall Street brokers. Self-styled masters of the universe. Michael Douglas Gordon Gekko wannabe motherfuckers figuring out new ways to rob hardworking people blind. Send those Enron assholes to jail for fucking life! You think Bush and Cheney didn't know about that shit? Give me a fucking break.

. . .

Fuck the priests who put their hands down some innocent child's pants. Fuck the church that protects them, delivering us into evil. And while you're at it, fuck J.C.! He got off easy—a day on the cross, a weekend in hell, and all the hallelujahs of the legioned angels for eternity. Try seven years in fucking Otisville, J.

Fuck Osama bin Laden, Al Qaeda, and backward-ass cave-dwelling fundamentalist assholes everywhere! On the names of innocent thousands murdered, I pray you spend the rest of eternity with your 72 whores roasting in a jet-fuel fire in hell. You towel-headed camel jockeys can kiss my royal Irish ass!

The established repetitive pattern eventually breaks and Monty's tone changes, "Fuck this whole city and everyone in it," Monty's voice now lament-filled. "Let an earthquake crumble it, let the fires rage, let it burn to fucking ash, and then let the waters rise and submerge this whole rat-infested place." Monty ends his tirade by turning his rage inward, "No. No. Fuck you, Montgomery Brogan. You had it all, and you threw it away, you dumb fuck!" Racist. Homophobic. And just generally xenophobic and hateful. And yet somehow the hate and anger get suffused by the beautiful. That is not to say that hate is "dealt with," or fully "resolved." Far from it. Rather what we have is a brilliant sublimation of abjection. How does Lee manage this masterful stroke? And I hope that the reader takes the additional effort to watch this sequence, because the text on its own does not fully capture the emotional and affective force of the cinematic sequence—complete in its full audio-visual power. That all said, I would suggest that there are strong affinities here with the French novelist Louis-Ferdinand Céline's hateful and violent prose. Céline, who gained some fame with his novel *Journey to the End of the Night* (1932), was a highly controversial figure. During the Second World War he openly supported the fascist agenda and even lent his literary talent to writing anti-Semitic pamphlets. Prior to his literary career, Céline studied medicine and started medical practice in the mid-1920s—and his familiarity with human anatomy and medicine informs some of his gruesome content.

The last third of Julia Kristeva's *Powers of Horror: An Essay on Abjection* focuses on Céline's work. While academics (especially in our discipline) have mobilized *Powers of Horror* to address the horror genre, what often gets overlooked is the latter third of Kristeva's text, which deals with Céline's anti-Semitic ravings, his vicious misogyny, violent imagery, and most significantly his rhythmic and musical style. Beyond the violent content, what Céline is known for is his broken passages, often marked by the use of ellipses, curt phrasing, and onomatopoeia. And it is just as much in the content of what Céline says, as how he says it that indicates where affect lies. Just to have a sense of what we are talking about here, here are some samples of Céline's writing cited in *Powers of Horror*. From *Death on the Installment Plan* published in 1936 (and to be clear the ellipses are in the original text):

> He sticks his finger into the wound . . . He plunges both hands into the meat . . . he digs into all the holes . . . He tears away the soft edges . . . He pokes around . . . He gets stuck . . . His wrist is caught in the bones . . . Crack! . . . He tugs . . . He struggles like in a trap . . . Some kind of pouch bursts . . . The juice pours out . . . it gushes all over the place . . . all full of brains and blood . . . splashing . . .[4]

And here from *Guignol's Band* (1944):

> My blood turns! . . . I stop breathing! . . . I stop moving! . . . I stand there hypnotized . . . he looks at me! . . . I look at him! Ah! but I'm thinking! . . . I'm thinking fast! . . .It's the midget! there against me! . . . It's him! [. . .] It's getting ready by itself! . . . my scheme . . . I concentrate . . .

> concentrate ... Not a word ... calm and collected ... .[. . .] We hear the train roaring ... it's coming! ... there in the darkness ... in the hole ... at my right ... Good! ... Good! ... Good! ... the train's approaching. It's roaring fiercely, crashing in, swelling up ... Brrr! Brrroom ... Good! Good! Good! ... It's near ... I look at Matthew opposite ... .[. . .] Bop! I hit him with my ass! the midget! up in the air! ... The thunder lets loose, passes over him!⁵

And then, illustrative of Céline's open anti-Semitism (and anti-Catholic attitudes) in his 1938 *School for Corpses*:

> The most shameless gambling joint for corn-holed Christianese the kikes have ever laid hands on ... [...] Christianic religion? Judeo-Talmudo-communism? A gang! The apostles? Jews. All of them! Gangsters all! The first gang? The Church! The first racket? The first people's commissariat? The Church! Peter? Al Capone of the Canticles! A Trotsky for Roman muzhiks! The Gospel? A code for racketeers.⁶

Analogous to the operation of aesthetics, racism, misogyny, homophobia, and xenophobia have everything to do with the subject experiencing (or uttering) hate, and nothing to do with the external object that is the ostensible target. Hateful speech (and most especially, in its tone, its resonance) discloses the internal dread of abjection. To spout anti-Semitic rhetoric says nothing of the Jew, and everything of the one that utters such things. But in order to quell this simmering hatred, at least for a moment, is to throw a latticework around the abject, which, as Kristeva cites at the beginning of her book, is a non-object. To name it, and thus to truly "deal with it," to fully neutralize the abject is impossible.

How is the non-object approached then? Kristeva suggests that it is in Céline's stylization of language where the abject is approached, found in "the polylogue of the Celinian symphony—a music, a web, a lacework."⁷ And it is in this musicality that shape is lended to the non-object. The external object is not in itself the subject's abject hatred, but rather serves as a host for the subject's abject rage, which locates its force, its affective charge, not just in the "host-object," but in the "polylogue" character of its utterance. In its musicality, or its resonance—the Kristevan semiotic. The Celinian text lends shape to abjection, not in name as such, but in the excess of the utterance, which "conveys the body, and even more so the sick body, to a beyond made up of sense and measure." The abject is not in the content necessarily, and in that sense is "[b]eyond the narrative," and is located in the "music, as breath of words, rhythm of sentences, and not only as metaphor of an imaginary rival where the voice of the mother and of death is hiding."⁸

There is no representation of abject hatred so to speak (there is no language of abjection), only placeholders, or provisional utterances where linguistic force, syntax, punctuation, slang and expletives lend it the semblance of figuration. "The vision of the ab-ject is," as Kristeva writes, "by definition, the sign of an impossible ob-ject, a boundary and a limit."[9] The apocalyptic vision that Céline offers, gestures to the impossibility of representing abject hatred, and yet the seeming never-ending compulsion to grasp onto it—slipping through his hateful fingers.

The images that Céline presents, the ideas and narrative content are but the carapace of hatred. As cognitivist behavioral therapists might say, "Anger is an emotional mask, it conceals other emotions." Hurt, insecurity, self-loathing, jealousy, seized by the abject lurks beneath the veneer of anger. The qualities of hateful abjection necessitate "deep transformations in syntax," precisely because what Céline strives to convey is not simply the surface of hatred (the sacrificial objects), but the "raw" feeling of hate itself, abjection. And to lend "form" to sensation, demands extra-communicative forms of expression. Thus, Kristeva concludes, "Céline's music is composed through the work of a syntactician; Céline the musician turns out to be a specialist in spoken language, a grammarian who reconciles melody and logic admirably well."[10] Céline "translates" an affective charge "into sound, on that articulation between body and language, on the catastrophe fold between the two, there looms up [as Céline says] 'my great rival, music.'"[11]

Colloquial speech, expletives, slang are often a shortcut to affect, precisely because the utterances are frequently not just the things themselves that they ostensibly signify but are laden with semiotic excess. As Céline says, "Slang is a language of hatred that knocks the reader out very nicely . . . annihilates him! . . . completely in your power! . . . he just lies there like an eight-ball!"[12] Kristeva concurs, "Slang produces a semantic fuzziness, if not interruption, within the utterances that it punctuates and rhythmicizes, but above all it draws near to that emptiness of meaning at which Céline seems to aim." Céline in effect "speaks" emotion and/or affect, and it is uttered not just through words, but also in how he musicalizes his diction. Kristeva emphasizes "that the colloquialism of Céline's prose does not only express an ideological position, it is also a stylistic strategy." And in this musicalization of words this "allows the signifier itself to hold the overflow of emotion that Céline wishes to exhibit on the plane of language. Thus, when he rebels against 'ideas,' it is in order to allow the appearance 'of spoken language's emotion through writing.'"[13]

The abundant use of ellipses in the Celinian text does not signify an absence, but a surplus of affect for which language cannot adequately express. And affect then manifests, not in the ellipses themselves (they do not serve as some sort of non-linguistic signifier, or symbolic representation), but rather by imposing a rhythmic regime over the narrative. Kristeva suggests that the function of the ellipse in the Celinian text "is to signal that, while the syntactical structure is normally complete, the enunciation, on the other hand, is not; it continues, becomes displaced, concatenates other clauses." Rather than signifying an absence, an omission, the ellipse "rather point[s] to the overflowing of the clause into a higher unit of enunciation, that of the message."[14] The message of sensation—of hate, of the abject. The ellipse then, in its insistence upon rhythmic breaks, introduces musicality into the text. Circumventing signification, as Kristeva observes, and emphasizing the poetic, the musical, the semioticizaton of discourse necessitates that Céline mobilize extra-linguistic signs, to prevaricate and smuggle feelings into the text.[15] "Once more," Kristeva reiterates, "the Celinian music proves to be 'written affect,' thanks to a syntactico-logical over-competence and to an additional complication of linguistic operations."[16] One would be mistaken to assume that the curt phrasing, the ellipses, the colloquial and crass language are the signs of a lack of literary competence, or of a simple vulgarity, but quite to the contrary, as Kristeva insists, what "we are dealing" with is not "a 'less' but with a 'more' of syntax. The syntactical capacity that is already there, to which 'regressive' strategies are superadded, may only be a competence (not necessarily explicit in the performance) of vulgar speakers."[17] The Celinian text is "nothing more than the effervescence of passion," that is to say, laden with affect. And it is in the "language we call style, where any ideology, thesis, interpretation, mania, collectivity, threat, or hope become drowned." In other words, the affective potential of the (Celinian) text is in its stylistic treatment, and this can even "overshadow" the narrative content. "Music, rhythm, rigadoon, without end, for no reason."[18] But if it is for "no reason," then it is for affect—an expression of feelings for which language is not fully capable of conveying.

Sam Levinson's 2018 film *Assassination Nation* is a highly stylized treatment of the millennial teen-girl experience. And toward the end of the film, we are presented with a comparable sequence to the one found in *25th Hour*. In *Assassination Nation* a hacker releases the data of half of the town of Salem—text messages, photographs, internet search histories. This destroys the reputation of public officials and students alike—violently tearing apart the social fabric. The town erupts into an unruly mob (the town's name is consequential), and our primary character, Lily, is accused of being the hacker. (Lily's name is equally as consequential.) Lily and her three friends are targeted in a home-invasion assault. Lily though manages to escape, arm herself to the hilt, free her friends (captured during the home-invasion), and then broadcast a message across some unspecified social media platform. In this broadcasted message Lily directly addresses the camera—a large American flag mounted behind her. The direct address, the content of the address, and the American flag bear the hallmarks of Monty's diatribe in *25th Hour*.

Directly addressing the camera, the 18-year-old Lily lambasts the hypocrisy endemic to American culture. "Don't take your hate out on me. I just got here," Lily implores. Lily admits that she is lost, not sure where to go or what to do:

> Because from the moment I arrived,
> all I was ever given were orders:
> Smile.
> Open up.
> Cross your legs.
> Spread your pussy.
> Speak softer.
> Speak louder.
> Be quiet.
> Be confident.
> Be interesting.
> Don't be so difficult.
> Be strong.
> Don't fight back.
> Be an angel.
> Be a whore.
> Be a princess.
> Be anything you want to be.
> Even the President of the United States of America.
> Just kidding.
> Fuck you.
>
> You still want to kill me?
> Rape me?
> Stab me?
> Shoot me?
> Let's go.
> Rally your fucking crew.
> Grab your guns and hide behind your masks.
> You want to do this in real life now?
> Give it your best shot.
> 'Cause you've prepared me my whole life for this.
> You may kill me.
> But you can't kill all of us.

In the litany of orders punctuated with, "Fuck you," as well as the direct address, the comparisons with *25th Hour* are fairly self-evident.[19] There is a degree of poetic intonation in the compendium of contradictory commands, coupled with Anohni's song "In My Dreams."

It does many of the things that Lee does in *25th Hour*—reflecting on the contradictory and hypocritical American project. On the one hand the dominant culture espouses the sanctimonious ideals established by the founders of the United States, while at the same time, whether articulated or not, institutionalizes white superiority coupled with racist, homophobic, and sexist beliefs. At the level of "political meanings" *Assassination Nation* approaches what we find in *25th Hour*, however, it does not quite command the same visceral force. My intention here is not to imply that Lee's film is (artistically) superior, but rather, through comparison, to illustrate the affective potential of musicalizing the cinematic experience. While the soliloquy in *25th Hour* offers "a 'more' of syntax," semiotizing the text through rhythm and enunciation (coupled with a rousing score), Lily's address is not embellished as much—it remains utilitarian, closer to "pure" communicative discourse, less musical than Monty's delivery. To make a turn on Kristeva's phrasing, there is "a 'less' of syntax" here. While they communicate similar messages, and share iconographic and compositional similarities, they "feel" different. The same can be said of the *Do the Right Thing* sequence referenced above—it too "feels" different, lacking that musicalization.

Figure 4.1 Top, *25th Hour* (Spike Lee, 2002); bottom left, *Assassination Nation* (Sam Levinson, 2018); bottom right, *Do the Right Thing* (Spike Lee, 1989)

To be abundantly clear I am not suggesting that Spike Lee is ideologically aligned with Céline—that would be utterly preposterous. Nor am I suggesting that Lee was influenced by Céline. Rather, Lee brilliantly captures—perhaps merely by happenstance—the "music, rhythm, rigadoon, without end, for no reason" in his *25th Hour* soliloquy. All the hate-filled rhetoric, the use of colloquial speech, slang, and expletives is all there. But most importantly, so is the rhythmic structure. "Fuck," which begins each new stanza, serves a double role. On the one hand, it serves as a punctuated break—and it is less the word "fuck," as it stands as an exclamation point placed at the beginning of the utterance. And in that sense it finds affinities with the use of ellipses in the Celinian text. On the other hand, the word "fuck" is "empty" of proper meaning, but instead is an utterance that holds, in its vocal expression, tremendous affective energy.

J. Lachlan Mackenzie re-affirms that "fuck" is often employed as an emotional amplifier. However, while "emotions play a vital role in human cognition and high emotional arousal and commitment can manifest themselves in the use of 'strong language,' the grammatical properties of swear words (and specifically of fuck and its derivatives) do not require any grammatical innovations. No evidence has been found here of any distinct 'grammar of emotions.'" Though it is important to note, as Kristeva will have it, while there might not be a grammar of emotions, emotions can manifest in syntax. Expletives are subject to grammatical constraints, and they can be integrated "seamlessly into existing structures."[20] (For an entertaining and informative discourse on "fuck"—its etymology, its use as an emotional intensifier, its cathartic potential, and its function in colloquial speech—see the first episode simply entitled, "F**k," on the Netflix 2021 series *History of Swear Words*.)

Each utterance of, "Fuck the . . .," belies the internal site of abjection. Whatever the object of hate might be—be it Sikhs and the Pakistanis, Chelsea Boys, Korean grocers, it makes little difference—there is a degree of "disingenuousness," because it is never really about the external object, rather it is all about Monty. And there is some acknowledgement of this, notably when Monty breaks or negates the established "Fuck the . . ." pattern, with "No. No." Which is immediately followed with a limited recognition in the closing stanza, "Fuck you, Montgomery Brogan. You had it all, and you threw it away, you dumb fuck!" And, of course, this is not to mention that all of this transpires in front of a mirror; and it is Monty's other, internal self (a violent return of the repressed?), his reflected self that is the sight/site of hatred. It reveals what Kristeva called elsewhere, the stranger within ourselves.[21]

Furthermore, the word "fuck," with its soft "pha" and its hard "c" ending necessitates a particular guttural force in its utterance. "Fuck," can be articulated in an affectively neutral tone, no different than how "truck," "tuck," "luck," "duck," and so on might be uttered. But this is not how it is mobilized in Monty's haranguing outburst. And, more often than not in billingsgate speech the word "fuck" is used to add pathos to the utterance. While "fuck" has some connotative meanings (usually associated with sexual intercourse) it is a very slippery signifier and is thus not used for "communicative" purposes necessarily, but rather as an emotive amplifier, which is effectively "empty," nearly lektonic. (In fact, in many cases the word can be excised without inhibiting the communicative value of an utterance. For example, "What the fuck is going on?" can simply be given as, "What is going on?" without any loss whatsoever to the meaning of the utterance. Rather what is "lost" here is the urgency, or the "feeling" of the utterance.) And thus, the word becomes the perfect vehicle for an affective expression. The exhalation of air in the "pha" coupled with the hard "c" that comes from the diaphragm and the back of the throat bears all the cultural connotations associated with it, but also the traces of the semiotic, of the body. In the same way that colloquialisms, slang, onomatopoeia in the Celinian text hold an excess of sensations, the mobilization of "fuck" is "to touch the intimate nerve, to grab hold of emotion by means of speech," and in this way Monty affectively charges the discourse, and transforms it, musicalizes the frenzied outburst.[22]

The musicality of the repeated refrains (backed by Blanchard's score) and their poetic structure provide an outlet for semiotic violence—something that perhaps approaches the sensate equivalent of parapraxis, a reflexive disclosure of feelings. Monty's ravings "bring the [abject] depths to the surface, carry emotional identity as far as signifying appearances, raise neural and biological experience up to social contract and communication,"[23] but in their form and textured delivery pollute the language with an affective charge. Although Kristeva is speaking about the Celinian text, she could just as well be speaking about Monty:

> the unbearable identity of the narrator and of the surroundings that are supposed to sustain him can no longer be *narrated* but *cries out* or is *descried* with maximal stylistic intensity (language of violence, of obscenity, or of a rhetoric that relates the text to poetry). The narrative yields to a *crying-out theme* that, when it tends to coincide with the incandescent states of a boundary-subjectivity that I have called abjection, is the crying-out theme of suffering horror. In other words, the theme of suffering-horror is the ultimate evidence of such states of

abjection within a narrative representation. If one wished to proceed farther still along the approaches to abjection, one would find neither narrative nor theme but a recasting of syntax and vocabulary—the violence of poetry, and silence.[24]

Just as with the Celinian text, Monty's diatribe brings together that "fascinating crest of decomposition-composition, suffering-music, and abomination-ecstasy."[25] This temporary negotiation of abject hatred, to bring it into existence and then allow it to sublimate (suffering to music), permits this nearly mystical transformation to take place where vulgarity and hatred are transmogrified into the beautiful. Along with the poetic nature of Monty's verse is Terence Blanchard's affecting score. Mentioned previously, though only in passing, Blanchard's score underpins and carries Monty's diatribe along. The score builds—along with Monty's vitriol and increasingly impassioned speech—arriving at a climax. Monty's poetic and musical expression, in its connection to the sensate body—from its rhythmic musicality to the guttural articulations of expletives, to its stylistic intensity—cuts to our core, touches us, perhaps (in a sense) fucks us. Taken altogether, Monty's soliloquy transforms suffering into music, and transforms abomination into ecstasy. Even despite the abject nature of the content, Lee's direct-to-camera address is illustrative of the beautiful.

Cunningham/Björk: "All Is Full of Love"

Where *25th Hour* negotiates hate, here we shall explore love, or if not love itself, then, attendant matters such as tender caressing. Where Monty's ravings attempt to negotiate an unwanted proximity (what abject hatred might amount to), love on the other hand is a desired proximity. As discussed in the previous chapter, Thom Yorke's scoring of Luca Guadagnino's 2018 film *Suspiria* approaches the feeling of touch, and especially touching associated with intimacy. And touching or caressing is not some phenomenologist's flight of theoretical fancy, rather soundwaves touch us, and as Anne Fernald suggests (again, cited in the previous chapter), sound is "touch at a distance."[26] Analogous to my discussion of Yorke's scoring, Björk's "All Is Full of Love," and specifically Chris Cunningham's music video for the Björk track, among others, through the use of rhythm and harmony has the capacity to resonate with us and our bodies—eliciting pleasurable feelings.

The British video artist Chris Cunningham established his reputation making music videos, commercials, and short video pieces (some intended for gallery installations), among other things. As James Leggott observes, "Cunningham (who was born in 1970) remains an elusive figure within British visual culture." And while Cunningham's versatility is broad, Leggot laments that his "relatively slim [output], and his seemingly slow work rate (and tendency to leave projects uncompleted or unreleased) has been a frustration for fans and commentators, particularly those who hoped he would channel his interests and talents into a full-length 'feature' film project."[27] Cunningham actually began his cinematic career early. At the age of 19, he worked in the special effects department for Clive Barker's 1990 film *Nightbreed*. He was also the lead sculptor of the alien for David Fincher's 1992 installment in the Alien franchise, *Alien*³. Even with this "relatively low" output and frustrating career trajectory, he secured something of a legendary reputation by spearheading the pre-production work developing the robots for Stanley Kubrick's *A.I.*, a film that never came to fruition.[28] All of this experience, whether it came to fruition or not, was channeled into the music video for Björk's "All Is Full of Love," which will be discussed at length below.[29]

Cunningham's 1997 music video for Aphex Twin, "Come to Daddy," was something of a "break-out" work for Cunningham. He would go on to make other music videos for the likes of Madonna and Portishead, among others. Much of Cunningham's work wields the potential to elicit an affective response—at both ends of the spectrum so to speak. While his work for Aphex Twin—including "Come to Daddy," and "Windowlicker"—and his video short *Rubber Johnny* emphasize deformed human bodies, grotesque bodies (that is, mixed forms), viscera, or what we might characterize as ugly human forms, Cunningham appears to be equally as happy in the realm of the beautiful.

The music video is ripe with the potential to elicit a strong affective charge, not least because of the power of music to quite literally touch us—sound waves in effect, rhythmically touch, caress, tickle our sensory system. As Steven Shaviro suggests, the cinematic and the music video, "*are machines for generating affect.*"[30] Furthermore, as Mathias Bonde Korsgaard adds, "Music videos often subvert the traditional structures of representational meaning that we confront in other audiovisual media, turning instead towards a concern with modulation, materiality, and the non-representational."[31] In the release from the imperative to narrate, or more broadly to represent, the music video through a myriad of techniques—be it through "radical" compositions (extreme close-ups, spinning cameras, tilting cameras, cameras and/or objects place in motion), or various effects applied to the image (either as part of mise-en-scène, or in post-production digital effects)—renders objects as fluid, disfigured, multiplied, layered, transformed/transforming, and so on. And this manipulation of the image can potentially cut in two ways: toward the ugly (the abject), or toward the beautiful. While Cunningham's *Rubber Johnny* and his music video "Windowlicker" lean in on the former (as stated previously), his music video for Madonna's "Frozen" is illustrative of the latter.

Cunningham's music video "Frozen" features the famous pop singer in the California desert landscape. Her long flowing black Victorian-styled dress billows in the wind, at various points her form (or is it her dress), morphs into flowing fabric, crows, a Doberman, a black liquid (blood?), shadows, doppelgangers. "Indeed, the persistent modulation of image, body, and voice in music video means," as Korsgaard observes, that "neither exists in a finite state of being but rather in an endless process of becoming."[32] And particularly in the state of becoming—becoming-crow, becoming-Doberman, becoming-black fabric, or even harmonizing vocalizations that dissolve into one another—these deterritorializations come undone from signification. Shaviro makes a similar observation about Godard's use of extreme close-ups, which tears the referent from the landscape of meaning. And cleaving the object from a larger context (and thus from meaning), invests these images "with a surprising, alien beauty; they are 'aestheticized' precisely to the extent that they insist before, and persist beyond, the act of recognition that stabilizes and rationalizes perception." In the deterritorialization of the object, be it through scale, composition, or in the fluidity of objects in-between "forces us to stop regarding them *as* referential objects."[33] And thus, with the "breakdown" of firm objects (clear categories, conceptual order) our aesthetic judgement is left to prehend the audio-visual referent (see the "On the Beautiful" chapter).

In addition to the fact that the music video is inextricably tied to the history of experimental cinema—think for instance of Kenneth Anger's work such as his 1965 short *Kustom Kar Kommandos*, or Bruce Conner's work including his music video for Devo "Mongoloid" (1978)—music videos are generally not governed by a narrative-imperative. Korsgaard adds further that "the cross-fertilizations between music and image in music video," also invites music video creators to liberate themselves from being squarely representational. And in this sense, music video creators are more akin to painters than to filmmakers (as conventionally conceived). While there is some implicit expectation that the painter (even an abstract painter) depict something in the world (to represent), at the same time, the painter (especially after photography was able to fix the lived-world) is given great latitude in how to depict the visual field. The music itself might already suggest a particular tempo or editing regime as it relates to specific musical features. "In most music videos," Korsgaard continues, "the image enters into a relation with a musical feature at some point or another, whether it is an aspect of rhythm, melody, harmony, musical structure, or something else." The visual material in its assimilation of the musical regime then, "becomes multiple in attempting to mirror the multitracked nature of music." Korsgaard concludes, "the musicality of the image assists in disrupting the standard ordering of vision as the dominant force of perception in audiovisual forms, giving birth to a specific kind of 'audio-vision' in which music and image mutually remediate each other."[34]

With music's innate tie to the lektonic—from the "meaninglessness" of instrumental utterances (a high-pitched wail of a violin, the twang of a guitar, the thud of a drum), to vocalized utterances that are empty of meaning ("hmmm"), to abstracted or "raw" visual signifiers untethered from representational regimes—coupled with the effort to "musicalize," the image invites the potential to elicit an affective response. "The aspiring synaesthetic perception offered in music video seems to further strengthen its affective potential—the cross-sensual and multimodal character of music video generates meanings that are more directly affective and less directly 'decodable.'"[35] The most affecting moments in "Frozen" come precisely at these instances that are not "decodable"—when Madonna's vocalizations are nothing more than "mmm," which is overlaid with her own voice (or is it a back-up singer?) and where multiple voices harmonize in that non-linguistic utterance. The visual track at these moments is "musicalized" as well, where for instance Madonna's dress "liquifies," and the definable geography of the body is (at least momentarily) lost.

Cunningham's music videos amplify the musicalization of the image. Whether it is the hilarious parodying of Matthew Barney's *Cremaster* films in "Windowlicker"—where cuts and movements are synched with the changing rhythmic patterns of the Aphex Twin track—or it is the sultry swooning of Björk's "All Is Full of Love," Cunningham, as Shaviro observes, "edits his videos more for effects of time and rhythm, than he does for narrative or meaning. 'All Is Full of Love' is best understood in terms of this reflex action, this synesthetic manipulation of sound and picture."[36] To emphasize this point further Shaviro cites Cunningham himself, who claims that there is no "intelligence behind" his work, and that he is "not trying to make a social statement or let people know what I think about things. The videos that I do are pure manipulation of sound and picture, and most decisions are made on a reflex action."[37] Although not couched in these terms, Cunningham is directed by the logic of sensation (to borrow Deleuze's phrase).

"All Is Full of Love" begins in almost exactly the same way "Frozen" does. The camera moves in an upward direction, scanning an "empty" space, set to a spare instrumental introduction, before locating our central character and the first vocalizations are uttered. While there is something of a narrative to be drawn from "All Is Full of Love"—an android is brought to "life" through tender caressing and kissing—but the "real meaning," if we insist upon locating meaning, is found in the feelings evoked by the music video. Echoing this point, Dean Lockwood similarly recognizes that, "Although Cunningham's music videos frequently feature narrative and can be conducive to a hunt for meaning, non-representational, affectively attuned orchestration of time, rhythm, and light appears, on the whole, to be much more important to his endeavour."[38]

The body, and its mutability, is something that preoccupies Cunningham's work. From his music videos like "Frozen," through his more "cinematic" work, or artworks such as *Rubber Johnny*, *Flex*, and even his design of the xenomorph in *Alien*³, and back again to "All Is Full of Love," the body is always sensual. Even with "All Is Full of Love," which features stark, clean androids, and robotic arms, set in a sterile industrial setting—think of some of the sets in *Star Wars IV: A New Hope* (George Lucas, 1977) and in particular the design of the stormtroopers—Cunningham somehow imbues his machines with tenderness and warmth. And the affinities with *Star Wars* is no coincidence. Cunningham explicitly acknowledges that *Star Wars* is a significant influence.[39] But again, even with the post-human android body, there is fleshiness, a sensorial system. And this manifests in at least two ways: through the face and the voice. As Lockwood notes, "the affective tone generated in this softening silky, milky world is of a piece with a sense of openness and vulnerability, an invitation to metamorphosis."[40]

The face of the two androids featured in "All Is Full of Love" are modeled on Björk's facial features. And while the androids retain their hard and smooth plastic qualities, the faces are at the same time expressive and fleshy. The face is the socialized presence, it offers "intelligible" expressions. But Cunningham gives us something in excess of a socialized face and offers what Deleuze refers to as the Figure (sensations). As Deleuze notes, "the Figure, being a body, is not the face, and does not even have a face. It does have a head, because the head is an integral part of the body. It can even be reduced to the head." And indeed, the robots in "All Is Full of Love," have "non-expressive" bodies—all mechanics, a solid white carapace for a body. In the same way that Francis Bacon dismantles the face, to reveal "the head or make it emerge from beneath the face," Cunningham does something similar.[41]

As already established, for all his technophilia (for example, interest in industrial machinery and robotics, and electronic music) Cunningham exhibits a clear fascination with (human) anatomy. In the same way that Bacon exposes the head-meat, revealing the meat behind the face, Cunningham—while he does his share of exposing the meat of the body (especially in *Rubber Johnny*)—also exposes the meat-voice, in his musicalization of the visual field. Lockwood views it similarly, "Cunningham's preoccupations with the structure and movement of the body—in effect, his music videos index what might be thought of as a study of sonic anatomy—have often been noted, both by Cunningham himself and by commentators on his work."[42] Lockwood recalls the 1996 music video for Autechre's "Second Bad Vilbel," which features an animalistic robot (as well as a monstrous alien—echoing the contours of the xenomorph and the disfigured titular character in *Rubber Johnny*). The robot is somewhere between a turtle and a dog, but what is notable is the stylistic treatment of the visual field—blurred, layered; seen through colored filters, television static, and raster lines—the camera tending to move in circular gestures, though often interrupted by an abrupt cut, or flash of color. In composition and movement there are some affinities with Bacon's 1952 painting *Dog*, where the central figure of the dog is obscured, blurred, set in the characteristic Bacon "blank" space, and encircled by green. The space, the vibrating figure of the dog, and the circular green marking are all echoed in Cunningham's "Second Bad Vilbel," and as Lockwood observes, the music video "works viscerally, affectively, rather than as representation or narrative."[43] Although nowhere as frenetic (the music does not call for it) "All Is Full of Love," similarly to "Second Bad Vilbel," explores the malleability of the body, where "we might experience our physical immediacy in new, perhaps posthuman, ways."[44]

The music gives shape to the visual regime. Cunningham immerses himself in the music and allows it to inform his approach to creating a music video. It is not simply the narrative or implied theme of the music—if there are any lyrics at all ("Second Bad Vilbel," for example, is nothing more than a rocking techno beat without any vocals)—but rather as Lockwood suggests, "an affective attunement. The 'universes' he evokes typically involve attunement with monstrous, nonhuman, or cyborg bodies." But as much as Cunningham demonstrates an interest in anatomy, "he places greatest emphasis on digital sculpture in post-production," Lockwood observes. "It is at the stage of post-production that his talents for manipulation of sound and image are most intensively practiced."[45] Cunningham's aesthetic is most notable in his brilliant art direction (specifically lighting, models, costuming, and set design) and his virtuosity in post-production—in the way he applies effects, his (often) frenetic editing, and the way that he slows or speeds up the image. "The mutability of temporality—accelerate and rupture—is a key aspect of Cunningham's synaesthetic anatomical sensibility. The human body, and the body which is the video itself, becomes a 'malleable "puppet" body open to control by another performer.'"[46] And this conception of Cunningham as master puppeteer, which Lockwood takes from Arild Fetveit, is an excellent way to approach "All Is Full of Love," as while there is narrative motivation for this conceptualization (the robotics onscreen manipulate the two android characters), it is nonetheless Cunningham that is pulling all the strings. Fetveit is specifically addressing Cunningham's music video for Portishead's "Only You," but the analysis is applicable to Cunningham's approach to music videos in general. "Cunningham, in effect, *dances* the bodies to the music by means of adjusting the speed of the footage in post-production. The implication of this dancing is not only to overrule the automated reproduction process audiovisual discourse is based upon."[47] This manipulation of the image in post-production recalls Erika Balsom's observation (cited in the previous chapter) that, even with technology that offers incredible visual fidelity, filmmakers "dirty" the image for stylistic and affective purposes.[48] It is from the editing suite that Cunningham pulls all the strings. The characters and inanimate objects in Cunningham's videos answer "to the rhythmic pulse of the music itself." Governed by the rhythm and tempo of the musical track, Cunningham "realizes new potentials for an exploration of fundamental rhythmic pulses—pulses that may inform both body movements and musical beats, and facilitate correspondences between them—like we see in dance closely synchronized to music."[49] And this is precisely what we find in "All Is Full of Love," where Björk's seductive crooning coupled with the mellifluous and rousing instrumentation is paired with Cunningham's gently sweeping camera movements and where Cunningham, in certain instances, ever so slightly slows the image speed to musicalize the image.

The lyrics for "All Is Full of Love" suggest a narrative and are pretty typical fare for pop music: "You'll be given love / You'll be taken care of / You'll be given love / You have to trust it." This is the opening stanza. Nothing particularly striking here—well-worn territory for pop music. The affective charge though does not stem from the lyrics, message, theme, or suggested story. Rather, as I have stated multiple times in the present volume, the affect emerges from how those lyrics are delivered: how Björk draws out utterances, how she harmonizes with her own voice (or a backup singer, just like the example from "Frozen" discussed above), and how this is paired with the instrumentation. As discussed of Mahalia Jackson and Thom Yorke in the previous chapters, harmonizing, as Lydia Goehr says, "strives to reunite alienated individuals with the collective."[50] When the older(?) android joins the main narrative, she sings in a slightly higher vocal range, but somehow the two voices harmonically fuse. And it is when the voices approach instrumentation, moving away from the utilitarian function of the voice to communicate, that they are imbued with affective potential. "Music is a deterritorialization of the voice," as Gilles Deleuze and Félix Guattari suggest, "which becomes less and less tied to language, just as painting is a deterritorialization of the face."[51] It is in the "less and less language" where affect emerges, for example, where the word "all" is stretched out to such an extent that the word begins to lose shape. "All" is nearly subsumed or obliterated by an extreme elongation of the "ahhh" before folding back into communicative discourse and ending with the consonant. The word "love," no surprise, is also given a similar treatment, elongated, and sung in a soaring manner. And it is in these instances where the voices are deterritorialized that sensations are elicited.

In his study of Bacon, Deleuze reflects on the power of music to elicit sensations. "Certainly music traverses our bodies in profound ways, putting an ear in the stomach, in the lungs, and so on. It knows all about waves and nervousness," Deleuze writes. Music though "involves our body, and bodies in general, in another element. It strips bodies of their inertia, of the materiality of their presence: it disembodies bodies." Deleuze then arrives at an understanding where the disembodied body and music resonate with one another, or "even of a bodily combat in music." While visual stimuli have the capacity to achieve similar affects, the nonmaterial sonorous qualities of music are better equipped. "In a sense," Deleuze concludes, "music begins where painting ends, and this is what is meant when one speaks of the superiority of music."[52] It is in the disembodied bodies, as manifest in noncommunicative utterances, where we encounter the semiotized voice that we find the sensate. And it is in the harmonization, the entanglement of multiple voices, where the "bodily combat" takes place. "We are no longer concerned with the difference between music and painting," Deleuze submits. "The important point is that the two sensations are coupled together like 'wrestlers' and form a 'combat of energies,' even if it is a disembodied combat, from which is extracted an ineffable essence, a resonance, an epiphany erected within the closed world."[53]

The visuals do advance the narrative elements or themes found in the lyrics, though, set within post-human android bodies. The face of both androids is modeled after Björk's facial features, and although stark and glossy white the androids are expressive—especially in their eyes and mouth. William Gibson apparently references Cunningham's androids. In Gibson's 2003 novel *Pattern Recognition*, as Lockwood observes, the "protagonist, Cayce, is staying in the Camden Town flat of her friend, Damien, 'director of music videos and commercials.'" Describing Damien/Cunningham's apartment, Lockwood goes on to add that parts of an eroticized female robot are scattered about his flat: "'Dreamlike things in the dawn half-light, their small breasts gleaming, white plastic shining faint as old marble. Personally fetishistic, though; she knows he'd had them molded from a body cast of his last girlfriend.'"[54] While the androids are clearly eroticized in exactly the way Gibson describes them, in Cunningham's music video there is far more to it than that. There is perhaps an overlap between the beautiful and the play with eroticism in the way that the androids are animated and how they are subsequently framed.

Cunningham situates his music video in a long tradition of sexualizing and fetishizing female-coded robots. And there is something deeply problematic in creating robots that are designed to be receptive to and subservient to their creators—a girlfriend without agency, a girlfriend that will never leave, a girlfriend that is subservient to wishes of its (male) creator. This positioning is not that far off from the plot of Bryan Forbes' 1975 film *The Stepford Wives*. While acknowledging this as problematic, nevertheless, Cunningham is gentle and loving in his approach. Insofar as the narrative is concerned, what appears to be happening is that the primary android appears to be in the final stages of production; various armatures fasten to the android's body, adjustments are made (when armatures spin, this is often timed with a strumming of an electric harp), and various parts are lubricated with a milky white liquid (a nod to the Alien franchise). A second android arrives on scene to initiate our primary robot; the second android offers up the love that is sung about, she is the one that takes care of our primary robot as recited in the lyrics. The pair enter an embrace, passionately kiss, and at one point "Björk" (or her robot avatar) digitally stimulates the other (in colloquial speech—fingers). In the latter moments of the video the pair are on their knees, prodded by various devices, and caressing one another—approaching what one might see in a "lesbian scene" in mainstream heterosexual pornography. There are affinities as well with the closing moments of Chan-wook Park's 2016 film *The Handmaiden*, where the coupling of female bodies is framed in a nearly identical manner (see Chapter 7). And in fact, Park was taken to task for his fetishistic treatment of his characters echoing the contours of heterosexual pornography. Cunningham, likewise, draws from the fetishistic vocabulary of porn.

Musicality 97

Figure 4.2 Left, *Björk: All Is Full of Love* (Chris Cunningham, 1999); right, *The Handmaiden* (Chan-wook Park, 2016)

This is further emphasized by the compositional strategy that Cunningham employs. In a number of instances Cunningham shoots the androids from a low angle. And thus, what is presented to us is a highly fetishistic depiction of female jawlines, half-cocked heads open and receptive to an erotic encounter, coy downward flirtatious glances, caressing hands on the buttocks of the other robot. (This might share something in common with the erotic choreography found in the chikan genre discussed in Chapter 6.) This kiss, as well, is not your standard Hollywood stage kiss, this is a fully invested kiss—deeply sensual, and despite being androids, this is a real kiss in its fleshy-tongue-oral-hand materiality. And although we are speaking about androids, the spirit or life-force of these inanimate things escapes through the eyes and mouth. It is the open mouth, as we find in Bacon's paintings, "that turns all meat into a head without a face. It is no longer a particular organ, but the hole through which the entire body escapes, and from which the flesh descends."⁵⁵ The hole manifests (visually) as a black void, but in its sonorous utterance reveals the meat-head. And it is not in the communicative utterances necessarily, but in the "raw" vocalization that "the body escapes from itself; that is, the way it escapes from the organism." The body escapes through that hole exposing "[t]he presence of a body without organs under the organism, the presence of transitory organs under organic representation."⁵⁶ Whether it is the mouth that is open to croon, or wide-open in an invitation to kiss, therein resides the sensate.

Conclusion: Musicalization and its Affective Potential

There are affinities between the manipulations of image and voice in the music video with what was dubbed "Extreme Cinema," or in its more localized form, "New French Extremity."⁵⁷ Extreme Cinema was a global cinematic trend emerging in the waning moments of the twentieth century and the beginning of the twenty first, emphasizing sex and violence. However, as I have argued elsewhere, while critics and scholars got hung up on the graphic content that these films traded in, more importantly these films often experimented with cinematic form, and this was especially true in those instances where explicit sex or violence was on display. For example, Extreme Cinema often experimented with sound design, "dirtying" the soundtrack with the use of drones (see for example, Gaspar Noé's 2002 *Irreversible*, Claire Denis's 2001 *Trouble Every Day*, Philippe Grandrieux's 1998 *Sombre*, Sion Sono's 2005 *Strange Circus*, and Peter Strickland's 2012 *Berberian Sound Studio*).⁵⁸ Extreme Cinema also experimented with the visual field, blurring the image, slowing the image, breaking with standard editing or compositional regimes, or the use of extreme close-ups where the marks of human geography (in particular) are lost or abstracted (see for example, György Pálfi's 2006 *Taxidermia*, Michael Winterbottom's 2004 *9 Songs*, and David Wnendt's 2013 *Wetlands*).

While many are quick to align Extreme Cinema with the likes of Pier Paolo Pasolini, Ingmar Bergman, Mario Bava, or other (European) "art cinema" filmmakers, and they are not necessarily wrong in their presumption, the experimentation with the visual and audio field in Extreme Cinema also has its roots in experimental cinema and music videos. James Leggott points to, among others, Tanya Horeck and Martine Beugnet, who recognized the impulse to elicit sensations from the stylized treatment of sex and violence. British art cinema, of which we might include Cunningham, can be placed within this lineage.⁵⁹ Leggot cites

Cunningham's own characterization of *Flex* (a 2000 video installation piece) "as a work encompassing 'blood, muscles, heavy breathing, spunk and God.'"[60] And Leggot observes that this echoes James Quandt's, "Flesh and Blood: Sex and Violence in Recent French Film," and from which the term "New French Extremity" was coined, referring to those French films at the turn of the millennium which were "suddenly determined to break every taboo, to wade in rivers of viscera and spumes of sperm, to fill each frame with flesh, nubile or gnarled, and subject it to all manner of penetration, mutilation, and defilement."[61] But as I argued previously, in my own co-authored *Extreme Cinema*, what got overlooked was the stylistic treatment of content. Extreme Cinema's experimentation with cinematic form shares affinities with the music video just as it does with European "art cinema"—and thus as much as we should consider Pasolini, we should also consider Bruce Conner and Anton Corbjin. And as oft repeated in this volume, affect is not simply the product of "strong" content, but form. This is all to say that all these various cinematic traditions have had varying degrees of interest in eliciting sensations through the stylized treatments of audio-visual material.

Musicalization of the cinematic demands the stylization of content. Whether it is love or hate, these emotions and their attendant affective experiences—goosebumps, tears, abjection—are elicited through musicalization. While the (narrative) content of the material might appeal to our emotions—be it hate or anger as articulated in Monty's tirade or love as expressed in Björk's "All Is Full of Love"—the affective experience, on the other hand, stems from an encounter with lektons, the rhythm and/or harmony of the audio-visual material. It is the form of the content, not the content in itself, that elicits the affective experience.

As demonstrated above, Spike Lee "articulates" abjection not in the content of Monty's hate-filled diatribe in *25th Hour*, but in the poetic delivery of his monologue. The affective force is located in the repeated rhythmic utterance, punctuated with one of the slipperiest of all English-language signifiers, "fuck." We find affinities with Kristeva's reading of Céline's text in her seminal book *Powers of Horror*. And just as with Céline's vicious and violent prose, written in that highly stylized form, Lee negotiates Monty's abject hatred, to "articulate" abjection and to sublimate it, and at the same time mystically transforms it into the beautiful. In Monty's direct address to the camera, Lee poeticizes his discourse and allows it to slip into musicality—amplifying its affective charge.

"All Is Full of Love," both in Björk's sensual singing and Cunningham's stylized treatment of the visuals, is loaded with affective potential. While the pop lyrics are simple, it is the harmonizing of Björk's vocalizations, where such utterances approximate instrumentation, and where the utterances begin to come undone from their communicative function, from which affect is born. The physical properties of music, in its resonant vibrations, rhythmically encounter the body as pulsating waves stimulating our nervous system. Music moves us—from dancing to near reflexive toe-tapping, or the bobbing of a head—and it moves us in part because it actually touches us. Cunningham accentuates the sensation of touch in his fetishistic treatment of the androids, and the choreography of the cinematography, which is only a stone's throw away from a "lesbian" porn scene in mainstream pornography, inviting a degree of erotic interest. And this approaches the subject of the following section and the chapters therein—sexual arousal.

Notes

1 Eric Shouse, "Feeling, Emotion, Affect," *M/C Journal* vol. 8, no. 6 (2005): no pagination. https://doi.org/10.5204/mcj.2443
2 Julia Kristeva, *Powers of Horror: An Essay on Abjection*, trans. Leon S. Roudiez (New York: Columbia University Press, 1982), 140.
3 Steven Shaviro, "Beauty Lies in the Eye," *Symplokē* vol. 6, no. 1/2 (1998): 99.
4 Louis-Ferdinand Céline, *Death on the Installment Plan*, trans. Ralph Manheim (New York: New Directions, 1966), 560. Cited in Kristeva, 150.
5 Louis-Ferdinand Céline, *Guignol's Band*, trans. Bernard Frechtman and Jack T. Nile (New York: New Directions, 1969), 219–20. Cited in Kristeva, *Powers of Horror*, 152.
6 Louis-Ferdinand Céline, *L'Ecole des cadavres* (Paris: Denoel, 1938), 140. Cited in Kristeva, *Powers of Horror*, 176.
7 Kristeva, *Powers of Horror*, 136.
8 Ibid., 146.
9 Ibid., 154.
10 Ibid., 192.
11 Ibid., 190.
12 Louis-Ferdinand Céline, *Entretiens avec le professeur Y* (Paris: Gallimard, 1954), 72. Cited in Kristeva, *Powers of Horror*, 191.
13 Kristeva, *Powers of Horror*, 191. Kristeva again cites Céline at the end of this passage, see Céline *Entretiens avec le professeur Y* (Paris: Gallimard, 1954), 23.
14 Kristeva, *Powers of Horror*, 198.
15 Ibid., 200.
16 Ibid., 203.
17 Ibid., 197.
18 Ibid., 206. Kristeva cites Céline's, *Rigadoon*, trans. Ralph Manheim (New York: Dell, 1974), 261.

19 There are also strong affinities with Paul McLean's 2020 short *Be A Lady They Said*. Available on Vimeo, February 23, 2020, https://vimeo.com/393253445.
20 J. Lachlan Mackenzie, "The syntax of an emotional expletive in English," in *Emotion in Discourse*, eds J. Lachlan Mackenzie and Laura Alba-Juez (Amsterdam: John Benjamins Publishing Company, 2019), 83.
21 See Julia Kristeva, *Strangers to Ourselves*, trans. Leon S. Roudiez (New York: Columbia University Press, 1991).
22 Kristeva, *Powers of Horror*, 137.
23 Ibid., 189.
24 Ibid., 141. Italics in original.
25 Ibid., 153.
26 Anne Fernald interview, "Sound as Touch," *Radiolab*, NPR, September 24, 2007, https://www.wnycstudios.org/podcasts/radiolab/segments/91514-sound-as-touch.
27 James Leggott, "Come to daddy? Claiming Chris Cunningham for British art cinema," *Journal of British Cinema and Television* vol. 13, no. 2 (2016): 244.
28 Ibid., 246. As noted in Leggott, Steven Spielberg picked up the project and released *A.I.* in 2001. Chris Cunningham is not officially credited in Spielberg's film, though the IMDB listing gives him as "special effects (uncredited)." It has been noted by some that Cunningham also worked on one or more of Barker's *Hellraiser* films—however, there are no listings for Cunningham on IMDB. The first *Hellraiser* film was released in 1987, which would likely make Cunningham either 16 or 17 during the production. The second installment of the *Hellraiser* films was released just a year later.
29 "All Is Full of Love," would become highly influential in its own right. As Benjamin Frisch reports in a *Slate* article,

> The Mecha-Nanny from Steven Spielberg's 2001 film *A.I. Artificial Intelligence* also has the look of a composited human face on a spindly, unfinished mechanical robot body. (Coincidentally or not, Cunningham did special effects work involving robots on the unfinished Stanley Kubrick version of the project.) The robots in the 2004 film *I, Robot* are similar enough that some fans called it "a blatant rip-off," although the producers never commented on the similarity. Neill Blomkamp's 2015 film *Chappie* has also been noted as ending with a riff on "All Is Full of Love." In another 2015 film, *Ex Machina*, Ava the robot also possesses the cutout style of human face on [a] thin mechanical body, and *Westworld*'s title sequence is an acknowledged homage.

Benjamin Frisch, "All Is Full of Björk Bots," *Slate*, January 23, 2018, https://slate.com/technology/2018/01/how-bjrk-robots-influenced-the-way-we-think-about-the-future.html
30 Steven Shaviro, "Post-Cinematic Affect: On Grace Jones, *Boarding Gate* and *Southland Tales*," *Film-Philosophy* vol. 14, no. 1 (2010): 3. Emphasis in original.
31 Mathias Bonde Korsgaard, "Creation and erasure: music video as a signaletic form of practice," *Journal of Aesthetics & Culture* vol. 4, no. 1 (2012): no pagination. https://doi.org/10.3402/jac.v4i0.18151
32 Ibid.
33 Steven Shaviro, *The Cinematic Body* (Minneapolis: University of Minnesota Press, 1993), 28. Emphasis in original. Shaviro is referencing "Godard's images, in extreme close-up, of a pebble held in a hand in *Weekend*, and of coffee swirling in a cup in *Two or Three Things I Know about Her*." Shaviro, *The Cinematic Body*, 28.

34 Korsgaard. Korsgaard draws the term "musical features" from Carol Vernallis and Kevin Williams. Vernallis, for example, suggests that nearly any "musical feature can be reflected in the music-video image." Carol Vernallis, *Experiencing music video: Aesthetics and cultural context* (New York: Columbia University Press, 2004), 79. Williams similarly frames this as "visualizing music." "Music is visually illustrated when the visual cuts on and/or around the beat, giving the visuals a feeling of tempo, rhythm, and texture (a common editing technique in music videos)." Kevin Williams, *Why I [Still] Want My MTV* (New Jersey: Hampton Press, 2003), 65.
35 Korsgaard.
36 Steven Shaviro, "The Erotic Life of Machines," *Parallax* vol. 8, no. 4 (2002): 22.
37 Chris Cunningham quoted in Shaviro, "The Erotic Life of Machines," 22.
38 Dean Lockwood, "Blackened Puppets: Chris Cunningham's Weird Anatomies," in *Music/Video: Histories, Aesthetics, Media*, eds Gina Arnold et al. (New York: Bloomsbury, 2017), 197.
39 "As for Lucas, Cunningham says in an interview: 'Star Wars is such a fucking fundamental influence in my work. It's all white costumes against black walls—everything's very classy.'" Cited in Shaviro, "The Erotic Life of Machines," 23.
40 Lockwood, 198.
41 Gilles Deleuze, *Francis Bacon: The Logic of Sensation*, trans. Daniel W. Smith (Minneapolis: University of Minnesota Press, 2004), 19.
42 Lockwood, 200.
43 Ibid.
44 Ibid., 275.
45 Ibid., 203–4.
46 Ibid., 205.
47 Arild Fetveit, "Mutable temporality in and beyond the music video: an aesthetic of post-production," in *Between Stillness and Motion: Film, Photography, Algorithms*, ed Eivind Røssaak (Amsterdam: Amsterdam University Press, 2011), 166.
48 Erika Balsom, "One Hundred Years of Low Definition," in *Indefinite Visions: Cinema and the Attractions of Uncertainty*, eds Martine Beugnet, Allan Cameron, and Arild Fetveit (Edinburgh: Edinburgh University Press, 2017), 87.
49 Fetveit, 166.
50 Lydia Goehr, *Elective Affinities: Musical Essays on the History of Aesthetic Theory* (New York: Columbia University Press, 2008), 56.
51 Gilles Deleuze and Félix Guattari, *A Thousand Plateaus: Capitalism and Schizophrenia*, trans. Brian Massumi (Minneapolis: University of Minnesota Press, 2005), 302.
52 Deleuze, *Francis Bacon*, 46–7.
53 Ibid., 57.
54 Lockwood, 198. Lockwood cites William Gibson, *Pattern Recognition* (New York: G.P. Putnam's Sons, 2003), 2; 5.
55 Deleuze, *Francis Bacon*, 23–4.
56 Ibid., 43.
57 See Aaron Kerner and Jonathan Knapp *Extreme Cinema: Affective Strategies in Transnational Media* (Edinburgh: Edinburgh University Press, 2016); Martine Beugnet, *Cinema of Sensation: French Film and the Art of Transgression* (Carbondale: Southern Illinois University Press, 2007); Tanya Horeck and Tina Kendall eds, *New Extremism*

in Cinema: From France to Europe (Edinburgh: Edinburgh University Press, 2011); and James Quandt, "Flesh and Blood: Sex and Violence in Recent French Cinema," *Artforum International* vol. 42, no. 6 (February 2004): 126–32.
58 See Lisa Coulthard, "Dirty Sound: Haptic Noise in New Extremism," in *The Oxford Handbook of Sound and Image in Digital Media*, eds Carol Vernallis, Amy Herzog, and John Richardson (New York: Oxford University Press, 2013), 115–26.
59 Leggott, 249–50.
60 Ibid., 250.
61 James Quandt, "Flesh and Blood: Sex and Violence in Recent French Cinema," *Artforum International* vol. 42, no. 6 (February 2004): https://www.artforum.com/print/200402/flesh-blood-sex-and-violence-in-recent-french-cinema-6199.

PART 2

5

On Sexual Arousal

Introduction: The Hidden Force of Allure

Arousal shares something in common with the Kantian conception of the beautiful. That is to say, the mechanics are similar. As we have already established (in the previous section on the beautiful), objects in themselves are not innately beautiful, or ugly for that matter. And in fact, we are often not even talking about objects necessarily, but rather the subject's own disclosure of pleasure drawn from some external referent. In his discourse on the Kantian beautiful, an individual "does not cognize the beauty of an object," Steven Shaviro notes in his book *Without Criteria*. "Rather, the object lures the subject while remaining indifferent to it; and the subject feels the object, without knowing it or possessing it or even caring about it."[1] In a similar fashion, then, the external referent is not innately arousing. But when an individual pronounces, "Oh, that's sexually arousing," or more likely in a more colloquial tone, "Oh my god, so fuckin' hot!" this discloses more about the subject making the utterance than it does about the referent. And thus, arousal poses a particular challenge—assuredly based in part on embarrassment—because to address arousal something is potentially revealed about the individual making the utterance.

In a similar rhetorical gesture, Shaviro (elsewhere) locates affinities between allure and Kantian aesthetics. Drawn from Graham Harman's discourse on allure, Shaviro recounts that allure trades in the currency of excess—an ephemeral non-assimilable surplus standing outside the objectal economy. "What seems to happen in every form of allure is that a special sort of interference occurs in the usual relation between a concealed sensual object and its visible symptoms." The arousing object appears to contain within it some other nearly mystical quality quite apart from the object in itself. Harman adds further, "If objects are what recede from us, qualities are simply defined as whatever does not recede, allowing us to bathe in them at every moment."[2] Harman describes this surplus—the force, or energy of allure—in almost mystical terms as a "dark agent," trading outside, alongside, or in the shadow of the economy of objects.[3] Harman frequently uses terms like "beneath," or "subterranean."

Elsewhere, but in similar terms, Harman characterizes allure as having an "archaic residue," noting that "perhaps metaphors, jokes, and beauty in general echo a process already underway in the most primitive inanimate sphere, and maybe they seduce us precisely with this archaic residue of causality—just as some hold that the mystery of the sea lies in its appeal to our distant ancestry."[4] "Metaphor" is an object that gestures towards something else. And, as far as I understand it, it is not the "something else," the corresponding object, that is necessarily at stake, but rather the gesture that directs us, it is the gesture that is the "dark agent" that invites us to locate that other meaning.[5] In many cases, jokes similarly operate through incongruity, which demands that we connect the incongruous ideas. The imperative of the joke, then, relies on this movement between ideas, failing to follow the gesture built into the joke might well prompt one to respond, "I don't get it." Thus, failure to "get it," indicates an inability to follow the gesture. Metaphors and jokes, however, are perhaps too abstract for our purposes here, and ultimately remain semiotic exercises.

The affinities between allure and beauty, on the other hand, offer a more productive comparison. Shaviro notes that the alluring object "does not just display certain particular qualities to me, but also insinuates the presence of a hidden, deeper level of existence." The alluring object possesses some kind of excess, beyond the mere qualities of the object itself.[6] Once again, as we found with metaphors and jokes, Shaviro points to the gestural force of allure (it "calls attention"), indicating the presence of surplus energy.

Shaviro appears to modify Harman's conceptualization of allure. Harman is an "object-orientated philosopher," which he proudly announces numerous times, and "rescues" the sensate by lending it the qualities of an object. No sooner than we recognize that allure is ephemeral stuff do "we begin to wonder what this ether of the senses may be," after which "we find only two basic possibilities." Harman posits that the first option "is that the qualities adrift in the world are made of an entirely different stuff from objects, which would leave us with a dualistic cosmos of objects and properties, perhaps along the traditional lines of form and matter." The second option, according to Harman, is that these "additional" qualities are objects in themselves. "This would give us a world filled with a single genre of reality known as objects, unaccompanied by any second, foreign principle."[7] While I actually find Harman's conceptualization of allure generally productive, like Shaviro, I find the former more convincing than the latter.

That all said, as Shaviro explains, "I experience allure whenever I am intimate with someone, or when I am obsessed with someone or something. But allure is not just my own projection."[8] Rather, alluring objects invite an intersubjective encounter, to brush up against us, to perhaps contaminate us. Harman speaks of allure as a kind of radioactive leakage emanating from the alluring object. "Like radiation seeping from the core of a blackhole, notes escape to some degree the 'event horizon' of an object and offer tantalizing hints as to what lies at its core."[9] Thus, as Shaviro recounts, objects retain something that is "deeper" than what can be grasped. "And the object becomes alluring, precisely to the extent that it forces me to acknowledge this hidden depth, instead of ignoring it."[10] Allure, as Harman notes, "is expressed in many ways, but each of its forms involves the separation of a thing from its innermost precious features: its notes."[11]

Allure, for Shaviro, might well be at its strongest when the subject has no familiarity or interpersonal relation with the external object—it is at its strongest when it is experienced vicariously. Rather than being premised on knowing (cognitively), allure possesses a near magical magnetism. The beautiful, or anything alluring, "seems to arise from a hypnotic underlying daemon, as if the object made use of the properties as secondary instruments at its command."[12] Allure—as it lies beneath, or interior to the object—has nothing to do with the utility of the object, or what an object might mean, or signify. Allure seduces, or even manipulates us. "The seducer mumbles something under his breath, refusing to repeat it when she asks him, drawing her ever further into the clutches of his sham secret—or perhaps the secret is real."[13]

"Vicarious allure is the ground of aesthetics," Shaviro insists, it is "a mode of involvement that is, at the same time, heightened and yet (as Kant puts it) 'disinterested.'"[14] The seemingly magical qualities of the alluring object go beyond any utility or function that the object might serve. The power of allure, then, does not rest in the object itself necessarily, but in its "hidden" qualities, what is in excess of the object itself. It is the residual qualities of an object that appeals to our senses—that is alluring. Shaviro, thus, aligns allure with the aesthetic experience. The qualities in excess of the object itself, the disinterested, the non-conceptual, and non-cognitive—operating outside language, the Symbolic, meaning—these place allure within the affective realm. I follow Shaviro's lead in his (perhaps willful mis-?)reading of Harman's text.

Allure, indeed, as Harman suggests, is nearly mystical in its operation, how it works on us. While allure effectively operates as a universal human experience, what one finds alluring, the triggering referent, is highly subjective—governed by any set of demographic, social-cultural, historical, or individual contingencies. And accordingly, any examples that I introduce in the present discussion will invariably be filtered through my own historic cultural heterosexual male lens. What is alluring to me, might not be alluring to the person sitting next to me on the bus. The human experience of allure, though, functions in the same way. Thus, to be abundantly clear then, any examples provided here are only examples (not "the" examples) and are merely intended to be illustrative of how the mechanics of allure work on us—and how the cinematic potentially capitalizes on our desire to be lured in.

Indeed, allure is seductive. If we examine the etymology of "allure" there is a sense of bewitching, or beguiling. *The Oxford English Dictionary* informs us that "allure" derives from the "Old French *alerrer* to deceive (a person) by insincere words . . . (Flanders, with change of conjugation) *alorir* to seduce (a person) (c1240), and (with prefix substitution) Old French *enleurer* to attract (a person) by deceptive means." The *OED* also invites us to compare, "Old Occitan *aloirar* to lure (a hawk)." And to follow the etymological path just a bit further, "lure" means, "To recall (a hawk) by casting the lure; to call (a hawk) to the lure." Allure, that dark agent that pulls us in, is a masterful magician—casting spells upon us. And before moving on, it is worth adding that "pretty" has similar connotations and etymology. The English word appears to be related to others such as the "Old Norwegian 'prettugr,'" meaning, "tricky, deceitful," or to the "Middle Dutch 'pertich'" meaning, "cunning, quick, lively," and its original English meaning being "cunning, crafty."[15] As we can infer this craftiness is in no way neutral, because as Rosalind Galt reminds us the connotative associations of the "pretty" are "close to witchcraft."[16]

Allure, as an almost mystical force, is the Siren's call—something that might not be "perceived" as such, but something that simply resonates with the body and seduces us. And this conception of allure, aligns, if not finds certain affinities with Susanna Paasonen's conception of "resonance." Paasonen is specifically interested in the subject of porn, but her conception is broadly productive. Set in contrast with that slippery term that us film scholars are prone to employ, "identification," rather Paasonen proposes "resonance as a concept for making sense of the movement between porn and its users. On the one hand, resonance describes the force and grab of porn—its visceral appeal and power to disturb. On the other hand," Paasonen adds, "resonance is at play in how users attach themselves to porn sites, images, videos, and texts and recognize some of the carnal sensations depicted on the screen." While Paasonen's attention is specifically the medium of online pornography, which requires a degree of active participation (for example, clicking, tapping, swiping, navigating, searching, uploading or downloading) the cinematic experience of viewing pornography nevertheless invites sexual excitation and carnal release. "With resonance," Paasonen wants "to tackle the interactive nature of such attachments, for the central question is pornography's power to touch and move us, to arouse our senses and interest alike." Paasonen argues this is not a matter of identification necessarily, where we put ourselves into the character's position, rather resonance is a shared sensory experience. "To resonate with one another, objects and people do not need to be similar, but they need to relate and connect to one another."[17] And this "connection" that Paasonen locates in resonance, echoes the present theorization of allure and its seductive force. Allure, like resonance, relies on aligned frequencies not necessarily identification.[18] Allure, like Paasonen's conception of resonance, has less to do with "being in the shoes" of the characters onscreen, or aligning with the character's gaze, and more to do with being on the same wavelength.[19] To have something resonate is to in a sense allow our internalized idealized objects to align with the exterior stimulus (this will be discussed later in relation to fetishism). "Failures" in allure, might manifest in those instances where an exterior stimulus and an internalized object fail to align, fail to resonate.

In addition, there are then some affinities with fetishism, and Harman's positioning of allure, that mystical "something" that stands in excess of the object, some veiled essence that bewitches and hails us. What makes John Legend so alluring, for example, is not Legend himself, but (parroting Harman's own phrasing here) the way that he might pronounce certain words, or "the specific curvature of a cheekbone," which in itself says nothing of Legend. "A dog becomes charming by the way it tilts its head when hearing commands, not through immaculate dogness; a crystal goblet is beautiful not for its drinking utility but for its superfluous diffraction of light."[20] It is not the object itself necessarily, but the idiosyncratic qualities that are in excess of the object, beyond its meaning (dogness), or function (device for drinking). The Kantian overtones are self-evident here. All the little "extra" things make John Legend the "sexiest man alive"—deemed by that guarantor of such things, *People Magazine*—and are not all the "little extra things" the stuff of fetishism? Or for that matter, attraction? And thus, I have arrived at my basic premise: Sexual arousal is largely, perhaps primarily, spawned by the economies of allure and fetishism.

Fetishism

Fetishism is a loaded term, there is no way around that. Moreover, it is often associated with negative connotations, especially in its mobilization by feminist film theorists. Most notably, Laura Mulvey ends her landmark essay, "Visual Pleasure and Narrative Cinema," by observing that some radical filmmakers—in their self-reflexive and materialist turn, as well as their overt engagement with politics—have rejected the sadistic and fetishistic gaze of conventional filmmaking. "There is no doubt," though, as Mulvey concedes, "that this destroys the satisfaction, pleasure and privilege of the 'invisible guest,' [that would be us] and highlights the way film has depended on voyeuristic active/passive mechanisms."[21] There is no need to dismiss Mulvey's conclusion—Mulvey I believe makes a persuasive case that women in narrative cinema are subjected to a fetishistic and/or sadistic gaze—nevertheless, what I do want to explore is the possibility for (visual) pleasure. And this might necessitate leaving open the possibility for a degree of cognitive dissonance—the intention, then, is not to discount the social critiques made by a whole range of (feminist) film theorists, but rather to focus our attention on (visual) pleasure. To add to this, an affective reading of cinematic material does not preclude social criticism, and in fact the things that might elicit arousal could very well be politically regressive. And in that sense, the present discussion is perfectly in keeping with the observations of feminist film theory. I concur with Mulvey's overall assessment that the cinematic fetishizes and offers up visual pleasure. Where we part company is the assumption that fetishism is inherently "bad." The sensate body can betray us, which to my mind is all the more reason to give serious consideration to the affecting experience, and how it functions even despite our best vigilance.

Paasonen is also critical of Mulvey's quick dismissal of visual pleasure. Where Mulvey's objective is to destroy visual pleasure (for political purposes to interrupt patriarchal objectification of the female body), as Paasonen observes, Mulvey leaves little to no room for the possibility "of visual pleasure in the positive spectrum, or of the more visceral sensations involved in encounters with film." Paasonen finds it peculiar that Mulvey's articulation of the male gaze is at once "affect-less," in its mechanical positioning of identification in the cinematic apparatus, but yet, at the same time, how it is "underpinned by affected dynamics: intensities of feeling that grab the viewer, resonate in the body and create connections to the things watched before one is even aware of them."[22] It is the fetish that "grabs" the viewer, that resonates with us, even if unconsciously.

Perhaps this is controversial, but I suspect that we all fetishize. It is unnecessary to apologize for fetishism or attempt to "save" fetishism—recouping it through some rhetorical gymnastics. It is possible, I believe, that we can negotiate this cognitive dissonance. It is possible to work within this (potentially) contradictory condition. Fetishism, as I have already posited, is one of the (primary?) ways that sexual arousal is elicited. We all have our "types," we all have our secret interests or fascinations, we all have those things that we consider "hot." Are these not just fetishes by some other name? And in my application of fetishism here, I am not fully beholden to the psychoanalytic conception of it, particularly in its relation to lack. In a similar gesture, Paasonen approaches my particular conception of fetishism in her discussion of habit. "To habituate means to accustom by frequent repetition or prolonged exposure: it is a matter of practice and process," Paasonen notes. "Habit stands for a recurrent, often unconscious pattern of behavior acquired through repetition." A preference for a particular "type," for instance, aligns with Paasonen's "recurrent . . . pattern of behavior." Paasonen adds, "Sexual practices are also a matter of habit—routines and choreographies that are repeated and tested. Although habits are contingent, they are not simply matters of choice."[23] The habit, like the fetish, stems from some unconscious desire—something that we might not even be capable of fathoming. Why is it that I like this or that thing? Why is it in my own sexual practices I repeatedly seek out BLANK? There may not be any "reason" for it, but the fetish offers us pleasure.

Assuredly these "types," fantasies, habits, and what is considered "hot" are all culturally complex, and do not reside within a personal vacuum. These are all deeply imbricated in a complex matrix of highly subjective predispositions entangled with the machinery of our respective cultural and historical context. Affective potentiality, then, is not transcendental, but culturally, historically, and subjectively contingent. The fetishistic economy, likewise, then, is part of this complex matrix located in both external and internal objects. And as much as the society of the spectacle supplies us with a menagerie of fetishistic spectacles to consume, we still (despite what Guy Debord insists) have some agency in the curation of our own internalized objects. Nonetheless, as Debord noted, the spectacle is masterful in its ability to assimilate, to reconstitute what falls outside the spectacle.

The fetish, even in Freud's discussion of it, is a source of pleasure. Freud notes that patients did not come to analysis for relief from a fetish, quite to the contrary, "the fetish made its appearance in analysis as a subsidiary finding." Indeed, the fetish only in very rare instances manifested "as symptoms of illness," but in fact the analysand was more often than not "quite content with them [that is, their specific fetish(es)] or even extol[led] the advantages they offer[ed] for erotic gratification."[24] The fetish, in the psychoanalytic setting, then, only materialized as an adjacent subject to the process of analysis—a reading of the analysand's individual proclivities. Often the disciplines of film and media studies and visual culture locate fetishism through a "reading" of the visual text. Berkeley Kaite in her discussion of fetishism frames the spectator's experience as an encounter. "The vocabularies of the photographic (and filmic) media . . . signify deferrals. That is, we know that what is missing from the text is as important as what is there." Kaite notes that it is the "reader," or in Mulvey's phrasing the "invisible guest," that "is one of the things missing from the text."[25] Citing Victor Burgin, Kaite notes that the viewer/reader brings something to the referent "because the 'visual medium' is 'invaded by language in the very moment it is looked at: in memory, in association, snatches of words and images continually alternate and intermingle.'"[26] It is in this "intermingling" where an internalized object might "latch onto" the cinematic referent. And this is where allure does its work, in the gestural force that links the internalized object and the cinematic referent, the force that (if only temporarily) fuses a link between the inside and outside objects, the catalyst for this intermingling.

This internalized object is the discursive repository that connects (or intermingles in association) with the exterior referent. Sexual arousal in the cinema problematizes my all-too-tidy divide between emotion (mind) and affect (body). Furthermore, sexual arousal also problematizes narrative—namely where the narrative is actually located. As much as narratives are supplied by the cinematic referent, narratives also reside within the viewing subject. A fetish is in effect an internal narrativized object. A fetish is the overvaluation of an object, and this subjective investment is rooted in a complex and fluid network of personal predilections and reinforced by a socially shared repertoire of erotically charged signifiers. As an illustrative analogy, perhaps one of the ways to think about fetishism is to imagine that it functions like the principle of cohesion in chemistry—where similar molecules pull together. Two separated droplets of water, for instance, will pull together through cohesive force. And just to clarify further, this analogy of cohesion operates according to the principle of two like things pulling together, which is different from magnetism, where opposite poles attract. Thus, our internalized and externalized objects pull together, and it is allure (like cohesive force) that draws these like internal/external objects together. This pull then corresponds to all the different gestural forces discussed above—the lure, calling attention, the bewitching, and so on. The effect of this bond—where there is a close match between the internal (my "type," what I consider "hot") and external objects—results in sexual arousal.

Harman's conceptualization of allure, which I discussed above, also works according to some nearly mystical force—an alchemical enticement, the force that fuels fetishistic pleasure. Harman argues that certain objects might be alluring as they possess some "charm." And once again, just as Galt suggested earlier, Harman notes that the word "charm" "should be heard with overtones of witchcraft rather than those of social skills. What is at issue is not some sort of people-pleasing faculty in things, but a sort of magic charm or elixir that we sense in each thing."[27] The power of allure, as Harman frames it, comes from within the interior of the object. The pull of allure occurs as a result of conflict "between the object and itself, between the monad [that is, its invisible qualities] and its own traits."[28] And it is in this tension that the force of allure calls to us. In its magnetic (or more accurately cohesive) appeal allure invites the subject and some external object (Harman frames it as two objects) to "enter into relation. They do not confront each other directly, but only brush up against one another's notes, like shadow governments communicating through encryptions or messenger-birds."[29] This encounter, or relation, is never a hard, concrete exchange between objects as such, but an ephemeral brush with the qualities of an external object that somehow manages to break free to greet the subject. This brushing encounter between the fetishistic internalized and the external object facilitates sexual arousal when these objects resonate. The very "result of allure," as Harman posits, "is to separate an object from its traits."[30] And yet "[w]hen we say that one object encounters another, what this means is that it makes contact with strife between the unitary reality and specific notes of its neighbor."[31]

The power of allure, in Harman's model is found widely, from humor, to metaphors, and beauty, but what is clear is that "all forms of allure resemble each other in their strong emotional impact upon us." Allure, then, seduces, attracts, grabs, or resonates with us and defines how we perceive an object.[32] The relations between internal/external fetishistic objects, driven together by allure, elicits erotic interest—for example, when my internalized ideal body-type finds a referent in an external object, be it representational form, or the lived-experience. There are strong affinities with Alfred North Whitehead's conceptualization of "prehension" (discussed in Chapter 2), prehension meaning a seizing, or grasping. And this also aligns with Paasonen's framing of resonance which she also associates with tactility: resonance "grabs" us (this is discussed in the following chapter).[33]

There is some experimental data that corresponds to my conceptualization of the interplay between internal/external fetishistic objects and the power of allure. In a study published in *Archives of Sexual Behavior*, Joana Carvalho and her co-authors observe, not so surprisingly, that the most intensely positive sexually arousing experiences actually necessitate some affinities between explicit sexual content "and an individual's sex scripts. That is, if the scenes portrayed in an erotic video match an individual's scripts, this individual may experience less negative affect, more positive affect, and higher subjective sexual arousal."[34] Carvalho's study showed explicit and non-explicit romantic clips to a small sample of men (29) and women (28). While watching the selected material participants were instructed at certain points to imagine their real-life sexual partner, and then at other times to imagine an encounter with someone other than their sexual partner. The study recorded self-reported subjective experiences, and also sexual physiological responses to the screened material and directed imagined experience. Carvalho and her team continue, "Consistent with these findings and interpretation, we expected that when instructed to imagine that the male actor is their real-life partner, women will experience less negative affect, more positive affect, and stronger sexual arousal to sexually explicit film stimuli." The authors of the study explain further that, "The instruction to imagine their real-life partner was expected to match women's sexual scripts leading to a deeper involvement and more positive affect during a sexually explicit film."[35] And in fact, the Carvalho study concluded that, "Women will experience higher levels of genital and subjective sexual arousal and stronger positive feelings when exposed to explicit films if these films are combined with the instruction to imagine the depicted male is their real-life sexual partner."[36] Although the study does not explicitly link fetishism with sexual arousal, what the study does do, however, is to examine the correlation between internal narrativized objects (for example, your real-life sexual partner in a certain scenario) and an external explicit referent.

Interestingly, many of the scientific studies on eroticism often frame the erotic encounter as a "scripting" of the sexual scenario—in effect, narrativizing the sexual experience. And even in our colloquial speech we talk about reaching climax, which corresponds to our general framing of (cinematic) narrative arcs. And while the study appears to reveal a gender difference, which the team acknowledges might be a product of gender socialization, there is, to borrow a Kantian phrase, subjective universalism. The operation is more or less the same (universal), though the particular referents are individually constituted (subjective), and thus inflected with socialized gender experiences. Regardless, this social science study gestures toward the interplay between internalized and external objects, and how their correspondence has the potential to elicit positive sexual arousal.

While the fetish is the object in itself, the attraction or allure is found in the form or style, in other words, how the object is presented to us. As stated previously, we all have our "types," or what we consider "hot." Imagine for a moment your ideal body-type presented in a biology textbook to illustrate human anatomy. In this context, let us say, that the figure is set against a flat white background, with high key lighting (eliminating all shadows), standing straight, centrally framed, and so on, even if the model were your "type," the affective charge might be lessened, or perhaps neutralized altogether.[37] If, however, this very same model was set in a more erotic setting, with more dramatic lighting, framed to emphasize particular curvatures of the body, then, miraculously, allure has the potential to do its work, eliciting a strong positive affective charge.

Mirror Neurons: Reinforcing Allure and Fetishism

Neurology offers some exciting new possibilities in thinking about the affective experience. Specifically, the research on mirror neurons supplements the present theorization of erotic arousal. Italian neurologist Vittorio Gallese, along with others, has identified mirror neurons, where a perceiving subject, upon witnessing some action (be it via visual or auditory stimulus), will activate the neural networks associated with the same action. This is not to suggest that human beings are mere automatons, but rather that neurology offers a tool, among others, that when qualitatively contextualized can lend further understanding to the affective and emotional appeal of the cinematic experience. The point is not to stake a claim to a universal human experience, but rather this supplementary methodological approach can point to some commonly shared experiences.[38]

The intention is to bring these neurological tools to bear on our understanding of "mental states—and intersubjectivity—the sharing of subjective states by two or more individuals," which occur, as experiments demonstrate, whether in a lived face-to-face encounter, or in some representational form (for example, the cinematic).[39] And it is my speculation here, taking these neurological findings into account, that the pornographic invites for an intersubjective experience, and thus a pleasing state of arousal. Gallese and others, though, as already suggested, are quick to disabuse us of any notion that neurology might offer some positivist or deterministic approach to the cinematic experience. "Mirror neurons and embodied simulation do not consist of stereotyped and undifferentiated responses," Gallese writes. "They are both context dependent and idiosyncratically linked to individuals' personal historical, social and biological identity." Gallese and his fellow researchers do not posit that there would ever be a preordained response to a witnessed activity. Rather a subject's response to external stimuli "to cultural artefacts is always characterized by a projective quality, related to how personal life history determines the development of embodied cognition, as the latter is the outcome of bodily habits and implicit memories."[40] Gallese wants to put to rest any notion that neurological findings can be taken on their own, and rather insists that these neurological studies investigating cultural activities be carefully framed to consider cultural, gender, and socio-political differences. "The scientific investigation of the mechanisms enabling the experience of cultural artefacts does not imply, let alone posit, cultural homogeneity: the same neurobiological mechanisms are likely at stake in every culture, as they are part of humans' biological fabric." However, even within the same culture, a myriad of individual differences needs to be allowed for, because the mirror neuron "mechanisms are plastic and bear the mark of each individual's personal identity, thus leading to personalized forms of embodiment."[41] Neurology alone, Gallese admonishes, cannot unravel the complexities of the human experience. "The truth is that neuroscientists do not yet have a clear model of how humans understand each other," Gallese and Hannah Wojciehowski admit in their co-authored article. The authors add that, "fMRI studies present yet another text to be interpreted; the information they convey is at times highly ambiguous and/or subject to multiple interpretations."[42]

Clearly, neurology is no panacea.[43] Any findings, as the study acknowledges, should "not be used to evaluate the aesthetic, artistic, social, or political value of movies." Thus, insofar as the "meaning" of cinematic content is concerned, this is the jurisdiction of film and media scholars and critics. While appreciating this distinction, Gallese and Michele Guerra's *The Empathic Screen: Cinema and Neuroscience* is a fascinating foray into a cross disciplinary venture between neurology and media studies. Gallese is a neuroscientist, while Guerra is a film scholar—both are based at the University of Parma (Italy). Gallese was instrumental in the discovery of mirror neurons, and the co-authored project brings the findings in neurology to the cinematic experience. Many of their observations align with some of the phenomenological work done by Sobchack, Marks, Barker, and Hanich.

Gallese and Guerra mobilize "embodied simulation" as a central configuration of the cinematic experience. Just as in our lived experience, the cinematic experience invites shared parallel affective and emotional "responses from inside our body, which are known as 'enteroception.'" Neurological studies demonstrate that cerebral regions associated with feelings "such as touch or pain and emotions such as disgust or fear activate when we recognize them in other people. It follows that a vast number of mirror mechanisms are present in our brain." Gallese and Guerra posit that "these mechanisms allow us to recognize others as similar to ourselves and therefore make possible a first level of non-linguistic interpersonal communication and comprehension through the creation of an 'intentional consonance.'"[44] (There might be affinities here between intentional consonance and the conceptualization of resonance discussed above.) In short, mirror neurons in a sense "reflect" what is perceived by external stimuli.

Elsewhere Gallese and another writing partner note that, "Observing an action causes in the observer the automatic activation of the same neural mechanism that is triggered by executing that action oneself." Gallese was among the first to determine that an external stimulus is mapped onto "recognizable" motor neural activity—what phenomenologists have referred to as carnal or sense memory. Even an action, or movement that is ostensibly "devoid of meaning for the observer" is nonetheless directly understandable to them "because it can be directly mapped onto the observer's motor representation, that is, on the same neural network the observer normally activates when executing the same motor act."[45] Thus, in the Japanese chikan pornographic genre (discussed at length in Chapter 6), when a character gropes another character's buttocks, this would correspondingly stimulate the neurons in the viewing subject—of touching and being touched regardless of the regressive narrative scenario. Moreover, Gallese and Guerra would even go as far as to say that even in this written account, this would activate the reader's (that would be you, your) mirror neurons. It is not necessarily that the viewing subject (or the reader/you) would "feel" the sensation of touch/touching, but that such an external stimulus would trigger a neural response without you necessarily being conscious of it.[46]

An external stimulus—simply seeing, hearing, imagining, or reading about something—wields the potential to trigger related neural activity. When, for instance, we witness India Stoker—in Chan-wook Park's 2013 film *Stoker*—grab for a key attached to a chain around her neck we, through embodied simulation, in effect grasp the key, although "our muscles are not activated and we do not make any movement." Gallese and Guerra hypothesize that "this motor simulation contributes significantly to our degree of identification with what is happening on the screen." Mirror neurons then can account for the empathic and immersive potential of the cinematic experience.[47] And if it was not already evident, but to be explicit, an external stimulus does not only activate visual parts of the brain. Rather what neuroscience has demonstrated is "that vision is multimodal: it encompasses the activation of motor, somatosensory and emotion-related brain networks."[48] And this shares affinities with some phenomenological approaches to the cinematic experience. I am thinking of course of Vivian Sobchack and what she has called the "cinesthetic subject," where the audio/visual encounter with the cinematic might stimulate perception in another sense.[49] Gallese's work offers further credence to the phenomenological approach, noting that, "Motor neurons not only cause movements and actions but they also respond to body-related visual, tactile and auditory stimuli, mapping the space around us, the objects at hand in that very same space, and the actions of others."[50] Striking an almost Deleuzian tone, to "lay one's eyes" on something, as Gallese insists, "betrays the haptic quality of vision: our eyes are not just optical instruments, but also a 'hand' touching and exploring the visible, turning it into something *seen by someone*."[51] In that sense, to watch the caressing of a character's ass in the pornographic genre, then, is in a sense to touch and to be touched.

Despite this, what is conspicuously absent from the Gallese and Guerra volume, though, is any substantive accounting of how mirror neurons might respond to sexual content. They make several passing glances at erotic content (and subsequent erotic interest in the viewing subject), but invariably sidestep the issue. "When we see the body of another person being touched, caressed, slapped, or wounded," Gallese and Guerra observe, "it activates those parts of our motor, somatic sensory, and visceral motor/limbic systems that normally guide our behavior and map the sensory motor, tactile, nociceptive, and interoceptive sensations that we personally experience." The authors add that their research indicates "that one of the cerebral areas that maps our tactile sensations is also activated by the tactile experiences of others with the same body part."[52] It is not a stretch, then, as I have already posited, to conclude that sexual content would have a similar effect on the viewing subject. (In an unpublished interview with Gallese, he confirmed this to me.)

Embodied simulation, in addition to finding affinities with the phenomenological approach to the cinematic, fascinatingly dovetails with Linda Williams's conception of body genres as well. Williams identifies melodrama, horror, and pornography as the constituents of the body genres. All three of these genres invite some sort of affective/emotional experience: the melodrama is a tear-jerker, horror jerks us around by causing us to jump from our seats, and of course pornography appeals to the spectator to jerk-off. Williams observes that of course that there are other cinematic genres that "both portray and affect the sensational body—for example, thrillers, musicals, comedies." However, Williams contends that the body genres, as popular and crass, are specifically crafted to elicit an affective experience from the viewing body. Furthermore, the perception of the body genres as low-brow is "that the body of the spectator is caught up in an almost involuntary mimicry of the emotion or sensation of the body on the screen along with the fact that the body displayed is female." Williams observes that the body genres almost invariably depict women "out of control"— they cry inconsolably in melodrama, scream hysterically in horror, and writhe uncontrollably in orgasmic pleasure in pornography. Thus, while other genres such as comedy might elicit an affective response, for example, when we witness a clown slip on a banana peel, the spectator "does not mimic the sensations experienced by the central clown. Indeed, it is almost a rule that the audience's physical reaction of laughter does not coincide with the often dead-pan reactions of the clown."[53] What is most fascinating here, is Williams's insistence that the body genres anticipate an "involuntary mimicry of the emotion or sensation of the body on the screen." And this insistence upon "involuntary mimicry," neatly corresponds with the conceptualization of embodied simulation prompted by the activation of mirror neurons.[54]

And to be clear, the sensate experience is not altogether divorced from understanding. Our shared experience of crying, jumping, or cumming brings us to some "sensate" understanding of the character's experience onscreen. "Embodied simulation is a mandatory, prerational, non-introspective process—that is, a physical, and not simply 'mental' experience of the mind, emotions, lived experiences and motor intentions of other people," Gallese and Wojciehowski write. In a phenomenological gesture, Gallese and Wojciehowski suggest that our understanding, or perception of the world is not only channeled through cognitive processes but also through our sensate body. "Embodied simulation challenges the notion that interpersonal understanding consists solely of our explicitly attributing to others propositional attitudes like beliefs and desires, which we map as symbolic representations within our own minds." Embodied simulation allows the spectator to resonate with the external stimulus having experienced "a similar emotion or sensation." Now in almost a Deleuzian turn, Gallese and Wojciehowski, echoing the body without organs (conceptually and in phrasing), note that embodied simulation in its sensual intersubjective encounters is "the Feeling of Body (FoB)." The FoB by virtue of the mapping of external stimuli "onto our own visceromotor and somatosensory systems" facilitates (carnal) empathy.[55] Gallese and Wojciehowski conclude that "the FoB is not to be uniquely conceived of as a mere sensing of how our body reacts to external stimuli. It is a bodily way of making sense of our social world." And thus, "Our interpersonal relations—both in daily life as well as with fictional characters—are marked by our bodily involvement (the FoB) with the actions, emotions and sensations acted and expressed by others."[56] Analogous to Williams's framing of involuntary mimicry, then, embodied simulation accounts for the often-intense bodily involvement in the viewing of pornography.

Furthermore, in my conceptualization of fetishism, where there is a "match" between an external object and an internalized ideal, this too corresponds to Gallese and Guerra's conceptualization of embodied simulation. Gallese, in his neurological work, notes that memory and imagination are made of the same fabric, "and this fabric has a lot to do with embodied simulation."[57] Whether it is an external stimulus, an imagined image, or an image recalled, these all wield the power to stimulate neural activity. "As with visual imagery, motor imagery also shares many features with its actual counterpart. Mentally rehearsing a physical exercise induces an increase of muscle strength to some extent comparable to that attained by a real exercise."[58] Are fetishistic fantasies nothing more than a rehearsal for some erotic encounter? "When we imagine performing a given action, several bodily parameters behave as if we were actually executing the same action." Other studies "have shown that heartbeat and breathing frequency increase during motor imagery of physical exercise. As with real physical exercise, these parameters linearly increase with the increase of the imagined effort."[59] Sex of course being the ultimate indoor sport, one would presume that both imagining it and its representation in the cinematic, would have an analogous effect on the body. One has probably had the experience of watching porn and recognizing (even without any biometric devices) a discernible elevated heart-rate, perspiration, trembling excitement, and not to mention excitation of the erogenous zone. Embodied simulation works directly on the nervous system, outside consciousness. The symptomatic response to pornography in the form of sexual arousal appears to speak to these reflexive and unconscious responses to the cinematic.

Conclusion: Embodied Simulation, Allure, and Fetishism

Allure and fetishism work together hand-in-hand—and embodied simulation appears to reinforce this economy of arousal. The fetish object may lie inert until the power of allure as a dark agent lures us in. As Harman discusses above, it is not the chalice in itself, but how the chalice refracts light that makes it beautiful; it is not the human form in itself, but in how it is framed, composed, contextualized that makes it "hot." This shares affinities with the Kantian conception of the aesthetic experience where the elicitation of the beautiful has nothing to do with the object, but rather discloses disinterested pleasure. While similar to the operation of the beautiful, arousal, though, relies on a repository of "ideal" (read: fetish) objects, what in colloquial terms we might call our "type(s)," and how that internalized object locates a correlating object in the external world. And we might not even have access to those internalized objects necessarily, veiled behind the curtain of the unconscious, and thus the arousing referent might feel mystical, or that it seemingly "came from out of nowhere." And it is allure that is the force that pulls these internal/external objects together, creating the potential to elicit arousal.

By way of a closing example, in Birdy Wei-Ting Hung's article, "Allure and Dissonance: Interracial Lust and 'Problematic' Pleasure," she considers the erotic charge of a curious scene found in Ming-liang Tsai's 2005 film *The Wayward Cloud*. In the article Hung discloses that Shiang-chyi's miming of making out with a watermelon elicited erotic interest in her.[60] This scene also plays on a few common fetishistic tropes: (1) the character's slow movement into the refrigerator, as if tentatively leaning in for a first kiss; (2) Shiang-chyi's cocked head, with the camera composition emphasizing the jawline; (3) the gently darting tongue (the tentative lick—again, like a first kiss, or an erotic encounter with a new sexual partner); (4) the kissing itself (the motion of the jaw, lips, tongue); and (5) the gentle sounds (for example, slobbery, and slight moan signifying sexual excitation). Similar to the reference to John Legend above, it is not simply Shiang-chyi, but how she is presented to us. It is not simply the kiss, it is how that kiss is depicted, both in terms of the cinematography and how Shiang-chyi performs it— from the tilting of her head to her rhythmic attack, to the sounds of wetness and subtle moans signifying pleasure. Embodied simulation is at play as well, in the sense that one (unconsciously) recognizes what it is to kiss and to be kissed, and mirror neurons reinforce the play between the fetishized object and the dark power of allure.

And it is fascinating that this scene is also followed with the porn shoot— part of the plot includes the shooting of a porn film starring the male protagonist, Hsiao-Kang, and an unnamed Japanese actress—which seems to reaffirm that we should take the watermelon kissing scene as erotic—a substitute for a sexual number/encounter. Interestingly, again, everyone is going solo. Shiang-chyi is kissing her watermelon, Hsiao-Kang is jerking off (watching the Japanese porn actress), and the Japanese porn actress is

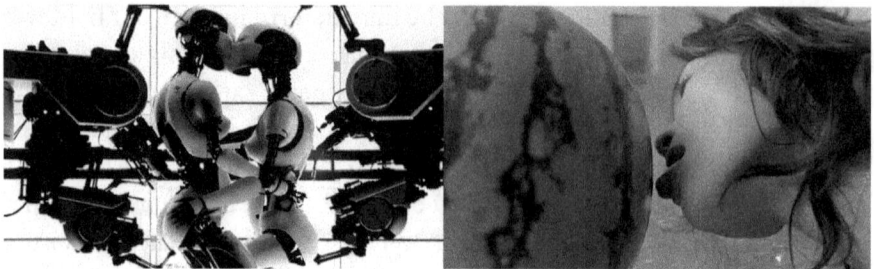

Figure 5.1 Left, *Björk: All Is Full of Love* (Chris Cunningham, 1999); right, *The Wayward Cloud* (Ming-liang Tsai, 2005)

in the middle of shooting a masturbation scene. All of these individuals presumably are all imagining substitutes—"writing" their own sex scripts. In particular, the suggestion is that Shiang-chyi and Hsiao-Kang are imagining having sex with one another—a foreshadowing of what happens at the end. The camerawork, the gesture(s) of the actress, perhaps the actress herself, the sound design—all these are fairly common fetishistic tropes that porn and mainstream cinema draw upon to elicit erotic fascination. And in Hung's disclosed arousal, there was some "unfathomable" (Hung's word) something, resulting from the pairing of some internalized fetishistic object that "clicked," or cohered with the exterior referent of Shiang-chyi's making out with a watermelon. Illustrative of this shared fetishistic economy is Chris Cunningham's music video for Bjork's "All Is Full of Love," discussed in the previous chapter. Although taken from a different angle—Shiang-chyi's watermelon kiss is similarly composed to that of the androids' heads, the ways in which their heads tilt, emphasizing the jawline, and how their mouths slack slightly agape while leaning into a kiss. Making out with a watermelon, I think it is fair to say, does not constitute a common fetishistic trope, however, in the framing, the camera movement, gestures performed, and the audio design Tsai draws out the alluring notes from the object—making this unusual encounter with a watermelon arousing. In a word, it is the form that is critical here.

What follows in the next two chapters is a discussion of the elicitation of sexual arousal (or at least erotic interest, a prelude to a physiological response): how fetishism and allure seduce the viewing body—reinforced by the mechanism of mirror neurons. Even in the most regressive manifestations of the pornographic genre, as I will discuss in Chapter 6 with the chikan (sub-)genre of Japanese porn, despite our better angels, the pull of explicit material wields the potential to elicit arousal. Chapter 7 features Chan-wook Park's 2016 film *The Handmaiden*, which draws from Pier Paolo

Pasolini's infamous 1975 film *Salò, or the 120 Days of Sodom*, and motifs found in the work of the Marquis de Sade, specifically Sade's novel by the same name *The 120 Days of Sodom*. And yet despite its sadistic elements, *The Handmaiden* is stunningly beautiful and an erotically charged film.

Notes

1 Steven Shaviro, *Without Criteria: Kant, Whitehead, Deleuze, and Aesthetics* (Cambridge, MA: MIT Press, 2009), 4.
2 Graham Harman, *Guerrilla Metaphysics: Phenomenology and the Carpentry of Things* (Chicago: Open Court, 2005), 150.
3 Ibid.
4 Ibid., 172.
5 In one of the more elucidating examples of metaphor, Harman writes:

> To say that "my pen is like a pencil" strikes far too closely to what we regard as the inner reality of these utensils, so that we pass straight to the total unity of the pen without jarring loose any of its elements. By contrast, "my pen is an avenging viper" is an obvious catachresis that cannot take us directly to the pen as we know it, but unleashes its ink as a kind of venom, its ramrod-straight figure as a degenerate serpentine form, and its sideways motion as a slithering movement toward polemical ambush. The point is not that metaphor and literal statements both fail to grasp any hidden literal meaning and therefore are equally metaphorical. What marks the difference between metaphor and literal language is that metaphor actually generates new objects rather than passing straight toward those already stockpiled in our midst. It liberates qualities or notes from their banal servitude to withdrawn objects and sets them loose as objects in their own right.

Harman, 163.
6 Steven Shaviro, "Post-Cinematic Affect: On Grace Jones, *Boarding Gate* and *Southland Tales*," *Film-Philosophy* vol. 14, no. 1 (2010): 10.
7 Harman, 154.
8 Shaviro, *Post-Cinematic* Affect, 9.
9 Harman, 185.
10 Shaviro, *Post-Cinematic Affect*, 9.
11 Harman, 211.
12 Ibid., 151.
13 Ibid., 152.
14 Shaviro, *Post-Cinematic Affect*, 9.
15 "Pretty," s.v. OED.
16 Rosalind Galt, *Pretty: Film and the Decorative Image* (New York: Columbia University Press, 2011), 7. Later Galt adds,

> The production of the pretty as a space of rhetorical exclusion depends heavily on its connection to the wrong kinds of bodies. Plato's cosmetics instantiate a connection of the untrustworthy image with the deceptive woman that has dogged the history of Western art, and the devices and tricks of the cinematic pretty oppose an overly fussy feminine mise-en-scène to the grandeur of the masculine exterior. Moreover, the classical binary of Attic authority versus overly flowery Asiatic rhetoric links decorative style both to the

> non-Western and, in the binary's modern forms, to effeminacy and sexual perversion. The politics of the pretty is therefore always engaged in a critique of gender, sexuality, and race as these terms have been imagined and codified through visual culture

(Galt, 20). Much later, though, Galt raises concerns about the bewitching power of the pretty:

> A hint of the pretty also lurks in the word charms. Like prettiness, charm implies magic, a form of pleasurable seduction that is outside of reason or agency. To be charmed is to be tricked, and the witchcraft of the charm closely affiliates the inferior unbeautiful aesthetic with the dangerous power of women and primitives.

And again later, Galt notes, "As with the etymology of the term pretty, when one deviates from the nobility of masculine meaning, witchcraft is never far behind" Galt, 55; 181.

17 Susanna Paasonen, *Carnal Resonance: Affect and Online Pornography* (Cambridge, MA: MIT Press, 2011), 16. Paasonen draws her conception of resonance from Susan Kozel. See Susan Kozel, *Closer: Performance, Technologies, Phenomenology* (Cambridge, MA: MIT Press, 2007), 24–6.
18 Paasonen, *Carnal Resonance*, 18. Also see Susanna Paasonen, "Grains of Resonance: Affect, Pornography and Visual Sensation," *Somatechnics* vol. 3, no. 2 (2013): 358.
19 See Paasonen, *Carnal Resonance*, 189.
20 Harman, 163–4.
21 Laura Mulvey, *Visual and Other Pleasures* (Bloomington: Indiana University Press, 1989), 26.
22 Paasonen, "Grains of Resonance," 354. Rosalind Galt is critical of Mulvey's objective to destroy visual pleasure:

> We can compare this approach with feminist theory, which in some of its more radical moments suggested that the only way to oppose the simultaneous overvaluation/ punishment of women in the image was to strip the image of visual pleasure or, indeed, of women. The logic underlying this politics is that the pristine image is more truthful, but although the rhetoric of the true voice is appealing, that logic is exactly the one that consigned racial and gendered others to the lesser realm of the pretty in the first place

Galt, 162.
23 Paasonen, *Carnal Resonance*, 254.
24 Sigmund Freud, "Fetishism," in *Sigmund Freud Collected Papers*, ed. James Strachey (New York: Basic Books, 1960), 198.
25 Berkeley Kaite, *Pornography and Difference* (Bloomington: Indiana University Press, 1995), 14.
26 Ibid. Kaite cites Victor Burgin, "Seeing Sense," in *Language, Image, Media*, eds Howard Davis and Paul Walton (Oxford: Basil Blackwell, 1983), 226.
27 Harman, *Guerrilla Metaphysics*, 137.
28 Ibid., 148.
29 Ibid., 174.
30 Ibid., 164.
31 Ibid., 175.
32 Ibid., 218.
33 Paasonen, *Carnal Resonance*, 186–7.

34 Joana Carvalho et al., "Gender Differences in Sexual Arousal and Affective Responses to Erotica: The Effects of Type of Film and Fantasy Instructions," *Archives of Sexual Behavior* 42 (2013): 1012–13. Carvalho references Donald L. Mosher and Barbara B. White, "Effects of committed or casual erotic guided imagery on females' subjective sexual arousal and emotional response," *Journal of Sex Research* vol. 16, no. 4 (1980): 273–99.
35 Carvalho et al., 1012–13.
36 Ibid., 1013.
37 Birdy Wei-Ting Hung, my research assistant, noted that this might be illustrative of the difference between "figure," and "Figure" in Deleuze's *Francis Bacon: The Logic of Sensation*: where the "soulless" image of human anatomy might be conceived of as a figure, the arousing image, on the other hand, in its resonating invitation is potentially an example of the Figure. See Gilles Deleuze, *Francis Bacon: The Logic of Sensation*, trans. Daniel W. Smith (Minneapolis: University of Minnesota Press, 2002).
38 This idea is drawn from Italian philosopher Paolo Virno referenced in Vittorio Gallese and Hannah Wojciehowski, "How stories make us feel: Toward an embodied narratology," *California Italian Studies* vol. 2, no. 1 (2011): no pagination. https://doi.org/10.5070/C321008974.
39 Gallese and Wojciehowski. See Vittorio Gallese, "Mirror Neurons and the Neural Exploitation Hypothesis: From Embodied Simulation to Social Cognition," in *Mirror Neuron Systems*, ed. Jaime A. Pineda (New York: Humana Press, 2009), 165.
40 Vittorio Gallese, "Embodied Simulation: Its Bearing on Aesthetic Experience and the Dialogue Between Neuroscience and the Humanities," *Gestalt Theory* vol. 41, no. 2 (2019): 124. See Vittorio Gallese, "Embodied simulation theory: Imagination and memory," *Neuropsychoanalysis* vol. 13, no. 2 (2011): 196–200; and Vittorio Gallese and Michele Guerra, *The Empathic Screen: Cinema and Neuroscience*, trans. Frances Anderson (Oxford: Oxford University Press, 2020).
41 Gallese, "Embodied Simulation," 124. See Hannah C. Wojciehowski and Vittorio Gallese, "Introduction," *Costellazioni: Rivista di lingue e letterature* 5 (2018): 9–22; and Vittorio Gallese, "A Bodily Take on Aesthetics: Performativity and Embodied Simulation Mechanisms," in *The Extended Theory of Cognitive Creativity*, eds Antonino Pennisi and Alessandra Falzone (Cham: Springer International Publishing, 2019), 135–49.
42 Gallese and Wojciehowski. See Gallese "Mirror Neurons and the Neural Exploitation Hypothesis," 165.
43 Even in the sciences, some have heralded warnings about the power of neurology and brain imaging approaches to all forms of human activity.

> A recent book entitled *Neuro-mania: il cervello non spiega chi siamo* (2009), by the Italian cognitive scientists Paolo Legrenzi and Carlo Umiltà, strongly criticizes the neurological positivism and determinism generated by the acritical application of the brain-imaging approach to practically all dimensions defining the human condition. These authors are right in emphasizing the limits intrinsic to the brain imaging approach, which does not directly measure neural activity, but can only estimate it indirectly by detecting how blood flow varies across different brain regions during perceptual, motor, or cognitive tasks.

Gallese and Wojciehowski.

44 Gallese and Guerra, *The Empathic Screen*, 4–5.
45 Gallese and Wojciehowski. See Vittorio Gallese et al., "Action Recognition in the Premotor Cortex," *Brain* vol. 119, no. 2 (1996): 593–609; and Giacomo Rizzolati et al., "Premotor Cortex and the Recognition of Motor Actions," *Cognitive Brain Research* vol. 3, no. 2 (1996): 131–41.
46 Gallese and Wojciehowski state:

> Most important for the purpose of our paper, the premotor cortex exhibiting the Mirror Mechanism is also involved in processing action-related words and sentences, suggesting that mirror neurons, together with other parts of the sensory-motor system, could play a relevant role in the semantics of language.

Gallese and Wojciehowski. See Vittorio Gallese and George Lakoff, "The Brain's Concepts: The Role of the Sensory-Motor System in Reason and Language," *Cognitive Neuropsychology* vol. 22 (2005): 455–79; Vittorio Gallese, "Before and Below Theory of Mind: Embodied Simulation and the Neural Correlates of Social Cognition," *Philosophical Transactions of the Royal Society of London B Series B: Biological Sciences* vol. 358 (2003): 517–28; Vittorio Gallese, "Il corpo teatrale: mimetismo, neuroni specchio, simulazione incarnata," *Culture Teatrali* vol. 16 (2008): 13–38; and Arthur Glenberg and Vittorio Gallese, "Action-Based Language: A theory of language acquisition, production, and comprehension," *Cortex* vol. 48, no.7 (2012): 905–22. Interestingly, Gallese and Guerra have hypothesized that language can in fact stimulate sensorial activity: in a recent fMRI study which demonstrated that the SI somatosensory cortex activated while reading linguistic metaphors concerned with texture, suggesting that comprehension of these metaphors could be perceptually "sensed" based on embodied simulation in the sensory systems. Gallese and Guerra, *The Empathic Screen*, 163.
47 Gallese and Guerra, *The Empathic Screen*, 70.
48 Vittorio Gallese, "Visions of the body: Embodied simulation and aesthetic experience," *Aisthesis. Pratiche, linguaggi e saperi dell'estetico* vol. 10, no. 1 (2017): 43.
49 Richard Cytowic cited in Vivian Sobchack, *Carnal Thoughts: Embodiment and Moving Image Culture* (Berkeley: University of California Press, 2004), 67.
50 Gallese, "Visions of the body," 43.
51 Ibid., 48–9. Emphasis in original.
52 Gallese and Guerra, *The Empathic Screen*, 37–8.
53 Linda Williams, "Film Bodies: Gender, Genre, and Excess," *Film Quarterly* vol. 44, no. 4 (Summer, 1991): 4.
54 My research assistant, Birdy Wei-Ting Hung was the first to point out the affinities between Linda Williams's body genres, which anticipate mimicry of what unfolds onscreen, and mirror neurons.
55 Gallese and Wojciehowski. See Vittorio Gallese, "The manifold nature of interpersonal relations," 517–28; Vittorio Gallese, "Embodied simulation: From neurons to phenomenal experience," *Phenomenology and the cognitive sciences* vol. 4, no. 1 (2005): 23–48; and Vittorio Gallese, "Intentional attunement: A neurophysiological perspective on social cognition and its disruption in autism," *Brain Research* vol. 1079, no. 1 (2006): 15–24.
56 Gallese and Wojciehowski.

57 Driehaus Foundation, "Vittorio Gallese Interview - Driehaus Symposium 2017," YouTube video, October 9, 2017, https://www.youtube.com/watch?v=us8mMKUi1cc
58 Gallese and Wojciehowski. See Guang H. Yue and Kelly J. Cole, "Strength Increases from the Motor Program: Comparison of Training with Maximal Voluntary and Imagined Muscle Contractions," *Journal of Neurophysiology* vol. 67, no. 5 (1992): 1114–23.
59 Gallese and Wojciehowski. See Jean Decety et al., "The Timing of Mentally Represented Actions," *Behavioral Brain Research* vol. 34, nos. 1–2 (1989): 35–42; and Jean Decety et al., "Vegetative Response during Imagined Movement is Proportional to Mental Effort," *Behavioral Brain Research* vol. 42, no. 1 (1991): 1–5.
60 Birdy Wei-Ting Hung, "Allure and Dissonance: Interracial Lust and 'Problematic' Pleasure," *Cinemedia*, June 4, 2020, https://cinemedia.media/allure-and-dissonance/.

6

Pornography
Erotic Disavowal, Regressive Content, and the Chikan (Sub-)Genre

> The experience of our actions, emotions and sensations and of those of others always takes place within a we-centric dimension.[1]
> — Vittorio Gallese

Introduction: I watched it, but I swear it didn't turn me on . . .

The affective experience shares strong affinities with the pornographic. After-all, if something is geared toward the body and its sensations, "porn" is often affixed as a suffix: food porn, poverty porn, war porn, and so on. Nonetheless, in the (sub)discipline of porn studies (within media studies), the affective experience has often been strangely overlooked, or even disavowed.[2] In many cases, the porn genre is subject to some version of content analysis. From queer theory and post-colonial theory to feminist film theory, porn studies has largely directed its attention to reading porn content in order to situate it within a cultural environment. And there is a near paradox in the analysis of pornography, because whereas "[p]ornography aims to create proximities between viewers and images," Susanna Paasonen observes, "content analysis is efficient in obscuring these proximities. Both content analysis and studies of representation can be critiqued for being based on and giving rise to a distance between the images studied and the one doing the study." The discourse of analysis, and the paradigms of content analysis and studies of representation, places a safe distance between the scholar and their subject of analysis. "When studying pornography, such a distance may create a comforting sense of safety as the imaginary line keeps the body genre and the carnal reactions that it evokes at bay." However, this distance comes at a price, because "the distance may keep the researcher from asking some crucial questions concerning the genre and its affective force."[3]

Often studies of representation or content analysis attempt to either "redeem" pornographic material because of its progressive potential, or to critique it as a manifestation of regressive political representations.[4] Lover or Hater. While I have no intention of dismissing these important socio-political interventions, and I do my fair share of content analysis, I nevertheless want to honestly engage with what is often left at the front door: the affective experience.[5] Regardless of the ideological implications of the pornographic material, the object of the genre is nearly singular in its intention: sexual arousal. And nowhere else do Steven Shaviro's admonishing words ring truer: "Beneath its claims to methodological rigor and political correctness, it manifests a barely contained panic at the prospect (or is it the memory?) of being affected and moved by visual forms."[6] To approach pornography through narrative and sociological paradigms of assessment often entails keeping the affective power of the pornographic at more than arm's length, marginalizing (or ignoring altogether) its effects on the body. And that is not to mention that the very intent of the genre is to elicit sexual arousal.

There have been some challenges to this focus on the ideological within porn studies though (as indicated in note 2). "Porn is both material and semiotic," Susanna Paasonen observes, "it involves fleshy intensities, conventions of representation, media technologies, and the circuits of money, labor, and affect." With the explicit exhibition of sex—and the attendant sounds and fluids—the pornographic genre addresses itself directly and affectively to the viewing body. "Through minute anatomical realism, it tries to mediate the sensory and to attach the viewing body to its affective loop: in porn, bodies move and move the bodies of those watching."[7] Paasonen's work is exemplary precisely because of her attention to social meanings and industrial practices (for example, internet distribution), all the while acknowledging porn's power to affect the viewing body.

Porn studies with some regularity privileges "alternatives" to mainstream pornographic production (as mentioned in the introductory chapter—what Tristan Taormino calls "organic, [or] fair-trade porn"[8]), to showcase resistance to perceived notions of heteronormative sexual fantasies.[9] Paasonen offers similar reflections, noting that studies of pornography should not be limited to content analysis in the pursuit of ascertaining "meanings," or how the genre "depict[s] and give[s] shape to social categories such as gender, race, or class (this aspect of the representational having been one of the most important foci in studies of pornography to date)." Rather Paasonen asserts that pornography should take into account "technologies of production and distribution, affective intensities and resonances, appeal, and force. Rather than being mutually exclusive or conflicting with one another, these perspectives support one another."[10] Importantly though, Paasonen insists that drawing stark divisions between "older" disciplinary trends which are rooted in structuralism, and the "newer" turn to affect, is equally as mistaken.[11] (And as we saw in the introductory chapter, this chronological conception is erroneous in itself as numerous early film theorists were interested in investigating the affective potential of the cinematic.)

Furthermore, Paasonen, acknowledges that there has never been a wholesale disavow of the affective experience in the study of pornography, but rather "it seems that relatively little has happened in conceptualizations of porn and its fleshy, sensuous appeal since Linda Williams's 1991 article on body genres and Richard Dyer's 1985 consideration of pornography as a genre 'rooted in bodily effect' and involving bodily knowledge."[12] The disciplinary imperative to locate meanings—in part a product of the methodological approaches applied to the analysis of porn—all but assures that the affective experience is skirted. "Analysis highlighting questions of meaning does not quite manage to grasp this excess and resistance—that is, the sensory, synesthetic, and visceral aspects of encountering images." And such attention to cultural meanings, arguably, is to miss the whole point of the genre.[13]

Williams has also gone back to reevaluate her own work. "In 1989 when I latched on to the term, 'frenzy of the visible,'" reflecting in a 2019 article, Williams recounts, "I was still inclined to join apparatus theorists in a blanket condemnation of the visible itself—a visible whose unprecedented techniques for creating the illusion of the real, seemed reprehensible for the false impression of mastery and control it engendered." Williams acknowledges that the (implicit) imperatives of the discipline directed her analytic approach, realizing that she fell in lockstep with "apparatus theory's condemnation of a regime of the visible that was too wedded to the then-current feminist and Lacanian critiques of Renaissance perspective considered as a form of ideological false consciousness—an illusion of mastery that filled a fundamental 'lack.'"[14]

Williams does not move entirely in the direction of theories of affect, nevertheless, she makes gestures in that direction. Williams turns her attention to e-motion and lust. The movies move us. And Williams reminds us that "the very word emotion (from Latin *emovere*, or agitate) derives from motion. Yet nowhere is this relation of motion to e-motion so evident as in hard-core moving-image pornography." The cinematic is laden with affective potential, pornography though in its choreography of movement and audio (soundwaves just being one other form of movement) generally cuts to the chase fulfilling the spectator's erotic interest, which Williams understands "as both the frenzied motions of sexual acts and as the e-motion accompanying them felt in the bodies of viewers," which brought about "the modern invention of . . . [the pornographic] genre."[15]

While we must acknowledge the regressive politics endemic to the pornographic genre, all at the same time the genre is, one might argue, exclusively geared towards eliciting pleasure. There is always a question about whose pleasure is being served, the presumption of course is that pornography is singularly focused on male pleasure. And it is more or less. But to preclude female pleasure from the consumption of pornographic material is also a perilous assumption—why close off avenues toward female sexual fantasies, or erotic interests? Why police sexual fantasies? Why is it automatically assumed that a woman who derives pleasure from politically regressive content is a "traitor" to her gender, or somehow deluded, naïve, or stupid?[16]

Undoing Gendered Presumptions and Unruly Bodies

There are entrenched gendered assumptions about the consumption of pornographic material. The presumption that male porn consumption is singularly focused on hardcore mainstream heteronormative sex is not wholly accurate. The "gangbang" or the "MMF three-way" scenario, for instance, might serve (unconscious) homoerotic interest. As recited in lyrics of the SNL Digital Short, "3-Way (The Golden Rule)," featuring The Lonely Island, Justin Timberlake, and Lady Gaga, "It's okay if it's in a 3-way / It's not gay when it's in a 3-way / With a honey in the middle, there's some leeway / The area's grey in a 1-2-3-way."[17] Categories on popular porn distribution sites like "shemale" also suggest that even for cis-gender men, sexual interests are fluid.[18] Likewise, the presumption that women favor "softer," more "romantic" narrative-invested pornographic material, or content that is more politically progressive is misplaced. Research in this area indicates that we cannot preclude the possibility that female pleasure can be drawn from politically regressive pornography.

Athanasia Daskalopoulou and Maria Carolina Zanette's study of female porn-consumption observes that it is too presumptuous to demarcate "women's from men's consumption, we find that women use pornography in a fairly similar way to men as reported in recent studies."[19] Based on their study, Daskalopoulou and Zanette report "that women also find pleasure in mainstream pornography, including hardcore categories, even though they do not always identify with the actors and stories." However, this is not to suggest that women that consume pornography have internalized misogyny, or that they are masochistic. Rather, Daskalopoulou and Zanette "find that porn tastes can be quite different from real-life sexual preferences. Consuming pornography in that sense allows women to explore sexual practices that they have not experienced in real life or do not necessarily intend to mimic."[20] Daskalopoulou and Zanette conclude that female porn consumers use it to elicit their own sexual excitation, and do not necessarily "identify" with it, or hope to enact what happens in porn in their own sex-lives.[21]

Susanna Paasonen also finds the distinction between male and female interest in the pornographic impractical. Paasonen finds "the notion of gendered structure of desire rather nonsensical in its attachment to a binary notion of difference (male and female) that grants no fluidity within the categories." There is no "monolithic point of reference (because no such point of reference exists)" in the pornographic genre. Paasonen puts it simply, concluding that, "Different things turn different people on, as any online session spent browsing through the available subcategories of online porn is likely to show."[22]

Furthermore, while there is an assumption that mainstream heterosexual pornography focuses on male pleasure, Kelly Denis notes that "[c]ontrary to conventional wisdom on the subject, the primary—even obsessive—focus of mainstream, heterosexual pornography is, in fact, female orgasm." As Williams explores in *Hard Core*, visual technologies, no sooner than they were invented, were quickly employed to capture the confessions of the (female) body. "One might even say that the history of visual technology is a prolonged quest for establishing proof of female sexual pleasure, attempting to render that which does not conform to perceptual conventions." Dennis goes on to assert that, because the female orgasm is ostensibly "invisible" the choreography of pornography displaces it for "what can be seen: i.e., onto both the 'hydraulics of male ejaculation' and the *expression* of ecstasy on the woman's face, often coupled in the film 'come shot' onto the face of the woman." Limited to what can be seen and heard, "women can only *look like* they are coming."[23] The male body, on the other hand, freely confesses to sexual arousal and gratification in both the exhibition of the erect penis and ejaculation. The male body cannot fake it.[24]

Pornography has developed a repertoire of visual choreographed events designed to elicit arousal from the spectator—compositions, mise-en-scène (including gestures, sexual positions, etc.), editing, and what might be overlooked but a soundscape that (like the visual design) intends to offer proof, or at least some evidentiary material of (female) excitation. The sounds associated with sex, especially those associated with female sounds in mainstream heterosexual porn, has been a significant focus in the porn industry, precisely because the female orgasm does not (generally) have the same evidentiary force that male ejaculate does. The proof is in the cum. It is a confession of the body—it is undeniable evidence of (male) sexual gratification. Thus, the porn industry has developed a choreography, or repertoire of aural/visual motifs that are designed to elicit pleasure from the spectator. The aural expressions from the female actress are intended (in part) to offer proof of excitation as a kind of substitute for what cannot be seen.[25]

"Ohhhh … fufufufufuuuuuuck … ahhhhh." A good deal of what is heard in the porn soundscape is lektonic (that is, a signifier without a signified). In other words, the utterances are "empty" of meaning. Consider, just as an example, "SARA LUVV EXTREME PASSIONATE ROUGH FUCK, CUMMING ON COCK MULTIPLE TIMES AND CUM SWALLOW," viewed over 19 million times, featuring the director/performer James Deen, and the actress Sara Luvv. Forty-five seconds into the clip, Luvv utters an extended, "ohhh… fu————ck."[26] The utterance in its elongation nearly loses hold of its communicative value. Supposedly symptomatic of Luvv's sexual ecstasy, she elongates the word "fuck," where the "pha" is pronounced, but is followed with a long instance of holding the breath interrupting the final utterance of the "k" consonant. And this nearly obliterates the integrity of the word. Obviously, we can attribute meaning, despite the impedance of clearly articulated language, "ohhh … fu————ck" means pleasure (whether "real," exaggerated, or acted), but linguistically, there is little communicative function as such. At three minutes and fifty seconds into the clip, Luvv utters, "Oh yes!" Even when discernable words are uttered such as, "Oh fuck!" "Oh shit!" "Oh god!" "Oh yes!" and so on, to a certain extent these words come undone, they lose their meaning. While an "Oh yes!" might say something like, "yes, keep doing that thing, that feels good." It is nonetheless, not quite that though, there is often more to it than that. It is often, "Yesssssss," the tone, the volume, the way that the word might be affected by a body that is out of breath, the way it might be drawn out, the way the word manifests with bodies thrusting together, for example at 8 minutes and six seconds Luvv extends, "Y-uh E-uh S-uh" stuttering over the "s." And this is not limited to Luvv's utterances, equally, Deen makes nearly identical utterances, for instance, "Fuck————me," at the forty-four second mark. And when Deen ejaculates, not all of his utterances are communicative as such, just, "uh oh!" emphasized in a lower guttural register, and immediately after cumming an, "Oh, my godddd," the latter consonant delivered in a quivering half-laugh. All of this "extra" stuff that is "added" to a signifier like "yes," is what Julia Kristeva would call the semiotic. That "yes" (or whatever word might be uttered) is entwined with the trace elements of the body—its breath, its musculature, its heart-rate, its spasmodic pulsations. Lektonic aural utterances are taken as a symptom of bodily pleasure. (The near "meaninglessness" of words in the pornographic genre also speaks to the global appeal of Japanese porn, which Pornhub reports was the most popular category in 2019. Assuredly, many consumers of Japanese pornography cannot understand what is said, but that hardly matters. The Japanese chikan genre is the subject of discussion below.)

Others have made similar observations. Sex, as Paul Ricoeur observes, "belongs to a pre-linguistic existence" of the human species. Even if the body engaged in sexual activity "mobilizes language, . . . it [nevertheless] crosses it, jostles it, sublimates it, stupefies it, pulverizes it into a murmur, an invocation. Sexuality demediatizes language; it is Eros and not Logos."[27] And indeed, the industry relies on "amplifying" (in every sense of that term) those aural utterances—it is called acting. But regardless if it is genuine, exaggerated, or even fake altogether, the aural utterances are intended to offer evidence of excitation, and thus elicit arousal in the spectator. And to be certain, pornography is not synonymous with sex, rather pornography is a genre with a set of conventions that are intended to elicit sexual arousal.[28] The spectator is in effect invited to participate in the feelings of pleasure—fueled by the economies of fetishism and allure and reinforced by the mechanism of embodied simulation.

Embodied simulation in particular, because it operates upon the neural system outside cognitive processes, speaks to the dissonance that might emerge in the consumption of porn.[29] Material that, at a diegetic level, is problematic might still elicit sexual arousal. Ariane Cruz, a self-described black feminist interested in kink (namely BDSM), has wrestled with this very issue. Cruz acknowledges in her own research that the arousing power of porn on the body is frequently at odds with the mind. "That is, frequently racist, sexist, and purely offensive material can and will arouse the body while simultaneously seeming to quash the mind." In her own history of examining and consumption of pornography, the depictions of black female bodies can be quite alarming (in American pornography). Cruz acknowledges the deeply troubling optics of a whipped and bound black body—the connotations of slavery are painfully self-evident—however, at the same time, does this then preclude Cruz (or others) from indulging in BDSM fantasies? Cruz grapples with this dilemma. And thus, even in particularly problematic scenarios, in the ways that the female black body "may be treated by her partner, positioned, framed, spoken to, clothed, and/or to her expression (or lack thereof) of her own sexual pleasure, there is the potential, albeit short lived, for physical arousal." Cruz adds, "My scholarly trained black feminist mind often futilely scolds my body for responding in such a manner."[30]

This tension that Cruz reveals—where an individual's taste in porn disagrees with their values—appears to be a fairly common experience.[31] In Paasonen's article, "'We watch porn for the fucking, not for romantic tiptoeing': extremity, fantasy and women's porn use," she explains that in 2017 she was contacted by a producer for the television series *Jenny+*, produced by the Finnish public service broadcasting company Yle, a popular lifestyle program promoting female body-positivity and health. The program surveyed "2438 women," Paasonen reports, "the overwhelming majority (1637) being women aged 20–40 years," which given the context "was high in a country of 5.5 million people."[32] Citing the 3.8 billion women on the planet, Paasonen warns against making assumptions about the desires, fantasies, and porn consuming habits of such a diverse population. Far too often we rely on gender-based assumptions about porn consuming habits, but as Paasonen finds in the *Jenny+* data, such studies upend our assumptions, finding that women enjoy "hardcore scenarios of control, domination and submission, or other content deemed marginal and extreme."[33]

Our unruly bodies potentially introduce a degree of dissonance between our most cherished beliefs and the affective experience. Paasonen offers similar observations and acknowledges this dissonance. Her conception of resonance (discussed in the previous chapter), does not aim to dismiss feminist interventions in the critiques of pornography, but rather to account for "surprising reverberations, affective intensities, and moments of being moved by dissonance inasmuch as by 'sympathetic vibrations.'"[34] The question remains though, what exactly is it, what are our bodies responding to, and how does the pornographic genre wield such tremendous power that it might short circuit cognitive judgement, and "speak" directly to our nervous system? The following sections, in part, attempt to address at least some of these questions.

Chikan: A Regressive Sub-genre of Japanese Porn

As referenced above, according to Pornhub's "The 2019 Year in Review," reports that, "For the last several years 'Lesbian' has been the most viewed category through most of the world, but this year 'Japanese' moved into first place."[35] Amongst male visitors "Japanese" was the most searched term/category, while it was third for female visitors to the popular porn distribution site. The Japanese porn industry is prolific and internet distribution makes it amongst the most widely consumed purveyors of pornographic material across the planet. (For an entertaining examination of the history of the Japanese video porn industry, see the Netflix series *The Naked Director*.)

Regressive content most certainly has the power to elicit sexual arousal, and to explore this issue I will focus on the Japanese chikan (sub-)genre. The Japanese chikan genre features the groping of (more often than not) a female character in a public setting. Chikan translates as "groper." In many cases chikan videos are set on a bus or a train where one or more female character is fondled and groped either by a singular male character, or by a group, often on a crowded train or bus. There are other variants on the chikan genre, which I will discuss momentarily. It often culminates in a full-on sexual encounter, but some scenarios are limited to fondling—ending with the female character, and/or the male character climaxing.

While the genre itself is not new, there appears to have been a revival of the genre in the last 15 years or so. The various public transportation companies that serve rail and subway systems in Tokyo began to introduce female only cars (during rush hour periods) in the early 2000s. "In train company surveys, a large percentage, often a majority, of women indicated they had been groped, with most incidents occurring on commuter trains," Mitsutoshi Horii and Adam Burgess report. "It is young women, especially school and university students, who appear to be the most common victims. According to the Gender Equality Bureau's survey (2000), 48.7% of women over 20 years old had at least one experience of being groped." Some studies have found that upwards of 70% of women surveyed report having been groped.[36] The effort to stop groping, along with a highly visible public awareness campaign, probably prompted renewed popularity in the chikan genre (a deeply regressive backlash). I have no intention to "save" the chikan genre, but rather to acknowledge the potential to elicit sexual arousal despite the fact that the content is offensive and depicts what in the "real-world" would be considered criminal behavior. And to be clear, there is a difference between a criminal act, and the fictional representation of a criminal act, which is what chikan is. Nevertheless, I have elected to focus on chikan precisely because this genre is so deeply problematic.

The chikan genre has antecedents in Japan's softcore tradition of pink films as well as manga and literary predecessors. Just for a moment, because it also speaks to the erroneous assumption that the chikan genre elicits pleasure from only male viewers we might consider, for example, Motomi Kado's "My Most Perverted Evening."[37] This is a story, in the manga format, that was written by a woman, supposedly drawn from a reader's real-life sexual encounter, published in a "ladies' comic." In contemporary parlance ladies' comics are called, *josei manga*, which is marketed for a female audience, some of which might include erotic/pornographic content. Deborah Shamoon discusses ladies' comics, including "My Most Perverted Evening," which features a female protagonist, Mayumi, who engages in sex with her boyfriend on a crowded train. The couple are caught, and while "Mayumi swears off exhibitionism at the end of the story," Shamoon adds, "the last frame indicates that she and her boyfriend will continue their sexual experimentation."[38] (As a side note, the chikan fantasy is also evident in "train themed" love hotels, where couples might go to act out such fantasies in a room that replicates a train car.[39]) While "My Most Perverted Evening" is by and large consensual (though Mayumi is ultimately made to suffer humiliation), many of the stories found in ladies' comics feature nonconsensual situations. "Dismissing ladies' comics as yet another example of patriarchal oppression," Shamoon urges that this "is a disservice to both the comics and their readers." Shamoon argues that ladies' comics put to rest "common myths about pornography, such as that women are not visually stimulated and that hard-core pornography necessarily proves harmful to women. Ladies' comics provide a unique example of what heterosexual women might find pleasure in looking at."[40] And as evident in the popularity of ladies' comics, including non-consensual and violent content, it would be an error to assume that chikan videos only appeal to men.

Another variant of the chikan genre (or if not properly chikan, then immediately adjacent to the genre) is massage. The massage industry in Japan is relatively popular and entirely mainstream. You can walk the streets of Tokyo and find completely "legitimate" venues offering massage services. In some cases, these venues, with their glass storefront, are entirely visible from the street—sometimes, though not always, a partition might be placed around the massage table to lend at least nominal privacy. In the pornographic chikan genre, though, as one might expect, an individual going in for a massage ends up getting more than they bargained for—and not just a "happy ending." In most cases women are given a massage, but the masseuse (either male or female, or sometimes even both with multiple masseuses) slowly works their way into the erogenous zones—massaging the woman's breasts, buttocks, inner thigh. The woman might initially resist, or feign shyness, but she invariably relents to the feelings of pleasure, and she is brought to climax. The encounters may or may not include penetrative sex. Some common scenarios include: mother-daughter scenarios (where the mother brings the daughter in for a massage); husband-wife scenarios (this can be quite comical—the oblivious husband gets an "innocent" massage, while behind a curtain his wife, who is likely unfulfilled by her partner, finds satisfaction with her masseuse); a coed stressed out about school or some sport injury; or a bored, sexually unsatisfied, or lonesome housewife who treats herself to a massage. Like the train/bus setting, with the massage scenario the female character is (at least to start) often a nonconsensual participant to the erotic touching, either voicing, "no," or through body-language resistant to the initial forays into erogenous zones. With the massage scenario, though, there is a degree of narrative motivation for the erotic encounter.

In yet one more common chikan scenario, and much closer to videos set on a train or bus, there is a smaller niche of Japanese pornography set in either a library or bookstore. Often it is set in a high school or college setting, where a woman is groped between shelves of books. The library scenarios— like those set on a bus or train—often seem wildly implausible, where other patrons might pass by completely unphased by the (supposedly) surreptitious erotic encounter. Again, very much like chikan videos set on a train or bus, the female character is often groped, and scenes often culminate in a full-fledged sexual encounter (with penetrative sex), but not necessarily. But just like the other two scenarios discussed here, the female character is often a nonconsensual participant. And like the other chikan scenarios the female character, who is often minding her own business browsing the bookshelves, is an unwilling party to the sexual encounter, but like the other situations she often relents and becomes ecstatically enthralled. Inescapably problematic to be certain, this is nevertheless how it is justified within the narrative context of chikan videos.

Anyone with the slightest moral compass would find the behavior exhibited in these pornographic videos to be wrong. And particularly if these were set in a "real life" situation, the overwhelming majority of us (at least one hopes) would find such behavior utterly reprehensible—criminal, in fact. In the context of the pornographic genre, however, some license is given to the content—pornography and personal fantasies, do not necessarily align with our ethical perspectives. Making a similar observation, Tristan Taormino, feminist porn icon, notes that "the libido is a tricky thing; what turns us on may be disconnected from or in opposition to our social and political values."[41] And clearly, judging by what is on offer (on sites like Pornhub, and other distribution sites), vast swaths of the population locate pleasure in problematic pornographic material.

As an example, let us review Kanie's 2015 film *Married Teacher Molester Train* featuring the actress, Reiko Kobayakawa.[42] And specifically, let us take an excerpt from this full-length film, erroneously entitled, "Abused in Bus," distributed on the Pornhub site.[43] (Very clearly the video is set on a subway car or JR [Japan Rail] train.) As often happens on these pornographic distribution platforms, excerpts are taken to cut to the chase, and to get straight to the affecting business. "Abused in Bus," is longer than most excerpted clips, running just over 26 minutes, and actually leaves the narrative contextualization in place, establishing that Kobayakawa's character is a high school teacher. I have selected this particular example, because it has been viewed over 7 million times, and exhibits many of the conventions associated with the chikan genre.[44] Kobayakawa plays a sexy teacher—white blouse, very short black skirt, and black high heels. Her all-male students gawk at her, muttering between one another. Students, twice no less, intentionally drop pens on the floor (pretending to be accidental) so as to sneak a peek under her skirt or down Kobayakawa's blouse as she bends down to retrieve the pens. The fetishistic treatment of Kobayakawa's body is played to the hilt—her short skirt emphasizes her legs and its snug fit emphasizes her buttocks, her blouse hints to her buxom figure, and her hair (tied back in a ponytail) and attire self-consciously play on the well-worn sexy teacher/librarian trope. The cinematography as well capitalizes on Kobayakawa's figure, and this is particularly true once she is on the train. Numerous shots are taken from a low angle to emphasize her legs and the hint of the curvature of her buttocks before it rises up behind the hem of her skirt. She often stands with her legs somewhat apart, to allow for flashes of undergarments (if viewed from the "right" vantage point—which of course the camera does).

"Abused in Bus" cuts straight from the classroom to the interior of a train. In many cases though, chikan videos that are set on a bus or train, emphasize the "authenticity" of the situation by surreptitiously shooting the female character at a real JR or subway station, or bus stop.[45] JR stations in particular lend a strong sense of verisimilitude, with the bustle of people and the various announcements and chimes associated with approaching or departing trains. Once on the train or bus, in most cases, the film cuts to a closed set, or as sometimes happens charts a private bus. Filling the bus or train carriage with numerous extras offers narrative motivation for the groping, where throngs of people are crushed together. One of the interesting elements in *Married Teacher Molester Train* is the use of mosaic censoring. While it is used as a means to retain a degree of decency to censor genital contact, as is the convention in the Japanese porn industry, what is specifically interesting here is that the faces of the other commuters are censored to preserve their anonymity as well. Although *Married Teacher Molester Train* is very clearly set on a closed set, and the other commuters are extras, the censoring of their faces lends a degree of "authenticity," suggesting that the scene is really taking place in public even though it is not. Mosaic censoring is sometimes used to blur out faces in masseuse videos too. It is also the convention of the Japanese news media to blur out people's faces in the background, or children, especially in a "sensitive" news story.

And the "authenticity" within the chikan genre is leveraged to authenticate the transgressive (criminal behavior) and sexual pleasure even despite the scenario. The gestures toward "authenticity" are only genre conventions, and in most cases chikan videos are transparent in their dissimulation. Paasonen interrogates the conception of authenticity in the pornographic genre. "Pornography sports the 'authentic presence' of arousal and orgasm with the aid of the documentary powers of photography and cinematography by promising to convey indexical traces of the events that have taken place." However, Paasonen observes, "any first-year media studies student will point out that pornography hardly just 'records' the acts performed for the camera." Rather, like any other genre, pornography is governed by a set of conventions and tropes. No genre is fixed, rather like all other genres, porn is subject to ebbing and waning trends, or evolutionary pressures (whether driven by technology, or the desire for novel approaches to revitalize a stagnating genre). Nevertheless, genres generally follow well-worn paths, meeting spectator expectations, and porn is no different in that respect. Porn is highly orchestrated and follows established choreography to optimize what can be seen and heard.[46] And not to be overlooked, the very framing of porn as "authentic" is in itself just yet one more convention of the pornographic genre.

Although *Married Teacher Molester Train* dispenses with the JR station setting, we find Kobayakawa on a moderately crowded train. Kobayakawa slowly rocks back and forth, jostled by the movement of the train (though clearly this is just acted). A fellow passenger mirrors the rocking gesture as well, and at first allows the outside of his hand to bump up against Kobayakawa's buttocks casually and lightly—what, especially on a crowded train, in normal circumstances might be passed off as an innocent accident. However, the light glance of the hand rests momentarily on Kobayakawa's buttocks, followed by a reaction shot indicating that Kobayakawa is aware that this is in fact no accidental glance of a hand, but a conscious gesture. Returning to the passenger's hand, now his hand in-facing, begins to make tentative light touches. Kobayakawa is clearly distressed by the groping and tries to slink away from the probing hand—even reaching back twice to brush away the intruder. But, of course, per genre imperatives, the coy groping continues, and slowly builds to firmer clutches, eventually the passenger yanks Kobayakawa's skirt up. Her buttocks more exposed (though she is wearing pantyhose and underwear) the passenger firmly massages Kobayakawa's ass. This is then followed by clitoral stimulus, the passenger making circular gestures with his right hand, his left hand now slinking beneath her pantyhose to massage her naked ass at the same time. Implausibly, other passengers take no notice of what is happening, as Kobayakawa's pantyhose are peeled away, and she begins to utter (though muted) reflexive expressions of arousal with increasingly heavy breath. The touching continues to amplify, leading to Kobayakawa's underwear being stripped away as well. The camera, this whole time (save the occasional cut to a reaction shot), is placed low to focus on the buttocks and (now by this point) exposed genitals. The passenger now really begins to work on Kobayakawa to bring her close to climax. A near extreme close-up offers evidence of Kobayakawa's excited state, by showing the passenger's fingers at her genitals, strings of viscous vaginal fluid thread between his stimulating fingers and her labia. In this increased state of excitement, the passenger begins to undress Kobayakawa unbuttoning her blouse, and removing her bra to expose and massage her breasts. Nearly entirely naked at this point, Kobayakawa is eventually brought to climax as she crumples to the floor after digital stimulation. From this point penetrative sex is initiated, though, Kobayakawa remains an unwilling party performing oral sex and then vaginal penetrative sex.[47] By some coincidence, one of the gawking students happens to be on the same train, and records a video of Kobayakawa on her

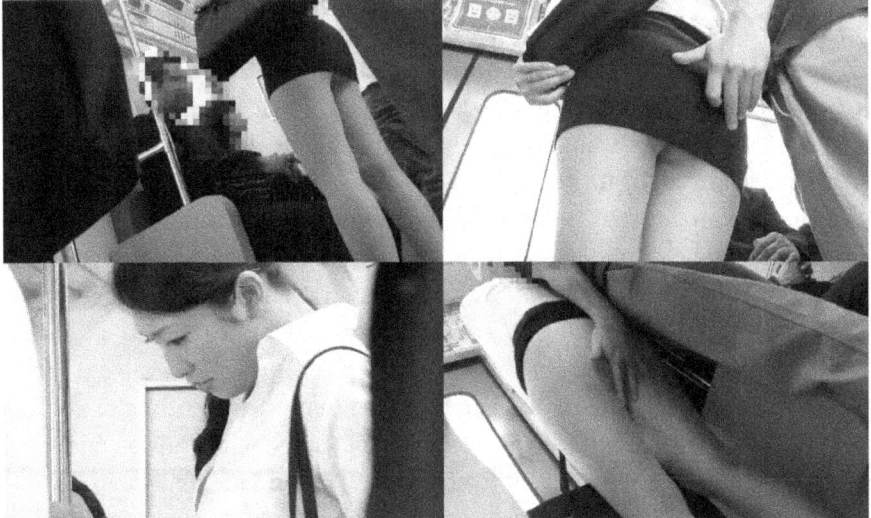

Figure 6.1 *Married Teacher Molester Train*, "Abused in Bus" excerpt (Kanie, 2015)

knees performing oral sex and (presumably) the rest of the sexual encounter on his phone.

Despite the narrative contextualization, the careful choreography of the chikan genre works hard to authenticate female excitation. In this excerpt, "Abused in Bus," approximately 15 minutes (or approximately 65% of the time) is given to touching and stimulating the female body, and 8 minutes to penile-penetrative sex.[48] There is (again despite the situation) an effort to focus on female excitation. As mentioned above, Dennis and Williams observe that mainstream pornography is on a never-ending quest to offer proof of female excitation, specifically female orgasm, which is generally invisible. The choreographed money shot—male ejaculate coupled with the woman's expression of ecstasy—is often taken as the substitute for what has no visible correlate.

Chikan videos are no different in this respect. And with the tropes of authenticity of the chikan genre female excitation is lent further substantiation in the setting—the "supposed" reality of the setting, whether that is a JR station, or a massage office—which confers a degree of authenticity to the whole. Roland Barthes called this the "reality effect." However, I do not want to suggest that the affective force rests in the supposed "authenticity" of the pornographic content. There are lots of examples of animated chikan videos that would likely elicit the same response without any pretension to authenticity—see for example Hiroshi Kimura's 2012–2015 animated series *Crimson Girls: Chikan Shihai*.[49]

More significantly, chikan videos tend to emphasize female vaginal moisture. As found in "Abused in Bus," a premium is placed on touching and fingers that are visibly wet by digital stimulation. Even in the context of a crowded train or bus, or a library/bookstore, evidence of female sexual arousal is often paramount. There is a "narrative" challenge though, how to demonstrate female excitation when the character must remain relatively composed and mitigate for aural utterances (lest attracting attention to the supposedly surreptitious erotic encounter)? While mainstream pornographic conventions rely on the carefully choreographed expressions of the female performer—specifically, in her aural and facial expressions—with the chikan genre these expressions are generally muted or toned down. Thus, in chikan videos there is an emphasis placed on vaginal secretions. Whether it is the male character that demonstrates for the camera the presence of vaginal fluids—for instance, using a close-up on the male actor's hand to offer evidence of wetness as we found in "Abused in Bus"—or vaginal expressions seeping through undergarments, or pooling on the floor, in many cases as a result of the male character's manual stimulation.

Coupled with what is made visible, there is often a "sloppy-wet" audio accompaniment that amplifies vaginal wetness. If not taken as an expression of orgasmic pleasure (female ejaculate, or other secretions), then, at the very least wetness (regardless if it is real or fake) signifies intensified sexual arousal in the female character. And in that sense, it serves as a correlate to the confessions of the male body—erect penis and ejaculate. And as a sidenote, another popular porn category is "squirting," which seems to play on exactly this fantasy—rendering female sexual pleasure visible.[50] The proof is in the cum.

"What is a pornographic film doing when it shows female wetness?" Eugenie Brinkema asks. "Nothing other than radically othering the image: the ontologic authenticity of the pornographic image has always been associated with the male body because it was the production of visible male stuff that marked that something 'real' had taken place." Chikan relies on female wetness as a signifier of excitation—that "real" female pleasure has taken place. The chikan genre is perhaps even compelled all the more because of the narrative situations, to prove excitation and as if to say, "Look, she really likes it." In mainstream heterosexual pornography, the affective experience is lent visual evidence. "The interior female sexual (and psychic) experience is a sort of hidden presence, not quite real, refusing to provide the authenticity by which the genre is defined. Her sexuality is not figurable, not sufficient." Brinkema then concludes, "In traditional pornography, female sexuality is not there."[51] What is there, though, is ontological realism as Brinkema posits it. And just to qualify this in clear terms, female excitation, or its signifier in the form of wetness, should not necessarily be conflated with female pleasure, but a physiological response to erogenous stimulation.

The point again, is not to justify rape, but rather to examine how the choreography of the scene short circuits ethical channels and speaks directly to the viewing body. While a conventional disciplinary analysis, often some form of content analysis, would direct our attention toward the narrative situation, what any conventional disciplinary approach would likely overlook is the affecting choreography, because again our discipline is so utterly transfixed on narratives and "meanings." A conventional disciplinary approach would ask us to consider what happens in *Married Teacher Molester Train*, and there would be nothing wrong with that, but what I am suggesting is that with an approach to pornographic material through affect theory, we are invited to consider how the content is presented to us, and why it might elicit arousal even despite the unethical narrative situation. Presumably, one could formulate some sort of narrative explanation to explain sexual arousal, probably around the fetishistic formulation of, "I know, but . . .," this, to my mind, seems insufficient. There is also the transgressive nature of the encounters presented in chikan videos—a violation of law and common decency.[52] (Transgression, and the wrong time and place, will be an important feature in our discussion of laughter in the coming chapters.[53])

What "speaks" to the viewing body though is not simply the narrative context (that is, rape, transgressive behavior, or exercising of power), and in fact if spectators truly considered the narrative content they very well might be profoundly turned off, but the choreography of sensuous touching is what appears to be the turn on. In fact, the narrative—or for that matter, the emotional state of the characters—is perhaps even irrelevant. The presentation of bodies, as Brinkema observes, "is not pornographic in itself, it's the way we represent it, or, a space is not pornographic in itself, it's the way we inhabit it, or, even, a pornography is not pornographic in itself, it's the way we materialize it."[54] And assuredly this is one of the central problems with the pornographic genre, and is its effacement of social actors, and the fetishistic treatment of bodies. (No significant revelation there.) That all said, though, while pornography might be "dehumanizing" as some of the most ardent anti-porn feminists have argued, this does not make pornography necessarily any less affecting.[55] And there is perhaps some peril in pretending otherwise.

It is worth noting that *Married Teacher Molester Train* ends with a textual disclaimer (though written in Japanese), that states that all participants were consensual parties, and that groping in real life is a crime. The disclaimer implores spectators "not to imitate" the events portrayed. The Pornhub excerpt, "Abused in Bus," does not have this disclaimer. In the pornographic genre it is the exhibition of bodies and evidence of physical arousal that is at stake. With the chikan genre, more often than not, female characters (whether desired or not) are subjected to long drawn-out caressing, which proceeds any explicit sexual encounter. This is perhaps most self-evident with the massage scenario, but in the chikan genre (regardless of the specific scenario) there is often an emphasis placed on caressing, on touching, and extended foreplay prior to penetrative sex—if that even takes place. While this is not always the case, in many cases there is a premium placed on the exhibition of female excitation, and this is particularly true of massage scenarios.

Conclusion: The Power of Embodied Simulation, Fetishism and Allure

Chikan emphasizes touching, and irrespective of the narrative content, it is this emphasis on touching that potentially elicits sexual arousal. Thus, it is in the choreography of pornography where mirror neurons might betray us—where the intersubjective encounter is mediated through body-to-body communication bypassing linguistic channels (that is, narrative meaning). It is in this highly contrived arrangement, that is designed to play on our "biological wiring," so to speak. And, in fact, human artifacts—from Édouard Manet's 1863 painting *Olympia* to contemporary hardcore pornography—in their crafted quality as cultural productions are "often more powerful than real life in evoking our emotional engagement and empathic involvement," Vittorio Gallese and Hannah Wojciehowski posit. The authors speculate that this is "because in aesthetic experience we can temporarily suspend our grip on the world of our daily occupations." Cultural productions, and perhaps most of all cinematic experiences (including pornography), invite us to "shut out" the world around us, and to free our perceptual and sensate faculties into carefully curated experiences that outshine our ordinary day-to-day experience. Gallese and Wojciehowski note that it is not simply "a suspension of disbelief," but the "aesthetic experience of art works," or by extension any cultural production, that might liberate embodied simulation to allow us to enter an intersubjective experience with the external referent. "When reading a novel, looking at a visual art work, or attending a theatrical play or a movie, our embodied simulation becomes liberated, that is, it is freed from the burden of modeling our actual presence in daily life."[56] Cultural production, even porn, amplifies the lived-experience; "drama is life with the dull bits cut out," as Hitchcock famously remarked. Pornography is no different, and generally speaking, is a fully curated experience without the drawn-out interpersonal negotiations, without the messiness, or without the awkwardness of real sex. And though politically problematic, the mediated image facilitates the suspension of ethical imperatives. Cultural productions allow us, from a safe distance, to approach this amplified version of the lived-experience. And thus, the appreciation of art (or any other human production) affords us the opportunity to close out the world—if only momentarily. "Through an immersive state in which our attention is focused on the narrated virtual world, we can fully deploy our simulative resources, letting our defensive guard against daily reality slip for a while."[57] The chikan genre invites us to experience sensuous touching outside of our ethical lived daily reality.

I would like to modify Gallese and Wojciehowski's claims here: (1) the authors emphasize, or privilege "art" and those cultural productions with some esteem, and (2) they focus on the fictional. I do not think it is necessarily the fictional scenario, or the artistic merit that is liberating necessarily, though assuredly none of those things hurt, but rather our ability to direct our attention to cultural productions rests in the mediated form, as a re-presentation of a lived experience. Documentaries, for example, have the power to be just as affecting as any other narrative mode (or any cultural production). Ostensibly, documentaries are not fiction, though, one might argue that narrativizing any historical account is already a manipulation of a real event. Be that as it may, and to return to our specific concern here, it is the cinematic treatment of sex, and most particularly the choreography established in the pornographic genre, that invites this intensified affective experience. And the chikan genre often plays on documentary tropes: handheld (often surreptitious) shots at a JR station, shots taken from a groper's phone, shots from hidden cameras (in a massage parlor), security camera footage (for example, at a station, a bookstore, or massage parlor lobby). And then, just more generally, while there might be some narrative arc of a particular pornographic video, what is most important is the documentation of "real" unsimulated sex. As Bill Nichols argues, pornography and ethnography share affinities in their epistemological mission to disclose the secrets of the human experience.[58]

One might assume at first glance that the pornographic genre is fairly straightforward, capturing human activity unmediated—in effect, *cinéma vérité* (or more accurately, and more often than not, direct cinema). Even if the framing scenarios are ridiculous or predictable, the sexual act itself is "real," right? Simply a document of a sexual encounter? Obviously, this is a naïve premise, even a fly-on-the-wall accounting of the sexual encounter is already a highly mediated event. The point, though, is not to take for granted that the pornographic genre is—no matter how much it dresses itself in the markers of "authenticity"—a highly controlled and manufactured cultural production. It is specifically crafted to elicit arousal in the spectator, and there are specific compositional and editing strategies that are employed to meet the expectations of the audience. And as Gallese insists, "any form of aesthetic experience induced by human relations to cultural artefacts is a mediated form of intersubjectivity, where the cultural artefact connects the subjectivity of the producer of the artefacts with that of their recipients."[59] In the writhing and ecstatic bodies, the touching, the kissing, the fucking, pornography is just another cultural artefact that works very hard to connect the bodies onscreen with the viewing body.

For better or for worse, mirror neurons are more or less deaf to narrative, and by extension to ethical considerations, and are instead responding to the "raw" exhibition of bodies touching one another. And again, it is the pornographic choreography that maximizes the potential for embodied simulation to take place. That is not to suggest that narrative context has no place in our perception of an external stimulus. Traumatized individuals that have been groped, for example, might not be capable of divorcing the "raw" sexual encounters found in chikan videos from the narrative situation—or their traumatic memories. Furthermore, the chikan scenario might not match an individual's sex script, or fetishistic erotic interests. "Embodied simulation mediates the capacity to share the meaning of actions, basic motor intentions, feelings, and emotions with others, thus grounding our identification with and connectedness to others."[60]

Embodied simulation opens us to potential intersubjective experiences, and to locate "carnal meanings" through the sensate experience. The representational form, which mediates an intersubjective experience, wins greater attention from the spectator and allows us to momentarily escape our immediate lived-experience and to direct all of our perceptive faculties to the sexual encounter onscreen. This is coupled by the fact, in many instances, that we are relatively stationary when we focus our attention on a cultural production, which "additionally boosts our embodied simulation. Our being still simultaneously enables us to fully deploy our simulative resources at the service of the immersive relationship with the fictional world, thus generating an even greater feeling of body." Immobilized, by virtue of lending our attention to the cinematic (or some other cultural production) and fixing our attention "we are more open to feelings and emotions." Gallese adds, "The specific and particularly moving experience generated when immersed in fictional worlds is thus likely also driven by this sense of safe intimacy with a world we not only imagine, but also literally embody."[61] In the case of pornography, for example, save for a straying wayward hand perhaps, our audio-visual processes lay transfixed on the sight/site of the external stimulus allowing us to enter this intersubjective exchange with the bodies onscreen.

Linda Williams's insistence that the body genres invite involuntary mimicry is lent further credence when placed in conversation with embodied simulation.[62] Furthermore, the choreography of pornography—with its curation of full body shots, close-ups (especially meat shots, reaction shots, forensic shots detailing digital stimulation), and money shots (including evidence of female excitation in the expression of vaginal fluids)—are designed to elicit arousal in the spectator, irrespective of the narrative contextualization. In the case of the pornographic genre, a narrative situation (such as it might be) is merely a thinly veiled excuse to get us to the affecting events. Gallese was amongst the first to demonstrate "that one of the cerebral areas that maps our tactile sensations is also activated by the tactile experiences of others with the same body part,"[63] which has profound implications for our understanding of how pornography might work on the viewing body.

Drawing from David Bordwell's firewall hypothesis (where even when a spectator is familiar with a film, a spectator might for example still be thrilled by a suspense sequence),[64] Gallese and Guerra recount, "when we watch a thriller, a horror movie, or even a particularly moving melodrama for the umpteenth time, we still experience the same emotions as we did during the first viewing, even though we know the movie like the back of our hand." Although it is left off the list of genres (I wonder why?), pornography (which we might know like the front of our hand) is just as likely to elicit arousal even after multiple viewings. In fact, individuals might return to a particular video, a specific scene, or a particular clip, precisely because they know it will spawn sexual arousal. Moreover, pornographic sub-genres are often highly orchestrated events that might differ very little from one another—if you have seen one chikan video set on a train, you have seen them all, more or less. Gallese and Guerra speculate that "intersubjective forms acting non-linguistically activate specific relationships each time with what we see, decoupled from what we already know."[65] Of the over 7 million viewings of "Abused in Bus," spectators, even if it is their first viewing, or their tenth viewing, know what is going to happen. It is pre-determined that Kobayakawa's efforts to resist the groper will amount to nothing; it is a given that the male passenger will fondle her and bring her to climax. This is the genre imperative. The chikan narrative terrain is well-worn and highly predictable, nonetheless, in the various touches (with particular attention to close-ups, and forensic details) it invites an intersubjective encounter that bypasses our critical cognitive faculties and speaks directly to our body.

As Williams has stated the pornographic genre does not play peek-a-boo with us. It emphasizes what is possible to see. The emphasis, then, on details—for example, the stress placed on vaginal fluids in chikan videos—requires the use of a close-up which "enhances and focuses the spectator's gaze on the more material aspects of the object being filmed, whether it be a face, a hand, a landscape, a building, or an artefact." Hands and faces are incredibly important in pornography, but so are asses and cocks, and as Gallese and Guerra note, "the cortical system that maps tactile sensations not only activates when we experience a form of contact, but also when we see another person having a similar experience."⁶⁶ And thus, when we watch, "Abused in Bus," we are not only watching Kobayakawa get fucked on a train, but in a sense, we feel it (as betrayed by our arousal): "we 'see' the tactile experiences of others with our visual system, but also with our motor and tactile system."⁶⁷ Gallese and Guerra argue that embodied simulation "reintroduces the role of empathy in the experience of moving images, particularly images that show caresses, touch, intimate contact; by unconsciously simulating the content of these images in . . . [the spectator's] brain–body, the spectator is able to establish an aesthetical relationship with them."⁶⁸ Although pornography lacks the psychological investment in characters that are supposedly the markers of "good" cinema, the pornographic genre, perhaps more so than any other genre, invites an immediate bodily resonance with the characters onscreen—a direct, immediate, sensate encounter. And in that sense, perhaps not an ethical empathy (as Gallese and Guerra seem to imply), but a carnal empathy. While we in the discipline of cinema and media studies might rely too heavily on and take for granted this conception of "identification," what we should perhaps begin to do is adopt the term "relationship"—because with embodied simulation we are entering a bodily relation with an external stimulus. And with embodied simulation it is less "identification," and more of an exchange, an intimate relationship of touch and being touched.⁶⁹

Paasonen likewise suggests that identification is not necessarily at play when consuming porn, offering resonance as an alternative. Porn resonates with us, or if it fails to elicit arousal, then, it might be perceived as dissonant—off putting, perhaps even disgusting. Paasonen adds that pornographic resonance can be fickle, fleeting, and fluid. "Through resonance, something grabs and moves me, and its power to move me makes me question my sense of mastery over what I view."⁷⁰ And that "something" grabs us (and the tactile analogy of grabbing is particularly interesting here), as it finds affinities with the operations of embodied simulation, and to prehension (meaning to seize, or to grasp—discussed in Chapter 2).

In addition to embodied simulation, of course fetishism has a lot to do with the appeal of pornography. "Abused in Bus," for example, is replete with commonly shared fetishistic signifiers—from the tight short skirt to the pantyhose and undergarments; to the curvature of Kobayakawa's body, to her legs, to the library/teacher trope (complete with glasses and tied up hair); to the acts performed and the expressions that accompany those acts, including vaginal secretions; and even to the transgressive setting and behavior. And assuredly there are yet other fetishistic things that might be listed here.

Our internalized depository of fetishistic objects has the potential to locate a correlate in "Abused in Bus"—and this might have very little, or nothing to do with the criminal scenario. The cohesive force of allure works on the viewing body, which is steeped in his/her own idiosyncratic fetishistic investments, reinforced by a cultural/historical moment that privileges certain fetishistic signifiers. When watching porn, the spectator might locate some affinities between their own internalized types, their sex scripts, or those things that they find hot, and the compendium of fetishistic tropes supplied by "Abused in Bus." Allure as a cohesive agent then couples internal/external objects together, and the result of this resonating pairing of objects is sexual arousal, even despite the unethical nature of the scenario.

Furthermore, our internalized depository of fetishistic objects—our dirty little secrets, our naughty fantasies—might stand in radical contrast with our most cherished beliefs. And the acts performed in porn might have no correlation whatsoever with what consumers of porn would ever want to act out in their lived experience (which is what Daskalopoulou and Zanette find in their research, discussed above). "Transgressive tastes" are not indicative of mass illness, but that the libido is complex and very well might stand in radical contrast with what our politics direct us in what we are "supposed to" like. Policing fantasies is not productive. Fantasies, or our internalized fetishistic investments, do not necessarily correspond with who we are as ethical people. What we are "supposed to" like, what is politically correct or progressive, might not always erotically resonate with us.[71] Furthermore, what is at stake here is not necessarily what turns us on, but how an external referent turns us on. There is often a degree of emotional distance to what is presented onscreen, because regardless of gender porn consumers are not identifying with the (morally corrupt) content, but rather locating a visceral resonance with the pornographic content facilitating sexual arousal.[72]

While there might be dissonance at the level of narrative in pornography, there very well might be resonance at the level of affect. One thing many film scholars and critics are quick to point to is the absence of psychological development of characters in porn, and while this is intended to be a dismissive gesture, indicating that this is the inherent flaw in the pornographic genre, rather this is its very function addressing itself directly to the viewing body (embodied simulation) and the affective experience of sexual arousal (fetishism and allure). Porn speaks directly to the sensing body. The following chapter focuses on Chan-wook Park's 2016 film *The Handmaiden*, which negotiates (within the diegetic narrative) female sexual agency and sadistic situations. Park explicitly peddles in fetishistic imagery and has been accused of replicating the fetishistic tropes found in mainstream heterosexual porn. And while there is a degree of tension between (narrative) dissonance and (affective) resonance in porn, with *The Handmaiden* we might find a harmony between narrative/emotional appeal and the affective experience even despite its sadistic content.

Notes

1 Vittorio Gallese, "Embodied Simulation: Its Bearing on Aesthetic Experience and the Dialogue Between Neuroscience and the Humanities," *Gestalt Theory* vol. 41, no. 2 (2019): 115. See Vittorio Gallese, "The 'Shared Manifold' Hypothesis: from mirror neurons to empathy," *Journal of Consciousness Studies* vol. 8, no. 5–7 (2001): 33–50; and Vittorio Gallese, "The manifold nature of interpersonal relations: The quest for a common mechanism," *Philosophical Transactions of the Royal Society of London Series B: Biological Sciences* vol. 358 (2003): 517–28.

2 Over ten years ago, Magnus Ullén in "Pornography and Its Critical Reception: Toward a Theory of Masturbation," made a similar observation, and in part attempts to repatriate the sensate within the analysis of pornography. A couple of years later, Julian Hanich in 2011 notices a shift in porn studies, "After a long period of tacit denial, porn studies has begun to acknowledge that pornography strongly affects the consumer's body." Julian Hanich, "Clips, clicks and climax: notes on the relocation and remediation of pornography," *Jump Cut: A Review of Contemporary Media* no. 53 (Summer 2011): no pagination. https://www.ejumpcut.org/archive/jc53.2011/Hanich2/text.html. Magnus Ullén, "Pornography and its Critical Reception: Toward a Theory of Masturbation," *Jump Cut: A Review of Contemporary Media* no. 51 (Spring 2009): no pagination. http://www.ejumpcut.org/archive/jc51.2009/UllenPorn/text.html. Ullén argues:

> A theory of pornography must thus be a theory of the mode of reading which the consumption of pornography habitually involves, which is to say that it needs to be a theory of masturbation ... To enjoy pornography, mere intellectual processing of the discourse is not enough: it calls for a mode of reading which involves the physical activity of one's body as well. In that sense, pornography is quite literally an interactive discourse. This discourse, much like the virtual reality of computer games, requires that the reader/consumer abolish the cognitive distance between the discursive and the historical present. The reader starts to act as if the two orders' separate temporalities were one.

Ullén adds,

> For pornography does not only talk about sex, it is a form of sex: masturbation. [Linda] Williams's perspective, be it noted, has the strategic advantage of making the study of pornography academically decent. For if it is really the case that pornography can be said to establish a mode of knowledge—as Williams, inspired by Foucault, claims in her first book—it also means that it can be seen as yet another text to be interpreted and hence easily incorporated by academic discourse.

3 Susanna Paasonen, *Carnal Resonance: Affect and Online Pornography* (Cambridge, MA: MIT Press, 2011), 133–4.

4 For a survey of "sex-positive" research and porn production see *The Feminist Porn Book: The Politics of Producing Pleasure*, edited by Tristan Taormino, Celine Parrañas Shimizu, Constance Penley, and Mireille Miller-Young (New York: The Feminist Press at CUNY, 2013).

5 Paasonen makes a similar gesture, "Content analysis, as I have deployed it, is valuable in mapping out regularities and recurrent elements in porn, but additional analytical tools are needed to grasp the ambiguity and plurality of the material studied." Paasonen, *Carnal Resonance*, 136.

6 Steven Shaviro, *The Cinematic Body* (Minneapolis: University of Minnesota Press, 1993), 14–15.

7 Paasonen, *Carnal Resonance*, 2.

8 Tristan Taormino, "Calling the Shots: Feminist Porn in Theory and Practice," *The Feminist Porn Book: The Politics of Producing Pleasure*, eds Tristan Taormino et al. (New York: The Feminist Press at CUNY, 2013), 261.

9 Paasonen, *Carnal Resonance*, 7.

10 Ibid., 8.

11 Ibid., 10–11.

12 Ibid., 13. See Linda Williams, "Film Bodies: Gender, Genre, and Excess," *Film Quarterly* vol. 44, no. 4 (Summer 1991): 2–13; and Richard Dyer, *Only Entertainment*, 2nd edn. (London: Routledge, 2002), 140.

13 Paasonen, *Carnal Resonance*, 13–14.

14 Linda Williams, "Motion and e-motion: lust and the 'frenzy of the visible,'" *Journal of Visual Culture* vol. 18, no. 1 (April 2019): 100.

15 Ibid., 97.

16 Moreover, pornography is, with some frequency, a part of committed long-term relationships.

> A 2009 study found that couples who used pornography together experienced a relationship climate high in eroticism, as they felt more comfortable expressing and acting on their sexual desires with each other; these couples also reported more sexual dysfunctions such as arousal issues and negative self-talk among females suggesting that these couples may have used pornography in order to compensate for arousal difficulties or decreased self-esteem. (Daneback et al. 2009)

Nicholas P. Newstrom and Steven M. Harris, "Pornography and Couples: What Does the Research Tell Us?" *Contemporary Family Therapy* vol. 38, no. 4 (2016): 418. Newstrom and Harris reference Kristian Daneback, Bente Træen, and Sven-Axel Månsson, "Use of pornography in a random sample of Norwegian heterosexual couples," *Archives of Sexual Behavior* vol. 38, no. 5 (2009): 746–53.

17 "3-Way (The Golden Rule)," Don Roy, Akiva Schaffer, and Jorma Taccone, *Saturday Night Live*, Season 36, Episode 22, May 24, 2011, 3 minutes. This is available on YouTube: https://www.youtube.com/watch?v=p9riv8_tfy4.

18 Susanna Paasonen, *Carnal Resonance: Affect and Online Pornography* (Cambridge, MA: MIT Press, 2011), 150. Similarly, David Church relates that openly gay filmmakers, "such as Chuck Vincent and the Amero Brothers" made straight porn, and observes that desire is fluid. David Church, *Disposable Passions: vintage pornography and the material legacies of adult cinema* (New York: Bloomsbury, 2016), 197.

19 Daskalopoulou and Zanette, 983. Daskalopoulou and Zanette cite Mark McCormack and Liam Wignall, "Enjoyment, exploration and education: Understanding the consumption of pornography among young men with non-exclusive sexual orientations," *Sociology* vol. 51, no. 5 (2017): 975–91.
20 Daskalopoulou and Zanette, 983. Daskalopoulou and Zanette cite Maria Gurevich et al., "Sexually progressive and proficient: Pornographic syntax and postfeminist fantasies," *Sexualities* vol. 20, no. 5–6 (2017): 558–84.
21 Daskalopoulou and Zanette, 983.
22 Paasonen, *Carnal Resonance*, 72.
23 Kelly Dennis, "'Leave it to Beaver': The Object of Pornography," in *Strategies for Theory: From Marx to Madonna*, eds R. L. Rutsky and Bradley J. Macdonald (New York: SUNY Press, 2003), 187. Emphasis in original.
24 Assuredly, cum shots in porn can be faked, whether that is through editing, or by some other means.
25 For a brief history of the cum shot see Susanna Paasonen, *Carnal Resonance: Affect and Online Pornography* (Cambridge, MA: MIT Press, 2011), 119–20.
26 "SARA LUVV EXTREME PASSIONATE ROUGH FUCK, CUMMING ON COCK MULTIPLE TIMES AND CUM SWALLOW," James Deen, *Pornhub*, 2021, 11 minutes, https://www.pornhub.com/view_video.php?viewkey=ph6036b8cbc4f0a.
27 Paul Ricoeur, "Wonder, eroticism, and enigma," *CrossCurrents* vol. 14, no. 2 (1964): 141.
28 Paasonen, *Carnal Resonance*, 244–5.
29 Although she does not explicitly address dissonance, Paasonen discusses the "affective stickiness" of material that might arouse disgust. See the section entitled, "Illegitimate Touchings," in Paasonen, *Carnal Resonance*, 239–41.
30 Ariane Cruz, "Pornography: A Black Feminist Woman Scholar's Reconciliation," in *The Feminist Porn Book: The Politics of Producing Pleasure*, eds Tristan Taormino et al. (New York: The Feminist Press at CUNY, 2013), 222. For more see Cruz's book, *The Color of Kink: Black Women, BDSM, and Pornography* (New York: New York University Press, 2016), 62. In her introduction Cruz notes that her first chapter, "The Dark Side of Desire: Racial-Sexual Alterity and the Play of Race," is

> interested in staging the unique theoretical and practical challenges of the unspeakable pleasures aroused in racial submission and domination that BDSM presents to black women specifically. I examine race play as a particularly problematic yet powerful BDSM practice for black women, one that unveils the contradictory dynamics of racialized pleasure and power via the eroticization of racism and what I term racial-sexual alterity.

Ariane Cruz, *The Color of Kink: Black Women, BDSM, and Pornography* (New York: New York University Press, 2016), 24.
31 Susanna Paasonen, "'We watch porn for the fucking, not for romantic tiptoeing': extremity, fantasy and women's porn use," *Porn Studies* (2021): 4. Similar to Cruz, a respondent in the survey addressed in Paasonen's article (discussed further in the text) notes:

> I'm no longer confused by this but in my 20s it felt wrong as a woman to like submission, to watch bukkake, gangbang, and group sex stuff; the porn advertised for women was always romantic, progressed slowly, came with romantic music and other "soft" stuff. Now on the verge of middle age it's no longer confusing or embarrassing to admit that this doesn't interest or arouse me, I skip all stuff advertised as being "for couples" [. . .] Sure, romantic porn has its place, it was closer to me as well when I was younger (in

my teens/twenties); surely most women would nevertheless watch something like that, and people like me who watch more, who have clearly their own taste, are in the minority among women . . . Or, I don't know, an interesting question, what kinds of porn do women like on average?

    Paasonen, "'We watch porn for the fucking, not for romantic tiptoeing,'" 4. On the tension between pleasure and politically regressive content Paasonen directs us to see: Karen Ciclitira, "Pornography, Women and Feminism: Between Pleasure and Politics," *Sexualities* vol. 7, no. 3 (2004): 281–301.

32 Paasonen, "'We watch porn for the fucking, not for romantic tiptoeing,'" 1. Paasonen adds that the *Jenny+* survey was "certainly of a much larger scale than my own previous studies of porn use in the country." Paasonen references her own co-authored published study: Susanna Paasonen, Katariina Kyrölä, Kaarina Nikunen, and Laura Saarenmaa, "'We hid porn magazines in the woods': Memory-work and porn consumption in Finland," *Sexualities* vol. 18, no. 4 (2015): 394–412. Furthermore, Paasonen acknowledges a number of flaws in the study, from the self-selecting nature of the survey (drawing from viewers of *Jenny+*), to the journalistic intent of the survey (and the lack of applied social science or academic methodologies).

33 Paasonen, "'We watch porn for the fucking, not for romantic tiptoeing,'" 2.

34 Paasonen, *Carnal Resonance*, 18.

35 "The 2019 Year in Review," *Pornhub INSIGHTS*, December 11, 2019, https://www.pornhub.com/insights/2019-year-in-review.

36 Mitsutoshi Horii and Adam Burgess, "Constructing sexual risk: 'Chikan', collapsing male authority and the emergence of women-only train carriages in Japan," *Health, Risk & Society* vol. 14, no. 1 (2012): 42.

37 Motomi Kado, "Watashi no ichiban etchi na yoru" [My most perverted evening], *Fizz* (February 1999), 107–50.

38 Deborah Shamoon, "Office Sluts and Rebel Flowers: The pleasures of Japanese pornographic comics for women," in *Porn Studies*, ed. Linda Williams (Durham, NC: Duke University Press, 2004), 89.

39 For a tour of Japanese love hotels, including a train-themed room, see this YouTube video: "LOVE HOTEL: JAPANESE TRAIN," posted by Sam in Tokyo, YouTube video, September 1, 2018, https://www.youtube.com/watch?v=uQ89EbzXKuw.

40 Shamoon, 99.

41 Tristan Taormino, "Calling the Shots: Feminist Porn in Theory and Practice," in *The Feminist Porn Book: The Politics of Producing Pleasure*, eds Tristan Taormino et al. (New York: The Feminist Press at CUNY, 2013), 263.

42 The director apparently typically goes by this singular name, Kanie. The name clearly plays on, "Kayne West." Elsewhere the porn director goes by the name, "Kanie Isuto" (Kayne East).

43 "Abused in Bus," Pornhub.com, posted 2017, accessed July 22, 2020, https://www.pornhub.com/view_video.php?viewkey=ph596778c623e3e (this link is defunct, see note 45 below). The full-length feature can be found at: https://hpjav.tv/72446/vec-125 accessed January 20, 2022.

44 Interestingly, during the time of drafting this and revising the viewing tally increased dramatically. Eventually though, this particular title was removed, and then reposted as, "Japanese MILF Gets Fucked on the Bus Wwith [sic] her Boyfriends." And this

too would eventually be taken down as well. On December 4th of 2020, an opinion piece ran in *The New York Times* that, as a result, has effectively hollowed out Pornhub's content. In his opinion column Nicholas Kristof reports that Pornhub hosted content featuring under-age individuals and nonconsensual acts. Kristof focuses on the story of Serena Fleites, who the columnist describes as "an A student in Bakersfield, Calif., who had never made out with a boy. But in the eighth grade she developed a crush on a boy a year older, and he asked her to take a naked video of herself." She was just 14 years old at the time. Apparently, this boy shared the video with some of his friends, and eventually somewhere along the way someone posted it to Pornhub. Pornhub, at least until mid-December (2020), allowed users, just like YouTube, to upload content. "A great majority of the 6.8 million new videos posted on the site each year probably involve consenting adults," Kristof speculates, "but many depict child abuse and nonconsensual violence." But Kristof adds that "it's impossible to be sure whether a youth in a video is 14 or 18, neither Pornhub nor anyone else has a clear idea of how much content is illegal." Due to these revelations, Mastercard pulled its relationship with the porn distribution site. Any visit to the site will reveal that the site is a pale shadow of its former self. Suspending any content that it cannot verify—specifically, that the parties involved are of age, and are consenting. Visitors to the site hoping to watch a video that they have seen in the past, might encounter the following message in its place: "Video has been flagged for verification in accordance with our trust and safety policy." See Nicholas Kristof, "The Children of Pornhub: Why does Canada allow this company to profit off videos of exploitation and assault?" *The New York Times*, December 4, 2020, https://www.nytimes.com/2020/12/04/opinion/sunday/pornhub-rape-trafficking.html.

45 In some cases, when not set on a bus or train, other techniques will be employed to suggest "authenticity." In Dera 3's 2016 film *Shrimp Warp: Aphrodisiac Massage Akiho Yoshizawa*, for instance, the filmmaker uses what appears to be security footage in the lobby of a massage office—timestamped, grainy black and white, a red dot indicating that the feed is being recorded. This is also coupled with an extensive interview by the massage therapist and the woman seeking their service. Other techniques include obviously surreptitiously placed cameras (for example, in a duffle bag, on a shelf).

46 Paasonen, *Carnal Resonance*, 80.

47 Demonstrations of "unwillingness," sadly might well also contribute to the "authenticity" of the scene. Although writing about "amateur" porn, Paasonen's reflections on sexual "failures" might resonate:

> In one recurring amateur video theme, attempts at anal sex are halted by—or carried out in spite of—screams of pain. Unlike the eloquently functioning bodies of commercial porn and anal penetrations taking place with seemingly no lubrication or warm-up, amateur bodies regularly fail to comply. They do not always desire, perform, or enjoy according to generic scripts and choreographies. These "failures" increase the sense of authenticity and realness associated with amateur videos and help to set them apart from commercial productions.

Paasonen, *Carnal Resonance*, 113.

48 Three-minutes of establishing narrative context, which is set in a classroom, as opposed to the train, is not included in this estimation.

49 See the first episode of Kimura's series *Crimson Girls*, listed as "Crimson Girls Chikan Shihai Episode 1," on the Pornhub site: https://www.pornhub.com/view_video.php?

viewkey=ph569d82306dabb (this episode had nearly 3.4 million views but was also removed as part of the hollowing out of Pornhub's video content [see note 44 above]).

50 My research assistant, Birdy Wei-Ting Hung, reminded me of this (sub-)genre in porn. Hung further adds that wetness is particularly evident in the massage scenario, where wetness is found not only in female expressions of pleasure, but also in the ample use of massage oil. See for example, "Minami Aoyama Luxury Aroma Oil Massage Part 3," Pornhub, accessed January 20, 2022, https://www.pornhub.com/view_video.php?viewkey=ph6049d9be89a3e.

As commonly featured in the chikan genre there is a clear emphasis on touching and caressing the female body. And the massage scenario, as seen in the video cited here offers dramatic squirting as a "proof" of female orgasm (or at least pleasure).

51 Eugenie Brinkema, "Celluloid Is Sticky: Sex, Death, Materiality, Metaphysics (in Some Films by Catherine Breillat)," *Women: A Cultural Review* vol. 17, no. 2 (2006): 152.

52 One of the most trafficked motifs in the pornographic genre are social transgressions. Murray Davis commenting on sexual behavior observes that,

> Although the thought that unsexy settings could ever become lascivious locales appalls many people, it arouses others. Those who prefer to intensify their sexual excitement by violating obsolescent social norms may copulate in unusual places—the bathroom instead of the bedroom, the floor instead of the bed, or a workplace like an office in the evening.

Davis adds, "Thus sex in unusual places (or times)—unusual because ordinary activities usually occur there (or then)—can intensify experiences of erotic reality by exaggerating its break with the surrounding everyday world." Murray Davis, *Smut: Erotic Reality/Obscene Ideology* (Chicago: University of Chicago Press, 1985), 25–6.

53 My research assistant, Birdy Wei-Ting Hung, made this connection between the appeal of transgression in pornography and comedy.

54 Brinkema, 152.

55 Andrea Dworkin and Catherine MacKinnon are the most well-known anti-porn feminists.

56 Vittorio Gallese and Hannah Wojciehowski, "How stories make us feel: Toward an embodied narratology," *California Italian Studies* vol. 2, no. 1 (2011): no pagination. https://doi.org/10.5070/C321008974.

57 Ibid. See Vittorio Gallese, "Il corpo teatrale: mimetismo, neuroni specchio, simulazione incarnata," *Culture Teatrali* vol. 16 (2008): 13–38; Vittorio Gallese, "Corpo e azione nell'esperienza estetica. Una prospettiva neuroscientifica," Postscript in *Mente e Bellezza. Mente relazionale, arte, creatività e innovazione* by Ugo Morelli (Turin: Umberto Allemandi, 2010): 245–62; and Vittorio Gallese, "Seeing art... beyond vision. Liberated embodied simulation in aesthetic experience," *Seeing with the Eyes Closed* (2011): 62–5.

58 See Bill Nichols's co-authored chapter (Nichols shares credit with Christian Hansen and Catherine Needham), "Pornography, Ethnography, and the Discourses of Power," in his *Representing Reality: Issues and Concepts in Documentary* (Bloomington: Indiana University Press, 1991), 201–28.

59 Vittorio Gallese, "Embodied Simulation: Its Bearing on Aesthetic Experience and the Dialogue Between Neuroscience and the Humanities," *Gestalt Theory* vol. 41, no. 2 (2019): 114.

60 Gallese and Wojciehowski.
61 Vittorio Gallese, "Visions of the body: Embodied simulation and aesthetic experience," *Aisthesis. Pratiche, linguaggi e saperi dell'estetico* vol. 10, no. 1 (2017): 47.
62 My research assistant, Birdy Wei-Ting Hung, was the first to point out this connection between embodied simulation and mimicry in Williams's conception of body genres.
63 Vittorio Gallese and Michele Guerra, *The Empathic Screen: Cinema and Neuroscience*, trans. Frances Anderson (Oxford: Oxford University Press, 2020), 38.
64 See David Bordwell, "This is your brain on movies, maybe," *Observations on film art* (blog), *David Bordwell's website on cinema*, March 7, 2007, http://www.davidbordwell.net/blog/2007/03/07/this-is-your-brain-on-movies-maybe/.
65 Gallese and Guerra, 54–5.
66 Ibid., 151.
67 Ibid.
68 Ibid., 170.
69 It has occurred to me that in my analysis of pornographic material, my analysis very well might verge on porn itself. This is something that Susanna Paasonen has also considered:

> In the context of pornography—a framework that Barthes probably would have refused to consider as an example—this kind of 'reading' involves desire for carnal resonance and openness to being moved and aroused. Writing in the mode of affectation and sticking close to the resonating object mean description as well as writing that itself borders on the pornographic. I was once asked if it upsets me that people may be sexually aroused when reading my essays on porn. My response was negative—no, this would not bother me too much—even if I was surprised that this might be the case (for surely those reading with the intent of arousal can find more gratifying texts to interface with).

Paasonen, *Carnal Resonance*, 198.
70 Ibid., 186–7.
71 See Jane Ward, "Queer Feminist Pigs: A Spectator's Manifesta," in *The Feminist Porn Book: The Politics of Producing Pleasure*, eds Tristan Taormino et al. (New York: The Feminist Press at CUNY, 2013), 134.
72 For Susanna Paasonen "fascination and resonance need not be seen as matters of identification," rather porn consumers are often looking for something that suits their mood. Paasonen, *Carnal Resonance*, 16.

7

Romance

The Handmaiden and its Arousing Spectacles

> Never may an act of possession be exercised upon a free being; the exclusive possession of a woman is no less unjust than the possession of slaves; all men are born free, all have equal rights: never should we lose sight of those principles; according to which never may there be granted to one sex the legitimate right to lay monopolizing hands upon the other, and never may one of these sexes, or classes, arbitrarily possess the other.
>
> — Marquis de Sade *Philosophy in the Bedroom*[1]

Introduction: The Romance Genre and an Overcoming of the Sadistic Gaze

Chan-wook Park's 2016 film *The Handmaiden* is exemplary of the (lesbian) romance genre, and while its narrative content and structure elicit a strong pleasurable emotional charge, its stylistic treatment (mise-en-scène, cinematography, and sound design) appeals to the viewing body—to the affective experience. Taken altogether—that is, the emotional and affective charge—this makes for a deeply pleasurable experience. With the romance genre obstacles are invariably thrown in the path of the protagonists impeding the way to their objective. And obstacles can come in many forms—often something that impedes the satisfactory coupling of the primary characters. More often than not, in mainstream cinematic narratives, a satisfactory conclusion ends with the characters' union, or its potential—marriage being the most obvious example of character unions.

"Whatever the barrier to the romantic union," Jackie Stacey observes, "the question which must sustain the narrative tension is: will they (and importantly, how will they) or won't they overcome it?" And in most cases the degree of the obstacle proportionally corresponds to the intensity of the emotional charge for the spectator. Similar to the melodramatic genre, as a narrative culminates "it is typically, although not exclusively, the heroine who suffers pain, loss, denial, self-sacrifice and punishment," Stacey notes. A satisfactory resolution to a romance narrative is predicated upon whether "the couple stay together in either literal or symbolic heterosexual marriage," if the obstacles cannot be overcome, or the price exacted for overcoming those obstacles is just too great, this will likely lead to a less than satisfactory denouement (within the narrative diegesis, and for the audience as well). "The function of these barriers is to produce narrative tension and to encourage audience involvement in a particular set of intense emotions. The pleasures of romances, then, involve audience participation in the desire for love to win out over these obstacles."[2]

Stacey writing specifically of the lesbian romance narrative notes that historically these films assimilate the "heterosexual formulae, [and that] lesbian romance films share some of their narrative structures." While all romance narratives introduce some kind of obstacle to a successful union between the characters, in lesbian narratives (as compared to their mainstream heterosexual counterpart) the obstacles are distinct: "heterosexual men, suicide, murder, neurosis, isolation, depression, homophobia and fear of discovery are among the favourites—not a very appealing line-up." Park's film checks all the pertinent boxes—save perhaps homophobia, which never appears to be an issue in *The Handmaiden*. "The most frequent obstacle to lesbian love in film romances," though, as Stacey emphasizes, "is the figure of the heterosexual man."[3] And this is absolutely the case in *The Handmaiden*, the two antagonists of the film—Count Fujiwara and Uncle Kouzuki—stand in the way of the union of our two female protagonists—Lady Hideko and her handmaiden Sook-hee Nam. Before addressing the affective charge of the film, and its potential to elicit arousal (and the beautiful), let me first address the film's emotional appeal, which is tied up in the film's narrative. One of the central obstacles presented for our female protagonists is the sadistic (male) gaze, and it largely falls upon Lady Hideko to usurp the gaze of the men that would seek to control her.

Park adapted *The Handmaiden* from Sarah Waters' 2002 novel *Fingersmith*. Sue Trinder, the protagonist of the novel, is a "fingersmith," which is to say a petty thief and pickpocket. Waters' narrative is set in London during the Victorian era. She is enlisted in a scheme to come into the service of a wealthy heiress, Maud Lilly, as her servant, in a plot to swindle the heiress out of her inheritance. Lilly at the age of 12 is commanded into the custodial care of her uncle, who is domineering and conscripts the girl to work as his secretary cataloguing his collection of pornographic literature. Richard Rivers, at times simply referred to as, "Gentleman," is the mastermind behind the plot: he intends to elope with Lilly, and after which have her committed to an asylum allowing him to seize her fortune. At least this is what is conveyed to Trinder. But, as chance would have it, Trinder and Lilly fall in love and independently equivocate over following through with Rivers' plot. The lover's affair between the women brings to light further erotic connotations for the title of the novel.

Park leaves many of the plot elements in place. The English/international title for Park's film, metonymically references Waters's title, and implicitly some of the erotic connotations as well. (The Korean title, Ah-ga-ssi, means, "The Lady.") Park sets the film in the 1930s during the Japanese colonial occupation of Korea, taking liberties with the original text.[4] Sook-hee (also given the Japanese name, Tamako), like her English counterpart Trinder, is an illiterate petty thief, living in a den of thieves. A fellow Korean conman and master-forger assumes the identity of a Japanese minor noble, Count Fujiwara, in a bid to swindle a Japanese heiress, Lady Hideko, out of her fortune. We learn that Lady Hideko's mother died giving birth to her, and she blames herself for it: "it's as if I strangled her myself," she says. (However, given all the lies and betrayals, it is quite possible that Lady Hideko—whether by her own accounting, or unwittingly by Kouzuki's scheming—is trading in yet one more lie.) As in the *Fingersmith* plot, the Count enrolls Sook-hee into his scheme, enlisting her to persuade Lady Hideko to marry the charlatan count. Lady Hideko's uncle, Kouzuki, is likewise a scoundrel and a charlatan, with a penchant for sadism.

Prior to where we enter the story, Kouzuki, a Korean, divorces his Korean wife (Miss Sasaki) in order to marry into a Japanese family, and assumes a Japanese identity—including taking on his wife's family name. (The divorce and marriage might have been on paper only—recounting what he has heard from the servants, the Count notes that Kouzuki "still share[s] a bed with" Miss Sasaki.) Kouzuki helps the Japanese annex Korea and is rewarded with a goldmine for his collaboration, subsequently funding his extravagant tastes. Kouzuki obsessively collects books, amassing a huge collection of erotic and sadistic literature. The domineering Kouzuki compels Lady Hideko's aunt to perform readings from his collection, before an audience of well-appointed men. The situation eventually drives Lady Hideko's aunt to suicide, hanging herself from a cherry tree, leaving Lady Hideko to assume her aunt's position. From the age of five, Lady Hideko had been trained to read from Kouzuki's collection. When we enter the story of *The Handmaiden*, Lady Hideko is a full-grown woman, but still under the custodianship of Kouzuki, and delivers rousing readings from Kouzuki's collection, just as her aunt did.

The initial plan, following her nuptials with Fujiwara, is to have Lady Hideko committed to an insane asylum. This is what we are led to believe in Part One of the film, as viewed from Sook-hee's perspective. The film, though, is broken into three distinct parts, and each successive part systematically undoes our understanding of the situation. With the second part of the narrative, we get a different perspective—this time from Lady Hideko's point of view. We learn that Lady Hideko and Fujiwara are actually collaborating to get out from under Uncle Kouzuki's thumb, and to have the naive Sook-hee placed into an asylum though committed under the name of "Lady Hideko." And, of course, Sook-hee makes things worse for herself, when interviewed by the asylum doctors—who are informed that she is Lady Hideko—by asserting that she is Lady Hideko's handmaiden, and when finally committed vociferously protests that she is not the Lady.

The third part of the narrative reveals that while Sook-hee and Lady Hideko both schemed against one another, during the course of their mutually duplicitous plotting, they genuinely fall in love with one another. The pair forge a plot of their own and make off with the fortune that is rightfully Lady Hideko's to begin with. The pair set sail for Shanghai, which at the time, was a bustling cosmopolitan city under Japanese rule—and within the popular imagination the "Paris of the East," and "known as a place of vice and indulgence."[5] "Paris," "vice," and "indulgence" are euphemistically associated with sexual freedom and queerness, thus, a fitting place for our same sex couple to freely live and love one another.

And it is in the blossoming of this relationship between Lady Hideko and Sook-hee where the erotic is explicitly on display. Lady Hideko's readings though are erotically charged as well, all the while offering a meta-cinematic critique of visual pleasure. The reading performances in *The Handmaiden* are clearly modeled after the Marquis de Sade's arrangement in his most infamous novel *The 120 Days of Sodom*. In Sade's novel four libertines (sadists) abduct 8 boys, and 8 girls to amuse (read: abuse) themselves. The libertines, along with supporting characters, take the whole crew to a remote and isolated chateau—utterly removed from the world. Four female storytellers entertain the libertines, conveying depraved tales to stimulate the libertines' imaginations. *The Handmaiden*, with its secluded manor, and the storytelling element share similar contours. Likewise, in 1975 Pier Paolo Pasolini faithfully adapted Sade's novel to the screen in his film *Salò*, though, recontextualizing it at the end of the Second World War in the Republic of Salò, a puppet regime established by the Nazis in northern Italy. (Pasolini was murdered two weeks following the release of the film.) Pasolini levels a critique of fascism and the failures in the Enlightenment project through the Sadean lens.

At the same time, though, Pasolini also issues a critique of the sadistic gaze, nearly contemporaneous and analogous to Mulvey's landmark essay,

"Visual Pleasure and Narrative Cinema." Taken straight from Sade's novel, a series of female storytellers convey stories, as if upon a stage, intended to elicit the erotic attention of the libertines. Pasolini includes a female piano player as well, to accompany the salacious tales. Pasolini, though, effectively turns the table on us toward the end of the film, when during the climactic moments of the film, each libertine takes turns watching the final tortures being executed in the courtyard below. Positioned in a Macintosh chair, the Duke, taking a pair of binoculars (effectively "opera glasses") watches the violent spectacle in close-up—the camera assuming the libertine's perspective via the binoculars. At one point though, the libertine turns the binoculars the wrong-way-around, and once again, the camera also assumes this view as well, and the distancing of the spectacle, along with the binoculars as an optical device, aligns our perspective with the sadistic libertines, their visual field, and the cinematic apparatus (embodied in the binoculars) that invites us to find pleasure in the spectacle of sexual violence. All these things together along with the stage-like setting, the female storytellers eliciting erotic interest, and the piano player (as if accompanying a silent film) evoke the cinematic and its invitation to indulge in voyeuristic and sadistic fantasies serving as a biting meta-cinematic critique of visual pleasure in narrative cinema.

Park assimilates many of these elements from Pasolini and Sade, however, while the latter two offer content that is hard to stomach, Park manages to accomplish Pasolini's critique of the voyeuristic and sadistic gaze, while at the same time preserving visual (and auditory) pleasure. The reading performances in *The Handmaiden* echo what we find in *Salò* and Sade's novel. Pasolini continually aligns the spectator's gaze with the libertines. Just as the storytellers are commanded to provide salacious tales to fuel the four libertines' imaginations, they also aim to captivate *Salò*'s spectators. Sade explains in *The 120 Days of Sodom* that the libertines assembled in a circular room every day to hear one of the storyteller's episodes—they each sat in recesses that faced the center of the room. The storyteller, set as if on a stage, sat in the center: "in this position she was not only well before the four niches intended for her auditors, but, the circle being small, was close enough to them to ensure their hearing every word she said, for she was placed like an actor in a theater, and the audience in their niches found themselves situated as if observing a spectacle in an amphitheater."[6] The reading performances in *The Handmaiden* find clear affinities with Sade's mise-en-scène.

Suk Koo Rhee suggests that the arrangement is inherently unequal. "In this inverted form of Bentham's panopticon," Rhee observes, "the individual in the centre is defencelessly exposed because of her physically lower

Figure 7.1 Top, *Salò, or the 120 Days of Sodom* (Pier Paolo Pasolini, 1975); bottom, *The Handmaiden* (Chan-wook Park, 2016)

position."[7] There is no doubt that Hideko has endured significant mental and physical abuse, and is subject to the power of the gaze. This however is not to say that this is all she is—she is not just a victim (a point that Rhee actually advocates for as well). As I will discuss momentarily, Hideko is in fact a master libertine herself, akin to Sade's character Juliette.

Keungyoon Bae suggests that "the most subversive element of the film is its engagement with erotica." While the readings, the placing upon a stage, her doll-like appearance, the strenuous training that Hideko endures from a very young age (under Kozuki's punishing gaze—and mental and physical abuse), undoubtedly subjugate her, she is completely without agency. Bae observes that in Part Two of the film, "Hideko's relationship with erotica" changes. During Hideko's reading of *The Sound of Bells on a Windless Night*, there is "a brief blackout, and for a short while, Hideko is able to be alone with the material that she reads." In this moment of reprieve from the male gaze "she closes her eyes as she narrates the story, without even needing to read the pages, describing the lovemaking between a lady and her maid." Bae suggests at this moment, Hideko, for the first time, is seen to mine "her own pleasure from the act of reading, as she is granted a brief respite from the voracious male gaze."[8] From this we learn that Hideko is not as naïve as she is made to appear in Part One of the film—and she enacts the very fantasies inscribed on the page in her own sexual relationship with Sook-hee. *The Sound of Bells on a Windless Night* foreshadows the concluding moments of the film—as well as the sexual encounter between the women seen twice (once from Sook-hee's perspective, and then again from Hideko's).[9] In addition, Hideko is not a passive object to be looked at, she actively looks.

Of particular note is the instance when Hideko secrets herself away behind a sliding screen, where she spies upon the Count and Kouzuki, as they talk in Kouzuki's library. The two schemers discuss the art of forgery, and the Count's nearly mystical seductive power, claiming that he could have any woman in the house—save one, Hideko, fully aware of her sexual orientation. (Though the Count coyly does not disclose the identity of the one that would refuse him to Kouzuki.) Speaking about his seductive powers, the Count explains, "I look at women's eyes. Only the eyes. They turn their gaze away, but then they always look back. If I were to slide under someone's covers tonight, only one woman here would refuse me." The Count appears to know that Hideko is spying on them, and as much as the Count is relaying this information to Kouzuki, he appears to be addressing Hideko as well. During this dialogue, we see that Hideko (in her hiding place) peers at the men through the modernist woodwork with opera glasses.[10] There are clear echoes from *Salò* here, where the libertines observe the final tortures unfolding from the high modernist Macintosh chair, using binoculars. During *The Sound of Bells on a Windless Night* reading, one of the patrons watches the Lady with opera glasses as she reads. Yet one more instance of a reversal. (Interestingly too, the Count is working on a forgery as he speaks, and has a magnifying glass positioned above his painting—the magnifying glass being yet another amplifier of the eye.) Despite all this, when Park offers an objective view from within the library, the camera dollies backwards to reveal the shoji screen below Hideko's perch, and we find that it is made in the pattern of a spider's web—one more suggestion that it is Hideko that is actually in control, luring the men into her web.

While many critics and scholars have suggested that Hideko's mind has been warped by her unusual education, what I would suggest is that she has become the craftiest of sadists. And to be clear, not a colloquial sadist (someone that derives pleasure from suffering), but rather an astute libertine as Sade envisions them. While Hideko treats Sook-hee with genuine erotic interest and affection (if not love), with the men Hideko spars with the male characters in the spirit of libertinage. With the Sadean libertine, sex and violence are not executed with capricious brutality. Rather the libertine is a cold rationalist, that is governed by reason, and is far more concerned with outstripping their "opponent" through intellectual mastery. Any violent or sexual conquest is the product of a well-executed plan, more in keeping with chess or a sporting match than "raw" animality.[11]

Rhee finds Lady Hideko's scrupulous training in libertinage under the custodianship of Kouzuki ironic, because as he observes, "unshackled by her education from sexual taboos, Hideko becomes free to act out exactly those forms of behaviour that Kouzuki has done so much to try to suppress in her." Rhee adds, "She not only becomes a fully sexual being but also initiates a lesbian relationship with her maid, undermining at one stroke her uncle's prolonged disciplinary and educational efforts."[12] I would read the situation from a slightly different perspective, it is not so much that Lady Hideko rejects or "undermines" her uncle's education, but rather that she proves herself to be a highly adept student. While Kouzuki is a sadist, in the clinical sense, he meets his match with Hideko—where the student becomes the master. Hideko, like Sade's Juliette, is a true libertine, and she gets precisely what she wants by outstripping all the men that would seek to control her. Overcoming the obstacle of the controlling (male) gaze, Lady Hideko and Sook-hee sail off to Shanghai together in a loving union, bringing the lesbian romance narrative to an emotionally pleasurable resolution.

Peddling in the Economies of Fetishism and Allure

While the sex scenes in *The Handmaiden* invite erotic interest, it is Park's self-consciously constructed images that are not explicitly sexual where I will focus most of my attention. There are specific instances in *The Handmaiden* where Park openly engages with the economies of fetishism and allure. But before I discuss the less than explicit sensual elements, let me first clear the air by discussing the sexually explicit scenes found in the film. The sex scenes are only a stone's throw away from what we might find in a mainstream heterosexual "lesbian" porn scene. And Park has taken some heat for his treatment of the sex scenes. For example, Laura Miller laments in her *Slate* review of *The Handmaiden*, that the sex scenes in Park's film are "disappointingly boilerplate," and adds that even after escaping the controlling grip of the two male antagonists, the women "fall back into the tired visual clichés of pornographic lesbianism, their bodies offered up for the camera's delectation in a carefully arranged exhibition that would fit right into Uncle's collection."[13] Miller is not altogether wrong in her assessment here. (As noted in Chapter 4, and to at least in part confirm Miller's point, there are clear affinities between Chris Cunningham's fetishistic treatment of female androids in Björk's music video "All Is Full of Love," and the framing of the female characters in *The Handmaiden* in the closing moments of Park's film.)

Shannon Keating, who cites Miller, echoes a similar sentiment, and specifically references the brief instances of scissoring as illustrative of the "inauthenticity" of the intimacy (and this is presumably "the tired visual clichés of pornographic lesbianism" that Miller is specifically referring to). "One of the reasons why scissoring is still such a popular depiction of lesbian sex," Keating claims, "is because scissoring looks 'real' to straight people." Keating concludes that heterosexual men presume that genital-to-genital contact is the only thing that counts for "real" sex, and thus, the scissoring motif is featured in "lesbian" scenes in mainstream heterosexual pornography. Whether it is "real" lesbian sex or not, there is an emphasis on proof of sexual excitation and pleasure, where after performing cunnilingus Sook-hee's chin is visibly wet—a signifier of and ostensible "proof" of pleasure. And in this sense, we might draw a connection to the pornographic, and its efforts to make (female) sexual excitation evident in the exhibition of wetness (a common trope, for example, in the chikan genre discussed in the previous chapter).[14]

While Keating takes issue with the depiction of lesbian sexuality, at the same time she does marvel at the beauty of Park's art design and visual composition. Commenting on the final scene, Keating notes that Sook-hee and Lady Hideko's "beautiful, lithe bodies are arranged in perfect symmetry, just like the room around them. The scene is an immaculately arranged tableau." But Keating rhetorically asks, toward the beginning of her article, "*Whose sex life looks remotely like this?*"[15] To insist upon, or to ask, "Is it real?" is to miss the point. It is a fantasy. Keating, though, in her critique of the heterosexual perspective insists that the "inauthenticity" of the "lesbian" sex somehow robs the material of its affective potential. In pointed terms, Keating assumes that non-lesbians assume that fingers do not count, and that Park (as a representative of male heterosexuality) emphasizes "genital-on-genital contact," because (as already noted) it comes the closest to approximating heteronormative penetrative sex. Keating goes on to lament that "tribbing, or using strap-ons" is a far more "authentic" lesbian experience. "For some reason," Keating adds, "strap-ons haven't caught on at all in either mainstream media or pornography made for straight men, and I'd wager that's because scissoring looks hot to guys, while a woman wearing a dildo could easily threaten straight men's egos." Keating presumes that a strap on connotes: "*Women and other queer and gender-nonconforming people can fuck each other better than you can. Sorry!*"[16]

What is troubling here is Keating's assumptions about what heterosexuals may or may not like. And as discussed in the previous chapter, in the chikan genre, the use of digital stimulation (tribbing) is a huge part of that specific sub-genre. Who is to say that straight men, or women for that matter, might actually be turned on by the use of strap-ons, or in fact use them in their own sexual practices? The implicit accusations regarding heterosexual presumptions about lesbian sex might be equally as true with respect to Keating's assumption about heterosexuals.[17] My former colleague Celine Parreñas Shimizu reads the scissoring differently and locates agency in the act. Drawn from Luce Irigaray's, "When our lips speak together," Shimizu views scissoring as the wrestling of power through "two lips touching," excising the phallic member from a female-to-female union.[18] Furthermore, such presumptions about sexual tastes are just not grounded in the lived-experience (of heterosexuals—with as many varied tastes and predilections as there are people). Individual pornographic preferences do not necessarily align with an individual's real-life sexual identification or tastes. As Paasonen observes, "While no direct connections can be presumed between a person's sense of sexual self and their patterns of porn consumption, there is also immediacy to sexual turn-ons that can make it difficult to detach them from ways of understanding the sexual self—and, consequently, one's very ways of being in the world."[19]

The critiques of *The Handmaiden* that fall back on a binary (straight and gay) conceptualization of pornography and pornographic consumption flatten out and overly generalize. "Heterosexual women write slash fiction (depicting romantic and sexual relationships between fictional characters of the same sex) falling under the category of gay erotica," Paasonen reminds us, "while women straight and queer watch gay porn and straight men enjoy variations of girl-girl action, dyke porn, and shemale action."[20] Rather than policing fantasies, as Lori Marso notes in her discussion of sadomasochistic pleasure (as found in Catherine Breillat's *Romance*, and the Amazon series *I Love Dick*), we should consider "which kinds of sex and which feelings are expected from romantic fantasies and what happens when different feelings emerge instead."[21] Real or not, the question really should be, how does *The Handmaiden* make us feel? And to Keating's question, "*Whose sex life looks remotely like this?*" I often ask this too in relation to heterosexual sex in mainstream television and cinema. Who has sex under sheets, strategically placed to cover naughty bits? The point being is that cinematic sex often has very little to do with how people actually fuck.

The lesbian sex scenes in *The Handmaiden* share affinities with the lesbian sex scene in Tony Scott's 1983 vampire film *The Hunger*. Scott's lesbian sex scene—featuring Catherine Deneuve and Susan Sarandon—is shot in slow motion, all flowing curtains and ivory sheets, a silver-framed full-length mirror oddly placed at the edge of the bed (to maximize what

170 Abject Pleasures in the Cinematic

the spectator can see). Soft warm lighting filtered through gauze curtains (covering the windows, and draped above and flowing down along the sides of the canopy bed), over-head shots revealing a mattress that mysteriously glows (warm white light glows through the sheets), a compendium of fetishistic shots (kissing upon the mouth and nipples, caressing, heads thrown back in ecstasy), and a dreamy score ("Viens mallika sous le dome," from Léo Delibes's opera *Lakmé*) accompany it all. (There are also vampire bites, it is a vampire movie after-all—this is where Deneuve as the queen-vampire turns Sarandon's character.) None of what we are given is "real" sex—this is the Playboy fantasy version of it. Between the mise-en-scène, the soundscape, and the bourgeois lifestyle, *The Hunger* trades in the aspirational aesthetics of a Playboy layout. This is not the "down and dirty" realities of sex, but a pasteurized vision of it that is self-consciously composed.

I have no intention of dismissing the arguments regarding the "authenticity," or the "inauthenticity" of the portrayal of lesbian sex in *The Handmaiden*. And I would presume that Miller and Keating are correct—that *The Handmaiden* does not accurately depict "real" lesbian sex. Taken on its own terms though, *The Handmaiden* is a (male) fantasy, and, like *The Hunger*, it openly peddles in the economy of fetishism. Keating praises Park, along with Abdellatif Kechiche and Todd Haynes (who have also recently included lesbian sexual encounters in their films), who at best have made an effort "to honor the beauty of queer female sexuality—but at worst, they're formalist experiments

Figure 7.2 Top, *The Hunger* (Tony Scott, 1983); bottom, *The Handmaiden* (Chan-wook Park, 2016)

in symmetry and duality (*Hey, they're having sex and they're both women! They look alike! See? Pretty!*) that can easily become flat-out fetishistic."[22] Regarding *The Handmaiden*, Keating is correct and let me go ahead and just take this a step further: it is fetishistic. But the assumption here is that fetishism is innately wrong. Keating implicitly establishes a zero-sum framework: there are either "authentic" depictions of lesbian sex, or "inauthentic" depictions.[23] And built into this logic is the assumption that somehow "authentic" sex is not fetishistic, whereas "inauthentic" sex is. Are the queer pornographic films of Shine Louise Houston any less fetishistic? Rather, Houston's films are differently fetishistic.[24] Furthermore, tied up in this all-or-nothing rhetoric, there is an assumption that only heterosexual men would find the fetishistic material in *The Handmaiden* arousing. Even if it is not a "real" portrayal of lesbian sex, is it remotely possible that spectators regardless of their orientation or gender identification might find the highly choreographed bodies sexually arousing? (And arguably, none of what we see in pornography is actually "real," but rather designed to elicit arousal.) As I have posited in an earlier chapter, there is the possibility to work within the realm of cognitive dissonance, where we can acknowledge the fetishistic economy (and some of the negative implications of that—objectification namely), and at the same time, locate pleasure in it. We need not arrive at an all-or-nothing conclusion.

The first, and highly emblematic scene, that openly peddles in fetishistic imagery takes place when Lady Hideko takes a bath in preparation for the arrival of Count Fujiwara. Sook-hee attends to the Lady in the bath, who is sucking upon a deep purple lollipop. Sook-hee relates that her aunt would give babies lollipops at bath-time so that they would associate bath-time with sweetness. Sook-hee even refers to the Lady as her baby. The infantilizing of Lady Hideko, the sucking upon the lollipop evokes what in Japan has been called the Lolicom (the Lolita complex), which references Vladimir Nabokov's novel *Lolita* with all the (transgressive) sexual connotations associated with it.

At one-point Lady Hideko, however, suddenly shrinks with a pained-expression and complains of a sharp tooth that is irritating the inside of her mouth. Sook-hee retrieves a thimble and begins to gently file down the sharp edge of the tooth. The procedure overflows with erotic tension—the positioning of hands, the way that the women tilt their heads, the attention given to their mouths, the lollipop, the in and out penetrative gesture of the filing finger, all these things (in themselves) already draw upon a cultural repertoire of fetishistic images.

Park is by no means the first to construct such fetishistic images, but in fact follows a well-worn tradition. Art historian and leading feminist scholar, Griselda Pollock, speaking of Rossetti's 1859 painting *Bocca baciata* (meaning "kissed mouth") speaks to this fetishistic vocabulary. Pollock notes that the title of the painting further isolates the lips, fetishisticly wresting the lips from the female figure as a whole. The title of the painting is taken from Giovanni Boccaccio's *Decameron*: "The mouth that has been kissed loses not its freshness; still it renews itself even as does the moon."[25] The fetishistic operation of isolating the lips metonymically invites us to populate the signifier with sexual connotations. "The mouth as ruby wound can function as a displaced sign of female sexuality, her genitals." The reference to "renewal" relative to the phases of the moon, reinforces the connotations here—via the menstrual cycle, and by association to sexuality. Pollock adds, "The mouth functions as a classic fetish, some sign which both involves and displaces visual knowledge of female genitals but can disavow the threat of that knowledge by harking back to another more comforting visual encounter and sensuous experience—that of looking up to the mother/female caretaker in the course of being suckled."[26] Such connotations invite us to reconsider the title of the score during the bath scene and Sook-hee's line of dialogue, "You are my baby, Miss."[27]

The chain of connotative associations with lips and breasts unsurprisingly leads to a particular shot of erotic contemplation for Sook-hee, and the spectator via Sook-hee's point of view. Sook-hee's mouth is thrown slightly agape in erotic astonishment (coupled with an audible expression of erotic-awe)

Figure 7.3 Top, *The Hunger* (Tony Scott, 1983); bottom, *The Handmaiden* (Chan-wook Park, 2016)

as she files the Lady's tooth, and this is immediately followed with a shot from Sook-hee's perspective first transfixed on the Lady's face then tilting downwards to gaze upon her naked breasts. The composition though is maximized for fetishistic pleasure: Lady Hideko's body glistens—the dewy droplets of warm bath water sparkle upon her breasts—and the bath water is sprinkled with crimson and purple flower petals. The bath scene is utterly replete with fetishistic images. The opulent setting, the decor, the bath-basin lined with linen, and not to mention Sook-hee being Lady Hideko's servant (the maid being a common fetishistic motif), all play to bourgeois fantasies of a lavish lifestyle, which is in itself a fetishistic vision.[28] And similar to *The Hunger*, referenced above, the setting is suffused in a soft warm light. The bath, the array of colorful bottles (containing various fragrances), the vase of flowers and flower petals, the wafting steam from the warm bath (which ever so slightly softens the image), these (and more) evoke the Playboy aspirational aesthetic, such as we found in Scott's *The Hunger*. All these elements are the basic vocabulary of fetishism—a shared global visual media vocabulary that might meet up with our individual compendium of things that we find appealing.

The bath scene is but one instance where Park consciously fabricates images that are steeped in fetishistic imagery. I will not go into detail here, but just to survey the film we might consider the fetishistic appeal of a number of other scenes. Recall, for instance, the short scene where Sook-hee escorts the lady to dinner—in an interior monologue Sook-hee marvels at the Lady's beauty. Walking behind her, Sook-hee gazes upon the Lady's bare back—revealed by a dress that dips down to her shoulder blades—and is completely awestruck. Following the dinner, the Lady dresses Sook-hee up in one of her dresses, furnishing the maid with make-up, jewelry, manicured hair, and hair pin, to which Hideko observes, "Dressed up, you look like a lady, too." After the Lady dresses Sook-hee up, the pair undress each other undoing buttons and corsets, Sook-hee at one point thinking to herself, "Ladies truly are the dolls of maids. All these buttons are for my amusement." And then, of course, there are the readings where Lady Hideko (and in one case, her aunt) are beautifully dressed—perfect living hina dolls. The film bursts at the seams with fetishistic imagery.

But this largely concerns content, what amplifies the affective charge of the scene is the mise-en-scène, cinematography, and subtle audio design. Returning to the bath scene, Park alternates between close-ups and near extreme close-ups. Captivated by Lady Hideko, we are given a shot in near extreme close-up of Sook-hee's lips, at one point she licks her lips with an erotic appetite. Sook-hee's lips at once offer an expression of erotic interest (in Hideko), and at the same time are offered as a fetishistic image for the spectator and Lady Hideko. The fetishistic framing of Sook-hee's lips is viewed through Lady Hideko's presumed perspective. Beads of spittle (or moisture of some kind—steam, perspiration?) rest upon Sook-hee's chin. The connotative associations of wetness and female sexual pleasure—specifically as it relates to Sook-hee's chin, and the act of cunnilingus discussed above—should not be overlooked here. The rhythmic movement of Sook-hee's head, too, takes on sexual connotations as she files down Lady Hideko's tooth. And as my research assistant, Birdy Wei-Ting Hung, notes, although Sook-hee is filing down a rough tooth, the contours of the act are suggestive of caressing, or massage. In close-up Lady Hideko gently caresses Sook-hee's elbow, as she performs her task. In a very tight close-up Lady Hideko, likewise, is caught in erotic contemplation, her mouth agape (with Sook-hee's finger in it), her gaze transfixed by Sook-hee's face mere inches from her own. Cutting to Lady Hideko's perspective, Sook-hee's eyes are caught in near extreme close-up, framed angularly across the screen. This series of shots, and the trading in erotic glances (in colloquial speech we might say, "eye-fucking"), is coupled with the subdued non-diegetic score, "You Are My Baby Miss," which plays low, and nearly tips over into the saccharine. Minimal in its instrumentation—violin, cello, and flute—the score pairs with the romantic mood, and the simmering eroticism that is budding between our two characters. The composition of shots, the lighting, and the score harbor the potential to elicit the beautiful, as well as our erotic interest.

In addition to the non-diegetic score, what is also notable here is Sook-hee's breath. Though it is subtle, as Sook-hee executes the procedure of filing down the sharp edge of Lady Hideko's bothersome tooth, her breath becomes increasingly labored—the kind of labored breath that is unmistakably associated with sexual excitation. Sensing her own palpable excitation, Sook-hee tries to conceal her attraction, at one point audibly swallowing, as if to tamp down the raw expression of her body, of sexual arousal. While we have the penetrative gesture of filing the tooth—with all of its sexual connotations plainly evident, and this might serve as a displacement of the meat-shot—as I have written elsewhere, this also elicits our erotic interest through the "meat sound."[29] "The allure of the sounds of pleasure," as Linda Williams observes in her landmark book *Hard Core*, "resides at least partly in the fact that they come from inside the body and are often not articulate signs (meaningful combinations of sound and sense) but, rather, inarticulate sounds that speak, almost preverbally, of primitive pleasures."[30] Indeed, the intensified exhalation of breath comes from within, it betrays the stirring of erotic interest, it stands as a lektonic marker of an elevated heart-rate and sexual arousal. Sook-hee attempts to conceal her erotic interest, to "keep it inside," but her excited exhalation stands as a confession of the body.

Allure does its work here. It is not Sook-hee, Lady Hideko, or their coupling as objects in the world that are alluring necessarily, but the "notes," as Graham Harman may put it, that emerge from their presence (that emerge from the fetishistic exhibition)—the ephemeral qualities that exceed the objects in themselves and that beckon us.[31] The compendium of fetishistic (disembodied) objects that are offered to us—eyes, lips, breasts, the Playboy aesthetic, and yes, even those "disappointingly boilerplate" arrangements as Miller has it—offer an opportunity for an intersubjective encounter, allowing us to brush up against the erotic objects and their notes. The labored breath in particular facilitates this encounter; breath is not communicative as such, nor is it an object, rather it is a lektonic referent that escapes the erotically charged object, a symptomatic signifier (without a proper signified) of sexual arousal. The bath scene, and the variously erotically charged fetishistic objects that populate it, becomes alluring, invites us to acknowledge what is hidden within the objects. And it is not even the individual fetishistic objects that elicit sexual arousal necessarily, but specifically how they are composed, how they are presented to us. Eyes, lips, or breasts on their own might have some utility (that is, meaning, or narrative information—this is Hideko's body, conveying to us that a character is looking at a specific object, and so on), but it is how they are presented that offers something in excess of the object itself, that bewitching veiled essence that elicits our erotic interest, if not outright sexual arousal.

The power of allure rests in its bewitching charm.[32] The alluring power in the bath scene comes from within the interior of what is presented to us. Allure in its cohesive properties invites an encounter between the erotic exhibition of fetishistic objects and the spectator, an erotic relation between the viewing body and the bodies onscreen. This ephemeral relation touches the viewing body, soliciting embodied simulation. The pull that allure forges creates a strong affective and emotional charge and invites our arousal.

There is, in effect, a meta-cinematic examination of the processes of fetishism and allure found in the storytelling sequences. In the latter storytelling sequence, the Lady sits upon a stage to read from Kouzuki's collection of erotic books before an audience of men. The stories that the Lady reads are salacious, described in one instance as "Sade-esque," explicitly designed to titillate the audience. As stated previously, the mise-en-scène, and the scenario (female storytellers conveying lascivious tales for the pleasure of well-appointed men) comes straight from Sade's *The 120 Days of Sodom*.

The affinities between Sade's infamous novel and *The Handmaiden* are self-evident, as cited above. Sade, in his description of the first storytelling, says that,

> The three storytellers, magnificently dressed as upper-class Parisian courtesans, were seated below the throne upon a couch, and Madame Duclos, the month's narrator, in very scanty and very elegant attire, well-roughed and heavily bejeweled, having taken her place on the stage, thus began the story of what had occurred in her life, into which account she was, with all pertinent details, to insert the first one hundred and fifty passions designated by the title of *simple passions*.[33]

While Lady Hideko is no Parisian prostitute nor scantly attired, she is beautifully dressed—hair up (in the manner of a seasoned geisha) decorated with sakura hair pins, brilliant red lipstick, white kimono with a bright red nagajuban (under-kimono), black gloves, and a white folding fan (with a tassel). The stage, the Lady's beautiful presence, and the content of the story that she reads are intended to invite erotic contemplation—for the men within the diegesis, and the spectator outside it.

A great deal of attention is given to intonation, breath, and the pacing of the storytelling. It is not simply the content of the stories that is emphasized, but how those stories are conveyed. Hideko as a youngster (perhaps 10 or 12 years-old) practices her reading with her aunt, Miss Sasaki, and Uncle Kouzuki. Hideko begins her reading, "When Jinlian finally took off her clothes, Ximen Qing examined her jade gate, to find it hairless white as snow and smooth as jade." Kouzuki abruptly interrupts, violently slamming his hand down on the table, and yelling at the child, "You must pause between words. Don't read like a dog lapping at his plate!" Now in a calmer tone he demands, "Listen to your aunt read." The camera dollies around, and as Hideko's aunt begins the reading there is a hard cut to a reading performance, restarting the story which Hideko had begun. The young Hideko at the back of the library, clutching her doll, listens to her aunt before an audience of men give a stirring reading of *Discovering the Secret Well*. In addition to the incredibly sultry reading of the story, it is at the same time beautifully matched with the mise-en-scène. Hideko's aunt continues the story, ". . . to find it hairless, white as snow, and smooth as jade. Tight as a drum, and soft as silk." At which point Miss Sasaki pulls a leaver, and the screens behind Hideko's aunt open, to reveal a Japanese garden, with snow falling covering the branches of a gnarled tree. The opening of the screens, the snowy garden all finding correlates to the anatomy described in the story. "Once he drew apart the curtains of flesh, the scent of well-aged wine emanated from within, and on fold upon fold of the red velvet interior, beads of dew were forming. Its center was dark and void, yet as if it had its own life, it twitched and twitched." While the content is fetishistic and potentially erotic on its own, its affective charge (whether it might elicit the beautiful, arousal, or perhaps even disgust) is in its delivery, the aunt's pacing, cadence, the rhythm of her enunciation—the musicalization of her voice (whether one understands what she says or not). And again, this is coupled with the beautiful mise-en-scène, the use of depth of field, camera movement, and of course a non-diegetic score featuring a tinkling piano to begin with and a violin that swells in the latter moments of the scene. Similar to Monty's delivery in *25th Hour*, discussed in a previous chapter, the affective charge stems from the various semiotized elements (those things that are "in addition" to the communicative value)—rhythm, musicalization of the voice, the non-diegetic score, light, color, cinematography and composition, and so on.[34]

It is not just the content, but the form of the text that elicits erotic interest (or the affective experience more generally). For Roland Barthes the presentation of a Sadean tableau vivant is what invites an encounter with the Sadean text. With the Sadean storytelling motif in the Sadean theater—even more so than most avant-garde theater (which strove to break down the boundaries between players and audience)—the spectator is lured into the narrative. Indeed, the spectators in a Sadean production are incorporated into the theatrical narrative as active participants, "instead of the actors jumping into the auditorium vulgarly to provoke the spectator," Barthes comments, "the spectator would go onto the stage and join in the posture: 'What a lovely group!'" It is here, in Sade, that Barthes witnesses the intransitive nature of the text, a text animated by the reader/spectator. We might extend this to *The Handmaiden*: the Sadean tale permits the storyteller and the spectator (inside the diegetic narrative and outside it) to encounter one another and to create the "scene and tableau."[35]

What is more, the men listening to Hideko's story are visibly aroused (they shudder, gasp, reflexively throw their jaws open, strategically position hats to conceal erections, shift in their seats), and at the same time during one of the storytelling scenes there are a series of curious cutaways—subjective shots of the men's own fantasies which find their correlate in Hideko's story. In these subjective cutaways, clearly spawned by the content of Hideko's story, the men place themselves in the position of the character in the Sadean story. This is the intransitive invitation that Barthes speaks of. Furthermore, this also visualizes the internalized fetishistic objects, or sex scripts that reside within the subject, which finds an external referent that mutually fuels the economy of fetishism and allure (as discussed in Chapters 5 and 6).³⁶

In the story that Hideko reads, a Duchess whips the male protagonist. As Hideko relates the story, she mimes the action, "The duchess raised the whip high in the air, and then . . ." raising her right hand, brandishing her fan, she suddenly and quickly brings her hand down in a whipping action. Hideko vocalizes the sound of the whip, which is echoed on the soundtrack with the sound of a riding whip slicing through the air and landing across bare flesh. This happens on three separate occasions, and with each mimed whip, a different male audience member places themselves into the story, with Hideko executing the lashes. Prior to this series of cutaways, there is another cutaway featuring a dialogue between the Count and Kouzuki, while Hideko, whipped red welts covering her naked ass, is strapped to a table. (And it is unclear if this particular cutaway is an imagined dialogue, or if it unfolds at some other point in the diegetic narrative.) Kouzuki quizzes the Count on the woman's fate, to which the Count responds that he pities her and that he would seek to comfort her with his caress. Kouzuki then suggests, "If you pity her so, why not take her place and let her whip you?" In the subjective cutaways that follow, this is in effect what happens—the men captivated by the story at the same time project themselves into the story imagining that they are the ones being whipped. And this projective gesture is, at the same time, illustrative of the operation of the economy of fetishism and allure, as well as embodied simulation. As much as Hideko is a doll, a

Figure 7.4 *The Handmaiden* (Chan-wook Park, 2016)

prop, a puppet, the men prove to be puppets of a different sort, willfully manipulated by Hideko's storytelling—an illustration of how embodied simulation invites an external audio/visual stimulus to play upon mirror neurons.

In the same way that Part Two of *The Handmaiden* undoes our understanding of events as portrayed in Part One, there are multiple reversals. This is what Rhee finds remarkable about *The Handmaiden*, where "the relationship between subject and object is presented as neither unilateral nor immutable but reciprocal. If the male guests imagine Hideko's body as a spectacle for their obscene fantasies," Rhee continues, "Hideko in her own way treats them as objects for her to control." Rhee argues that Hideko wields an affective force over the men in the audience that, and I might add to this the spectators of *The Handmaiden* as well, "respond to Hideko's words like marionettes whose strings she is pulling." Hideko is not simply there as a passive object to-be-looked-at, but she actively surveys the audience, staring them individually in the eye—including us the spectators.[37] Hideko controls the erotic economy and is the master of her own destiny.

Conclusion: Harmonizing of Emotion and Affect

As stated earlier, the sex scenes in *The Handmaiden* sit just adjacent to "lesbian" sex scenes found in mainstream heterosexual pornography. However, as I have discussed, most of the affecting work happens in the menagerie of fetishistic images where allure can do its work. And more than this, the affective force of the film is not necessarily found in its instances of eroticism, but rather in its harmonizing with the emotion of sheer joy! "*The Handmaiden*," as Simon Abrams recounts, "feels like a film that was designed with the goal of provoking emotions from viewers."[38]

Many of the (non-explicit) fetishistic moments are embellished further to emphasize their affective charge. In the "ladies truly are the dolls of maids" scene, for example, Sook-hee and Lady Hideko take turns taking off each other's Victorian corset dress. Similar to the bath scene (as discussed earlier), the camera angle switches between Sook-hee and Lady Hideko's perspectives, fetishisticly framing the other's body parts in close-ups. The choreography of gazes and mise-en-scene emphasize the nape of the neck (hair done up), shoulder, the back of each of the women as their wandering hands undo the tiny buttons, the laced-up back, and finally a full bareback. Lady Hideko once even runs her fingertips from Sook-hee's shoulder to the center of her back causing her to reflexively shudder in erotic pleasure.

Sook-hee's voice-over, like the sweet, sensual bedroom talk, whispers in an airy tone: "If I undo the buttons and pull out the cords, then, the sweet and soft things within, those sweet and soft things— If I were still a pickpocket, I'd slip my hand inside." Coupled with Sook-hee's inner monologue and the compendium of fetishistic images is the richly embellished audio-design.[39] The romantic non-diegetic score, "The Sweet Things Within," with its tinkling piano, delicate flute, and collection of plucked and wailing string instruments invites the beautiful, while the amplified diegetic sound—the friction between fabric, clothes sliding off bare skin, intimate whispering—emphasizes touch. Throughout this scene, Sook-hee and Lady Hideko never directly touch each other's skin (the Lady never removes her gloves), but the audio-design suggests intimate caressing. The various lektons (for example, the sound of buttons being undone, clothes falling off bare skin) invite an encounter with the beautiful and at the same time elicit erotic interest. Though crass, think of the reliance of the audible sounds of wetness in the chikan genre (discussed in the previous chapter), however in this case the collection of embellished sounds are indexical signs of touch, of caressing.

Clearly *The Handmaiden*, if it does not elicit outright sexual arousal, at the very least intends to peak the spectator's erotic interest. And it might be that the intensity of that sexual arousal correlates with the emotional charge of the narrative. With *The Handmaiden* there is a sense that the film harmonizes affect and emotion.[40] Emotion is "durational." The emotional appeal, or charge is built around the development of the characters and the maturation of their relationship, and the overcoming of the obstacles placed in their path. It takes a degree of time to appreciate our characters' personalities, to understand their individual desires/goals. Our emotional investment is premised on whether the character arcs arrive at their desired objective (or not). Our emotional response typically aligns with the character's (or characters') objective. We are elated when blockages are cleared away so that the characters might consummate their relationship. We are frustrated, disappointed, or saddened when things fall apart, and the obstacles prove too challenging to overcome. These emotional responses rely on unfolding events and require time to ferment and are an essential part of the romance genre. In *The Handmaiden*, the primary obstacle in the narrative are the male characters that seek to control Lady Hideko and Sook-hee, and cleave the relationship between them. Lady Hideko in particular, however, proves to be a skilled Svengali in her own right, and out-schemes the men that plot against her. The emotional satisfaction stems from the overcoming of these obstacles and the consummation of the union between our primary characters.

Affect, on the other hand, happens in isolated instances—the bath scene, the various instances where Park openly peddles in fetishistic imagery, and, of course, the sex scenes. One of the most affecting moments in the film has nothing to do with sexual arousal but occurs when the Lady and Sook-hee make their escape when Kouzuki attends to business at his gold-mine for a week. In this incredibly powerful moment, immediately before running away the Lady brings Sook-hee to the library. The Lady presents to Sook-hee a book that she reads for her uncle's reading performances. Unable to read Japanese (though it appears that the Lady has taught Sook-hee to read Korean), Sook-hee flips through the pages and eventually finds a picture meant to replicate Hokusai's 1814 woodblock print, "The Dream of the Fisherman's Wife," but the face of the ravished woman, in the Hokusai forgery, is made to look like Lady Hideko, wearing the blue spinel earrings (a gift from the Count earlier in the film). "Is this what you've been reading to that dirty old man and those gentlemen?" Sook-hee asks. Without uttering a word, tears welling up in the Lady's eyes, she affirms Sook-hee's query. Sook-hee directs her rage toward the book, and at first Lady Hideko hesitates (trained to treat the books with the greatest of care from an early age) as Sook-hee tears the pages from the book's binding. At this moment, the non-diegetic score, which begins with string instruments, plays low and begins to swell eventually accompanied by a piano. This initiates Sook-hee's rampage through Kouzuki's library, specifically targeting erotic illustrations—tearing pages from books, shoving books off their shelves, lacerating book pages with a knife, shredding scrolls, tipping over a vitrine, pouring ink over illustrated scrolls, dumping books in a pool of water. Lady Hideko stares in awe, but eventually joins in the vindictive vandalism. As she looks on in amazement, Lady Hideko reflects in an interior dialogue, "The savior who came to tear my life apart. My Tamako. My Sook-hee!" This interior reflection is coupled with the penultimate gesture: Sook-hee, wielding a metal bar, decapitates a sculpture of a snake which stands at the entrance of the library. The snake is associated with Kouzuki, a clear representation of phallic power—Sook-hee assumes the position of the castratrice.[41] The non-diegetic score amplifies, becomes richer at this exact moment, swells with passion, and accompanies a hard cut, cutting between the interior of the library (a site of oppression), to the open verdant fields. At a low stone wall, presumably marking the boundary of Kouzuki's estate, Lady Hideko (Kouzuki's lifelong captive) pauses. Sook-hee, stacking suitcases before the wall so that the Lady might traverse the barrier with ease, escorts her over the wall. (The wall being a literal manifestation of an obstacle that needs to be overcome to secure the union between the two women.) The pair of women, now free, laugh and run through the field as the non-diegetic score swells. This scene of liberation is an instance of harmonizing affect and emotion. While the castrating instance marking the overcoming of the main obstacle figures as an emotional high point, the score elicits the beautiful. Coupled together the emotional elation is accompanied by an affecting score that invites a visceral experience—tears, goosebumps.

Not only do the women overcome their obstacles, but they also turn the very things that would oppress them into agents of liberation and/or pleasure. The ben wa balls, used to punish Hideko as a child, and featured in the story *The Sound of Bells on a Windless Night*, become instruments of pleasure in the closing moments of the film. As Celine Parreñas Shimizu notes, the pair locate their agency "through sex."[42] The years of reading Sade (or Sade-esque) literature proved useful in Lady Hideko's own libertinage and fueling her own sexual fantasies. Sook-hee's underworld network proves useful in executing the pair's escape (including finding a forger capable of replacing Lady Hideko's photograph for Count Fujiwara's)—allowing Lady Hideko to assume Count Fujiwara's identity using his stolen passport.[43]

Addressing Donna Deitch's 1985 landmark lesbian romance film *Desert Hearts*, which is recognized as among the first mainstream films to depict a positive lesbian romance, Jackie Stacey laments that in its wake no films appeared to capitalize on its critical and market success. While Deitch's film laid the foundation for the popular lesbian romance film, Stacey bemoans that no films appeared to follow in its footsteps. Stacey concludes that "the popular lesbian romance film is a virtual contradiction in terms," because there has been an absence of films that mobilize "... recognizable Hollywood conventions' and 'appreciated by lesbian audiences,' lesbian to denote 'some kind of female same-sex desire,' and romance to mean 'the sexual and emotional union of two characters having successfully overcome certain obstacles which the audience believed they might not.'" Stacey closes, wondering, "Perhaps future films will prove me wrong."[44] Although long overdue, I would propose that *The Handmaiden* is precisely the film that Stacey has been waiting for.

Notes

1 Marquis de Sade, *Justine, Philosophy in the Bedroom, and Other Writings* (London: Arrow Books Limited, 1991), 318.

2 Jackie Stacey, "'If You Don't Play, You Can't Win' *Desert Hearts* and the Lesbian Romance Film," in *Immortal, Invisible: Lesbians and the Moving Image*, ed. Tamsin Wilton (New York: Routledge, 1995), 71.
3 Ibid., 71–2.
4 Park has explained in interviews that he felt compelled to relocate the story in Korea and Japan precisely because the BBC had already adapted Waters' book. See for example, "Park Chan-wook on relocating Sarah Waters' *Fingersmith* to Korea," interviewed by Henry Barnes, *The Guardian*, May 17, 2016, https://www.theguardian.com/film/2016/may/17/park-chan-wook-on-relocating-sarah-waters-fingersmith-to-korea.
5 Kristin Baird Rattini, "A Short History of Shanghai," *The New York Times*, 2006, https://archive.nytimes.com/www.nytimes.com/fodors/top/features/travel/destinations/asia/china/shanghai/fdrs_feat_145_5.html.
6 Marquis de Sade, *The 120 Days of Sodom and Other Writing*, trans. Austryn Wainhouse and Richard Seaver (New York: Grove Weidenfeld, 1987), 237–8.
7 Suk Koo Rhee, "The Erotic-Grotesque versus Female Agency in Colonial Korea in Park Chan-wook's *The Handmaiden*," *Canadian Journal of Film Studies* vol. 29, no. 2 (2020): 121.
8 Keungyoon Bae, "Admitting an Attraction: Colonial Villainy, Visuality, and *The Handmaiden* (2016) as Critique," *International Journal of Korean History* vol. 25, no. 2 (2020): 184–5. Jia Tolentino, "*The Handmaiden* and the Freedom Women Find Only with One Another," *The New Yorker*, October 29, 2016, https://www.newyorker.com/culture/jia-tolentino/the-handmaiden-and-the-freedom-women-find-only-with-one-another. Regarding Hideko's subjugation, Bae says, "She is relegated to the role of mannequin or prop within their male fantasies; at one point the film literalizes her circumstances by showing her demonstrating a sex position with a mannequin to provide visual aid for the guests." Bae, 184.
9 As my colleague, Steve Choe notes,

> In the final scene, Hideko and Sook-hee make love using four small silver bells attached to a string. Earlier in the film, Hideko reads from a piece of erotica called, *The Sound of Bells on a Windless Night*, in the library for a group of potential book buyers. They reappropriate the content of Kouzuki's pornography for their own pleasure at the end of the film, taking the written word and reworking it into the visual and auditory means of the cinema. For Waters, this act of reappropriation, an act that overturns the exploitation of women typically associated with pornography, constitutes the "feminist essence" of the film.

Steve Choe, "Park Chan-wook's Critique of Moral Judgment: *The Handmaiden* (2016)," *Studies in the Humanities* vol. 44 nos. 1–2 & vol. 45, nos. 1–2 (2017–2018): 35.
10 Rhee reads the waiving slates of wood, through which Hideko peers, differently; he views them as "behind the bars of the window, suggesting captivity." Rhee, 123.
11 Slavoj Žižek, "Kant with (or against) Sade," in *The Žižek Reader*, eds Elizabeth Wright and Edmond Wright (Oxford: Blackwell, 1999), 287.
12 Rhee, 125–6.
13 Laura Miller, "*The Handmaiden* Park Chan-wook takes on Sarah Waters' brilliant, intricate novel *Fingersmith*," *Slate*, October 20, 2016, https://slate.com/culture/2016/10/park-chan-wooks-the-handmaiden-based-on-sarah-waters-fingersmith-reviewed.html.

14 Regarding wetness and female sexual excitation also see Eugenie Brinkema, "Celluloid Is Sticky: Sex, Death, Materiality, Metaphysics (in Some Films by Catherine Breillat)," *Women: A Cultural Review* vol. 17, no. 2 (2006): 149.
15 Shannon Keating, "The Spectacle of Lesbian Sex in Prestige Cinema," *BuzzFeed*, Nov 25, 2016, https://www.buzzfeed.com/shannonkeating/the-handmaiden-and-lesbian-sex-scenes (italics in original).
16 Ibid.
17 Miller makes similar assumptions (critiquing *The Handmaiden* via a comparison to Waters' novel):

> *Fingersmith* is about, among other things, the insurrectionary freedom to be found in invisibility. Waters' title, Victorian slang for pickpocket, is also a punning reference to the dexterity of the lesbian hand, an erotic implement so much better at coaxing forth female pleasure than any tool the novel's men have at their disposal. (Not that these guys care much about the real pleasure of real women, caught up as they are in the organized, artificial ecstasies of Maud's uncle's pornographic library.)

18 Celine Parreñas Shimizu, *The Proximity of Other Skins: Ethical Intimacy in Global Cinema* (New York: Oxford University Press, 2019), 174. Irigaray writes in her poetic article, "You'll say to me, why talk? We feel the same thing at the same time. Aren't my hands, my eyes, my mouth, my lips, my body enough for you? Isn't what they say to you sufficient? I could say yes, but that would be too easy. It has been said too often to reassure you/us." Luce Irigaray, "When our lips speak together," trans. Carolyn Burke, *Signs: Journal of Women in Culture and Society* vol. 6, no. 1 (1980): 76.
19 Susanna Paasonen, "'We watch porn for the fucking, not for romantic tiptoeing': extremity, fantasy and women's porn use," *Porn Studies* (2021): 7. Paasonen references Martin Barker, "The 'Problem' of Sexual Fantasies," *Porn Studies* vol. 1, nos. 1–2 (2014): 143–60.
20 Susanna Paasonen, *Carnal Resonance: Affect and Online Pornography* (Cambridge, MA: MIT Press, 2011), 150.
21 Lori Marso, "Feminist Cringe Comedy: Dear Dick, The Joke Is on You," *Politics & Gender* vol. 15, no. 1 (2019): 122.
22 Keating.
23 Keating argues for greater representation in the media:

> One suspects that having more women in decision-making film roles—behind or in front of the camera; ideally, in the director's chair—would result in more lesbian sex scenes where individual characters' point of views are privileged; where we don't just see porny wide shots of bodies; where women don't see each other as reflections of themselves, but as complex and full-blooded other humans. All the better if those female decision-makers are queer themselves. If that were the case, we'd likely see way more queer sex scenes involving queer people across the gender presentation spectrum. (Hideko does don a great male disguise at some point, but she's out of it and having super-femme sex again soon enough.)

A greater diversity of voices is always welcomed. But that's not exactly what Keating and Miller are arguing for: rather, their argument is that Park's film (as well as Kechiche and Haynes) should have been something other than what they are. Something that would presumably appeal to them. Moreover, their commentaries have the ever so slight scent of racism. Keating writes, earlier in her text, "While we are placed into Sook-hee and

Hideko's perspectives at certain times during their sexual encounter—which is more than many other films can say—the big, dramatic moments reveal their entire bodies, in all their slim, hairless glory." And to add to this, Keating describes the female characters as having "lithe bodies," and that they "look alike." The hint of judgemental body-shaming about an Asian female body type, coupled with phrases such as, "*They look alike!*" which is not that far off from "they all look the same to me," is somewhat troubling. Yes, the reflection motif is part of the plot, yes at certain points (for example, when the Lady dresses Sook-hee up) they are meant to look alike, but this is coupled with Keating's judgmental tone, and from my perspective teeters on the edge of the offensive. Keating references (via hyperlink): Martha M. Lauzen, "The Celluloid Ceiling: Behind-the-Scenes Employment of Women on the Top 100, 250, and 500 Films of 2015," *Center for the Study of Women in Television and Film* (San Diego: San Diego State University, 2016).
24 See specifically Houston's *Crash Pad* series (2006–2008).
25 Boccaccio cited in Griselda Pollock, *Vision and Difference: Femininity, Feminism and the Histories of Art* (New York: Routledge, 1990), 128.
26 Pollock, 128.
27 The baby motif is interesting. At the beginning of the film, we learn that in addition to being thieves, Sook-hee and her adoptive family sell abandoned Korean babies to the Japanese. Gazing upon one of her compatriots, Sook-hee laments, "Gguet Dan hates feeding the children her breastmilk. If it were me, it'd be different. If only I had breastmilk, I'd feed each and every one of them till they're full." Additionally, during the second sex scene (actually, it's the same sex scene, just viewed from Hideko's perspective this time), Sook-hee says, "I wish that I had breastmilk so I could feed you."
28 Jia Tolentino similarly observes in her *New Yorker* review, "Their [Sook-hee and Hideko's] relationship builds through ashes of fetishistic typology: the two women are alternately baby and mother, master and servant, doll and child, and doubles of each other." Jia Tolentino, "*The Handmaiden* and the Freedom Women Find Only with One Another," *The New Yorker*, October 29, 2016, https://www.newyorker.com/culture/jia-tolentino/the-handmaiden-and-the-freedom-women-find-only-with-one-another.
29 Aaron Kerner and Jonathan Knapp, *Extreme Cinema: Affective Strategies in Transnational Media* (Edinburgh: Edinburgh University Press, 2016), 33–4.
30 Linda Williams, *Hard Core: Power, Pleasure, and the "Frenzy of the Visible"* (Berkeley: University of California Press, 1989), 126.
31 Graham Harman, *Guerrilla Metaphysics: Phenomenology and the Carpentry of Things* (Chicago: Open Court, 2005), 211.
32 Ibid., 137.
33 Sade, *The 120 Days of Sodom and Other Writings*, 266.
34 David Mai, one of my former graduate students, was the first to link the significance of enunciation in the storytelling back to the discussion of *25th Hour*.
35 Roland Barthes, *Sade/Fourier/Loyola*, trans. Richard Miller (New York: Hill and Wang, 1976), 156.
36 My research assistant, Birdy Wei-Ting Hung, was the first to make this connection between the cutaways here, sex scripts, and the economy of fetishism and allure.
37 Rhee, 122. Regarding Hideko's gaze Rhee adds,

> Hideko's counter-gaze, it turns out, can unsettle her viewers as much as her affective power excites them sexually. In the scene where she recites the tale of the deadly act

of sexual intercourse between the Duchess and her lover, for instance, Hideko pauses at a crucial moment for a duration that feels uncomfortably long. During the awkward pause, she gazes unabashedly at her audience for the emotional changes that her erotic words are causing in them. Under her blunt gaze, these men try to hide the evidence of their sexual arousal by shifting in their sitting positions or by placing hats over their crotches. When Hideko resumes her narration, the camera slowly zooms in on her flustered male viewers, giving the impression that Hideko's own eyes are refocusing on each of them in order to see them better in their not-very-flattering state. By "refus[ing] to return and restore the image of authority to the eye of the power," to borrow Bhabha's terms, Hideko here challenges the imperial patriarchal authority.

Rhee, 122. Homi Bhabha, *The Location of Culture* (London: Routledge, 1994), 100.
38 Simon Abrams, "Park Chan-wook's Films Push the Boundaries of Sex and Violence—But That's Not His Intention," *Esquire*, October 18, 2016, https://www.esquire.com/entertainment/q-and-a/a49691/park-chan-wook-interview-the-handmaiden/.
39 Sook-hee's whispering approaches what is found in ASMR videos, which for some elicits frisson, comparable to the experience of going flush with goosebumps while listening to music. See this study: Alexsandra Kovacevich and David Huron, "Two studies of autonomous sensory meridian response (ASMR): The relationship between ASMR and music-induced frisson," *Empirical Musicology Review* vol. 13, nos. 1–2 (2019): 39–63.
40 I credit this concept of "harmonizing emotion and affect" to my graduate student Jeffrey E. Martin.
41 See Barbara Creed's chapter "The Femme Castratrice: *I Spit on Your Grave, Sisters*," in her landmark book *The Monstrous Feminine* (London: Routledge, 1993), 122–38.
42 Shimizu, *The Proximity of Other Skins*, 181.
43 "This kind of idea of two women using men and using what men have to punish them," Park says, "this idea of subversion was certainly something that I thought would be interesting." Cited in Rhee, 127.
44 Stacey, 84.

PART 3

8

On Laughter

Introduction: Sorry, I Can't Help It, It's in my Ape DNA

Common sense dictates that laughter is synonymous with comedy. And, of course, a good joke, or a good *SNL* skit might cause us to double over with laughter. However, we actually laugh for a whole lot of reasons, and for things that are not funny in the least. Aristotle erroneously posited that, "mankind alone is ticklish both because of the thinness of his skin and because he is the only one of the animals that laughs."[1] Other primates laugh, other mammals laugh—though the vocalization of non-human animals is different. Laughter is effectively hardwired into the human experience. Individuals that suffer from hemiparalysis, for example, leave neural pathways intact "between the brain and face. When asked to grin, these patients produce crooked smiles—only one side of their face responds. However," as neurobiologist and psychologist Robert Provine observes, "they produce a normal, symmetrical smile if tickled or amused by a joke—the ongoing social stimuli activate intact neuronal pathways that are beyond conscious control." Provine suggests that with hemiparalysis "we glimpse the otherwise invisible hand of the ancient neurological puppeteer that controls spontaneous laughter and smiling."[2] Provine points to our ancient biological heritage, where, just as we can observe in contemporary great apes, laughter signals play—signaling between sparring parties, and the larger community, "we're just playing." Smiling and laughing are an important part of nonlinguistic communication.

Laughter has a social function, and as cited above, is deeply rooted in our primate ancestry. It is not an accident that we are inclined to erupt in vocalized laughter when in a group, as compared to when we might be alone. Like yawning, laughter can be strangely contagious. In 1962, for example, at a girl's boarding school in Kashasha Tanzania students broke out in uncontrollable fits of laughter—one girl apparently broke out in spontaneous laughter, and this initiated a chain reaction. The laughter soon spread, infecting others in the town as well. "In one village," as recounted by Jad Abumrad of *RadioLab*, "217 people start[ed] to laugh, and cry. A second boarding school . . . [had] to shut down, and no one knows why."[3] Whatever the reason—and it does not appear that a definitive reason was determined in the Kashasha case—laughter can be quite contagious.

Laughter communicates to our fellow humans, "I am with you." And assuredly we have all been in a situation where, surrounded by laughter, we might wonder, "What!? What's so funny?" Is there anything lonelier, more alienating than not being in on the laugh? Plato also viewed laughter as potentially dangerous—a threat to regimes of power. Laughter is a form of non-linguistic communication. Sophie Scott, a cognitive neuroscientist, in a TED Talk entitled, "Why We Laugh," observes that we laugh quite a lot. "You do it so often, you don't even notice it. Everybody underestimates how often they laugh," Scott tells us, "and you're doing something, when you laugh with people, that's actually letting you access a really ancient evolutionary system that mammals have evolved to make and maintain social bonds, and clearly to regulate emotions, to make ourselves feel better."[4] A volume on pleasurable affects would thus be remiss not to cover the subject.

While we certainly might be prompted to laugh in response to a joke, more often than not we laugh at the most banal, and deeply unfunny things. We are less likely to laugh by ourselves (as already stated). "Laughter is a social act," Provine insists, "involving members of their group (their companions), and eye contact is an important link in this social pas de deux."[5] As Provine suggests, laughter is in effect a social dance. Sit down at an academic conference, and a presenter might say something kind of snarky or snide, but nothing particularly funny, nevertheless, predictably a small wave of chuckles will wash through the attendees. I find this phenomenon actually quite annoying, though despite my annoyance, I get caught up in it too. But what I have come to realize is that this is less about responding to some "high-brow joke," rather what this really is, is a social cue, "I get it!" "I am (we are all) in the club." I join in the laughter precisely because I want to be in the club, to be recognized by my peers.[6] Although addressing the collective experience in the movie theater, and drawing from Michael Tomasello, Julian Hanich observes that this sort of collective laughter serves as a "'communicative *display*,' an indicator without intention, but it can also be a 'communicative *signal*,' intended and strategically selected for a social motive."[7]

Just like our encounter with sexual or erotic content, our bodies can betray us. Whether laughter reaffirms gender stereotypes, or we are responding to something that is politically incorrect, laughter is not necessarily in our conscious control. While we might find something politically regressive, or perhaps just sadistic in nature, despite our better angels it might nonetheless still cause us to laugh. And like tears, laughter can be prompted by narrative content, or with an encounter of the non-object (the abject). Often the non-object, or the abject, elicits from us a sense of disgust. Take, for instance, the *Tosh.0* episode, "Results of the Memorabilia Dump," where Daniel Tosh showcases individuals consuming things such as sour milk, whole jars of mayonnaise, cockroaches, and so on.[8] In the same sequence, Tosh features his tour manager, Andrew Wantuck, who drinks and eats all sorts of things that by volume (for example, a pint of non-dairy creamer), or measured against the conventional Western palette (for instance, pig bung, pig snout, a cow's penis, a chicken head) might be perceived as disgusting. This particular segment culminates, in the fashion of *Jackass*, with Wantuck drinking iced tea mixed with horse ejaculate. The segment by most measures might be disgusting, prompting nausea perhaps, and if not full-blown nausea then wincing or a furrowing of the brow, but also in all likelihood laughter as well.

Laughter neutralizes disgust. "All theoreticians of disgust are, at the same time," as Winfried Menninghaus insists, "theoreticians of laughter." As much as laughter is a vital human experience, so too is disgust, and laughter appears to be the polar complement that counteracts disgust. Laughter serves as a "sudden discharge of tension," which like vomiting can facilitate a distancing, discharging, or purging of disgust.[9] Like tears too, laughter can be prompted for a myriad of reasons: a defense against disgust, a response to fear, embarrassment, a response to a joke or some other humorous scenario (narrative), tickling, and so on. And as this partial list of things that make us laugh indicates, it would actually be a mistake to solely equate laughter with humor, as already noted we laugh for so many reasons.

Philosophical Approaches to Laughter: Superiority, Incongruity, and Relief

There are a number of general philosophical lines of thought on laughter: superiority, incongruity, and (cathartic) relief. And as for the latter, laughter might come as a response to stress, to embarrassment, to injury, to awkwardness, or as Menninghaus already noted above, to disgust. In his discussion on the "audience effect," Julian Hanich notes that laughing out loud can serve a protective function. "It is not at all a response to something funny, but rather serves to laugh something *away*." And similar to Menninghaus's observation that compares laughter to vomiting, Hanich views laughter, in certain instances, as a mechanism to push the offending referent away. Hanich asks us to consider those instances of being startled in a thriller or encountering dread or disgust either in horror or gross-out comedy. "These are moments in which the spectator is suddenly overcome by an overly obtrusive aspect of the—phenomenologically speaking—*under*-distanced film." Inferring a relation between the fight or flight reflex, laughter might serve as a defensive gesture. "In these instances," Hanich says, "the viewer feels overwhelmed, 'cornered,' and constricted, and as an answer suddenly and wholly intuitively reacts with laughter." Echoing Menninghaus's observations, Hanich continues, "As an eruptive, expressive, outward-directed response to an otherwise unanswerable mini-crisis, laughter relieves and liberates the viewer's constricted, beleaguered body by distancing the shocking, horrific, or disgusting film." Hanich insists that this is no theoretical or metaphorical gesture, rather "the film is *experienced* as overly close, just as the lived-body is *experienced* as constricted." Hanich notes that the very act of laughing enacts the defensive gesture, laughter "after all, [is] an expansive outward movement of the body that goes along with exhalation—we try to get rid of what seems to be *too close*." Thus, Hanich concludes, "When the film is felt as too shocking, horrific, or disgusting, laughter can work as a relief response to emotions like fear or disgust in the sense of a *reduction of tension*."[10]

Freud's discourse on jokes—where laughter exercises taboos, repressed sexual tension/anxiety, and/or hostility—also concerns the discharge of repressed feelings. And just to be abundantly clear, Freud is more interested in jokes and how they relate as a mechanism to disclose the secrets of the unconscious, rather than on laughter necessarily. That said, interestingly, Freud (drawing from Kuno Kischer) does from the outset of his discourse, place jokes immediately adjacent to aesthetic judgements.[11] Freud though ultimately locates affinities between dream-work—which relies on the processes of condensation and displacement—and what he terms "joke-work." The joke, like the dream, relies on "[i]ndirect representation—the replacement of a dream-thought by an allusion, by something small, a symbolism akin to analogy—is precisely what distinguishes the mode of expression of dreams from that of our waking life."[12] In the same way that dreams smuggle repressed material into our consciousness (via our recollection of dreams in waking life), jokes analogously offer a means by which to exorcize unconscious content. Dreams and jokes, however, clearly operate in completely different realms. While dreams happen while we are asleep, beyond our control, they are also obfuscated through the mechanism of the "unconscious mental processes . . . A joke, on the other hand, is the most social of all the mental functions that aim at a yield of pleasure." Furthermore, while jokes rely on condensation and displacement, at the same time for them to function in a social economy this necessitates a degree of clarity that is readily understood amongst company. "A dream still remains a wish, even though one that has been made unrecognizable; a joke is developed play." Freud adds, "Dreams serve predominantly for the avoidance of unpleasure, jokes for the attainment of pleasure; but all our mental activities converge in these two aims."[13] Freud concludes that the pleasure in jokes is located in its expenditure of transgressive material.[14]

Mikhail Bakhtin—who is discussed at length in the following section of this chapter—also positioned laughter found in the carnivalesque experience as a critical mechanism for common people to effectively "blow-off steam." This is especially true of Bakhtin's framing of the carnivalesque where, in a socially sanctioned time and place, common folks were given license to lambast and ridicule figures of authority. Where all things base—from eating and drinking to excess, to the sexually crass to all other kinds of vulgarity—were celebrated and invited raucous laughter. The carnivalesque afforded common folk an opportunity to "let their hair down," and to poke fun at the regimes of power.

Herbert Spencer, an English philosopher, positions laughter within the network of the nervous system, wherein the system necessitates the expenditure of surplus energy lest inviting some deleterious effect. Where some reflexes are intended to elicit specific bodily responses—for example, in the elicitation of fight or flight—laughter, on the other hand, has no function as such. Striking an almost Kantian tone, Spencer states that, "Strong feeling, mental or physical, being, then, the general cause of laughter, we have to note that the muscular actions constituting it are distinguished from most others by this, that they are purposeless." Generally, Spencer observes, "bodily motions that are prompted by feelings are directed to special ends; as when we try to escape a danger, or struggle to secure a gratification. But the movements of chest and limbs which we make when laughing have no object."[15] Although contemporary psychological and neurological studies suggest that laughter indeed serves an important social function, communicating to our fellow humans a sense of comradery, nevertheless, Spencer situates laughter as a healthy "venting" of the nervous system without an object.

When encountering a referent that invites us to laugh, Spencer interestingly outlines the physiological effects that accompany it. As the intensity of the laughter increases, this recruits additional involuntary expressions of the body. Spencer observes that:

> The upper limbs are set in motion. Children frequently clap their hands in glee; by some adults the hands are rubbed together; and others, under still greater intensity of delight, slap their knees and sway their bodies backwards and forwards. Last of all, when the other channels for the escape of the surplus nerve-force have been filled to overflowing, a yet further and less-used group of muscles is spasmodically affected: the head is thrown back and the spine bent inwards—there is a slight degree of what medical men call opisthotonos.[16]

We could add to this if the laughter is sufficiently intense, we might buckle over, fall to the ground, roll about, shed tears, abdominal muscles might contract so much that it induces pain, and even lose bladder control. And even in the most intense fits of laughter, we might declare, "Oh, boy, I needed that." Laughter as medicine—relief. In short, laughter relieves pent-up nervous energy.

The incongruity theory was held by a range of philosophers, among them James Beattie, Immanuel Kant, Arthur Schopenhauer, and Søren Kierkegaard. Kant, for instance, posits that, "*Laughter is an affect arising from a strained expectation being suddenly reduced to nothing.*"[17] Kant actually offers a couple of jokes to convey the conception of incongruity, the first of which is racist, the second is set at a funeral: a wealthy man preparing for a funeral service laments, "the more money I give my mourners to look sad, the merrier they look."[18] Analogous to the formula that Kant identifies, contemporary stand-up comedy often relies on the same incongruity: a set-up is followed by a punchline that is in some fashion incongruous, or otherwise defies our expectation.

Kant suggests that the abstract conceptualization of incongruity corresponds to what takes place in the musculature and the interior of the body. Moving from one concept to some incongruous concepts relates to the "movement in the bodily organs [which] is associated sympathetically with all our thoughts." The incongruous gesture of a joke, or situation, may result in the relaxing and tensing-up "of our viscera, which communicates itself to the diaphragm (and resembles that felt by ticklish people), in the course of which the lungs expel the air with rapidly succeeding interruptions, resulting in a movement beneficial to health." It is the bodily sensation of laughter, not the "meaning" of any given joke or situation that calls upon our cognition, but laughter in its own right that is significant for Kant.[19] Kant verges on the "relief theory," here, and in fact he reflects on Voltaire who "said that heaven has given us two things to compensate us for the many miseries of life, hope and sleep." Kant goes on, "He might have added laughter to the list."[20] Kant concludes that, "We may, therefore, as I conceive, concede

Epicurus the point that all gratification, even when occasioned by concepts that evoke aesthetic ideas, is animal, i.e. bodily sensation."[21]

Henri Bergson's *Laughter, An Essay on the Meaning of the Comic* is perhaps the most well-known discussion of laughter. Bergson, reflecting on the nature of laughter, notes that if we wish "to understand laughter, we must put it back into its natural environment, which is society, and above all else we must determine the utility of its function which is a social one."[22] Bergson straddles the line between the incongruity and superiority theory. While Bergson's focus on elasticity or flexibility might be framed as relating to incongruity, at the same time, laughter is also positioned as a social corrective. In sum, humans are expected to be fluid in their movements and their social engagements, and when individuals become too rigid or mechanical, and thus incapable of retaining "proper" flexibility, this might open the door to laughter. "Indeed, it is in this sense only that laughter 'corrects men's manners.' It makes us at once endeavour to appear what we ought to be, what some day we shall perhaps end in being."[23] Particularly illustrative of this is *The Office* (both the British original series and the American series) and *Curb Your Enthusiasm* (discussed further in the following chapter). Laughter comes as a response to the male protagonists that are utterly inflexible, often taking things quite literally and incapable of reading social cues, or stubbornly executing a plot despite all the social signs that scream: "Stop!"[24]

Bergson also associates laughter with ugliness, or more generally with deformity. "Suppose, then, we intensify ugliness to the point of deformity, and study the transition from the deformed to the ridiculous." Bergson adds that "some hunchbacks, for instance, will excite laughter . . . *A deformity that may become comic is a deformity that a normally built person could successfully imitate.*"[25] Presumably there is ugliness that could go too far, but some degree of ugliness might elicit laughter. "By toning down a deformity that is laughable, we ought to obtain an ugliness that is comic."[26] The caricaturist detects some "imperfection," and the caricaturist renders "it visible to all eyes by magnifying it."[27]

As one might imagine the "superiority theory" is fairly self-evident, in the way that laughter subjects one to some sort of ridicule or humiliation. Although Thomas Hobbes objected to it on moral grounds, Hobbes effectively establishes the "superiority theory," in his *Leviathan*. There is only one very brief discussion of laughter in the volume, though, Hobbes writes:

> *Sudden glory,* is the passion which maketh those *grimaces* called LAUGHTER; as is caused either by some sudden act of their own, that pleaseth them; or by the apprehension of some deformed thing in

> another, by comparison whereof they suddenly applaud themselves. And it is incident most to them, that are conscious of the fewest abilities in themselves; who are forced to keep themselves in their own favor, but observing the imperfections of other men. And therefore much laughter at the defects of others, is a sign of pusillanimity. For of great minds, one of the proper works is, to help and free others from scorn; and compare themselves only with the most able.[28]

Hobbes draws affinities between laughter and weeping. In both cases, laughter and weeping, these "are sudden motions."[29] Laughter, for Hobbes, is spawned by some degree of animus, or in a sense of "fitness," compared to some infirmity.

I suspect that laughter works in all of these various ways, and I do not intend to argue for one philosophical line of thought over another. While I will give considerable attention to Bakhtin (and thus, one iteration of the relief theory), that only relates to the attention of the present volume on (positive) affective experiences in abject material. When commenting on laughable cinematic content from a conventional methodological paradigm any of these theories related to laughter might be applied. Let us briefly consider Margret Cho's stand-up routine *Revolution*, for example, where she relates the nearly religious experience of witnessing her friend give birth. Cho expresses awe at the generative powers associated with women, "You see how powerful women are, that we bring forth life!" At the moment of birth Cho explains, "At that moment she was creation, she was life, she was God." However, this "magical moment" is suddenly shattered, Cho gives a loud exhalation of air with a "Pow!" and exclaims, "Her pussy exploded!" On stage, to allow for the audience's laughter to linger, she enacts the frantic inspection of her own body, and her surroundings to look for pieces of that explosive pussy. Noting (with some derision) that, "They had to sew it back together!" This too she mimes stitching in exaggerated gestures—in fact, this is not a totally uncommon phenomena, where an episiotomy is performed (an incision between the vagina and anus is made to increase the birthing opening), or as apparently happened in the instance that Cho relates, where vaginal tearing took place and required stitching to close. Aligning the female reproductive organs with the monstrous, Cho flatly declares, "Franken-pussy." And then, loudly and in a somewhat guttural voice echoing the lines from James Whales's 1931 adaptation of *Frankenstein*, "It's alive!" Cho ends her routine announcing that, "I am not a breeder."

We could argue that any of the three philosophical approaches are evident in the "Franken-pussy" routine. The initial jolt of laughter comes from the quick and incongruous shift from the sacred to the profane, from the spiritual to the earth-bound realities of biology. At the same time, the derision about "sewing it back together," in a sense elevates us above the raw materiality of the (female) body. Furthermore, when Cho mimes the stitching of the vaginal tear, she mimes biting the thread (rather than cutting with scissors). This gesture situates the birthing mother in the animal kingdom, and comparatively places Cho (and us as outside onlookers) as human. And, of course, the routine ends with Cho's declaration, "I am not a breeder." And while I do not believe Cho had any malicious intent, nevertheless, the "raising above," might be viewed as evoking the superiority theory of laughter. And finally, the "Franken-pussy" stand-up bit exercises anxieties about the generative powers of women—a power that only God and women possess. Horror and comedy are often called upon to negotiate the (patriarchal) anxiety elicited by the pregnant and generative (female) body (this is the thesis of Barbara Creed's landmark book *The Monstrous-Feminine*). And in this regard, Cho's routine exorcizes social anxieties and thus invites a reading via the relief theory. We can also see how these three approaches to humor might be applied, even to the same routine.

In this admittedly brief, and by no means exhaustive survey of the different philosophical approaches to laughter, we have found that the theories of incongruity and superiority are always already bound up with meaning. With the theories of incongruity and superiority we are, whether consciously or not, working within the objectal economy. And thus, we are never far from concepts, from narrative contextualization, or social meanings. Theories of relief, in some instances, negotiate the non-objectal economy—disgust, the abject, the (Kristevan) semiotic, states of becoming, the grotesque body. Notably, while Freud's discourse on humor is positioned among the theories of relief, the Freudian conceptualization of the subject is rooted in the objectal economy. Hostility or sexual aggression is directed toward an object. And this is one of Kristeva's major contributions, greatly expanding the psychoanalytic scope to consider those experiences that fall outside the Symbolic. Mikhail Bakhtin, discussed at length below, often evokes the non-object in the various forms of becoming, and the grotesque body.

Mikhail Bakhtin: The Carnivalesque and the Grotesque Body

With respect to the present volume, though, and with incongruity and superiority in particular, there is a reliance on narrative contextualization. Without dismissing these approaches to laughter—assuredly incongruous experiences elicit laughter, as does witnessing some failure or misfortune that invites laughter spawned by a sense of superiority—there are many things though that elicit laughter that are not necessarily bound up in narrative, in meanings (be it political, social, or linguistic). A joke is bound up with narrative, and socio-cultural meanings. And like the melodrama, which invites the feeling of sadness coupled with tears in response to a narrative situation (for example, a character is too late), a joke elicits an emotional response accompanied with the reflexive bodily response of laughter. However, the present discussion is less about the comedic genre, but instead we turn our attention to laughter elicited from the body caught in excess: leaking, consuming, procreative, deformed, broken. In short, what Mikhail Bakhtin called the "grotesque body."

And to be clear, Bakhtin's conception of the grotesque should not be confused with the contemporary colloquial understanding of the term (for example, gross, disgusting, the "ew factor"), rather the cultural and literary theorist draws on its original meaning. Our word, "grotesque," derives from the Italian, "grotto," meaning cave. During the Renaissance, curious explorers discovered in the ruins (read: caves) of the Roman empire, capricious designs decorating the walls of buildings. The designs freely mixed human, animal, architectural features, foliage, and festoons. Thus, drawn from the word "grotto," meaning "cave," these came to be known as "grotesques." Upon their discovery, they were copied and widely replicated. And we can still find them today—on the back of playing-cards, printed on flatware, public buildings erected in the 19th century assimilating classical designs (though, the grotesques fall outside the scholarly conception of the classical). In truth though the grotesques never went away, and the art historical narrative of "discovery" is something of a contrivance. Similar capricious designs survived, following the fall of Rome, in medieval culture—caricatures, pagan imagery assimilated by the Church, designs found on churches and illustrated manuscripts. In sum, Bakhtin's conception of the grotesque body—related to those capricious Roman designs—is one that is open to the world, where the human form is not an individuated entity set apart from the world, but rather a rhizomatic figure that is inextricably imbricated with the world all around us.

With the Renaissance and the proliferation of Enlightenment ideas, the conception of the human condition underwent a dramatic paradigmatic shift. Whereas the Enlightened subject is conceived as discrete, somehow "above" or "outside" the natural world, the medieval continental conception imagined the subject as open to the world, always in the state of becoming. Grotesque realism, as Bakhtin frames it, "never presents an individual body; the image consists of orifices and convexities that present another, newly conceived body. It is a point of transition in a life eternally renewed, the inexhaustible vessel of death and conception." Bakhtin continues, "the grotesque ignores the impenetrable surface that closes and limits the body as a separate and completed phenomenon. The grotesque image displays not only the outward but also the inner features of the body: blood, bowels, heart and other organs." While the modern conception of the body imagines that we are self-contained entities, closed off from the world, the medieval conception of the body was wholly different. "The outward and inward features are often merged into one." Bakhtin reminds us further that "grotesque imagery" figures a body that cannot be extricated from the web of life, and the perpetual flow of matter. "In the endless chain of bodily life it retains the parts in which one link joins the other, in which the life of one body is born from the death of the preceding, older one."[30]

In Bakhtin's survey of the Rabelaisian text, which he reads as emblematic of the carnivalesque, he notes that the cycle of life is a common feature. "The old dying world gives birth to the new one," Bakhtin observes. "Death throes are combined with birth in one indissoluble whole." Downward movement is coupled with upward movement, this is typical of the carnivalesque—clowns that descend into a summersault (the head lowering only to rise again) or taking a pummeling only to rebound rejuvenated. "This process is represented in the images of the material bodily lower stratum; everything descends into the earth and the bodily grave in order to die and to be reborn." With everything from consumption to defecation, from fucking to childbirth, the lower stratum is the site of the base behavior and renewal. The carnivalesque emphasizes images and motifs that signify the flow between consumption and excretion, between death and life.[31] Although Bakhtin only uses the term once, in short what carnivalesque celebrates is the cycle of life.[32]

The cycle of life is a source of laughter in the carnivalesque. *South Park*'s "A Very Crappy Christmas," features Mr. Hankey, a (literal) piece of shit, and his son Cornwallis. Mr. Hankey tries to explain to his boy, who is unsure of his role in life, that all life is interconnected. Cornwallis does not see himself reflected in the media, and laments, "I'm nothing but crap." To which Mr. Hankey explains, "But crap is everything." And at this point Mr. Hankey breaks into song: "Everything that lives on earth poos in some way. And that's how the cycle happens each and every day." Mr. Hankey, still in song, narrates the cycle—how consumption produces excrement, and how excrement in turn fertilizes, and as Mr. Hankey sings, "So that it can spring to life and become food for the land!" Mr. Hankey interrupts the song and explains further, "You see, son? You're not an insignificant part of life! You are life!" Still unsure, Cornwallis asks, "But how can I be that giraffe and blade of grass? Or a human? I don't control what they do." Mr. Hankey asserts, "Just like your heart beats without you thinking about it, so do your giraffes and humans do what they do. Without you even thinking about it! But it is all one life form. It is all you." Cornwallis, enlightened, exclaims, "I think I see now!" And belts out in song again, and suddenly in an unusually deep voice, the pair ending in a duet, "Which becomes the dinner part of humans, and turn back to poo again. That's the circle, the circle of poo."[33] The musical number in literal terms narrates the cyclical nature of life—a core concept of the carnivalesque. Interestingly too, with the father-son relationship, we have the cyclical process as well. And following Cornwallis's epiphany, suddenly his voice deepens signifying maturation—turning, and turning back again. With the carnivalesque conception of time, birth and death, or consumption and excrement (as articulated in the "circle of poo"), are in a constant open-ended process. Death is not an end necessarily, but pregnant with the potential for re-birth.

What the cycle of life also points to is a different conception of time. Bakhtin at a number of moments talks about vertical and horizontal time. With the Enlightenment and the conception of human progress, time is conceived as unfolding on a horizontal axis. The carnivalesque conception of time, on the other hand, is vertical. The Renaissance "destroyed" this vertical conception of the world Bakhtin says. The Renaissance "transferred to one single plane, and the higher and lower stratum became relative. The accent was placed on 'forward' and 'backward.'"[34] The carnivalesque conception of time, and the human experience within it, invites a rhizomatic worldview. Matter is not fixed necessarily, but rather always in motion, and the human subject is caught in a constant state of becoming. And in this open network of flowing matter, there is the potential for laughter in precisely the way that towering intellect Mr. Hankey explains.

And this rhizomatic vision of time also manifests in the spatial field as well. The marketplace in particular is a networked site, where the line between players and spectators dissolves, and there is an egalitarian perspective amongst participants. The public square or the marketplace is one of the central sites of carnivalesque culture. Set in contrast with official discourse—be it official governmental administration, courts, or the Church in all of its manifestations—billingsgate culture is the site of the folk experience, laughter, colloquial speech, slang, vulgarity. Imagine, for instance, eavesdropping on a conversation in a shopping mall food-court. Now imagine stepping into a courtroom. The types of speech will vary dramatically. While in the courtroom one would expect reasoned discourse, expressed in full and coherent sentences, in the shopping mall food-court, on the other hand, one is far more likely to encounter willful violations in grammar and syntax, and colloquial discourse. Set in contrast with the marketplace, the sites of official regimes of authority "the palaces, churches, institutions, and private homes were dominated by hierarchy and etiquette, but in the marketplace a special kind of speech was heard, almost a language of its own, quite unlike the language of Church, palace, courts, and institutions." The speech associated with these places is very different. And while regimes of authority policed "official" discourse, even those of higher rank were not immune to the "push back" from folk discourse. "On feast days, especially during the carnivals, this force broke through every sphere, and even through the Church, as in 'the feast of fools.' The festive marketplace combined many genres and forms, all filled with the same unofficial spirit."[35]

Billingsgate culture, or the marketplace, represented a site of freedom set apart from the rigid structures of official law and language. The marketplace represented a folk-space, which afforded common people a "utopian realm of community, freedom, equality, and abundance."[36] Furthermore, and perhaps most importantly, the marketplace invited common people to drop official pretenses and etiquette, to set aside social standing and deference, and to communicate with one another freely. Billingsgate culture "led to the creation of special forms of marketplace speech and gesture, frank and free, permitting no distance between those who came in contact with each other and liberating from norms of etiquette and decency imposed at other times."[37] This facet of the carnivalesque invited an openness—in effect the line between actor and spectator dissolves, and all become participants. And this alleviation from social constraints is pregnant with laughter.

Conclusion: We Laugh for So Many Reasons . . . But *Reason* Isn't Necessarily One of Them . . .

We do indeed laugh for so many different reasons. We might laugh at an incongruous punchline or laugh at someone's misfortune (consciously or not) insisting upon our superiority, or in some sort of "defensive" gesture to ward off embarrassment, or as a means to negotiate the abject, the non-object, the grotesque body, disgust. We might laugh in social situations to affirm solidarity with present company. Whatever the case might be, laughter almost invariably makes us feel good. It is generally a pleasurable experience. While there is no linguistic "meaning" as such to the vocalization of laughter—the rhythmic exhalation of air, "ha, ha, ha, ha," means nothing—the generally pleasurable experience of laughter is the meaning.

Jure Gantar situates laughter immediately adjacent to the Kantian beautiful. The object that elicits laughter is not innately laughable or funny, but rather laughter says something about the one that laughs. Gantar cites Charles Baudelaire, "The comic and the capacity for laughter are situated in the laugher and by no means in the object of his laughter."[38] The ethics of laughter rests then in the subject that laughs. However, as found in erotic stimulation (as discussed in the previous section), and as already stated above, our bodies can betray us. Laughter has the capacity to reveal things about the subject that laughs, displaying "our innate prejudices or, even more damningly, as a public projection of our desire to distance ourselves from the Other and suppress the difference."[39] While this very well might be true, my intention here is not to police laughter, or to locate the "deeper" political meaning of laughter, but rather to investigate how the cinematic elicits laughter beyond the comical situation (that is, via jokes or the comedic genre).

Again, in the same way that problematic pornographic content might elicit sexual arousal (as discussed in the previous section), against our own best vigilance the cinematic has the capacity to bypass our ethical circuitry, and "speak" directly to the body. What might offend a standard ethical position may still be affecting. There is very much the possibility for cognitive dissonance in the affective realm. For instance, whether we care to admit to it or not, the depiction of a violent sexual encounter might wield the potential to elicit arousal. Pornography, of course, is littered with all manner of ethically fraught encounters (see the discussion of the chikan genre in Chapter 6), and even when a scenario violates ethical norms, and even when we might consciously acknowledge it ("This isn't right!"), our body is potentially deaf to such ethical reasoning. It is too simple to cast aspersions on the producers of material that is ethically fraught, and it is equally as tawdry to dismiss giddy spectators as depraved. Rather, for those of us interested in studying the affective potential of the cinematic what is at stake is revealing the cinematic strategies that are affecting. The point here is that we need not surrender to radical relativism, but rather to honestly engage with how the cinematic affects us. Simply because a referent is ethically fraught does not make it any less deserving of critical attention. In fact, precisely because it is ethically fraught, this obliges us all the more to critically engage with it—to determine how it operates, to identify common tropes, and to apply an appropriate critical paradigm that is capable of negotiating the affective experience. The policing of politically regressive material, if we cannot address how the material makes us feel, will be as successful as the "war on drugs." Simply criminalizing drugs, without understanding why people seek out drugs in the first place, is short-sighted and fails to take the whole picture into account. What follows is an investigation into problematic content that invites laughter.

Notes

1. Aristotle, *On the Parts of the Animals I-IV*, trans. James G. Lennox (Oxford: Oxford University Press, 2004), 69.
2. Robert R. Provine, *Laughter: A Scientific Investigation* (New York: Viking, 2000), 52–3.
3. "Laughter," *RadioLab*, NPR, February 25, 2008, https://www.wnycstudios.org/podcasts/radiolab/episodes/91588-laughter.
4. Sophie Scott, "Why We Laugh," TED video, filmed March 2015, https://www.ted.com/talks/sophie_scott_why_we_laugh?language=en.
5. Provine, 46.
6. Shankar Vedantam explains that this sort of "polite laughter," triggers neural activity that suggests that subjects—when they hear such laughter—are thinking, effectively asking themselves, "What's really going on here?" And the neural response to full-blown belly laughter is altogether different. Shankar Vedantam, Laura Kwerel, and Tara Boyle, "Laughter: The Best Medicine," *Hidden Brain*, NPR, September 28, 2020, https://www.npr.org/2020/09/25/916997530/laughter-the-best-medicine.
7. Julian Hanich, *The Audience Effect: On the Collective Cinema Experience* (Edinburgh: Edinburgh University Press, 2018), 191. Emphasis in original.
8. "Results of the Memorabilia Dump," Scott Zabielski, *Tosh.0*, Comedy Central, Season 4, Episode 10, April 3, 2012, http://www.cc.com/video-clips/udsd0f/tosh-0-andrew-eats---uncensored.
9. Winfried Menninghaus, *Disgust: The Theory and History of a Strong Sensation*, trans. Howard Eiland and Joel Golb (New York: State University of New York Press, 2003), 10–11.
10. Hanich, 196. Emphasis in the original.
11. Sigmund Freud writes,

    > The characterization of jokes which seems best to satisfy Fischer himself is as follows: A joke is a playful judgement. By way of illustration of this, we are given an analogy: just as aesthetic freedom lies in the playful contemplation of things. Elsewhere the aesthetic attitude towards an object is characterized by the condition that we do not ask anything of the object, especially no satisfaction of our serious needs, but content ourselves with the enjoyment of contemplating it. The aesthetic attitude is playful in contrast to work. It might be that from aesthetic freedom there might spring to a sort of judging released from its usual rules and regulations, which, on account of its origin, I will call a "playful judgement," and that in this concept is contained the first determinant, if not the whole formula, that will solve our problem.

    Sigmund Freud, *Jokes and Their Relation to the Unconscious*, ed. James Strachey (New York: Basic Books, 1960), 10.
12. Ibid., 89.

13 Ibid., 179.
14 Ibid., 236.
15 Herbert Spencer, *Essays on Education and Kindred Subjects* (Auckland: Floating Press, 1911), 590.
16 Ibid., 592.
17 Immanuel Kant, *The Critique Of Judgement*, trans. James Creed Meredith (New York: Oxford University Press, 2007), 161. Italics in original.
18 Ibid.
19 Ibid., 162.
20 Ibid., 162–3.
21 Ibid., 163.
22 Henri Bergson, *Laughter: An Essay on the Meaning of the Comic*, trans. Cloudesley Brereton and Fred Rothwell (New York: The Macmillan Company, 1914), 7–8.
23 Ibid., 17.
24 See Pansy Duncan, "Joke work: comic labor and the aesthetics of the awkward," *Comedy Studies* vol. 8, no. 1 (2017): 47.
25 Bergson, 23. Italics in original.
26 Ibid., 24.
27 Ibid., 26.
28 Thomas Hobbes, *Leviathan* (New York: Oxford University Press, 1929), 52.
29 Ibid.
30 Mikhail Bakhtin, *Rabelais and His World*, trans. Helene Iswolsky (Bloomington: Indiana University Press, 1984), 318.
31 Ibid., 435.
32 Bakhtin writes, "In these last moments and in the language of the expiring organism, death becomes a moment of life, receiving an expressive reality and speaking with the tongue of the body itself; thus, death is entirely drawn into the cycle of life." Bakhtin, 359.
33 "A Very Crappy Christmas," Adrien Beard, *South Park*, Season 4, Episode 17, December 20, 2000.
34 Bakhtin, 363–4.
35 Ibid., 154.
36 Ibid., 9.
37 Ibid., 10.
38 Jure Gantar, *The Pleasure of Fools: Essays in the Ethics of Laughter* (Montreal: McGill-Queen's University Press, 2005), 12–13. See Charles Baudelaire, "On the Essence of Laughter, and, in General, on the Comic in the Plastic Arts," in Robert Corrigan ed., *Comedy: Meaning and Form* (San Francisco: Chandler, 1965), 316.
39 Gantar, 13. Julian Hanich makes a case for evaluating the ethics of laughter, noting that sometimes we need to be cognizant of when we have to "walk away" so to speak, especially in the case of collective group laughter. See Hanich, 213.

9

Body Humor
Dick Pics in Cringe Comedy and the Carnivalesque Grotesque Body

Introduction: There's a Time and Place . . .

There are different iterations of body humor, everything from slapstick to gross-out humor. Often with body humor the body is out of control, a body that is excessive, eliciting laughter. Watching people vomit, for example, can be side-splittingly hilarious. Kitao Sakurai's 2020 *Bad Trip* includes a scene with vomiting. Jeff Tremaine, known as a director/producer for the *Jackass* franchise, is one of the producers of *Bad Trip*, and the hallmarks of *Jackass* are evident in Sakurai's film. While *Bad Trip* has a clear narrative through-line—by comparison the *Jackass* television spots and films are by and large episodic with little or no narrative trajectory—what *Bad Trip* does is to stage scenarios in public to elicit "authentic" responses from social actors. And in this sense *Bad Trip* is closer to the *Bad Grandpa* films (a spin-off of the *Jackass* franchise).

In sum, *Bad Trip* is a bromance road movie, where our central protagonist, Chris, enlists his best friend Bud to travel from Florida to New York City in pursuit of his high school crush. At one of their stops along the way, they stop at a huge country western bar called the "Electric Cowboy," complete with a dancefloor, and rows of pool tables. Chris pounds shot after shot and becomes increasingly intoxicated. He climbs to a loft above the bar, yet another drink in hand, and publicly professes his affection for Bud. Predictably, Chris teeters over and falls (approximately 8 feet) into a disguised set piece (obviously, pre-positioned for this stunt, and designed to break his fall). The bar erupts in gasps, Bud helps Chris to his feet, and a woman, stating that she is a nurse, comes to evaluate his condition. With a circle of onlookers, Chris cups his hands to his mouth, and twice ejects a torrent of vomit that spatters the crowd. As part of *Bad Trip*, the scenario is in effect a prank played in good fun—and in fact at the end of the film, as the credits roll, the cast and crew reveal to the social actors the reality of the situation, and everyone has a good laugh. There are numerous other examples of vomiting that invite laughter: the YouTube video, "Man Drinks Ipecac,"[1] a scene in *Family Guy* that is premised on that same YouTube video,[2] the Lardass sequence in *Stand by Me* (Rob Reiner, 1986), the Mr. Creosote scene in *Monty Python's The Meaning of Life* (Terry Jones and Terry Gilliam, 1983), numerous SNL skits, and so on.[3] In these instances, laughter is elicited from the vomiting body—a body that convulses, that is out of control, that leaks.

There are also instances in cringe comedy, where the cringe stems from the carnivalesque presentation of bodies—in addition to being out of control, bodies might also be out of place and/or temporally misaligned. In some instances of cringe comedy, we find that dicks (and/or penile emissions) are in the "wrong place" and "wrong time"—think, for instance, of Bobby and Peter Farrelly's 1998 film *There's Something About Mary* and the painful zipper incident, or the "Is that hair gel?" moment. Or the apple pie in Paul and Chris Weitz's 1999 film *American Pie*. As for the latter, it is not simply that Jim attempts to fuck an apple pie, which on its own might be cringy, but the fact that his father catches him in the act that makes for the intense "cringy-ness" of the scene. The laughter emerges from the "wrong place" and "wrong time." While the scene is "out of place" for any number of different reasons, not least of which is that the euphemistic "pie"—slang for pussy—is taken literally, thus Jim's dick is in the "wrong place," but of course that the event is also "mis-timed" wherein Jim's father interrupts a private moment of intimacy.

The present chapter focuses on the instances where the grotesque body (a body that is excessive), or the inopportune exhibition of dicks in cringe comedy elicits laughter. As for the latter, beyond this literal meaning of dick pics, I also include in my discussion here narratives that feature penises (or penile emissions). Regardless, whether the literal or figural conception of the dick pic, in all cases, laughter might be elicited from dicks in the wrong place at the wrong time. In either case, whether discussing the carnivalesque and the grotesque body, or dick pics in cringe comedy, all of these have a relationship with time and place. While the carnivalesque makes temporal and spatial allowances for the exhibition of the grotesque body, cringe comedy, on the other hand, is premised on the violation of social norms governing the time and place for dicks to appear.

Cringe Comedy: Dick Pics

Cringe comedy is based on an emotional response—typically embarrassment. But like the melodramatic, which couples emotional pathos with tears, cringe comedy often elicits a reflexive bodily response such as: averting one's eyes, a furrowed brow, a guttural groan, hands thrown up in front of the eyes or mouth, a grimace with clenched teeth, or perhaps a mouth thrown agape. Cringe comedy more often than not stems from (social) meaning—based upon some understanding that an individual has committed some sort of social *faux pas* or responds awkwardly to some social situation. Awkwardness, to paraphrase Jason Middleton's conceptualization of it in his *Documentary's Awkward Turn*, is the rupture of smooth social discourse, where divergent perceptions of the world come into full focus.[4] To this we might add a sense of time, where these differing perceptions come into view at inopportune moments. The prefix of the term "awkward," "awk," most likely stems from the Swedish for "turned the wrong way, back foremost."[5] The suffix refers to movement. Thus, a turned around, or mixed-up movement. And in the Bergsonian conception of laughter (as discussed in the previous chapter), which emerges from the "inflexibility" of a social actor, we might see how awkwardness—be it actual physical movement, or in a more figurative sense having to do with a lack of social grace—is ripe for Bergsonian laughter.

Pansy Duncan applies Bergson's principle to cringe comedy—television programs like *The Office,* and *Curb Your Enthusiasm* being particularly emblematic. The male leads in these programs—in *The Office* David Brent (in the British version) and Michael Scott (in the American version), and Larry David in *Curb*—often fail to read social cues and lack a degree of social "flexibility" that ultimately leads to laughable and cringy conflicts. (In the following chapter, the inflexibility of these cringy characters is compared to Charles Stoker in Chan-wook Park's 2013 dramatic thriller *Stoker*.) In *The Office* "awkwardness arises from" David and Michael's "strenuous yet incompetent efforts at playfulness." Larry, on the other hand, "is characterized by his all-too literal adherence to a series of ethical and social edicts." Larry's inflexibility in navigating the social landscape leads him to believe, as Pansy Duncan summarizes, "that drycleaners should always return garments; that public property should not, under any circumstances, be defaced; that no true friend would steal shrimp from another's take-out container; and that if someone says they do not want a birthday present, they may be readily taken at their word."[6] With *The Office* and *Curb Your Enthusiasm*, laughter is born out of the characters' mechanical responses to situations that require nuance and social grace—of which David, Michael, and Larry have very little, or none at all. (There are female versions of this brand of cringe comedy, see for example Rebecca Wanzo's discussion of the HBO series *Girls* and the web-series *The Mis-Adventures of Awkward Black Girl.*[7])

Again, these are all related to social meaning, and thus are not purely affective experiences. Our understanding of the situation, like tears accompanying the emotional encounters in melodrama, is complemented by an affective bodily response. Social situations demand some degree of social grace, and an appreciation of the social context. A dick pic might actually be perfectly acceptable if it circulates in "proper" erotic economies (for example, certain queer social networks, solicited private exchanges). A dick pic, outside these sanctioned venues (just like the strictures of the carnivalesque), violates social mores and has the potential to elicit cringy laughter. As I use the term here "dick pics" includes the colloquial usage of it—selfies featuring an individual's (often erect) penis, which is then sent to someone via messaging or some sort of social media app—but also, the appearance of penises (or penile emissions) in the course of a narrative film. In this latter case, just as dick pics sent via messaging or social media apps, dicks in cringe comedies appear unwelcomed, at an inopportune moment; they are out of place, they tear asunder the divide between public and private space, between the everyday and the erotic.

Regarding dick pics sent via text messaging or some social media app, these are often delivered with some misguided amorous intent. Dick pics, as Susanna Paasonen and her co-authors note, serve "as an online variation of cat calling: in both instances, the men involved may frame their actions as a compliment taking the form of sexual interest, yet these nevertheless fail to be recognized as such."[8] The assumption here is that dick pics circulate in a normative heterosexual economy, where men (or adolescent boys) send women (or adolescent girls) dick pics. As already inferred, this leaves aside how dick pics circulate in male-to-male queer cyber-cultures, and dick pics that might in fact be solicited between consenting parties.[9] Paasonen and her co-authors observe that "desired dick pics may smoothly facilitate intimate exchanges and accelerate the reverbs of sexual desire in all kinds of contexts." Paasonen and her colleagues encourage us to consider the social contexts within which dick pics circulate, rather than assuming that the dick pic is a "simple exercise of misogynist energy." They encourage us to reframe the dick pic as "a complex, multivalent object that is not so readily defined."[10]

The dick pic as a means to facilitate an intimate encounter is found in Sam Levinson's HBO series *Euphoria* (2019–), which actually has a remarkable number of instances with full frontal male nudity for a televised series. The primary character, Rue, is a young woman in high school, who struggles with substance abuse issues. Rue's best friend, Jules, is a young man who presents and identifies as a young woman.[11] In the episode, "Made You Look," Jules has been texting with a young man laying the foundation for a "real life" encounter and a potential intimate relationship.¹² As the online relationship develops, eventually, Jules's cyber-interlocutor sends a dick pic. Jules shares the dick pic with Rue at the school cafeteria, but Rue is skeptical of its veracity observing that there is nothing in the picture to compare to scale. Jules protests, "This is an objectively big dick!" With this Levinson cuts to a classroom, where Rue breaks the fourth wall and addresses us directly. At the front of the class with a pointer, Rue offers a semiotic lesson on dick pics, visually aided by an old-school slide-projector slideshow. Rue breaks down dick pics into two basic categories: solicited and unsolicited. The former she insists only makes up 1% of all dick pics sent. Rue continues to inform us, that within that 1% of dick pics there are three distinct categories: "terrifying," "horrifying," and "acceptable." Before anyone might stop to ask her, Rue, recognizes that the difference between "terrifying" and "horrifying" might seem virtually indistinguishable, but she insists that while "terrifying" dick pics might alter us to basic hygiene issues, "horrifying," on the other hand—cutting to the ramblings of Charles Manson—points to, "a life-or-death situation." Rue walks us through a series of dick pics labeling them either terrifying or horrifying. Levinson cuts back to the cafeteria and to the objective narrative diegesis, Jules having pulled up another dick pic Rue observes, "Wow. Okay. His dick is the size of an Evian bottle." Rue nods her head, takes a beat and adds, "Well, the lighting is nice. His room looks clean. Looks well groomed." "Right!" Jules agrees. "Yeah," Rue confirms, "I am beginning to understand the appeal." The dick pic, in the right time and place, might actually invite erotic interest.

While the dick pics discussed in *Euphoria* constitute that very slender percentage of solicited exchanges, in most instances dick pics arrive uninvited and unwelcomed. Some women have responded to this phenomenon in humorous ways—as Jessica Ringrose and Emilie Lawrence summarize, aiming to "shed light on sexism through exposing and criticising them [that is, dick pics] via satire."¹³ In response to the phenomena of dick pics (and other forms of online sexual harassment), some feminists have taken aim

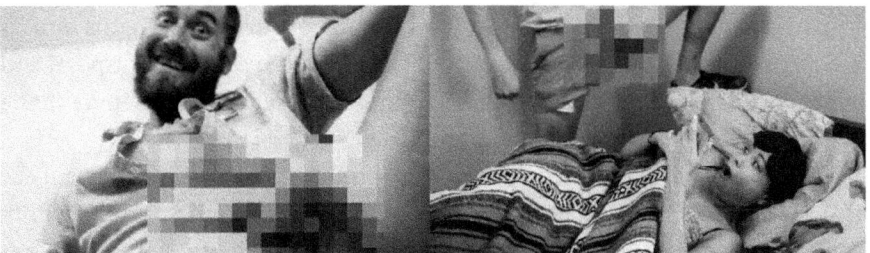

Figure 9.1 *What if men harassed women IRL like they do online?* (Miranda King, 2016)

at dick pic senders, and/or have reoriented dick pics and changed their affective charge. For example, in a short satirical video, *What if men harassed women IRL [in real life] like they do online?* (Miranda King, 2016), produced by ByeFelipe, men appear unceremoniously and at inopportune moments slinging their junk in close proximity to women on their computers or phones.[14] In one instance, a woman just waking up to check her phone, finds a man hovering above her with his penis dangling inches from her face. Another woman out for a run, is accosted on the street by a man in a black trench coat who exposes himself—finding a police officer, the woman is summarily dismissed and blamed for the harassment because of her attire. "Such approaches draw attention to the disconnect between digital and offline social norms, inviting a recognition of such behaviour as harassment."[15]

Whitney Bell created an exhibition entitled, "I didn't ask for this: A lifetime of dick pics," by printing out over 200 dick pics sent to her and other women. The exhibition space was modeled after Bell's own apartment, demonstrating how pervasive and intrusive dick pics can be, suggesting that, "Even when she's alone, in the privacy of her own home, she's not safe."[16] Bell explains that, "It all sort of began with a really beautiful dick shadow picture I was sent by a guy I was seeing. I sent it to one of my friends who said, 'That picture is so beautiful it should be in a museum.' That's when I thought of having a gallery of dick pics."[17] However, unsolicited dick pics are something different altogether. "I love a good dick," Bell explains. "I just don't love harassment."[18]

Madeline Holden, a self-identified lesbian, runs http://critiquemydickpic.tumblr.com/ where she genuinely critiques dick pics, commenting on things like props, lighting, composition (echoing what is found in Rue's critique of the dick pics sent to Jules in *Euphoria*). "Because people send in their images for critique that become spaces for in-depth aesthetic and humorous discussion," Ringrose and Lawrence contend that, Holden's critiques open, "an entirely new relationship to the penis by reorienting it and leaving space for many diverse readings of the dick pic." The authors add, "Beyond simply rejection or parody of dick pics, by turning the penis into an object of complex humorous debate and analysis, the meaning, import, and effect of dick pics are transformed—a significant political manoeuvre made possible through feminist digital mediation."[19]

Bell suggests that it is male privilege, and an exercising of power (not really sexual interest) that license men to send dick pics. And I think that Bell is correct, but I might add that dick pics are often stupidly conceived (consciously or not) as a form of potlatch. Potlatch being a form of aggressive gift giving, where the recipient is positioned as a debtor relative to the giver. Georges Bataille discusses this in relation to Native American practices, where disputes, rivalries, even wars might be resolved through potlatch. No different from commerce, potlatch, as Bataille explains, is "a means of circulating wealth, but it excludes bargaining. More often than not it is the solemn giving of considerable riches," Bataille explains, and as with some Native American groups a chief might offer a gift to "his rival for the purpose of humiliating, challenging and obligating" the receiving party. Upon receipt of the gift, "The recipient has to erase the humiliation and take up the challenge." The recipient is thus socially obligated to return the gesture, and is expected, "a short time later, by means of a new potlatch, [to offer a] more generous [gift] than the first." The recipient is obliged to "pay back with interest."[20] And this is precisely how men often conceive of dick pics.

There is an implicit expectation of reciprocity—that the female recipient will return the gesture in kind, and (although wildly outlandish) even reciprocate it with a real-world sexual encounter. The patently transactional (male) conception of sending dick pics, without an ounce of social grace, invites us to view these encounters through a Bergsonian lens. Dick pic senders are Larry Davids: they take an "all-too literal adherence" to the implied logic of potlatch, having offered a gift, they demand something back in return. Without diminishing the aggressive nature of dick pics, and the potential for the receiver to take the "gift" as a form of sexual harassment, nonetheless, the crackpot transactional stance, makes the dick pic sender an object of laughter. The dick pic sender in their endeavor to engage a party in potlatch, as Murray Davis observes in relation to "pick-up" schemes, "becomes too 'mechanical,'" sounding a Bergsonian tone, "too deaf to the feedback cues that tell a person how to synchronize his rhythm with her partner's."[21] Bergson's emphasis on flexibility, on an individual's capacity to "read a room," to properly understand the social context and to function accordingly, laughter serves as a social corrective.[22] With cringe comedy, and real-world dick pics, our better angels want to scream out, to extricate the (male) individual from some monumental lapse of social grace, but stubborn mechanical inclinations (which govern poor decisions) are fodder for laughter, especially in cringe comedy.[23]

The Netflix animated series *Big Mouth*, like *Euphoria*, also includes an instance of adolescent sexting, and the implicit potlatch associated with it. The program features middle-school children caught in the midst of puberty. The characters are shadowed by their respective "hormone monster," often counseling the youngsters, though sometimes with the most ill-advised plot. In the episode, "How to Have an Orgasm," Cherry, Andrew's "kissing-cousin," sends an image of her cleavage to the horny adolescent boy. Maurice, Andrew's hormone monster, insists that he reciprocate with a dick pic. Maurice pulls out the *Etdickquette Manual* and reads from it, "Here we go, cleavage pic gets [taking a beat] a dick pic in return." Andrew still waivers, and Maurice clarifies, "Well, it does say, if there's no nip, an abs pic will suffice." But Andrew knows that his physique is not exactly his best asset. After several of his own attempts, it becomes clear that Andrew cannot get a flattering image. Maurice steps in, and in the guise of a smarmy moustached pornographic photographer, conducts a photoshoot. The pair review their work and select an image to send. After sending the dick pic, Andrew frets over the delayed response from his cousin, but as they are waiting Andrew's father is heard from downstairs, "Barbara, why'd you upload all these pictures of pink mushrooms?" As it turns out, the photos were all sent to the family's shared cloud service. Andrew's parents confront Andrew, "You pervert! You took pictures of your thing?!" Andrew's father exclaims. Andrew naturally attempts to deny it. The exchange is interrupted when Cherry responds to Andrew's text. "You sent this filth to your cousin?!" Andrew's infuriated father asks. At first Andrew responds, "No," but then his curiosity gets the better of him, "What did she say?" To which Andrew's mother responds, "Andrew, are you trying to kill me?" The appearance of a dick pic in a familial (or work, or some other social) setting can add to the intensity of the cringe-factor.[24] The division between erotic milieus and "proper" social contexts—domestic, familial, work, school, and/or everyday social milieus—are generally intended to remain clear and distinct.

While the exchange between Cherry and Andrew is consensual, the appearance of dick pics on the family-shared cloud network is inopportune. Though dated and flawed in numerous ways, Murray Davis's book *Smut* nonetheless offers a productive means of speaking about time and place relative to sexuality. Davis characterizes his discussion of sexual relations as a "sexual phenomenology." Davis draws upon Alfred Schutz's distinction between the everyday life-world and a secondary "other-worldly" dimension of "dreams, fantasies, and science."[25] Davis following Schutz's example, divides "the experience of the world generated by our ordinary round of life as 'everyday reality,'" set in contrast with "our actual or potential sexual activities as 'erotic reality.'"[26] Generally speaking, as already suggested above, these different modes of reality are intended to remain separate and distinct, and the instances where these modes of reality trespass upon one another might elicit any range of emotions. If erotic reality trespasses upon everyday reality this might invite anything from disgust to embarrassment, and in the converse situation where the everyday invades erotic reality this has the potential to "spoil the mood." To maintain social norms and the individual social mores that govern interpersonal relations, as Davis observes, "erotic reality and everyday reality must each be whole and self-contained."[27] Moreover, it is imperative that in erotic reality individuals "must be synchronized more closely than everyday time." Davis continues, "Each participant must continually try to harmonize his or her personal sexual rhythm with the partner's, during both the active [erotic] periods and their interludes."[28] Notions of space change as well with erotic reality, where the intensity of the erotic moment dramatically narrows one's focus and attention to the wider world. "The boundaries of consciousness contract to the room, bed, and body; whatever lies outside these concentric spatial zones of awareness— Where is my husband now? Is the door locked?—cease to be matters of concern."[29]

Davis wrote *Smut* well before the days of the Internet, let alone cellphones, and communication via social media platforms. Nevertheless, one can quickly discern the significance for the bifurcation of everyday reality and erotic reality, and how the cellphone and social media apps might facilitate the all-too-easy intrusion of one mode of reality upon another. Davis observes that the shift from everyday reality to erotic reality is generally gradual. And an unsolicited dick pic would uniformly transgress the socially measured transition—the move between everyday reality and erotic reality requires a social negotiation, typically premised on linguistic and nonlinguistic cues, and following culturally and historically established patterns of behavior. Davis observes that "it comes as a shock for someone to experience the sudden intrusion of other people's sex organs into his or her visual field. The abrupt appearance of the chaotic genitals . . . produces a reaction that could be called 'genital shock.'"[30] The unsolicited dick pic, more often than not, elicits genital shock precisely because of the intrusion upon everyday reality. Furthermore, the abrupt shift from an exchange between "socialized bodies," to "the naked unsocialized body" can be startling and upsetting.[31] The intensity of the shock likely correlates to the spatial context in which a dick pic is received. At work, school, the familial setting (e.g., at the dinner table), out in public (e.g., on public transportation) a dick pic might elicit intense genital shock, on the other hand, in the privacy of one's own space (e.g., a bedroom, behind closed doors), while still potentially shocking, it nonetheless might elicit a different degree of shock. Time could play a role as well, a dick pic received first thing in the morning, might not elicit the same response in the evening.[32]

Just briefly to return to Spike Lee's 2002 film *25th Hour*, discussed at length in Chapter 4, Monty's haranguing hate-filled diatribe might find affinities with the way that laughter might turn away an inopportune appearance of a dick. In the long laundry list of referents that elicit Monty's abject ire is the appearance of dicks in public spaces including public access television. Monty rants, "Fuck the Chelsea Boys with their waxed chests and pumped-up biceps, going down on each other in my parks and on my piers; jiggling their dicks on my Channel 35!" Monty in his musicalized repetition (each stanza beginning with "fuck") throws a lattice work around the abject referent, allowing suffering to tumble into music (or poeticized speech), and at least for the time being, cast away, sublimated. Laughter serves a similar function, as a defensive gesture to turn away the offending dick and the genital shock that it might elicit.

Receiving an unsolicited dick pic is liable to engender an immediate visceral response. The timing and the context could very well determine how the dick pic is affectively charged. Additionally, the tactile nature of smartphones, for instance, bring—though mediated via a screen and digital coding—a dick into physical proximity of the receiver, especially when received in a space that is not private. And thus, we have anecdotal accounts of individuals, especially women, throwing their phone upon receipt of a dick pic, as if the phone itself was the offending object.[33] In a qualitative study of adolescent sexting, one young female participant in the study noted that there are "temporal limits of consent in relation to sexting and indicates that the lack of consent is part of what makes the receiving of unsolicited dick pics feel intrusive and unpleasant."[34] In the context of an unsolicited dick pic, disgust is a likely response, but this might be quickly followed with laughter as a way to resolve that repulsion. (The qualitative study seems to confirm this, as participants reflect on issues related to sexting, and dick pics specifically, and after relating experiences the participants often break out in laughter.) Laughter can serve as a means of exorcizing disgust (or displeasure), to push it out, from deep within the body to expunge, to purge the body of some abject presence.[35] Upon being startled, an individual might let out a shriek, or some other kind of utterance and reflexive bodily response (often miming some kind of defensive gesture—holding a phone with a fully extended arm or turning the phone screen away from the eyes), but then quickly follow it with laughter.

There are affinities between laughter and screams. Julian Hanich reminds us, "it is not the same if people scream out loud or laugh about something, but both reactions have in common that they are explosive, expansive, eruptive responses." Hanich adds that "[t]his is also one of the reasons why horror and humor in the splatter film, as well as disgust and humor in the gross-out comedy, go together so well."[36] We very well might add cringe comedy and the inopportune emergence of a dick, which might at first elicit a recoiling quickly followed by a laugh to Hanich's list. Whether received in a "proper" erotic context, or in an indecorous social context, a dick pic has the potential to elicit an affective experience. Susanna Paasonen and her co-authors agree, "Particularly where women are concerned, unsolicited dick pics are predominantly understood as ruptures in networked communication that make expected forms of sociability come to a halt and be recalibrated, often in highly antagonistic ways."[37]

Although not featuring proper dick pics as such, Mikkel Nørgaard's 2010 film *Klown* illustrates how the sudden emergence of a dick might elicit a strong cringy charge. *Klown* could never have been made in the United States, because at the center of the plot is a young boy, Bo, and his small penis.[38] The focus of the narrative is on Frank and Casper. The film is premised on a Danish television series by the same name (*Klovn* in the Danish). The television series ran for six seasons (2005–2018). In Zach Baron's *New York Times* review of the film, he aptly compares the Danish series to Larry David's *Curb Your Enthusiasm*.[39] Frank Hvam and Casper Christensen, the creators and stars of the popular Danish series, transform bad choices into an art—bad choices being fertile ground for cringe humor. When the creative team behind the television series began, they made a list of twenty taboo subjects, which served as a driving theme for an episode, and subsequently pursued with all the gusto and buffoonish fervency of chimps in heat. Themes included, as Hvam explained, "from racial issues to cannibalism to pedophilia to cancer, Down syndrome, all kinds of terrible things." The creative team, though, never felt capable of handling a child in the series, "We thought it would be too brutal to bring in a child into our universe." As they matured (as comedic storytellers) they imagined themselves capable of moving to the big-screen and to incorporate a child into one of their misadventures, as Hvam explains, "without it all exploding."[40]

In the film version, Frank has knocked-up his girlfriend, Mia, but he has thus far proved himself less than capable of being a father. In an effort to prove his paternal potential, Frank takes his girlfriend's 12-year-old nephew, Bo, on a previously planned canoe trip. Or, more accurately, it is not so much that he "takes Bo along," but rather he effectively abducts the near-adolescent boy. The canoe trip, though, was originally intended to be an adults-only buddy-adventure, as Casper phrases it, "Tour de Pussy." Bo is emasculated (before he is even properly a man), he is ridiculed for having a small dick, and pees sitting down, to which Frank asks, "What are you?

A girl?" Frank, Casper, and Bo's dicks all make inopportune appearances, and are fuel for cringy laughter.

Just to recount some of their misadventures: after seeking shelter at a woman's country home, following a capsizing, Casper with his classic Nordic-good-looks seduces their host. While all three are in bed, Casper and their host engage in sex, while Frank desperately tries to ignore them, but Casper coerces Frank into the action who (upon Casper's insistence) sticks his finger into their host's ass. Casper is thrilled to have experienced a threesome (and specifically the porn-fantasy of DP), but their host is not amused in the morning, and asks the crew to leave. Frank discovers Casper—who presents as the suave womanizer, deeply invested in his own heteronormative veneer—in a compromised position: fucked by a male high school teacher (who is chaperoning a group of students on an outdoor school trip). These are just some of their misadventures, and of course Mia and Casper's partners find out when Bo runs away after he overhears Frank and Casper ridiculing the boy for his small dick. Although Frank and Casper look for the boy, they have been drinking and are stoned out of their minds. Bo ends up nearly drowning in a lake and is taken to a hospital. Mia and Casper's partners soon discover the truth of some of their misadventures, but Frank ends up taking the fall: sentenced to six months in jail (for a robbery at gunpoint—to get a toy car for Bo), Mia breaks up with Frank, and Frank takes responsibility for the threesome letting Casper off the hook.

At the end of the film, it is assumed that all is resolved: Frank is out of jail and reconciled with his girlfriend, Bo is on the road to becoming a man, he pees standing up, and his dick has grown in the intervening time. At Bo's confirmation party, the boy, reflecting fondly on the misadventure, presents a slideshow on his computer. Bo only has a few pictures to share, but luckily Casper has left his phone with Frank. (Casper is off philandering with a woman, leaving his phone with Frank so that his wife cannot readily locate him.) Casper's photos present himself, Frank, and another buddy in the most compromising positions: Casper at a high-end brothel posing with nude prostitutes, Casper fucking a prostitute, Casper giving the male high school teacher head, Frank pulling at and posing with Bo's small penis. The slideshow scene elicits a significant cringe. While the pictures of Bo's penis were intended to blackmail the boy to keep him quiet about Frank and Casper's bad behavior, the other images were likely intended as trophies—documenting Casper's various sexual conquests. And in the context of bragging with friends, or kept as private mementos, most of these images—perhaps save the pictures featuring Bo's penis—would not elicit a cringe. But in the context of a confirmation party, with polite company, with

Casper and Frank's life-partners present (exposing their infidelity to family and friends), the "cringy-ness" is nearly overwhelming. The experience of watching the slideshow, cut with the shocked expression of the guests, invites us to join in the affective cringe.

Within the diegetic narrative, in the context of Bo's confirmation party no less, there is "cringy-ness." But there is also an extra-diegetic cringy-ness too, as a spectator, having assumed that the worst has come to pass, and Frank in particular has been punished for his misdeeds, we are affected all the more by the sudden reemergence of dicks in the closing moments of the film—a sudden return of the repressed, or genital shock. And it should come as no surprise that the inopportune return of Frank, Casper, and Bo's dicks come via a phone. *Klown*'s cinematic narrative, and its sudden and inopportune appearance of dicks, echoes the sudden appearance of an unsolicited dick pic on your phone. And just like the appearance of unsolicited dick pics—revulsion, a throwing away of the phone, or turning of the screen with an outstretched arm—we too might reflexively respond to the closing moments of the film with revulsion, we might shrink, contort our bodies, avert our eyes, groan, or utter a "tisk," but in the end we are also inclined to laugh. This laugh though, might not be characterized as a "humorous laugh" as such, but a defensive laugh—a reflexive gesture to push the offending referent away.

As I stated at the outset, cringe comedy is undoubtedly premised on an emotional response—one has to understand social decorum to appreciate the violation committed. But it is the presence of the dick—the unsocialized naked body intruding upon a social context—that amplifies the affective charge. This is analogous to the melodramatic genre. Recall, for example, the discussion of Douglas Sirk's 1959 film *Imitation of Life* in a previous chapter, where Sarah Jane arrives at her mother's funeral. The narrative content in itself is sad, but it is Mahalia Jackson's performance of her 1959 spiritual, "Trouble of the World," which greatly enhances the affective charge of the scene. In the instances of cringe comedy cited above, when dicks make their inopportune appearance it greatly intensifies the affective experience.

"Dick pics are ambiguous and malleable in their uses and meanings while simultaneously remaining literal, obvious, and fixed in that which they represent," Paasonen and her co-authors observe. "This paradoxical ambiguous literalness is key to the frictions involved in the accumulation and interpretation of dick pics in social media."[41] The literalness of the dick, and especially an exposed dick in a social context (outside of erotic circulation), is not simply sophomoric, but it also invites carnivalesque laughter. Wherever we find laughter and cursing, "particularly in a familiar environment, . . . speech is filled with bodily images," Mikhail Bakhtin observes. "The body copulates, defecates, overeats," and our colloquial "speech is flooded with genitals, bellies, defecations, urine, disease, noses, mouths, and dismembered parts."[42] But even the carnivalesque in its celebration of the genitals and the lower stratums has limits. During carnival in New Orleans, women in particular are invited to expose themselves in exchange for beads, which outside the context of Mardi Gras would be socially inappropriate. Thus, within a particular context public nakedness might well be acceptable. Cringe comedy generates laughter more often than not because a character violates some social norm, and as discussed above, the appearance of dicks outside the economy of an intimate erotic exchange might invite laughter. Often within cringe comedy we want to shout out to the character, "Stop! You are about to do something incredibly stupid." Furthermore, there is the potential encounter with cringy material, which might elicit a whole range of other reflexive responses—a lurching backward, an aversion of the eyes, an audible groan. In either case though—whether it is processed as disgusting, even arousing, or humorous—laughter might be a common response to a dick pic. There is a time and place for everything. The affective response to dick pics—be that disgust, "cringy-ness," laughter, or some combination of these things—violates this simple "time and place" social principle. The violation of time and place shares affinities with the carnivalesque, which is precisely about mapping the terrain and temporal moment when social mores are set aside. In the following section, I will discuss the carnivalesque allowances made on platforms such as YouTube, and television programs such as *Tosh.0*.

The Grotesque Body and Carnivalesque Laughter: *Tosh.0* and Ricky Berwick's YouTube Channel

The affective charge of cringe comedy and specifically dick pics stems from dicks being in the wrong time and place, while the carnivalesque is a celebration of transgressions—particularly as it relates to the lower stratums—within a specific time and place. And it is precisely the time and place of the carnivalesque that prompted Umberto Eco's critique, and the throwing of a wet blanket over the Bakhtinian conception of the carnivalesque—which was something of a "golden child" in the 1980s and 1990s.[43] Celebrated by scholars as liberating and revolutionary, Eco reminds us that the carnival was a state-sanctioned activity and viewed from a particular perspective seen as a mechanism of control—allowing common folk to "blow-off steam" and actually reinforce the established social order and regimes of power. The carnival was always authorized, and thus never truly transgressive. "If the ancient, religious carnival was limited in time, the modern mass-carnival is limited in space: it is reserved for certain places [for example, Las Vegas], certain streets, or framed by the television screen."[44] Television at the time Eco was writing served as a site of carnivalesque pleasures, but more than ever in the contemporary moment social networking platforms, including YouTube or TikTok, are the sites of billingsgate culture, the site where transgressive behavior is often showcased. Eco is correct, that there is nothing "revolutionary" in the carnivalesque, and Eco would just assume to rain on the carnivalesque parade (so to speak), but as I (and my then co-author, Jonathan Knapp) have stated elsewhere, "by most measures, laughter feels good, and we would not presume to rob the viewing body of that pleasure."[45]

We find the coalescence of the televisual and social media in the Comedy Central program, *Tosh.0* (2009–2020). Hosted by Daniel Tosh, the program showcases videos from the Internet, and is emblematic of the carnivalesque in the televisual medium.[46] ABC's *America's Funniest Home Videos* (1989–) is a clear predecessor to *Tosh.0*, however, while *AFV* is known for its wholesome family-friendly fun, the Comedy Central program sets itself apart by being willfully crass. The *Tosh.0* program in effect curates videos often featuring epic fails, people simply doing dumb shit, people fighting, or saying the most ridiculous things. Before a live studio audience, Tosh then—miming what happens in YouTube comments—offers snarky commentary. In some instances, Tosh will echo the activities found in the selected video clip in a short skit (often involving his writing staff), but recontextualized in some fashion. In an occasional recurring segment, "Is It Racist?" Tosh will feature a video that often rehearses racial stereotypes, and then either has a panel of people representing different racial groups or enlists his live audience to determine if something is racist or not. Each episode is anchored either with a "CeWEBrity Profile," or a "Web Redemption" segment, where Tosh invites individuals featured in a video to "redeem" themselves and reenact in some fashion the activity found in the video, though often with a more heroic, positive, or happy ending.

Cognitive neuroscientist Sophie Scott in a TED Talk, "Why We Laugh," unintentionally, parrots the format of the *Tosh.0* program. Scott underlines the social function of laughter, as a way for humans to enter an exchange with one another through extra-linguistic cues, in effect to say, "I get you." At about three-quarters through her talk, Scott shares a video where a German man (only dressed in Speedo swimming trunks) prepares to jump into a swimming pool that is iced over. The man jumps, cannonball butt first, but the ice is thicker than anticipated and the man lands with a hard audible thud, not so much as a crack is made in the ice. The man's friends recording the stunt burst into laughter, the cameraperson doubles over momentarily, and the TED audience upon the initial impact gives a loud collective, "Oh!" immediately followed by laughter. Scott offers her reflection, "The thing I really like about that is it's all very serious until he jumps onto the ice, and as soon as he doesn't go through the ice—but also there isn't blood and bone everywhere—his friends start laughing." But Scott then speculates that if in fact the man got hurt, that "we wouldn't enjoy watching that. That would be stressful. Or if he was running around with a visibly broken leg laughing, and his friends are going, 'Heinrich, I think we need to go to the hospital now,' that also wouldn't be funny." Scott then attributes social meaning to the laughter, "The fact that the laughter works, it gets him from a painful, embarrassing, difficult situation, into a funny situation, into what we're actually enjoying there."[47]

While I concur with Scott's general contextualization, with respect to the social function of laughter, where Scott is incorrect, though, is her assumption that watching someone get hurt would preclude laughter. There are numerous examples of videos featured on *Tosh.0* that feature individuals enduring grievous bodily harm: visibly broken limbs, dislocated joints, teeth knocked out, even dying. The *Tosh.0* program clearly demonstrates, despite our better angels, that watching people get hurt, humiliated, or otherwise compromised can be a source of laughter. In his stand-up routine *Happy Thoughts*, which aired in 2011, Tosh asks at one point, "My first thought [when learning a person was decapitated by a roller coaster] was 'How am I going to make this funny for everyone?'"[48] And closer to the video that Scott presents, just to offer one example, *Tosh.0* features a Web Redemption episode entitled, "Roof Jump," where two young women, Nichole, and another (unnamed) young woman jump off a roof into a pool.[49] Nichole, however, in her hesitant timidity falls short of the pool, and when she hits the pavement an audible crack is heard having broken both of her feet (both her heel bones shattered). In the Web Redemption we learn that because of a lack of insurance, Nichole never had corrective surgery to restore the full use of her feet. (The American health system at its best!) The episode is not as laugh out loud funny as some other episodes, but it rebuts Scott's insistence that if Heinrich were hurt "that . . . wouldn't be funny"—watching people get hurt, even sustaining injuries with life-long consequences, can in fact invite laughter. In Nichole's web redemption, which is fully fabricated, she jumps out of a window, several floors up, and this time over-shoots the pool, her legs tangle unnaturally and a small pool of blood appears around her head.

Daniel Tosh, in his stand-up routine, and with his television series *Tosh.0* courts controversy. Some critics have simply dismissed his comedy as empty shock, accusing him of crossing ethical lines.[50] Tosh regularly traffics in racial and ethnic stereotypes, and homophobic and misogynistic tropes. It is worth noting that Tosh codes himself as queer and invites the spectator (and show participants) to speculate about his sexuality. Tosh though never clarifies, and leaves things intentionally ambiguous. That all said, Tosh flouts the norms that are generally policed by self-appointed deputies of politically correct speech/thinking. Some scholars, though, like Jared Champion, have positioned Tosh as potentially progressive for his unmasking of some of the ugliest facets of the human experience (especially in American culture—though videos come from around the globe).

The *Tosh.0* program certainly entertains the "superiority theory" of laughter (discussed in the introduction to this section on laughter). Phenomenologist Graham Harman effectively argues for the "incongruity theory" of laughter, and against the "superiority theory." And in so doing, Harman has diagnosed me, and millions of others as sociopaths. Taking a cue from Bergson's discourse on laughter, Harman argues (like Scott) that watching some mishap befall an individual might elicit laughter within limits. If the individual endured severe injury this would dampen any potential for laughter, unless of course, as Harman comments, you happen to be a "stone-hearted sadist with limitless capacity for enjoying the destruction of others. But most of us are sufficiently sympathetic to our fellow humans that the situation has to be harmless enough to grant us a sort of permission to laugh." Harman continues to argue that an innocent stumbling might elicit laughter, so long as the individual "is not grotesquely injured in the process." Harman qualifies his position, noting that if the individual is not likable, pompous perhaps, then this might give us license to laugh as "an aspect of justice," or if the situation creates such a stark contrast between the individual, their station, and the calamity that befalls them that we are invited to laugh. If the individual, Harman adds, were our enemy we might be inclined to laugh at them, even if they endured some injury. "But only a sociopath would laugh if the tripping man were actually a child, a severely handicapped person, one's own grandfather, someone known to be terribly down on his luck, or a star athlete toasted throughout the nation." The referent that invites us to laugh, Harman insists, "must be implicitly contemptible, beneath our station in the world in some respect."[51]

By Harman's measure I am clearly a sociopath. Harman, as do many others (including Scott cited above), says what we are "supposed to" say, what is expected of a "high brow" academic or as a representative of "polite society," but let us be honest this does not reflect what actually happens in our lived-experience. *Tosh.0*—or any quick survey of the Google search, "epic fails," for that matter—will reveal a vast compendium of hilarious misadventures that in fact do end with children hurt, the disabled falling, individuals that end up with broken bones and/or are permanently disfigured, even death. Let us just briefly consider Tosh's video breakdown entitled, "Elevator Rascal."[52] A video, clearly taken from a security camera feed, shows an individual in a mobility scooter just missing an elevator. The person on the elevator, perhaps seeing the disabled person approaching, apparently pushed the "close door" button in his face. The man on the mobility scooter races to catch the elevator, ramming the door and aggressively pressing the button trying to catch the elevator as it rises out of frame. Understandably frustrated, the man reverses and rams the elevator door, twice more. But the third time the man rams the elevator doors he busts straight through the doors and disappears down the elevator shaft. In fact, the man died as a result, although this is inferred it is not explicitly acknowledged in the *Tosh.0* episode.[53] Regardless if we know the outcome or not, the video is, for me, laugh out loud funny. It is confirmed, I am a stone-cold sadist, a certified sociopath.

While the superiority theory of laughter is a viable line of argumentation with respect to the *Tosh.0* program, what I would posit is that the grotesque body and the carnivalesque are key to the production of laughter in the series. In addition to the stereotypes and misogynistic-based humor, the program also trades heavily in bodies in excess: "epic fails," people with a deformity (be it through a birth-defect, or injury), a handicap, bodies that leak, are out of control, spasm. What ties this chaotic collection of videos together is the carnivalesque: billingsgate language, the dressing down of regimes of power, the violation of social mores, grotesque bodies. YouTube, and other similar social media platforms, being one of the contemporary iterations of the medieval marketplace, creates an opportunity for individuals to communicate with one another outside the dominant media regime.

In the *Tosh.0* episode, "Ricky Berwick" (season 9, episode 11), which aired June 6, 2017, Tosh hosts Ricky Berwick, who has Beals-Hecht syndrome—a congenital disease that disfigures bone structure, resulting in severe scoliosis and restricted joint movement. Berwick has a very pronounced hump on his back, somewhat snarled teeth, his eyes do not necessarily align, and a tongue that rivals Gene Simmons's.[54] Although unable to walk upright, Berwick is nonetheless relatively agile, moving on his hands and knees. When in a public setting though he is often seen in a mobility scooter. Berwick on his YouTube channel features himself in short scripted skits, going on excursions, performing "stunts," or eating. Eating tends to be particularly exaggerated and is often presented in near extreme close-up to emphasize his gnashing teeth, saliva, and darting tongue. When eating he tends to breathe heavily, smacks his mouth, consciously chews with his mouth open (often allowing bits of partially chewed food to fall out of his mouth), drools, slurps. His diet is the stuff of a nutritionist's nightmare: French fries and chicken nuggets from McDonalds, chocolate chip cookies, cheese puffs, and even on some occasions he combines these together. And it is not simply what he eats, but how much and how he does it that slips into carnivalesque territory.

Tosh brings Berwick on for a "CeWEBrity Profile," the program created a set that is somewhere between *Pee-Wee's Playhouse* and a "proper" children's television program. A large caricatured version of Berwick's face is mounted at the back of the set; the large cut-out features Berwick's mouth wide open with his tongue made into a slide.[55] Although I highly doubt the designers of Berwick's set knowingly made a nod to the carnivalesque scenario, by happenstance the Berwick set echoes the medieval tradition of designing the theatrical stage as a gaping mouth—as in the gaping mouth of Hell. The set, with its gaping mouth set reflects the carnivalesque conception "of the grotesque body." Bakhtin explains:

> The front of the stage presented a platform that occupied the entire first floor of the structure and symbolized the earth. The backdrop was formed by an elevated set which represented heaven or paradise. Beneath the platform representing the earth there was a large opening, indicating hell, covered by a broad curtain decorated with a huge mask of the devil (Harlequin). When the curtain was pulled back, the devils jumped out of Satan's gaping jaws, or sometimes out of his eyes, and landed on earth. In 1474 the author of a mystery gave these stage directions, "Hell must be represented in the form of huge jaws which open and shut when needed."[56]

As was the convention, the gaping jaws of Hell would be "located in the very center of the stage and at the level of the spectators' eyes, [and this would be] . . . familiar to every mystery play audience." The medieval audience anticipated that the most "amusing and comic protagonists" would emerge from the gaping jaws of hell.[57] Interestingly, when the CeWEBrity Profile proper begins, following Tosh's introduction, Berwick slides down out of the caricatured mouth and down the tongue-slide. Tosh soon follows, inexplicably wrists bound by duct-tape. This staging—with our "amusing and comic protagonists" emerging from the gaping mouth—invites us to reconsider Berwick's body, snarled teeth, tongue, and cackling laugh as characteristically devilish. Furthermore, Berwick's caricatured head is surrounded by abstracted illustrations of heavenly purple, baby blue, and mint-green clouds, echoing the conventional backdrop of the medieval stage. If that were not enough, the set is bedazzled with bright red candy dispensers, lights, and clowns.[58]

Berwick plays the role of what Bakhtin referred to as the "comic monster." Berwick's body and gait stand in radical contrast with the normative human figure and posture. Berwick understands that he is differently-mobile and his relation to the conventionally conceived healthy human profile, allowing, as Bakhtin says, "people [to] play with terror and laugh at it." Berwick though in his self-awareness invites us not so much to laugh at him, but to laugh with him. Berwick plays up his role as "comic monster," or even clown, by cackling like a witch, laughing like a banshee, presenting his naked torso to expose his very distinct hump and other bodily deformities, his animalistic gait, his eating habits, and his general antics (e.g., getting into a faux "cripple fight" in a shopping mall). Berwick's exaggeration and clowning around invite us in to negotiate the monstrous other, making it "impossible to determine where the defeat of fear will end and where joyous recreation will begin." All kinds of deformities, Bakhtin recites, "such as protruding bellies, enormous noses, or humps, are symptoms of pregnancy or of procreative power. Victory over fear is not its abstract elimination; it is a simultaneous uncrowning and renewal, a gay transformation. Hell has burst and has poured forth abundance."[59] Berwick is this body of abundance—from his hump to his eating, he exemplifies the grotesque body (not as disgusting) but one that is open to the world, that exhibits the body's connection to the ecosystem. The hump on his back is suggestive of pregnancy, a swelling, or a body in the state of becoming. The rabid and exaggerated demonstrations of eating, likewise, emphasize the fluid boundary between inside and outside, and the never-ending economy of energy and matter that flows through the entities that inhabit the Earth in the cycle of life (or as cited in the previous chapter the "cycle of poo").

The grotesque body (a body always in a state of becoming, as a body that consumes and excretes), is a body that is exaggerated, dismembered or enlarged, and these are the traits of the carnivalesque body too. Berwick, as already stated, is often eating (too excess), and also excretes—be it spittle, or boisterous farts. Tosh asks in his CeWEBrity Profile with Berwick what the worst thing is day-to-day for Berwick, something that Berwick wished that abled-body people knew about his life. Without skipping a beat, Berwick says, "Messy shits." Tosh goes on to ridicule Berwick, "You know why you have messy shits—can I be honest Ricky, your diet! Just pure garbage." Again and again, it comes back to the lower stratums, to consumption (garbage diet) and excretion (messy shits). Bakhtin observes of Rabelais, the medieval author of *Gargantua and Pantagruel*, that he "depicts hunchbacks with humps of huge proportions, or monstrous noses, abnormally long legs, gigantic ears." In fact, one of the characteristics of Beals-Hecht syndrome is elongated limbs, and large ears. Berwick is torn straight from the pages of a Rabelais novel—exemplary of the carnivalesque figure.[60] But it is not simply the superficial outward exhibition of a non-normative body, but in how Berwick decides to present his body. His eating—presented in extreme or near extreme close-up. The "clowning around." A body out of control—farting, drooling, heavy breathing. Interestingly as well, the CeWEBrity Profile ends with the hands of a clock striking midnight, and Berwick presented with a giant McNugget along with a huge pouch of ketchup. (Giants and their eating habits are another common carnivalesque trope.) Evoking the *Gremlins* narrative, Tosh wonders aloud, "I thought you weren't supposed to eat after midnight." Pausing for a short beat, "Or get wet." Berwick fiendishly responds, "Don't tell me what to do!" Berwick bites into the McNugget—ketchup smearing across his face and dribbling on his shirt—and as Berwick feverishly consumes the McNugget, multiple Berwicks appear, like in *Gremlins*. It is a manifestation of a central carnivalesque theme: consumption, excretion, procreation, renewal.

Beyond what is featured on the *Tosh.0* episode, many of Berwick's videos are set in shopping malls, Walmart, or McDonalds. Berwick celebrates life, and flouts social mores of official "polite" society in our contemporary iterations of the public square or marketplace. "The marketplace was the center of all that is unofficial," Bakhtin observes, "it enjoyed a certain extraterritoriality in a world of official order and official ideology, it always remained 'with the people.'"[61] Berwick's jaunts to shopping malls and the like are almost invariably about this celebration of the people. In some of his shopping excursions—buying an obscene amount of Reese's Pieces, for instance—the quantity and the quality of the food evoke the carnivalesque, which of course is associated with feasts, and overindulgence. But in addition, the venues are also carnivalesque sites. In his video, "FORTNITE ON WHEELS," Berwick mounts two gaming laptops onto his mobility scooter and asks (young) folks in a Walmart to play the videogame with him.[62] In one exchange, while preparing to play *Fortnite* he enlists his fellow player to help him get a win, "You got to carry this fuckin' cripple," Berwick says. His fellow player chuckles, and assures him, "I got you." Games played in the marketplace are another carnivalesque trope. "In the popular marketplace

Figure 9.2 "Ricky Berwick," John Elerick and James Patton, *Tosh.0*, Comedy Central, Season 9, Episode 11, June 6, 2017

Figure 9.3 "Ricky Berwick," John Elerick and James Patton, *Tosh.0*, Comedy Central, Season 9, Episode 11, June 6, 2017

aspect of the feast a substantial place was held by games (cards and sports, as well as by various forms of fortune-telling, wishes, and predictions)."[63] At the end of "FORTNITE ON WHEELS," Berwick needs to charge his laptops, locating outlets in a shopping mall. Speaking to the camera, "I get to play *Fortnite* with all these people, with all these people. I love people!" He asks if the camera is off, assured that it is (though it is not), he slumps into his seat, and says, "I hate these people." Praise mixed with abuse is yet one more carnivalesque trope.[64] People recognize Berwick (many noting that they have watched his videos). Some pose for selfies with him. And regardless if it is a passing exchange, a selfie, playing a videogame together, or being wrangled into some in-store hijinks, the folks that Berwick interacts with become participants. Blurring the boundary between players and participants is likewise a central custom of the carnivalesque.

While the superiority theory of laughter might well be applicable to *Tosh.0*—unquestionably, the program trades heavily in derision and humiliation—at the same time, there is more to the program than just that. The superiority theory of laughter, even in its most abstract sense, is always related to (social) meanings, or narrative. Whether it is implicit or explicit we are often invited to laugh at the mishaps, misfortunes, or missteps of others. However, without dismissing any of these potential readings, there is also something more "immediate," or "direct" in many of the videos that are showcased on the *Tosh.0* program. What prompts laughter is not always based in "meanings" as such, but in the grotesque body—such as what we find with Berwick, or clips featuring a body grievously injured, leaking, broken, or otherwise compromised—which precedes any conceptual comprehension.

This shares affinities with Alfred North Whitehead's conceptualization of "prehension." There is an immediacy in this conceptualization of "prehension," where the external referent is apprehended by sensory systems prior to conceptualization. Although with more sophisticated fare in mind, Martine Beugnet notes that "the cinema of sensation" re-frames cinematic material that is "often undervalued," but nonetheless has "the ability to reach a spectator's mind through the intelligence of the affective."[65] Vivian Sobchack, from a phenomenological perspective, offers a similar idea, which she has referred to as "carnal comprehension," in effect, a sensorial intelligence that "knows" before the referent is cognitively "known."[66] It would reason that the "intelligence of the affective," "carnal comprehension," or "prehension" is attuned to the body—both in the way that bodies are presented, and also in how the viewing body receives an external referent.

The various becomings, the grotesque bodies—particularly as they approach the abject as "[t]he in-between, the ambiguous, the composite"[67]— these are in fact states (of being), processes, rather than "things," or proper objects. Hence my use of "referent," gesturing toward an external stimulant, which is not necessarily a thing or object. What potentially spawns laughter (or disgust), then, is not Berwick (as an object in the world), but the way he eats—the drooling, the heavy breathing, farts, burps, the ravenous way he devours chicken nuggets or French fries, which approaches the animalistic. And while this might entertain the superiority theory of laughter—inviting laughter as a form of "sudden glory" in response to Berwick's infirmity—from the carnivalesque perspective Berwick elides the modern subject conceived as self-contained, which transcends the natural world. Berwick's body and behavior challenge this conception of the human experience, and with the porous, grotesque, and generative body (humps and other deformities read as "outgrowths," or signifying pregnancy—potency, reproductive, growing) we are invited to laugh. It is not necessarily Berwick that we are laughing at, but the eclipsing of the self-contained subject and the shared grotesque experience. We are rather invited to laugh with Berwick, because the presentation of the grotesque body is not "abnormal" as such, but instead an exaggerated expression of the human experience in general. We are not laughing at Berwick, because we are Berwick. Though exaggerated, Berwick merely demonstrates the realities of the lived-experience for all of us—an abject body that leaks, oozes, consumes, excretes, fornicates, inescapably trapped in the cycle of life, and the rhizomatic natural world.

Conclusion: Wrong/Right Time and Place

Just as with the sexual excitation elicited from porn with problematic content, what elicits laughter does not necessarily align with our ethics. Lori Marso offers a similar observation, "Comedy is dangerous, and maybe especially so for feminists, who are too often said to be humorless and not often enough 'in on' the joke." Marso adds that there are affinities with erotic interest here, because "[j]ust as we might not want to explore what, why, and how something turns us on, we also worry about what makes us laugh."[68] We are socially conditioned not to laugh at others—especially, those with disabilities—and yet, despite the social injunction, the *Tosh.0* program proves over and over again that the carnivalesque exhibition of the grotesque body solicits our laughter despite our ethical inclinations. Whether it is Ricky Berwick or a kid with a visibly broken arm, the broken body, the body that is malformed, invites carnivalesque laughter. Obviously, just by being featured on the *Tosh.0* program, a video (even a video featuring grievous bodily injuries) within a carnivalesque framing is already contextualized, lending a degree of license for our laughter. The carnivalesque serves as the "proper" time and place for such affordances despite the mandates of polite society. Whether it is right or wrong, in our everyday encounters with the disabled body we might feel sympathy or pity, and more often than not we would find it inappropriate to laugh whether at or with them. In the context of the carnivalesque, however, we are granted license to laugh.

Be it on the *Tosh.0* program, or Ricky Berwick's own YouTube channel, for instance, the carnivalesque—which frames the grotesque body within a specific time and place—opens up the possibility for laughter.

As discussed in this chapter, laughter often corresponds to a particular temporal and spatial context. A dick pic outside of erotic economies might elicit disgust and/or laughter precisely because it appears at an inopportune moment. Interestingly, there are affinities with Linda Williams's conception of body genres, especially horror. Each of the respective body genres have a temporal element. With the melodramatic genre characters arrive too late, in porn they are right on time, but with horror characters arrive too soon—startling the character (and the spectator). In much the same way that Rue instructs us in *Euphoria* (discussed above), dick pics arrive too soon, unexpected, inopportune, and thus startle, offend, elicit disgust, and perhaps also invite laughter.[69] Furthermore, cringe comedy and its reliance on awkwardness, as exemplified in programs like *The Office*, invite laughter with instances of protracted "dead air" that, as Middleton observes, "compel[s] the viewer to feel time."[70] While cringe comedy creates "gaps in time"—for instance, sitting for some duration with an inappropriate Michael Scott joke—the dick pic is intrusive and often materializes suddenly, and at the wrong time.

Notes

1 "Man Drinks Ipecac," posted by nikmueller12, YouTube video, January 28, 2009, https://www.youtube.com/watch?v=M4vS4UWZ0nQ.
2 "8 Simple Rules for Buying My Teenage Daughter," Greg Colton, *Family Guy*, Season 4, Episode 8, July 10, 2005.
3 For more on laughter and vomiting see my forthcoming chapter: "Sadistic Laughter: A Case for 'Non-Ethical' Viewing," in *Violence Reader*, ed. Steve Choe (Cham: Palgrave Macmillan, 2022).
4 Jason Middleton, *Documentary's Awkward Turn: Cringe Comedy and Media Spectatorship* (New York: Routledge, 2013), 1.
5 "Awkward," s.v. *OED*. For a discussion of "awkwardness" see Adam Kotsko's book-length essay *Awkwardness* (Washington: Zero Books, 2010). Also see Jason Middleton's *Documentary's Awkward Turn: Cringe Comedy and Media Spectatorship* (New York: Routledge, 2013).
6 Pansy Duncan, "Joke work: comic labor and the aesthetics of the awkward," *Comedy Studies* vol. 8, no. 1 (2017): 47.
7 Rebecca Wanzo, "Precarious-Girl Comedy: Issa Rae, Lena Dunham, and Abjection Aesthetics," in *Abjection Incorporated: Mediating the Politics of Pleasure and Violence*, eds Maggie Hennefeld and Nicholas Sammond (Durham, NC: Duke University Press, 2020), 64–85.

8 Susanna Paasonen et al., "The dick pic: Harassment, curation, and desire," *Social Media+ Society* vol. 5, no. 2 (2019): 2.
9 As a brief example see: The queer character, Marquees of Queensberry, in "The Yung and the Restless," episode of *Mike Tyson Mysteries* says after a short flurry of text exchanges, "Oh, hello, dick pic at 11:00 in the morning?" He chuckles to himself, "How am I supposed to respond? 'Impressive'? Mmm, you know what? Yeah, I'll write 'impressive.'" Queensberry complains that he's been sitting around for days with nothing to do, "and then the second you get a nice hard cock like this on your phone, you're on a GD mystery." "The Yung and the Restless," *Mike Tyson Mysteries*, Season 4, Episode 9, July 28, 2019.
10 Paasonen et al., 8.
11 In fact, in the first couple of episodes Jules's gender is probably, by most viewers, just assumed to be female. Refreshingly, Jules just is—at least for a good stretch of the series. Later in the series we get some of Jules's backstory, revealing something of her gender identification. The inclusion of a trans character appears to be a marker of Sam Levinson projects. Bex is treated similarly in *Assassination Nation* (2018).
12 "Made You Look," Sam Levinson, *Euphoria*, Season 1, Episode 3, June 30, 2019.
13 Jessica Ringrose and Emilie Lawrence, "Remixing misandry, manspreading, and dick pics: Networked feminist humour on Tumblr," *Feminist Media Studies* vol. 18, no. 4 (2018): 686. Ringrose and Lawrence cite Joanne Gallivan, "Group Differences in Appreciation of Feminist Humor," *Humor* vol. 5, no. 4 (1992): 369–74.
14 "What if men harassed women IRL like they do online?" posted by Bye Felipe, YouTube video, June 7, 2016, https://www.youtube.com/watch?v=y-pNFCcIxow. Established by Alexandra Tweten after one too many noxious online encounters, Bye Felipe originated as an Instagram account, intended to be an "empowering guide to navigating the hazards and horrors of online dating."
15 Andrea Waling and Tinonee Pym, "'C'mon, No One Wants a Dick Pic': exploring the cultural framings of the 'Dick Pic' in contemporary online publics," *Journal of Gender Studies* vol. 28, no. 1 (2019): 76.
16 Alison Stevenson, "This Woman Turned Her Collection of Unsolicited Dick Pics into an Art Show," *Vice*, April 15, 2016, https://www.vice.com/en/article/ppxjem/this-woman-turned-her-collection-of-unsolicited-dick-pics-into-an-art-show.
17 Whitney Bell interviewed by Alison Stevenson, "This Woman Turned Her Collection of Unsolicited Dick Pics into an Art Show," *Vice*, April 15, 2016, https://www.vice.com/en/article/ppxjem/this-woman-turned-her-collection-of-unsolicited-dick-pics-into-an-art-show.
18 Bell.
19 Ringrose and Lawrence, 700.
20 Georges Bataille, *The Accursed Share: An Essay on the General Economy Vol. 1, Consumption*, trans. Robert Hurley (New York: Zone Books, 1988), 67–8.
21 Murray Davis, *Smut: Erotic Reality/Obscene Ideology* (Chicago: University of Chicago Press, 1985), 65.
22 Henri Bergson, "Laughter," in *Comedy: An Essay on Comedy* (Baltimore: Johns Hopkins University Press, 1980), 71.
23 See Duncan, 47.
24 Morten Birk Hansen Mandau, "'Directly in your face': a qualitative study on the sending and receiving of unsolicited 'dick pics' among young adults," *Sexuality & Culture* vol. 24,

no. 1 (2020): 79–80. Jon Lucas and Scott Moore's 2019 film *Jexi* includes an instance where the primary character's apparently sentient and jealous phone digital voice assistance, Jexi, sends a picture of his dick to all his co-workers, making for an encounter with "cringyness."
25 Davis, 3.
26 Ibid., 5.
27 Ibid., 9.
28 Ibid., 15. Davis continues to add,

> "As soon as one partner's rhythm gets out of phase with the other's, they must readjust it immediately; otherwise accelerating disrhythmia will soon shatter the entire experience." With erotic time the stars have to align, "the two partners must harmonize both desire and availability. When desire for sex is mutual, neither may be available; when availability for sex is mutual, neither may desire it."

Davis, 15; 20.
29 Davis, 20.
30 Ibid., 58.
31 Ibid., 58–9.
32 Davis observes that specific times might "block-off" the possibilities for the emergence of erotic time: "Uneroticizing times in our society include 'day-time' ('At least pull down the shades!'), 'worktime,' ('Stop fooling around: we've got work to do!'), and 'mealtime' ('Now? How nauseating! Besides everything'll get cold')." Davis, 17. Also see Mandau, "'Directly in your face,'" 75.
33 See Mandau, 79. Recounting upon a study of young men and women and their feelings about dick pics: "Laura describes how the experience of unexpectedly receiving a dick pic shocked her so much that she instantly threw her smartphone away. This reaction can be interpreted as an attempt to momentarily detach herself from the embodied relation she has with her smartphone by making the device physically distant." Mandau, 79.
34 Mandau, 80.
35 Winfried Menninghaus, *Disgust: The Theory and History of a Strong Sensation*, trans. Howard Eiland and Joel Golb (New York: State University of New York Press, 2003), 10–11.
36 Julian Hanich, *The Audience Effect: On the Collective Cinema Experience* (Edinburgh: Edinburgh University Press, 2018), 197.
37 Paasonen et al., 7. The authors immediately add to this, "Yet, unsolicited dick pics are equally part of the everyday uses of hook up apps used by same sex attracted men. Receipt of unsolicited dick pics in this context is more commonly experienced as disinterest and boredom than harassment." Paasonen et al., 7.
38 Apparently, Steve Morrissey agrees with me on this point. I had already drafted this when I stumbled on his review of the film. See Steve Morrissey, "Review: Klown aka Klovn: The Movie," *Movie Steve*, September 27, 2013, https://www.moviesteve.com/klown-2010/. Though having said that *Klown* could never be made in the US, apparently there are plans for an American remake in the works. As reported in *Variety*, Sacha Baron Cohen is attached to the American remake. "Todd Phillips, the director of *The Hangover*," Zach Baron reports, "is producing an American version of *Klown* for Warner

Brothers, with Danny McBride, of HBO's *Eastbound & Down*, on board to write the script and star." Zach Baron, "Rakes' Debauched Progress in Denmark," *New York Times*, July 20, 2012, https://nyti.ms/LyiHkJ. Dave McNary, "Sacha Baron Cohen *Klown* Remake Sells Out all Foreign Markets," *Variety*, November 17, 2016, https://variety.com/2016/film/markets-festivals/sacha-baron-cohen-klown-remake-sells-1201921177/.

39 Zach Baron, "Rakes' Debauched Progress in Denmark," *New York Times*, July 20, 2012, https://nyti.ms/LyiHkJ.
40 Ibid.
41 Paasonen et al., 8.
42 Mikhail Bakhtin, *Rabelais and His World*, trans. Helene Iswolsky (Bloomington: Indiana University Press, 1984), 319.
43 Robert Stam's 1989 book, *Subversive Pleasures: Bakhtin, Cultural Criticism, and Film*, is particularly emblematic. It is also possible to read Judith Butler's landmark 1990 book *Gender Trouble* through the carnivalesque lens, in Butler's championing of gender transgression, queerness, and the interrogation of established gender norms. See for example, Clive Thomson, "Bakhtin and Feminist Projects: Judith Butler's *Gender Trouble*," in "Bakhtin: Carnival and Other Subjects," ed. Myriam Díaz-Diocaretz, special issue, *Critical Studies* vol. 3, nos. 1–4 (1993): 210–28.
44 Umberto Eco, "The Frames of Comic 'Freedom'," in *Carnival!*, ed. Thomas A. Sebeok (New York: Mouton, 1984), 6.
45 Aaron Kerner and Jonathan Knapp, *Extreme Cinema: Affective Strategies in Transnational Media* (Edinburgh: Edinburgh University Press, 2016), 94.
46 The series had been renewed for four more seasons, but new executive leadership at Comedy Central have elected to go a different direction, and in a surprise move canceled the program. As reported in the *Hollywood Reporter*,

> On the linear network, *Tosh.0* has ranked as the top original comedy Tuesdays among men 18–34 in every cable year since it launched. The January four-season renewal was not the first time the series has received a multiple-year pickup. *Tosh.0* was renewed for three seasons back in 2018. The series will end its run after 11 years and more than 250 episodes, making it the longest-running weekly live-action show in Comedy Central's history.

Lesley Goldberg, "*Tosh.0* Canceled as Comedy Central Reverses 4-Season Renewal," *The Hollywood Reporter*, August 20, 2020, https://www.hollywoodreporter.com/news/tosh-0-canceled-as-comedy-central-reverses-4-season-renewal.
47 Sophie Scott, "Why We Laugh," filmed March 2015, TED video, https://www.ted.com/talks/sophie_scott_why_we_laugh?language=en.
48 Cited in Jared N. Champion, "'This Kindergarten Country of Ours': Daniel Tosh's Postmodern Social Politics," *The Journal of Popular Culture* vol. 51, no. 3 (2018): 596.
49 See "Roof Jump," Scott Zabielski, *Tosh.0*, Comedy Central, Season 6, Episode 10, April 22, 2014, 22 min.
50 During a 2012 routine at Los Angeles's Laugh Factory, for instance, Tosh insisted that anything could be made funny. A woman in the audience blurted out, "Actually, rape is never funny!" To which Tosh responded, "Wouldn't it be funny if this girl got raped by, like, five guys right now?" While some commentators and comedians voiced support for Tosh, others suggested that this was just one more instance of his disregard

of social mores. Cited in Jared N. Champion, "'This Kindergarten Country of Ours': Daniel Tosh's Postmodern Social Politics," *The Journal of Popular Culture* vol. 51, no. 3 (2018): 596. As a possible example of a "rape joke," see the "Massage Chair," episode of *Robot Chicken* (season 2, episode 9), which parodies commercials for the fabric softener Snuggle, running on television in the 1980s. In the *Robot Chicken* episode, a man is doing laundry, when who should appear from the washing machine, but the Snuggle's bear. Touching the bear, the man observes, "oh, so soft . . ." and takes the bear to a room and fucks it behind closed doors. The bear is heard protesting as the man has his way with it. This actually happens twice. There are perhaps a couple of different things that make this particular scenario "acceptable": (1) *Robot Chicken* self-consciously uses "bad" stop-motion animation (often using known action-figures)—and thus clearly not real, (2) the object of assault is a teddy bear (not a human being), and (3) the recognizable commercial compels us to read it through the lens of parody. All these things place the horror of rape at some distance, and thus allow us to approach it as humorous. That all said, just as stated in the *chikan* chapter, someone who has experienced sexual assault may find no comfort in the "distancing" devices employed in this sketch. And, in fact, even some who has never experienced sexual assault might not find it funny.
51 Graham Harman, *Guerrilla Metaphysics: Phenomenology and the Carpentry of Things* (Chicago: Open Court, 2005), 131.
52 "Bed Intruder," Scott Zabielski, *Tosh.0* Comedy Central Season 3, Episode 1, January 11, 2011, http://www.cc.com/video-clips/84kxht/tosh-0-elevator-rascal.
53 "Killed by a temper tantrum: Wheelchair man plunges to his death down elevator shaft after ramming lift doors," *Daily Mail*, October 8, 2010, https://www.dailymail.co.uk/news/article-1318802/Korean-man-wheelchair-falls-death-missing-lift.html. In Tosh's snarky commentary he says that the man demonstrates "that he is 'handicapable' of plunging to his death."
54 There are more affinities between Berwick and Simmons: both are clowns. Think for example of Kiss in their full makeup and outfits. Is this not the stuff of clowns? Between the exaggerated makeup, clothing, and tongue isn't Simmons a clown?
55 The caricature is yet another common trope of the carnivalesque, with its tendency toward exaggeration and its use as a political tool to dress down figures of authority.
56 Bakhtin, 348.
57 Ibid.
58 As one of my graduate students, Flor Marmolejo, pointed out, the set design has the connotations of elevating Berwick to a figure of the clown, instead of a fool. And thus, we are not laughing at him, but with/because of him.
59 Bakhtin, 91.
60 Ibid., 328.
61 Ibid., 153–54.
62 Ricky Berwick, "*FORTNITE* ON WHEELS," YouTube video, May 13, 2018, https://www.youtube.com/watch?v=8XDJLMCSY4Q.
63 Bakhtin, 231.
64 Bakhtin writes:

> The popular-festive language of the marketplace abuses while praising and praises while abusing. It is a two-faced Janus. It is addressed to the dual-bodied object, to the dual-bodied world (for this language is always universal); it is directed at once to the

> dying and to what is being generated, to the past that gives birth to the future. Either praise or abuse may prevail, but the one is always on the brink of passing into the other. Praise implicitly contains abuse, is pregnant with abuse, and vice versa abuse is pregnant with praise.

Bakhtin, 415.

65 Martine Beugnet, *Cinema and Sensation: French Film and the Art of Transgression* (Edinburgh: Edinburgh University Press, 2007), 178.
66 Vivian Sobchack, "What My Fingers Knew: The Cinesthetic Subject, or Vision in the Flesh," *Senses of Cinema* no. 5 (April 2000): no pagination. http://sensesofcinema.com/2000/conference-special-effects-special-affects/fingers/.
67 Julia Kristeva, *Powers of Horror: An Essay on Abjection*, trans. Leon S. Roudiez (New York: Columbia University Press, 1982), 4.
68 Lori Marso, "Feminist Cringe Comedy: Dear Dick, The Joke Is on You," *Politics & Gender* vol. 15, no. 1 (2019): 108.
69 I would like to acknowledge David Mai for connecting the temporal elements associated with body genres and the dick pic.
70 Middleton, 141–2.

10

Conclusion
The Limitation of Theories of Affect
with contributors Birdy Wei-Ting Hung and David Mai[1]

Introduction: The Limitation of Theories of Affect

This project was in a sense hamstrung from the very start. There is an inherent difficulty in "translating" the sensate experience into words. And the very nature of scholarly discourse anesthetizes the very things that are identified as cinematic examples capable of eliciting an affective experience. Inherently impoverished, no matter the methodology, analytic discourse will never fully apprehend the affective experience. As Susanna Paasonen suggests in her writing on pornography, the affect theorist acts as a ventriloquist "speaking on behalf of something that does not speak." Paasonen adds that, "translations from the carnal and the tactile to the visually perceived and the linguistically articulated are never fully accomplished. There is a perpetual gap between how things look and feel and how they can be described."[2] This impoverishment is precisely what leads some phenomenologists to resort to such virtuosity in their prose, as well as a reliance on analogy and simile. However imperfect, written scholarship is what we are left with, and we cannot let the perfect be the enemy of the good—and thus, despite the limitations, I have made an effort to synthesize a theorization of the affective experience by drawing from a wide range of eclectic sources.

Regardless, though, the affective experience is inherently subjective. Not only is it contingent upon individual dispositions, but also subject to cultural and historical contingencies as well.[3] Individual tastes vary widely. A particular piece of music might move one to tears, while leaving another filled with ennui. A particular kink in the pornographic genre might elicit frenzied arousal in one person, while leaving another utterly disgusted. A particular "epic fail" potentially incites tumultuous laughter in one, while leaving another aghast at the pitiful sight. While there is no universal affective experience, there is what Immanuel Kant termed "subjective universalism," accounting for the human capacity to be sensually perceptive—a power that Kant calls "taste." What follows is a closing summary of the ideas presented in this volume, after which I have included a discussion of an experimental exercise to highlight the affective experience with a particular focus on Chan-wook Park's 2013 film *Stoker*.

The Beautiful

Immanuel Kant is an affect theorist. His conception of the beautiful is a theory of affect. Kant's *Critique of Judgement* is an exploration of the aesthetic experience, "aesthetic" etymologically coming from the Greek "relating to sense perception, sensitive, perceptive."[4] Additionally, the Kantian conception of the aesthetic experience pertains to the sensate divorced from our cognitive faculties, what Kant terms disinterestedness. The experience of the beautiful is in effect a disguised expression of sensual pleasure. A genuine beautiful experience—to well-up with tears, to go flush with goosebumps, to reflexively gasp—says nothing of the external referent that elicits the sensation, the aesthetic experience "contributes nothing to knowledge."[5] The aesthetic experience has nothing to do with the utility or "meaning" of an object, but in the pleasurable sensations that it elicits.

The beautiful is ultimately subjective. And to declare that this or that thing is beautiful says nothing of the object, but instead discloses the feeling of pleasure in the subject. We might not share the same experience necessarily, but the aesthetic experience is in itself universal. Although the beautiful cannot be fathomed cognitively, to "prehend," in Alfred North Whitehead's terms, is to be affected by another entity prior to, or even outside its cognition. The aesthetic or affective experience is "triggered" by some external referent, and is not a thing, object, or concept, but rather an event, a state of being, to feel pleasure.[6] As discussed throughout the present volume, more often than not, the elicitation of an affective experience derives from how something is presented to us, not necessarily what it is.

The beautiful is a paroxysmal response, outside our conscious control, and thus our sensate bodies might very well betray us. Take, for instance, Monty's hate-filled diatribe in Spike Lee's 2002 film *25th Hour* (discussed in Chapter 4 on musicality), where Monty unleashes a torrent of vile hate-speech, and yet in its musicalized delivery manages to tumble into the beautiful. And we might scold our bodies for such a response, but what is important to recognize is that the beautiful (or the affective experience generally) is divorced from moral judgements. What is beautiful should not be confused for what is considered (morally) good, or agreeable. To locate pleasure in Monty's diatribe in no way "condones" the content of what he says, but rather acknowledges the visceral experience elicited from the musicality of the sequence. Thus, despite the abject content, the form elicits the beautiful—a disguised expression of pleasure manifesting in goosebumps. In short, affect often manifests in the stylistic treatment of a subject—the way a scene is lit; the saturation of color; movement, be it camera movement or choreography within the mise-en-scène; and perhaps the most potent aesthetic stimulant—musicalization, whether that is the musicalization of the visual field as often found in music videos, or the rhythmic or harmonic treatment of the audio material.

Sound is a sensual experience: sound waves are transmitted through air, literally touching our sensate bodies (not just our ears). And this is perhaps how music moves us, because it actually touches us. Even when music is accompanied with lyrics, which connote meaning, we nevertheless resonate with music not solely through the content (that is, meanings, words, narrative), but often the audible lektonic (that is, a signifier without a signified) referent—rhythm, melody, harmony, instrumentation (including the human voice). While linguistic utterances are "coded sound," for Anne Fernald even spoken language is not necessarily "about" something—rather, as sound it is effectively "touch at a distance."[7] Consider Thom Yorke's entrancing three-note triad in Luca Guadagnino's 2018 film *Suspiria* (discussed in Chapter 3). The affective charge is located in the combination of melodic rhythm, with its repetitive triads, coupled with the haunting harmonics in Yorke's delivery of the lyrics. "This is a waltz thinking about our bodies / What they mean for our salvation," Yorke croons with his slightly strained vocals and his extended utterances beginning to tear the individual words from their communicative function pivoting toward musicalization. In the instrumentation too, Yorke's falsetto delivery of the lines, "Here and now, death still behind a wall" harmonizes with the piercing pale wispy shrill of a flute. "Here and now" harmonically intertwining with (read: touching) the airy flute. It is the "raw" musicality that has the capacity to move us, to touch us, to invite the experience of the beautiful.

The affective experience can be multifold and even at times seemingly contradictory—for example, the mingling of the beautiful and erotic arousal, or the beautiful and the abject. Chan-wook Park's 2013 film *Stoker* does this. Interestingly, *Stoker* (discussed at further length below) gestures to other filmmakers such as Pier Paolo Pasolini and Alfred Hitchcock. India Stoker, our primary female protagonist "reclaims" sensual pleasures in a shower scene of her own, and despite being complicit in murder (though arguably self-defense), unlike Marion, she is not punished for her pleasure and brings herself to climax.[8] India is about to be raped, but her uncle arrives and with his belt forces the assailant's head backwards until his neck breaks. In the shower India rehearses the violence in her mind and appears to locate sexual gratification in the killing, climaxing as she recalls the audible snap of her assailant's neck. The shower scene—in the composition, slow motion, and musical scoring—invites the possibility of encountering the beautiful and potentially erotic interest despite the abject nature of the content.

Similarly, the Black Mass scene in Guadagnino's *Suspiria* vacillates between the beautiful (especially in Yorke's scoring) and eroticism, all despite the gruesome content. Set to Yorke's "Unmade," the film is set in slightly slow-motion and seen through a crimson filter as Susie gently caresses her breasts/chest, her mouth agape, and her head slightly tilted up—the framing emphasizing her jawline. Susie's heavy breathing suggests an ecstatic state, as she tears open her vulva-chest-heart, which is accompanied with the complex layering of female moaning (tortured and/or in ecstasy) and Susie's proclamation, drawn out in a thin wispy voice, "I am mother." Along with the cinematography and composition, the interwoven sounds—diegetic, subjective-diegetic(?), and non-diegetic—spiral around and around, encircling us, touching us in auditory embrace, vacillating between the abject, the beautiful, and all at the same time inviting sexual interest.

Arousal

The mechanism of Kantian aesthetics and arousal are similar. Objects in themselves are not intrinsically beautiful or arousing and arousal materializes with an encounter of the fetishistic object coupled with the magical seductive force of allure. The alluring object beckons us and seduces. A sense of bewitching or beguiling can be found in the etymology of "allure," rooted in the Old French to seduce or trick. Like an inviting seductive wink, allure casts spells on us. Similar to the Kantian conception of the beautiful, because it is not the object in itself that is alluring, but allure is a mysterious "force." Allure as a dark agent, grabs our attention, seducing us with a gesture to its own unfathomableness.

Akin to the formulation of the beautiful, arousal is also a disguised expression of pleasure. Arousal says very little about the thing deemed arousing, and actually reveals more about the aroused subject. While arousal is a universal experience, what allures us is highly subjective, governed by social-cultural, historical, or individual contingencies. Furthermore, arousal is not about "identification," but as Paasonen suggests: "resonance." Paasonen argues that resonance is at play between porn and its consumers. Porn does not demand its consumers to identify, comprehend, or sympathize with the characters/performers, and while apparatus theorists position cinematic spectators relative to the gaze, on the other hand, as Paasonen proposes, porn "grabs" us and resonates with our own erotic interests independent of our gender or sexual orientation. Paasonen surveys the practice of consumers of online pornographic content, but the conception of resonance was productive for us and our consideration of arousing cinematic material in Chapters 5, 6, and 7. Though online porn requires a certain level of participation from its consumers (for example, clicking, swiping, tapping), the cinematic experience also potentially resonates with us "and grabs [us] as intensities sensed in the body before we even know what got us."[9]

Similar to Whitehead's conception of "prehending" (as discussed in Chapter 2 "On the Beautiful"), arousal might not be "comprehended," but something that resonates with our sensate bodies before we are cognitively aware of it. Further, erotic resonance does not require that viewers locate affinities with the arousing referent, but as Paasonen notes, "they need to relate and connect to one another."[10] Rather than putting ourselves into a character's position, resonance is a shared sensory experience that connects. And arousal very well might not even align with our own sense of self, in fact, we very well might be aroused by material that runs completely counter to our most firmly held political values.

In Chapter 5 "On Sexual Arousal" I posited that sexual arousal is spawned by the economies of allure and fetishism. A fetish is the overvaluation of an object, and in our investment in the overvalued object we habitually return to it over and over again in our pursuit of (sexual) gratification. Paasonen briefly discusses habituated patterns in porn consumption and sexual practices. I view her conception of "habit" as effectively synonymous with fetishism, or if not synonymous then bearing strong affinities.[11] The repetition in the pornographic genre is not simply a lack of imagination, but that the oft-recycled scenarios (for example, chikan—discussed in Chapter 6), visual choreography, and employment of particular body-types often align with the preferences of porn consumers. Our cognitive selves might fully disagree with the transgressive content, and as Mulvey rightly claims female bodies are often fetishized objects to be consumed, nevertheless, our bodies can betray us and locate pleasure in the politically regressive. The experience of arousal is in itself universal, but we all have different preferences, our "types," our fantasies. And these "types," or fantasies might be commonly shared—though culturally and historically contingent. Like molecular cohesion where two droplets of water will pull together through cohesive force, our internalized narrativized objects (fetishistic preferences, those things that we consider "hot") cohere with the external stimulus. To paraphrase Laura Kipnis, we might not be able to clearly "name" our fetishized objects, or to comprehend why a certain thing is alluring, because the economies of allure and fetishism work in part in the realm of the unconscious.[12] But we need not reduce our sensate bodies as identification-biased machines, as Paasonen observes in her own encounter with online porn: "Depictions of bodies heaving in the throes of sex may resonate with my somatic archives without these bodies being similar to mine in terms of gender, age or ethnicity."[13] To resonate is to connect, to allow our internalized narrativized objects (that is, fetishistic objects) to align with external stimuli. Allure and fetishism thus work hand-in-hand, and when the internalized narrativized object and the external stimuli "harmonize," the result of this bond is arousal.

Allure is not an object but resides in form and style—the way in which fetishistic objects are presented to us. Take, for example, the reading performances in Park Chan-wook's 2016 film *The Handmaiden* (discussed in Chapter 7). In the scene where our female protagonist Hideko (as a youngster) practices reading with her aunt, a series of body parts are read in a flat tone, "Man. Woman. Eye. Nose. Mouth. Ear. Shoulder. Nipple. Navel." These body parts, especially in their flat delivery, do not invite erotic interest. As they continue to recite from the book, Hideko repeats after her aunt, but she stumbles over "penis, vagina"—cutting to Hideko's perspective to an open book with a wood block print of an erect penis and two vulvas—causing the pair to break into incongruous laughter. Hideko and her aunt are then brutally disciplined by Uncle Kouzuki's smothering gloves, presumably because the potentially fetishistic terms were not delivered in the "right" alluring manner. In another scene shortly thereafter, Uncle Kouzuki again scolds, "Don't read like a dog lapping at his plate!" instructing Hideko to read in the proper form—that is to say, to read in an alluring tone (discussed in Chapter 7). (In addition, the musicalized delivery of the stories, though different in content and form, recalls the discussion of the French novelist Louis-Ferdinand Céline and the comparison made to Spike Lee's *25th Hour*, discussed in Chapter 4.[14]) Hideko's affectless reading as a youngster is set in vivid contrast with the alluring form of her delivery as a mature performer (as well as her aunt)—through intonation, pace, and her sultry feminine voice the erotic content of the narratives is deeply embellished making it all the more alluring.

As discussed in Chapter 7, Park clearly places *The Handmaiden* in conversation with Pier Paolo Pasolini's infamous 1975 film *Salò, or the 120 Days of Sodom*. However, where Pasolini aligns the viewer's gaze with the libertines', in *The Handmaiden* Hideko, while onstage to-be-looked-at, actually meets the gaze and returns the look—the external diegetic viewers (those watching *The Handmaiden*) and the diegetic audience within the narrative are subject to Hideko's sadistic gaze. In one of the stories that Hideko reads, a Duchess whips the male protagonist, and echoing the contents of the story, Hideko quickly brings her hands down in a whipping gesture, while vocalizing the sound of the whip. In a montage, a series of close-ups of freshly whipped asses are shown, followed by the male audience members reflexively throwing their mouths agape and ecstatically exhaling. Each of Hideko's audio-visualized whipping gestures appears to "connect" with the men's internalized fetishized object. Allure is at work in the form of the audio-visual material, and this is in effect what happens—for the men within the diegesis, they are captivated by the story, and at the same time project themselves into the story, imagining that they are the ones being whipped. Internalized narrativized objects and external stimuli thus resonate, even if only temporarily. And this projective gesture is illustrative of the operation of embodied simulation.

As discussed at some length in the introductory chapter and Chapter 5, in association with academics from the humanities and other scientists, the neurologist Vittorio Gallese has theorized the concept of embodied simulation. There are affinities here with the conception of "kinesthetic empathy."[15] Based on his (and others') discovery of mirror neurons, Gallese has found that exterior stimuli such as watching someone grabbing an object would trigger the same neural activity in the individual witnessing it.[16] Gallese and others suggest that the recognition of another being invites the experience of embodied simulation, and it is not necessarily recognized consciously, nor is it "felt" necessarily, but is processed by our neural sensory system, and affords us the possibility to encounter the external stimulus not through linguistic means (that is, through meaning, narrative, concept), but instead through an interpersonal body-to-body form of communication.[17]

Applying these neurological findings to the experience of watching pornography, it is not a stretch to conceive that the grasping of an erect cock would stimulate the neural network system associated with touch and being touched—of touching or having one's cock touched.[18] And this sensorial engagement enhances our ability to "resonate" with what is happening onscreen.[19] As already suggested here, though to emphasize the point, with embodied simulation the external stimulus does not only activate the visual areas of the brain, but rather our vision is multimodal, and activates "motor, somatosensory and emotion-related brain networks." Motor neurons respond to all manner of stimuli, be they visual, auditory, or tactile.[20] Gallese's findings lend credence to Deleuze's insistence that, in the presence of the sensate, "the eye becomes virtually the polyvalent indeterminate organ that sees the body without organs (the Figure) as pure presence."[21]

Pornography in its presentation of the sexual encounter, as an encounter with the sensate, invites the spectator to share in the sexual experience, as the neurons associated with the same body part are activated.[22] Embodied simulation further problematizes the supposed "dispassionate" content analysis of the porn scholar—focusing on the political or cultural "meanings" of the genre and disavowing the affective experience. The sensate body can tell no lie, and often betrays us—we might be sexually aroused by politically regressive content or buckle over in laughter at someone's expense.

Laughter

It would be a mistake to solely equate laughter with humor. As discussed in Chapter 8, there are three common philosophical lines of thought on laughter: superiority, incongruity, and (cathartic) relief. While these three theories of laughter might overlap, superior and incongruous laughter operate within the objectal economy. Laughter is often a social dance. We gesture to our present company with a laugh: "I get it!" We offer our laughter to show our emotional support (signifying, "I am with you"), or sometimes our disagreement and/or contempt ("Haha. Not funny." Or "You're an idiot."). "LOL" and "LMAO"—Internet slang for "laugh out loud," and "laugh my ass off," with interesting Bakhtinian overtones, connoting the mouth and the lower body stratum—serve as a supportive nod to our interlocutors. The object that elicits laughter might not be funny whatsoever, yet we very well might be inclined to laugh nonetheless in a social setting. Generating superior and incongruous laughter involves a cognitive process—premised on being able to read social cues and situations, to in effect communicate, "I understand you," or "I get it." In these cases, laughter pertains to social proximity: an attempt to reinforce the social fabric (to be included in the group) or draw boundaries (to exclude).

We laugh for many reasons, sometimes even without any "logical reason," but rather as a defensive gesture in response to a non-object, the abject. The theory (or theories) of relief negotiates social anxiety, or an encounter with the non-objectal economy—disgust, the abject, the (Kristevan) semiotic, states of becoming, the grotesque body. In their own ways the genres of horror and comedy navigate the anxiety that the pregnant and generative (female) body elicits in (patriarchal) culture. Laughing out loud can serve a protective function, as phenomenologist Julian Hanich observes on the "audience effect," noting that we are just as likely to laugh at something that is funny, as we are inclined "to laugh something away." Hanich invites us to consider the sudden shock experienced in a horror film, or the instances in a gross-out comedy that elicit disgust, where in either case laughter might be mobilized to keep the offending referent at bay. Inferring a relation between the fight or flight reflex, the sudden encounter of the abject is akin to a "mini-crisis," which triggers our intuitive laughter as a defensive gesture. Hanich insists that this is no theoretical or metaphorical gesture, rather "the film is *experienced* as overly close," and the very act of laughing is "an expansive outward movement of the body that goes along with exhalation—we try to get rid of what seems to be *too close*." Thus, Hanich concludes that laughter works toward "a *reduction of tension*."[23] As in horror, laughter often follows a scare in the cycle of tension and release. Yet, this type of laughter often does not occur with solitary viewing, and it is almost as if we are signaling to the other members of the audience a collective release—pointing again to laughter as a reflexive social form of communication.

Ethically problematic material can elicit laughter. And it is not necessarily because the referent is funny necessarily, but laughter serves to neutralize disgust, to relieve the tension when encountering the abject. And this potentially aligns with Mikhail Bakhtin's conceptualization of the grotesque body, or grotesque realism. Bakhtin's utilization of "grotesque" should not be understood in its contemporary meaning. Etymologically, "grotesque" comes from the Italian "grotto," meaning cave, referring to cavernous Roman ruins where decorative designs were uncovered. These capricious designs did not differentiate between inside and outside, did not respect categories—animal and foliage, animate and inanimate—"the body swallows the world and is itself swallowed by the world."[24] And in the free mixing of things, grotesque realism is illustrative of the constant flow of things, of constant becomings, where the ingestion of one thing gives rise to something else. Death and rebirth, as Bakhtin observes, happen simultaneously at the carnival, where, "In all these events the beginning and end of life are closely linked and interwoven." And the abundant food at the carnival also points to the grotesque body that consumes, defecates, regenerates. Bakhtin continues, "copulation, pregnancy, dismemberment, swallowing up by another body—all these acts are performed on the confines of the body and the outer world, or on the confines of the old and new body."[25] Different from the modern conception of the individuated subject, Bakhtin's grotesque bodies are open to the world in a rhizomatic manner, embedded in the cycle of life—or as Mr. Hankey would have it, "the cycle of poo" (discussed in Chapter 8). Rather than the Renaissance's horizontal vision, Bakhtin's carnivalesque conception of time is vertical. Matters are not fixed, but constantly moving, transforming, becoming, in a perpetual cycle. The deformed, consuming, leaking, excreting body (discussed in Chapters 8 and 9) has the potential to threaten the neat-and-tidy conception of the modern human body form, inviting abject laughter.

As illustrated in Chapter 9 laughter often comes as a response to the right/wrong place and time. For instance, dick pics that arrive at inopportune moments, or in those sanctioned instances and places afforded by the carnivalesque. But laughter is also a defensive gesture, to ward off that which is too close—abject. Chan-wook Park's 2013 dramatic thriller *Stoker* features our female protagonist, India Stoker, and her sexual awakening, which is intwined with Charles, her uncle.[26] The incest trope lurking in the background threatens to be "too close," prompting us to laugh the taboo away. While the musicality of audio-visual material touches our sensate body, thus inviting the disinterested beautiful experience, Park's fetishistic choreography also lures us with a wink. Multiple affects are potentially at play—goosebumps, arousal, disgust, and laughter can be triggered simultaneously.

"There is something rotten in Denmark!" There are slight hints of *Hamlet* in *Stoker*, where Uncle Charlie usurps his brother's position and seduces his widowed wife. At the dinner table in a coy but knowingly transgressive comment, Charles says, "I want to know my brother's wife." At the same time, while Uncle Charlie seduces his sister-in-law Evelyn, he also shows unnatural interest in his niece India. The play of seductions makes the social awkwardness palpable—the camera, at multiple times, frames Charles between the two women. Over the dinner table, Uncle Charlie offers, "Now, can I get you anything else, maybe some ice cream?" India replies with a dismissive tone, "No," immediately corrected by Evelyn with a better mannered, "No, thank you." Mother and daughter thus throw Uncle Charlie (framed in the middle) polite smiles to spell away the social awkwardness. India fondling the phallic wine bottle (a 1994 vintage, consciously selected as it is the year of India's birth), as Uncle Charlie intently stares at his niece, eye-fucking her, India wonders aloud, "What do you want from me?" Charles simply insists that he merely wants to be friends, but India responds, sliding his glass of wine back to him, that, "We don't need to be friends. We're family." Although not played for laughs, Charles is only a stone's throw from Larry

David in *Curb Your Enthusiasm*, Michael Scott, or David Brent in the British and American versions of *The Office*, who each fail to recognize their violations in social etiquette, which results in cringy laughter. (The examples of cringe comedy—such as *Curb* and *The Office*—are discussed in Chapter 9.) Our laughter is an attempt to place distance between ourselves and the socially awkward. While the characters in these cringe comedies are oblivious to their social *faux pas*, Charles appears to be completely self-aware perhaps making the dinner scene doubly troubling: not only is Charles venturing into transgressive territory, he does it consciously so. And thus, while *Stoker* is by no means funny in the way that we might think of *The Office*, it potentially invites laughter to keep the transgressive at a distance. This is precisely what we found in the Kerner Sense Survey, discussed in the following section.

Conclusion: The Kerner Sense Survey as an Experimental Approach to the Shared Affective Experience

> My ears hear what others cannot hear. Small, faraway things people cannot normally see are visible to me. These senses are the fruits of a lifetime of longing. Longing to be rescued. To be completed. Just as the skirt needs the wind to billow, I'm not formed by things that are of myself alone. I wear my father's belt tied around my mother's blouse. And shoes which are from my uncle. This is me. Just as a flower does not choose its color we are not responsible for what we have come to be. Only once you realize this do you become free. And to become adult is to become free.
> — India Stoker in *Stoker* (Chan-wook Park, 2013)

As noted at the beginning of this chapter, there are limits to what affect theory can do in "translating" the affective experience. And by way of a conclusion, I offer an experimental exercise, a "Sense Survey," which I (Kerner) have conducted in some of my classes for the past handful of years in an effort to measure the affective experience. There is no pretense to being "scientifically rigorous," but rather it is more about opening up possibilities for a discussion of the sensate experience, to illustrate the commonly shared instances where the cinematic elicits affect. I have conducted my Sense Survey a number of times in a large lecture setting in a proper theater, and with a handful of different films. For the present discussion I will focus on my experience of screening Chan-wook Park's 2013 film *Stoker*.

Just to briefly familiarize ourselves with the example, beyond what has already been discussed above, Park's film features India Stoker, whose eighteenth birthday is overshadowed upon the news of her father's (Richard) unexpected death. At the funeral, and subsequent wake, Charles Stoker, Richard's younger brother, makes an appearance. Uncle Charlie, as India knows him, is veiled in mystique, his background is only revealed in later flashbacks. Although effectively a stranger, Uncle Charlie quickly insinuates himself into the family.

Stoker elicits the beautiful through its cinematography, composition, editing, and its mobilization of musicality. Our primary character, India, is hyper-sensitive, as she informs us in the opening voice-over (cited above) that she can see and hear what others cannot, that "These senses are the fruits of a lifetime of longing." Furthermore, as we found in Park's 2016 film *The Handmaiden*, *Stoker*—while nowhere as explicit—also invites erotic interest. As much as *Stoker* is about India's (sexual) maturation and transformation as a character—"to become adult," or to become sexually awakened, or perhaps becoming a vampire(?) (vampirism often employed as a trope of sexual awakening)—from the very start the narrative is about the affective experience, which Park infuses into the cinematic form.

And as discussed in Chapter 7 "Romance," Park's *The Handmaiden* draws from Pier Paolo Pasolini's infamous 1975 film *Salò, or the 120 Days of Sodom*, accomplishing Pasolini's critique of the voyeuristic and sadistic gaze, as well as following the contours of *Salò*'s plot with the titillating reading performances in Uncle Kouzuki's secluded estate. Similarly, *Stoker* shares certain affinities with Pasolini's 1968 film *Teorema*, where a mysterious man arrives at a wealthy family home and individually seduces each family member. Following the outlines of *Teorema*'s plot, in *Stoker*, Uncle Charlie as referenced above arrives at the Stoker family estate on the occasion of his elder brother's death. At least to start Charles is an enigma, and seduces his newly widowed sister-in-law, Evelyn Stoker, and his niece India Stoker. The seductions in *Stoker* initiate something of an existential crisis in each of the characters, similar to what is found in *Teorema*. The seductions in *Stoker* suggest that Charles is a vampire—the surname is a clear reference to Bram Stoker, the author of *Dracula*.

In addition to these paratextual references, there are also nods to Alfred Hitchcock's 1960 film *Psycho*—a frozen corpse in the basement, a roadside motel (where a murder takes place), and a shower scene (referenced earlier). Like *The Handmaiden*, *Stoker* is sumptuously beautiful, and includes elements that invite erotic interest. To my surprise, though, as noted in the Sense Survey, when screened the film also elicits laughter, perhaps less in response to something that is "funny," and instead as a defensive gesture to keep the horror, dread, or the erotic at bay. The dinner scene, referenced above, in fact generated a measurable laughter-spike in the Sense Survey.

But I have gotten a bit ahead of myself, let me detail what my Sense Survey is, and what it does. In order to keep the Sense Survey as simple as possible, I capitalized on free and easily accessible technology. While far from perfect (for numerous reasons discussed later), the Sense Survey, nevertheless, is designed to track the affective experience of watching a film in a classroom/theatrical setting.[27] Using Google Forms, I designed a very simple form listing various affective experiences and levels of intensity. The intensity level is on a scale of 1 to 3. As noted on the survey itself, "On this scale 1 indicates that something is bubbling—sensing the emergence of goosebumps without them materializing, the emergence of laughter only materializing with a slight grin, and so on. A 2 on this scale indicates a clear materialization of the affective experience—tingling body, watery eyes. And a 3 indicates that you've had an intense response—an actual tear running down your face, flush with goosebumps, and so on." The affective categories on the survey are: laughter, goosebumps, tears (happiness), perspiration, tears (sadness), disgust, "I felt something . . .", and a blank field to write-in something. Students could use their mobile phone, or

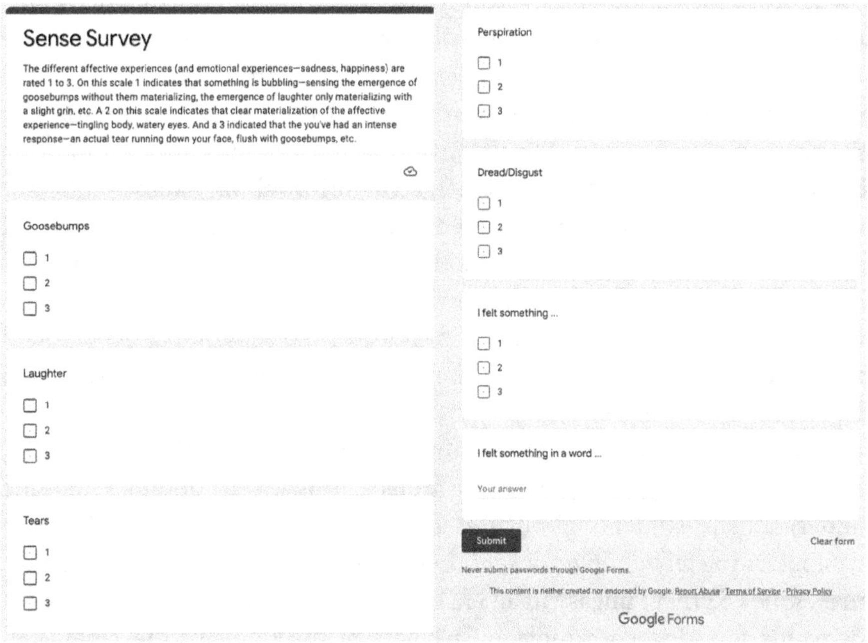

Figure 10.1 Kerner Sense Survey

some other Internet-enabled device to record their affective experiences as the film played. The Google Form automatically timestamps the data in a spreadsheet allowing us to see, in real time, affective spikes or apparent lulls in stimulus. By synchronizing the playtime of the film to the timestamped data we were subsequently able to match the affective experience with the film. Prior to the screening students are encouraged to submit as many responses as they like and are informed that the data are completely anonymous.

One of my (Kerner) teaching assistants for my Spring 2018 Critical Studies course, David Mai, assisted in visualizing the data to make the collected responses productive. Mai has continued to work with me on this, refining the survey, and reflecting on the pedagogical and scholarly utility of it. What we (Kerner and Mai) dubbed a "hit," corresponded to an individual response. Immediately upon tapping the "submit" button an affective response was recorded, and with each submission, the form would reload to allow the student to make another submission. During the Spring 2019 semester, we conducted a Sense Survey during the screening of Park's film *Stoker*. When the screening concluded we were left with over 630 hits. The question, then, was what to do with this data? Mai decided that the clearest way to interpret the data was through a heat-map visualization.

The Sense Survey graphs a linear timeline progression of the film on the x-axis, divided in one-minute intervals, while the y-axis is the sum of the hits within that single minute-along with the intensity of the hit. The Sense Survey attempts to slice the complexity of the recorded experience of the screened material into legible information. This specific visualization of the sense survey captured the affective trajectory of the collective viewing body of the audience. The use of cinemetrics brings about radically different modes of viewing a film and representations of the filmic text as a body—a body of frames, of movements, or colors. The visualization of data may not be the same kind of representation as found in cinematic representation (iconic), but data representation (an index of the sensational experience) is another way to make an image. The Sense Survey's heatmap visualization represents a body of sensations.

What is conspicuously absent from the option for affective experiences, as one might have noticed, is erotic arousal. This was by design. Querying undergraduate students about potential sexual arousal—even when the data is completely anonymous, and even as a tenured professor—frankly, makes me (Kerner) uneasy in an era of "more woke than thou," and student demands for trigger warnings. (Isn't part of the point of the cinema to be emotionally and affectively moved? Of course, I have no desire to

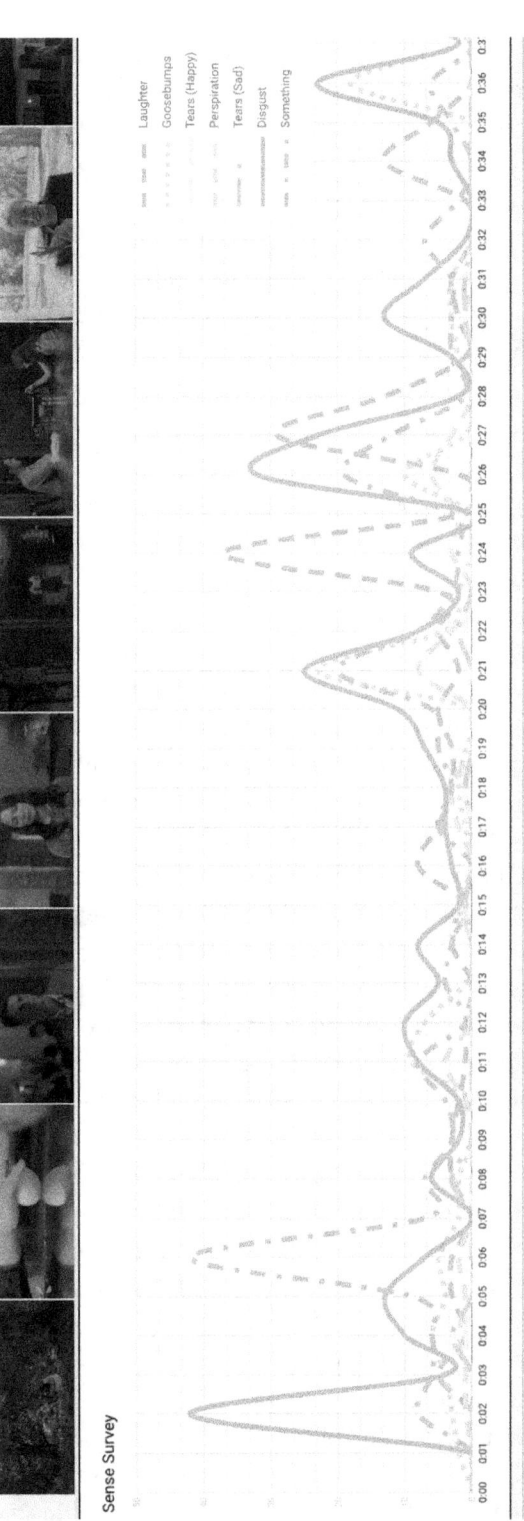

Figure 10.2 Kerner Sense Survey responses to a screening of Chan-wook Park's 2013 *Stoker* (Spring 2019)

"traumatize" students, which I have been accused of, but I fail to understand the compulsion to shield oneself from the emotional power and the affective potential of the cinematic. As numerous scholars have noted: the cinema is an emotion-machine.[28]) The "I felt something..." category was intended to record some sort of feeling (be that emotional or affective) that the student could not quite put a finger on. It was also intended as a coy (or perhaps a not so thinly veiled) work-around for the excluded erotic arousal category. However, what eventually did happen was that students posted comments, using the fill-in space, such as: "Hawt," "still hawt," "Super hawt," or erotically suggestive emojis (for example, face with mouth agape, eggplant, a smiling horned demon, tengu).

There are several limits to the Sense Survey. Clearly, one of the Achilles heels of the Sense Survey is that it is entirely reliant on self-reporting. Self-reporting might introduce a series of additional interrelated issues: (1) The operation of the Sense Survey necessitates that the spectator removes their attention from the screened material. And this is especially true if they elect to enter some word or phrase to articulate their feeling (beyond the simplified affective traits listed in the survey). (2) Timing. There might very well be a "lag" in the time that the affecting referent is presented and when the affecting experience is recorded in the survey. (3) Immersion. This could potentially cut two different ways (at least): on the one hand, the Sense Survey effectively asks the participants to turn their attention away from the very material that is being assessed as affecting, and on the other hand, the cinematic material very well might be so immersive that the participants fail to respond. And (4) Fatigue. As the screened material progresses, there is a chance that participants will become fatigued with the Sense Survey.[29] In addition to these "practical" problems, there is also the reliance on the individual respondents to be "honest"—even though the data is completely anonymous, respondents may not feel comfortable reporting what they are in fact feeling.

Furthermore, as with many experimental studies (that rely on college students as subjects), the sample population is very narrow—at least in terms of age range. Most of the participants were in their early 20s. In this specific case, the course is designed for Juniors. San Francisco State University, however, is a majority minority campus and the Cinema major largely reflects this. There is a general gender imbalance in our major (approximately 60/40) though, tending to skew toward the male demographic. That all said, aside from the very narrow age range, in other respects the sample group is fairly large and diverse. In addition to the Sense Survey, we (Kerner and Mai) discussed in the future the possibility of including a demographic survey too, in order to determine the racial, cultural, and gendered nuances of the audience as a collective viewing body. Collecting demographic data would bring the study of affect into conversation with the spheres of race, culture, class, gender, and sexual orientation. This too might allow us to potentially locate some of those demographic contingencies discussed in the present volume.

Additionally, the Sense Survey "cleans up" and quantifies an experience that is inherently "messy." Paasonen reflects on a similar "problem" in her own research on online pornography, recounting that in creating pie charts to summarize the grammar of pornography (for example, sucking, humping), felt that the exercise was somewhat absurd and "seemed far removed from the actual material discussed." While the charts served a utilitarian function, at the same time, Paasonen found it difficult to reconcile the apparent paradox that was "transform[ing] explicit sexual representations into tidy graphics. The ample visual landscape of body parts and bodily fluids is simply effaced." Encoding affective experiences, and the messiness of sex in particular, into abstracted visual data sets "translate[s] pornographic material into something easily distanced and approachable, and when faced with them, it is easy to resort to the position of an outside observer."[30] Although the Sense Survey is different in many regards to Paasonen's own research, it is important not to lose sight of the inherent "messiness" that lies behind the Sense Survey data. Quantifying the affective experience into a graph "simplifies" the inherent complexities of the lived-realities of a sensorial encounter.

Nevertheless, the Sense Survey is a useful tool in recognizing specifically affecting cinematic moments, and how specific cinematic strategies wield the potential to stimulate the sensate body. The objective is not to name objects, rather the Sense Survey is useful in isolating commonly shared moments in a film that elicits an affective experience amongst viewers—to identify affective events, or shared resonance. For example, one of the surprising moments that elicited a strong response in the Sense Survey comes when India cracks a hardboiled egg. There was nothing particularly obvious in the narrative content that would elicit a strong visceral response, but rather what appeared to elicit the intense response was the sound design. It illustrates (to the students) just how important that specific embellishments (for example, sound design, color, composition) are—that is to say the stylistic treatment of the material. It is not simply that India is rolling a hardboiled egg across a table, but in how the audio design (affectively) "amplifies" the content. The material itself is rather banal, but this mundane moment elicits a strong response in how it is treated. Again, the point is not to create a taxonomy of affective things/objects, which Eugenie Brinkema warns against (as I have cited previously), but rather to call our attention to the cinematic form that is pregnant with affective potential.[31]

My Critical Studies course, where I have conducted the Sense Survey, is a large class (anywhere from 80 to 120 students) and meets separately in smaller sections of 20 students led by a graduate student to discuss that week's course material. Days after the screening, Mai observed a few of the secondary discussion sessions. When the graduate instructor would choose a timestamp with a high number of hits, the corresponding scene often showcased an audiovisual embellishment that amplified the affective content. If nothing else, the Sense Survey proved an interesting teaching tool that allowed students—without having to reveal anything about themselves personally—to discuss the results of the anonymous data. Identifying scenes that elicited a strong affective response allowed the graduate student instructor to focus the discussion. Students were prompted to interrogate the cinematic material that was revealed to be affecting in the data—not just what was happening in terms of narrative content, but how the cinematic forms are choreographed: sound design, the scoring, the composition, the lighting, the editing, and so on.

For example, after India stabs a male student's palm with a sharpened pencil, followed by an extreme close-up of India sharpening that same

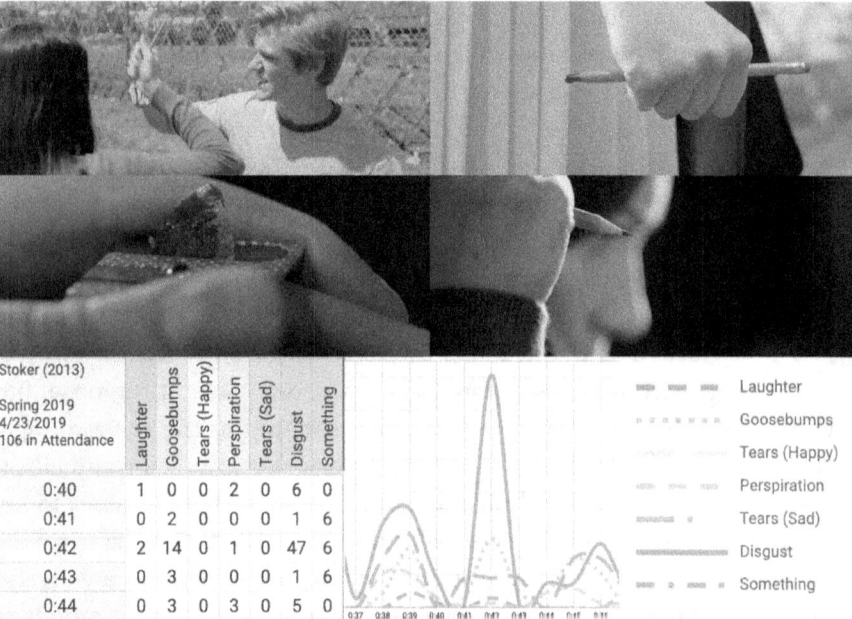

Figure 10.3 Kerner Sense Survey responses to a screening of Chan-wook Park's 2013 *Stoker* (Spring 2019)

blood-stained pencil, this elicited a wide range of affective responses: laughter 2 hits; goosebumps 14 hits; tears (happiness) 0 hits; perspiration 1 hit; tears (sadness) 0 hits; disgust 47 hits; and "I felt something . . ." 6 hits. Bringing the data to the section, and isolating the scene, students were able to discern that it was not simply the stabbing, or the sight of the blood-stained pencil, but rather upon close review it was in fact the audio design that elicited the strong visceral response. The extreme close-up of India turning the pencil with the wooden shaving peeling off a bloodied pencil tip is accompanied by (an obviously highly embellished) squishy audio design. As India turns the pencil against the face of the blade, the edge of the sharpener strips off more and more of the blood-soaked layer with a sickening sound that might be likened to that of flaying skin. What was particularly interesting was the students' choice of words in describing the affecting sound design: students would compare the sounds of the inorganic objects (that is, sharpening the pencil) to food and other edible material. The wetness of the audio design is crucial here in eliciting the strong affective response.

Aurel Kolnai's *On Disgust* observes that disgust is often triggered by proximity, an undesired closeness through touching, seeing, or smelling. Disgust elicited from an aural source though is, for Kolnai, harder to conceive.[32] Despite Kolnai's reservations, the elicitation of disgust through sound that suggests softness or wetness, connotes transition, the slipping between states, solidly coherent/dissolving putrefaction, but also eating as indicated in some of the student responses. Eating is yet another form of transition, and the erasure of boundaries between inside and outside. And interestingly, wetness can also elicit erotic interest (as discussed in Chapter 6 and 7).[33] Wetness appears to vacillate between disgust and erotic fascination precisely because it is suggestive of the breakdown of boundaries—be that in kissing/fucking (erotic), or eating/drinking, putrefaction/dankness (disgust). (And this vacillation evokes the Bakhtinian principle of grotesque realism discussed in Chapters 8 and 9.) In the case of the bloodied pencil the squishy sound brings the negative connotation of wetness into close proximity, and "by creating overwhelming and dislocating loudness, unwanted intimacy, and over-proximity" as Lisa Coulthard observes, invites disgust. And it is worth noting again, that not only is the audio-design amplified (louder than would be natural), but it is also "amplified" through the use of the extreme close-up.[34] Demonstrating that affect is located in the form.

The Sense Survey marks points of (conflicting?) affective convergences. The shot of the blood-stained pencil opens up Park's musicalized montage: India opens her tarnished brass pencil case, followed by a one-second insert shot of Mrs. McGarrick's frozen corpse in the freezer located in the

254 Abject Pleasures in the Cinematic

basement. (Mrs. McGarrick's frozen corpse in the basement is perhaps yet one more reference to *Psycho*.) This is followed with Uncle Charlie's silhouette, and juxtaposed with an extreme (or near extreme) close-up shot of India's eyes, his voice is heard in reverb, "Too cold down there?" All the while the rattling of the freezer laces the soundscape. Notably, as India curiously observes Mrs. McGarrick's (Bakhtinian) grotesque body (which is carefully positioned amongst a collection of frozen meat), her heavy-loaded breath suggests sexual interest. And this coupling of Eros and Thanatos is also worked into the sound design, because when India opens the piano (associated with the erotic—with the duet discussed below) once again the rattle of the freezer is heard. Interestingly, the sound design playfully amplifies our affective experience beyond disgust, potentially sliding toward the realm of arousal. And while the affective experience might manifest differently from individual to individual—while one chuckles, the other experiences goosebumps, or ambiguously "feels something"—the peaks tend to converge at specific affecting moments. The variation in responses offers an example of the Kantian conception of "subjective universality" (discussed in

Figure 10.4 Kerner Sense Survey responses to a screening of Chan-wook Park's 2013 *Stoker* (Spring 2019)

Chapter 2).³⁵ To add to this, the blood-stained pencil scene in *Stoker* is choreographed as a prelude to the piano duet scene (discussed below), which is clearly fraught with erotic tension. While there was a noticeable response in the Sense Survey, the responses varied dramatically.

Philip Glass composed the "Duet" for *Stoker*, and his "trademark triplet arpeggios"³⁶ recall Yorke's hypnotic tracks in *Suspiria*. "Duet" was performed by Sugar Vendil and Trevor Gureckis, the latter having worked for Glass for six years. The choreographed body movement of the two piano players was by design—Glass intentionally composed the track so that "one player has to put his arm around the other player."³⁷ Clare Nina Norelli observes, a "dissonant harmonic interval" is heard three times, before India starts to play the three-note motif, which we have heard a few times earlier in the movie.³⁸ With the duet, Charlie sits right next to India, sharing a small piano bench. And per the requirements of the piece, at one point Charlie reaches around India to play at the far end of the keyboard. Their bodies are so close to each other, though, never really touching. The duet enacts caressing, as the players wrap around each other, and notes swirl round and round (again, very similar to what we find in Thom Yorke's score for *Suspiria* discussed in Chapter 3). The erotic charge of the piece is made transparent in India's obvious sexual excitement—the way she reflexively tilts her head back, eyes at certain moments closed (abandoning the world to sensuous pleasure), the parted lips, the licking of lips, the curling of her feet, the slow rhythmic rocking, and her labored breath. The three-note triad and lektonic utterances in effect "translate" the non-linguistic expressions of India's pleasures. The duo playing is choreographed to elicit a strong emotional and affective response, despite the fact that nothing explicit is depicted, what Park offers us is caressing, touching, fucking through the musicalization of the image and Glass's "Duet." The piano duet scene elicited all of the affective categories in the Sense Survey—from goosebumps (17 hits) to disgust (21 hits) to "I felt something . . ." (23 hits) and everything in-between. While the scene presumably aims to elicit the beautiful and perhaps erotic interest, which is confirmed in the survey, what the Sense Survey also reveals is that the affecting experience can be multimodal and highly subjective.

The Sense Survey visualized the affective pulse of the film. Anecdotally, I can report that students found the Sense Survey productive. The vast majority of our students focus on production, and more than one student seeing the spikes in affective responses and how those directly correlated with the critical scholarship that we were reading, said, "Well, maybe this theory stuff isn't bullshit after all."

Laura Mulvey in her landmark essay, "Visual Pleasure and Narrative Cinema," proclaims in the conclusion that, "The first blow against the monolithic accumulation of traditional film conventions (already undertaken by radical filmmakers) is to free the look of the camera into its materiality in time and space and the look of the audience into dialectics and passionate detachment." Mulvey concedes though, that this undoubtedly "destroys the satisfaction, pleasure and privilege of the 'invisible guest,' and highlights the way film has depended on voyeuristic active/passive mechanisms."[39] There is, within our disciplinary DNA, an inherent distrust of the cinematic—with its seductive powers to bewitch and to stupefy us. Rosalind Galt observes that feminist film theory focuses its attention on the female masquerade and "locates political critique on the surface," and in our attention on the surface image leads to the iconoclastic logic within our discipline. And thus, the imperative in our discipline is to distance ourselves from the material and resist its seductive powers. As Galt recites, "The image in its imageness is the problem, a seductive surface that cannot be trusted unless it can be made to speak against itself. Only by keeping our distance can we be rational, make readings, be masculine."[40] Something very similar occurs with respect to affect, especially pleasurable affects associated with abject material. Being affected by the cinematic, insofar as our disciplinary DNA tells us, is synonymous with being duped. But as Paasonen notes, "a scholar studying porn who is never aroused by it is as anomalous and misplaced a creature as a researcher studying comedy who is never moved to laughter or a scholar working on horror who fails to jump or flinch." It is not that the affective experience is more "important" than the potential "meanings"—each is important in their own ways and may in some fashion work hand-in-hand with one another—nevertheless, to neglect, or to feign scholarly aloofness, is to fail to fully appreciate the power of the cinematic.[41] Turning our attention to affect, as I have stated at various points in the present volume, does not require us to abandon our critical perspective, but this should not necessarily come at the expense of all the pleasures that the cinematic has to offer. It is time for a significant paradigm shift in our discipline!

Notes

1 In many instances the text in this concluding chapter is truly a team effort, but there are other instances where specific contributions are named within the text.
2 Susanna Paasonen, *Carnal Resonance: Affect and Online Pornography* (Cambridge, MA: MIT Press, 2011), 201.
3 See David Church's *Disposable Passions* for a discussion of the shifting sexual tastes in American porn consumption, fueled by social, individual, economic, and legal factors.

David Church, *Disposable Passions: vintage pornography and the material legacies of adult cinema* (New York: Bloomsbury, 2016), 132–44.
4 "Aesthetic," s.v. *OED*.
5 Immanuel Kant, *Critique of Judgement*, trans. James Creed Meredith (New York: Oxford University Press, 2007), 36.
6 Melissa McMahon, "Beauty: Machinic repetition in the age of art," in *A Shock to Thought: Expression after Deleuze and Guattari*, ed. Brian Massumi (New York: Routledge, 2002), 46. McMahon references Immanuel Kant, *Critique of Judgement*, trans. W. S. Pluhar (Indianapolis: Hackett, 1987), 30.
7 Anne Fernald interview "Sound as Touch," *Radiolab*, NPR, September 24, 2007, https://www.wnycstudios.org/podcasts/radiolab/segments/91514-sound-as-touch.
8 There is also a nod to Brian De Palma's 1976 film *Carrie* as well.
9 Susanna Paasonen, "Grains of Resonance: Affect, Pornography and Visual Sensation," *Somatechnics* vol. 3, no. 2 (2013): 357.
10 Paasonen, *Carnal Resonance*, 16. Paasonen draws her conception of resonance from Susan Kozel. See Susan Kozel, *Closer: Performance, Technologies, Phenomenology* (Cambridge, MA: MIT Press, 2007), 24–6.
11 Paasonen, *Carnal Resonance*, 254.
12 Laura Kipnis, *Bound and Gagged: Pornography and the Politics of Fantasy in America* (Durham, NC: Duke University Press, 1999), 197.
13 Paasonen, "Grains of Resonance," 360.
14 David Mai was the first to link the significance of enunciation in the storytelling back to the discussion of *25th Hour*.
15 Paasonen summarizes:

> The notion of somatic archives also comes close to that of kinesthetic empathy—that is, feeling sensations in one's body that are similar to those watched on the screen or in front of oneself. In kinesthetic empathy [referencing Laukkanen], the sight of other people moving calls forth responses in one's own body. To a degree, such empathy is central to the "body genres" discussed by Williams and Dyer that aim to move the viewers' bodies. This motion is largely precognitive, based on the capacities and affordances of the body, [citing Nigel Thrift] for the 'roiling mass of nerve volleys prepare the body for action in such a way that intentions or decisions are made before the conscious self is even aware of them.' As I see it, this is not a modality of identification with characters or narrative but one of corporeal, fleshy relationality and resonance.

Paasonen, *Carnal Resonance*, 202–3. See Anu Laukkanen, "Hips Don't Lie? Affective and Kinaesthetic Dance Ethnography," in *Working with Affect in Feminist Readings: Disturbing Differences*, eds Marianne Liljeström and Susanna Paasonen (London: Routledge, 2010), 131; and Nigel Thrift, *Non-Representational Theory: Space / Politics / Affect* (London: Routledge. 2008), 7.
16 Vittorio Gallese and Hannah Wojciehowski, "How stories make us feel: Toward an embodied narratology," *California Italian Studies* vol. 2, no. 1 (2011): no pagination. https://doi.org/10.5070/C321008974. See Vittorio Gallese et al. "Action Recognition in the Premotor Cortex," *Brain* vol. 119 (1996): 593–609; and Giacomo Rizzolati et al., "Premotor Cortex and the Recognition of Motor Actions," *Cognitive Brain Research* vol. 3, no. 2 (1996): 131–41.
17 Vittorio Gallese and Michele Guerra, *The Empathic Screen: Cinema and Neuroscience*, trans. Frances Anderson (Oxford: Oxford University Press, 2020), 4–5.

18 Gallese and Wojciehowski. See Vittorio Gallese and George Lakoff, "The Brain's Concepts: The Role of the Sensory-Motor System in Reason and Language," *Cognitive Neuropsychology* vol. 22, no. 3 (2005): 455–79; Vittorio Gallese, "Before and below 'theory of mind': embodied simulation and the neural correlates of social cognition," *Philosophical Transactions of the Royal Society B: Biological Sciences* vol. 358 (2003): 517–28; Vittorio Gallese, "Il corpo teatrale: mimetismo, neuroni specchio, simulazione incarnata," *Culture teatrali* 16 (2008): 13–38; and Arthur M. Glenberg and Vittorio Gallese, "Action-based language: A theory of language acquisition, comprehension, and production," *Cortex* vol. 48, no. 7 (2012): 905–22.
19 Gallese and Guerra, 70.
20 Vittorio Gallese, "Visions of the body: Embodied simulation and aesthetic experience," *Aisthesis. Pratiche, linguaggi e saperi dell'estetico* vol. 10, no. 1 (2017): 43.
21 Gilles Deleuze, *Francis Bacon: The Logic of Sensation*, trans. Daniel W. Smith (Minneapolis: University of Minnesota Press, 2004), 45.
22 Gallese and Guerra, 37–8.
23 Julian Hanich, *The Audience Effect: On the Collective Cinema Experience* (Edinburgh: Edinburgh University Press, 2018), 196. Emphasis in original.
24 Mikhail Bakhtin, *Rabelais and His World*, trans. Helene Iswolsky (Bloomington: Indiana University Press, 1984), 317.
25 Ibid.
26 Anecdotally, Mai recalls during a screening of *Stoker* students awkwardly laughing at India's shower masturbation scene—trying to laugh the taboos away.
27 We are aware of similar experimental studies, however, one of the things that behavioral, neurological, and psychological sciences often fail to truly appreciate is the full audio-visual experience of the cinematic. A small screen and headphones, is a poor substitute for the fully embodied spectatorial experience. Audio design in particular should be felt, not simply just heard. Simply relying on headphones suggests an inherent bias in many studies that naively presume that narrative meaning matters more than the cinematic form. Some of the experimental studies also involve subjects strapped to cumbersome biometric devices, or compel subjects to stare at a specific focus point (for example, to record pupil dilation). Furthermore, a number of studies use extracted clips, rather than screening cinematic material in its entirety. While I (Kerner) have emphasized the significance of momentary aesthetic ruptures in the narrative that might elicit an affective experience—the affective experience strikes like lightning, it's not a sustained experience—I would not go so far as to suggest that we should sacrifice the integrity of a unified cinematic piece. Placing an affective experience in context, not necessarily narrative context, but aesthetic context remains important. Furthermore, the lab setting is no match to a theater equipped with a high-end projector and sound system. This is not to suggest that an affective experience cannot happen in a relatively "sterile clinical environment," clearly it can. Furthermore, we freely admit that most individuals are not consuming cinematic material in a theatrical setting. Clearly affective experiences are had on small devices with equipment that nominally passes as a sound system (for example, earbuds). Porn is probably more often than not consumed on smaller devices, and yet still gets the affective job done. The point remains though, that the relative impoverishment of the laboratory setting does not bring the full range of cinematic aesthetic strategies to bear.

28 See for example Ed S. Tan, *Emotion and the Structure of Narrative Film: Film as an Emotion Machine* (Mahwah, N.J: Erlbaum, 1996).
29 Mai notes that this is borne out in the Sense Survey too, with the amplitude of the peaks being noticeably lower on average in the latter half of the screenings.
30 Paasonen, *Carnal Resonance*, 135.
31 Eugenie Brinkema, *The Forms of the Affects* (Durham, NC: Duke University Press, 2014), 130–1.
32 Aurel Kolnai, *On Disgust* (Chicago: Open Court, 2004), 48.
33 For the acoustic slip between disgust and eroticism see: Lisa Coulthard, "Acoustic Disgust: Sound, Affect, and Cinematic Violence," in *The Palgrave Handbook of Sound Design and Music in Screen Media: Integrated Soundtracks*, eds Liz Greene and Danijela Kulezic-Wilson (London: Palgrave Macmillan, 2016), 190.
34 Coulthard, 188.
35 Kant, 43.
36 Clare Nina Norelli, "Scores on Screen: Piano Lessons: Death and Desire in Park Chan-wook's *Stoker*," *Notebook Column* (blog), MUBI, September 4, 2018, https://mubi.com/notebook/posts/scores-on-screen-piano-lessons-death-and-desire-in-park-chan-wook-s-stoker.
37 Richard Guerin, "Glass Notes: Love Is in the Air," *glass notes* (blog), philipglass.com, July 9, 2014, https://philipglass.com/glassnotes/love-is-in-the-air/
38 Norelli.
39 Laura Mulvey, *Visual and Other Pleasures* (Bloomington: Indiana University Press, 1989), 26.
40 Rosalind Galt, *Pretty: Film and the Decorative Image* (Columbia University Press, 2011), 256.
41 Paasonen, *Carnal Resonance*, 23.

Bibliography

"The 2019 Year in Review," *Pornhub INSIGHTS*, December 11, 2019. https://www.pornhub.com/insights/2019-year-in-review.
Adorno, Theodor W. *Aesthetic Theory*. Translated by Robert Hullot-Kentor, edited by Gretel Adorno and Rolf Tiedemann. Minneapolis: University of Minnesota Press, 1999.
Adorno, Theodor W. "Functionalism today." Translated by Jane O. Newman and John H. Smith. *Oppositions* 17 (1979): 30–41.
Ahmed, Sara. "Creating Disturbance: Feminism, Happiness and Affective Differences." In *Working with Affect in Feminist Readings: Disturbing Differences*, edited by Marianne Liljeström and Susanna Paasonen, 31–44. London: Routledge, 2010.
Ahmed, Sara. *The Cultural Politics of Emotion*. New York: Routledge, 2013.
Altieri, Charles. "II Affect, Intentionality, and Cognition: A response to Ruth Leys." *Critical Inquiry* vol. 38, no. 4 (2012): 878–81.
Andrew, Dudley, ed. *The Image in Dispute: Art and Cinema in the Age of Photography*. Austin: University of Texas Press, 1997.
Andrews, David. *Theorizing Art Cinemas: Foreign, Cult, Avant-Garde, and Beyond*. Austin: University of Texas Press, 2013.
Aristotle. *On the Parts of the Animals I-IV*. Translated by James G. Lennox. Oxford: Oxford University Press, 2004.
Ashton, Sara, Karalyn McDonald, and Maggie Kirkman. "Pornography and Women's Sexual Pleasure: Accounts from Young Women in Australia." *Feminism & Psychology* vol. 29, no. 3 (2019): 409–32.
Bae, Keungyoon. "Admitting an Attraction: Colonial Villainy, Visuality, and *The Handmaiden* (2016) as Critique." *International Journal of Korean History* vol. 25, no. 2 (2020): 175–88.
Bain, Alexander. *The Emotions and the Will*. New York: D. Appleton & Company, 1876.
Barthes, Roland. *Sade/Fourier/Loyola*. Translated by Richard Miller. New York: Hill and Wang, 1976.
Bakhtin, Mikhail. *Rabelais and His World*. Translated by Helene Iswolsky. Bloomington: Indiana University Press, 1984.
Balsom, Erika. "One Hundred Years of Low Definition." In *Indefinite Visions: Cinema and the Attractions of Uncertainty*, edited by Martine Beugnet, Allan Cameron, and Arild Fetveit, 74–89. Edinburgh: Edinburgh University Press, 2017.
Barker, Martin. "The 'Problem' of Sexual Fantasies." *Porn Studies* vol. 1, nos. 1–2 (2014): 143–60.

Baron, Zach. "Rakes' Debauched Progress in Denmark," *New York Times*, July 20, 2012. https://nyti.ms/LyiHkJ.
Barss, Patchen. *The Erotic Engine*. Toronto: Anchor Canada, 2011.
Bataille, Georges. *The Accursed Share: An Essay on the General Economy Vol. 1, Consumption*, translated by Robert Hurley. New York: Zone Books, 1988.
Baudelaire, Charles. "On the Essence of Laughter, and, in General, on the Comic in the Plastic Arts." In *Comedy: Meaning and Form*, edited by Robert Corrigan. San Francisco: Chandler, 1965.
Bell, Whitney. "This Woman Turned Her Collection of Unsolicited Dick Pics into an Art Show." Interviewed by Alison Stevenson. *Vice*, April 15, 2016. https://www.vice.com/en/article/ppxjem/this-woman-turned-her-collection-of-unsolicited-dick-pics-into-an-art-show.
Belodubrovskaya, Maria. "The Cine-Fist Eisenstein's Attractions, Mirror Neurons, and Contemporary Action Cinema." *Projections* vol. 12, no. 1 (Summer 2018): 1–18.
Bergson, Henri. *Laughter: An Essay on the Meaning of the Comic*. Translated by Cloudesley Brereton and Fred Rothwell. New York: The Macmillan Company, 1914.
Bertelsen, Lone, and Andrew Murphie. "An Ethics of Everyday Infinities and Powers: Félix Guattari and Affect and the Refrain." In *The Affect Theory Reader*, edited by Melissa Gregg, and Gregory J. Seigworth, 138–58. Durham, NC: Duke University Press, 2010.
Beugnet, Martine. *Cinema of Sensation: French Film and the Art of Transgression*. Carbondale: Southern Illinois University Press, 2007.
Billig, Michael. *Laughter and Ridicule: Towards a Social Critique of Humour*. Thousand Oaks, CA: SAGE Publications, 2005.
Black, Joel D. "Levana: Levitation in Jean Paul and Thomas De Quincey." *Comparative Literature* vol. 32, no. 1 (1980): 42–62.
Bocher, Moshe, et al. "Cerebral activation associated with sexual arousal in response to a pornographic clip: a 15O–H2O PET study in heterosexual men." *Neuroimage* vol. 14, no. 1 (2001): 105–117.
Bondanella, Peter. *A History of Italian Cinema*. New York: Continuum, 2009.
Bordun, Troy Michael. "The End of Extreme Cinema Studies," *Canadian Review of Comparative Literature* vol. 44, no. 1 (March 2017): 122–36.
Bordwell, David. "The Viewer's Share: Models of mind in explaining film." In *Psychocinematics: Exploring Cognition at the Movies*, edited by Arthur P. Shimamura, 29–52. New York: Oxford University Press, 2013.
Bordwell, David. "Brains, bodies, and movies: Ways of thinking about the psychology of cinema." *Observations on film art* (blog). *David Bordwell's website on cinema*, April 29, 2020. http://www.davidbordwell.net/blog/2020/04/29/brains-bodies-and-movies-ways-of-thinking-about-the-psychology-of-cinema/.
Bordwell, David. "Mirror neurons and cinema: Further discussion." *Observations on film art* (blog). *David Bordwell's website on cinema*, August 16, 2020. http://www.davidbordwell.net/blog/2020/08/16/mirror-neurons-and-cinema-further-discussion/.
Bordwell, David. "This is your brain on movies, maybe." *Observations on film art* (blog). *David Bordwell's website on cinema*, March 7, 2007. http://www.davidbordwell.net/blog/2007/03/07/this-is-your-brain-on-movies-maybe/.
Bourdieu, Pierre. *Distinction: A social critique of the judgement of taste*. Translated by Richard Nice. Cambridge, MA: Harvard University Press, 1984.

Brinkema, Eugenie. "Celluloid Is Sticky: Sex, Death, Materiality, Metaphysics (in Some Films by Catherine Breillat)." *Women: A Cultural Review* vol. 17, no. 2 (2006): 147–70.

Brinkema, Eugenie. "Laura Dern's Vomit, or, Kant and Derrida in Oz." *Film-Philosophy* 15, no. 2 (2011): 51–69.

Brinkema, Eugenie. *The Forms of the Affects*. Durham, NC: Duke University Press, 2014.

Bruno, Giuliana. *Atlas of Emotion: Journeys in art, architecture, and film*. New York: Verso Books, 2018.

Buck-Morss, Susan. "Aesthetics and Anaesthetics: Walter Benjamin's artwork essay reconsidered." *October* vol. 62 (1992): 3–41.

Burgin, Victor. *The end of art theory*. London: Macmillan International Higher Education, 1986.

Butler, Judith. *Gender Trouble*. New York: Routledge, 2002.

Carroll, Noël. "Ethics and comic amusement." *British Journal of Aesthetics* vol. 54, no. 2 (2014): 241–53.

Carroll, Noël. "On some affective relations between audiences and the characters in popular fictions." In *Empathy: Philosophical and psychological perspectives*, edited by Amy Coplan and Peter Goldie, 162–84. New York: Oxford University Press, 2011.

Carroll, Noël. "Film, Emotion, and Genre." *Philosophy of Film and Motion Pictures: An Anthology*, edited by Noël Carroll and Jinhee Choi, 217–33. Hoboken: Wiley, 2009.

Carvalho, Joana, et al. "Gender Differences in Sexual Arousal and Affective Responses to Erotica: The Effects of Type of Film and Fantasy Instructions." *Archives of Sexual Behavior* 42 (2013): 1011–19.

Castello-Branco, Patricia. "Pure Sensations? From abstract film to digital images." *Animation* vol. 5, no. 1 (2010): 25–40.

Céline, Louis-Ferdinand. *Death on the Installment Plan*. Translated by Ralph Manheim. New York: New Directions, 1966.

Céline, Louis-Ferdinand. *Entretiens avec le professeur Y*. Paris: Gallimard, 1954.

Céline, Louis-Ferdinand. *Guignol's Band*. Translated by Bernard Frechtman and Jack T. Nile. New York: New Directions, 1969.

Céline, Louis-Ferdinand. *L'Ecole des cadavres*. Paris: Denoel, 1938.

Céline, Louis-Ferdinand. *Rigadoon*. Translated by Ralph Manheim. New York: Dell, 1974.

Champion, Jared N. "'This Kindergarten Country of Ours': Daniel Tosh's Postmodern Social Politics." *The Journal of Popular Culture* vol. 51, no. 3 (2018): 595–614.

Choe, Steve. "Park Chan-wook's Critique of Moral Judgment: The Handmaiden (2016)." *Studies in the Humanities* vol. 44, nos. 1–2 (2017) & vol. 45, nos. 1–2 (2018): 20–37.

Church, David. *Disposable Passions: vintage pornography and the material legacies of adult cinema*. New York: Bloomsbury, 2016.

Ciclitira, Karen. "Pornography, Women and Feminism: Between Pleasure and Politics." *Sexualities* vol. 7, no. 3 (2004): 281–301.

Colver, Mitchell C., and Amani El-Alayli. "Getting aesthetic chills from music: The connection between openness to experience and frisson." *Psychology of Music* vol. 44, no. 3 (2016): 413–27.

Connolly, William E. "I The Complexity of Intention." *Critical Inquiry* vol. 37, no. 4 (2011): 791–8.

Cooper, Sarah, Paúl M. Velazco, and Hunter Schantz. "Navigating in Darkness: Human Echolocation with Comments on Bat Echolocation." *HAPS Educator* vol. 24, no. 2 (2020): 36–41.
Coulthard, Lisa. "Acoustic Disgust: Sound, Affect, and Cinematic Violence." In *The Palgrave Handbook of Sound Design and Music in Screen Media: Integrated Soundtracks*, edited by Liz Greene and Danijela Kulezic-Wilson, 183–93. London: Palgrave Macmillan, 2016.
Coulthard, Lisa. "Dirty Sound: Haptic Noise in New Extremism." In *The Oxford Handbook of Sound and Image in Digital Media*, edited by Carol Vernallis, Amy Herzog, and John Richardson, 115–26. New York: Oxford University Press, 2013.
Creed, Barbara. *The monstrous-feminine: Film, feminism, psychoanalysis*. London: Routledge, 1993.
Cruz, Ariane. "Pornography: A Black Feminist Woman Scholar's Reconciliation." In *The Feminist Porn Book: The Politics of Producing Pleasure*, edited by Tristan Taormino et al., 215–27. New York: The Feminist Press at CUNY, 2013.
Cruz, Ariane. *The Color of Kink: Black Women, BDSM, and Pornography*. New York: New York University Press, 2016.
Daneback, Kristian, Bente Træen, and Sven-Axel Månsson. "Use of pornography in a random sample of Norwegian heterosexual couples." *Archives of Sexual Behavior* vol. 38, no. 5 (2009): 746–53.
Das, Lina. "I felt raped by Brando." *The Daily Mail*, July 19, 2007. https://www.dailymail.co.uk/tvshowbiz/article-469646/I-felt-raped-Brando.html.
Daskalopoulou, Athanasia, and Maria Carolina Zanette. "Women's Consumption of Pornography: Pleasure, Contestation, and Empowerment." *Sociology* vol. 54, no. 5 (2020): 969–86.
Shier, David. "Why Kant Finds Nothing Ugly." *The British Journal of Aesthetics* vol. 38, no. 4 (October, 1998): 412–18.
Davis, Murray. *Smut: Erotic Reality/Obscene Ideology*. Chicago: University of Chicago Press, 1985.
De Boever, Arne. "Losing Face: Francis Bacon's *25th Hour*." *Film-Philosophy* vol. 16, no. 1 (2012): 85–100.
Decety, Jean, et al. "The Timing of Mentally Represented Actions." *Behavioral Brain Research* vol. 34, nos. 1–2 (1989): 35–42.
Decety, Jean, et al. "Vegetative Response during Imagined Movement is Proportional to Mental Effort." *Behavioral Brain Research* vol. 42, no. 1 (1991): 1–5.
De Quincey, Thomas. *Confessions of an English Opium-eater and Other Writings*, edited by Robert Morrison. Oxford: Oxford University Press, 2013.
De Quincey, Thomas. *Suspiria De Profundis*. Blackmask Online, 2001. http://public-library.uk/ebooks/28/2.pdf.
Deleuze, Gilles, and Félix Guattari. *A Thousand Plateaus: Capitalism and Schizophrenia*. Translated by Brian Massumi. Minneapolis: University of Minnesota Press, 2005.
Deleuze, Gilles. *Cinema 1: The Movement-Image*. Translated by Hugh Tomlinson and Barbara Habberjam. Minneapolis: University of Minnesota Press, 1997.
Deleuze, Gilles. *Francis Bacon: The Logic of Sensation*. Translated by Daniel W. Smith. Minneapolis: University of Minnesota Press, 2002.

Dennis, Kelly. "'Leave it to Beaver': The Object of Pornography." *Strategies for Theory: From Marx to Madonna*, edited by R. L. Rutsky and Bradley J. Macdonald, 187–224. New York: SUNY Press, 2003.

Dew, Oliver. "'Asia Extreme': Japanese Cinema and British Hype." *New Cinemas: Journal of Contemporary Film* vol. 5, no. 1 (2007): 53–73.

Dreyfus, Hubert, and Sean Dorrance Kelly. *All Things Shining: Reading the Western Classics to Find Meaning in a Secular Age*. New York: Free Press, 2011.

Duncan, Pansy. "Joke work: comic labor and the aesthetics of the awkward." *Comedy Studies* vol. 8, no. 1 (2017): 36–56.

Dyer, Richard. *Only Entertainment*. 2nd edn. London: Routledge, 2002.

Eco, Umberto. "The Frames of Comic 'Freedom.'" In *Carnival!* edited by Thomas A. Sebeok, 1–10. New York: Mouton, 1984.

Eisenstein, Sergei. "The Montage of Attractions." In *The Eisenstein Reader*, edited by Richard Taylor, 29–34. London: BFI, 1998.

Eleftheriotis, Dimitris, and Gary Needham, eds. *Asian Cinemas: A Reader and Guide*. Honolulu: University of Hawai'i Press, 2006.

Fetveit, Arild. "Mutable temporality in and beyond the music video: an aesthetic of post-production." In *Between Stillness and Motion: Film, Photography, Algorithms*, edited by Eivind Røssaak, 159–86. Amsterdam: Amsterdam University Press, 2011.

Flanagan, Martin. *Bakhtin and the Movies: New Ways of Understanding Hollywood Films*. New York: Palgrave Macmillan, 2009.

Foucault, Michel. "Preface." In *Anti-Oedipus: Capitalism and Schizophrenia*, by Gilles Deleuze and Félix Guattari, xiii–xvi. Translated by Robert Hurley, Mark Seem, and Helen R. Lane. Minneapolis: University of Minnesota Press, 1983.

Foucault, Michel. *Aesthetics, Method, and Epistemology: Essential Works of Foucault* Vol. 2. Edited by James Faubion. Translated by Robert Hurley et al. New York: The New Press, 1998.

Freud, Sigmund. *Jokes and Their Relation to the Unconscious*. Edited by James Strachey. New York: Basic Books, 1960.

Freud, Sigmund. *Sigmund Freud Collected Papers*. Edited by James Strachey. New York: Basic Books, 1960.

Frisch, Benjamin. "All Is Full of Björk Bots," *Slate*, January 23, 2018, https://slate.com/technology/2018/01/how-bjrk-robots-influenced-the-way-we-think-about-the-future.html.

Fulmer, Ellie Fitts, and Nia Nunn Makepeace. "'It's Okay to Laugh, Right?': Toward a Pedagogy of Racial Comedy in Multicultural Education." *Penn GSE Perspectives on Urban Education* vol. 12, no. 1 (2015): 38–53.

Gallese, Vittorio. "A Bodily Take on Aesthetics: Performativity and Embodied Simulation Mechanisms." In *The Extended Theory of Cognitive Creativity*, edited by Antonino Pennisi and Alessandra Falzone, 135–49. Cham: Springer International Publishing, 2019.

Gallese, Vittorio. "Bodily framing." In *Experience: Culture, Cognition, and the Common Sense*, edited by Caroline A. Jones, David Mather, and Rebecca Uchill, 1–15. Cambridge, MA: MIT Press, 2016.

Gallese, Vittorio. "Embodied Simulation: From neurons to phenomenal experience," *Phenomenology and the cognitive sciences* vol. 4, no. 1 (2005): 23–48.

Gallese, Vittorio. "Embodied Simulation. Its Bearing on Aesthetic Experience and the Dialogue Between Neuroscience and the Humanities." *Gestalt Theory* vol. 41, no. 2 (2019): 113–27.

Gallese, Vittorio. "Intentional attunement: A neurophysiological perspective on social cognition and its disruption in autism." *Brain Research* vol. 1079, no. 1 (2006): 15–24.

Gallese, Vittorio. "Mirror Neurons and the Neural Exploitation Hypothesis: From Embodied Simulation to Social Cognition." In *Mirror Neuron Systems, The role of mirroring processes in social cognition*, edited by Jaime A. Pineda, 163–90. New York: Humana Press, 2009.

Gallese, Vittorio. "The manifold nature of interpersonal relations: the quest for a common mechanism." *Philosophical Transactions of the Royal Society of London Series B: Biological Sciences* vol. 358, no. 1431 (2003): 517–28.

Gallese, Vittorio. "Seeing art. . . beyond vision. Liberated embodied simulation in aesthetic experience." In *Seeing with the Eyes Closed*, edited by A. Abbushi et. al., 62–5. Berlin: Association of Neuroesthetics, 2011.

Gallese, Vittorio. "The 'Shared Manifold' Hypothesis: from mirror neurons to empathy." *Journal of Consciousness Studies* vol. 8, no. 5–7 (2001): 33–50.

Gallese, Vittorio. "Visions of the body: Embodied simulation and aesthetic experience." *Aisthesis. Pratiche, linguaggi e saperi dell'estetico* vol. 10, no. 1 (2017): 41–50.

Gallese, Vittorio. "Vittorio Gallese Interview - Driehaus Symposium 2017." YouTube video, October 9, 2017. https://www.youtube.com/watch?v=us8mMKUi1cc.

Gallese, Vittorio, and George Lakoff, "The Brain's Concepts: The Role of the Sensory-Motor System in Reason and Language." *Cognitive Neuropsychology* vol. 22, no. 3 (2005): 455–79.

Gallese, Vittorio, and Hannah Wojciehowski. "How stories make us feel: Toward an embodied narratology." *California Italian Studies* vol. 2, no. 1 (2011): no pagination. https://doi.org/10.5070/C321008974.

Gallese, Vittorio, and Michele Guerra. *The Empathic Screen: Cinema and Neuroscience.* Translated by Frances Anderson. Oxford: Oxford University Press, 2020.

Gallese, Vittorio, et al. "Action Recognition in the Premotor Cortex." *Brain* vol. 119, no. 2 (1996): 593–609.

Gallivan, Joanne. "Group Differences in Appreciation of Feminist Humor." *Humor* vol. 5, no. 4 (1992): 369–74.

Galt, Rosalind. *Pretty: Film and the Decorative Image.* New York: Columbia University Press, 2011.

Gantar, Jure. *The Pleasure of Fools: Essays in the Ethics of Laughter.* Montreal: McGill-Queen's University Press, 2005.

Gibson, William. *Pattern Recognition.* New York: G. P. Putnam's Sons, 2003.

Goehr, Lydia. *Elective Affinities: Musical Essays on the History of Aesthetic Theory.* New York: Columbia University Press, 2008.

Goldberg, Lesley. "*Tosh.0* Canceled as Comedy Central Reverses 4-Season Renewal." *The Hollywood Reporter*, August 20, 2020. https://www.hollywoodreporter.com/news/tosh-0-canceled-as-comedy-central-reverses-4-season-renewal.

Goldstein, Avram. "Thrills in response to music and other stimuli." *Physiological Psychology* vol. 8, no. 1 (1980): 126–9.

Gregg, Melissa, Gregory J. Seigworth, and Sara Ahmed eds. *The Affect Theory Reader.* Durham, NC: Duke University Press, 2010.

Guerin, Richard. "Glass Notes: Love Is in the Air." *Glass notes* (blog), philipglass.com, July 9, 2014. https://philipglass.com/glassnotes/love-is-in-the-air/.

Guins, Raiford. "Blood and black gloves on shiny discs: new media, old tastes, and the remediation of Italian horror films in the US." *Horror International* (2003): 15–32.

Gurevich, Maria, et al. "Sexually progressive and proficient: Pornographic syntax and postfeminist fantasies." *Sexualities* vol. 20, nos. 5–6 (2017): 558–84.

Hallam, Lindsay. "Touching the Colour and Sound of Your Body's Tears: Affect and Homage in the Neo-Giallo." *Filmtidsskrft* vol. 16, no. 9, October 22, 2017, http://www.16-9.dk/2017/10/touching-the-colour/.

Hanich, Julian. "Clips, clicks and climax: notes on the relocation and remediation of pornography." *Jump Cut: A Review of Contemporary Media* no. 53 (Summer 2011): no pagination. https://www.ejumpcut.org/archive/jc53.2011/Hanich2/text.html.

Hanich, Julian. *The Audience Effect: On the Collective Cinema Experience*. Edinburgh: Edinburgh University Press, 2018.

Harman, Graham. *Guerrilla Metaphysics: Phenomenology and the Carpentry of Things*. Chicago: Open Court, 2005.

Hasson, Uri, et al. "Neurocinematics: The neuroscience of film." *Projections* vol. 2, no. 1 (2008): 1–26.

Hasson, Uri, et al. "Intersubject synchronization of cortical activity during natural vision." *Science* vol. 303, no. 5664 (2004): 1634–40.

Havas, Julia, and Maria Sulimma. "Through the gaps of my fingers: Genre, femininity, and cringe aesthetics in dramedy television." *Television & New Media* vol. 21, no. 1 (2020): 75–94.

Helens-Hart, Rose. "Promoting fan labor and 'all things Web': A case study of *Tosh.0*." *Transformative Works and Cultures* vol. 15 (2014): https://journal.transformativeworks.org/index.php/twc/article/view/491.

Heller-Nicholas, Alexandra. *The Giallo Canvas: Art, Excess and Horror Cinema*. Jefferson, NC: McFarland and Company, 2021.

Hester, Helen. *Beyond Explicit: Pornography and the Displacement of Sex*. New York: SUNY Press, 2014.

Hobbes, Thomas. *Leviathan*. New York: Oxford University Press, 1929.

Hogarth, William. *The Analysis of Beauty*. Edited by Roland Paulson. New Haven: Yale University Press, 1997.

Horeck, Tanya, and Tina Kendall eds. *New Extremism in Cinema: From France to Europe*. Edinburgh: Edinburgh University Press, 2011.

Horii, Mitsutoshi, and Adam Burgess. "Constructing sexual risk: 'Chikan', collapsing male authority and the emergence of women-only train carriages in Japan." *Health, Risk & Society* vol. 14, no. 1 (2012): 41–55.

Hung, Birdy Wei-Ting. "Allure and Dissonance: Interracial Lust and 'Problematic' Pleasure." *Cinemedia*, June 4, 2020, https://cinemedia.media/allure-and-dissonance/.

Hye-Knudsen, Marc. "Painfully Funny: Cringe Comedy, Benign Masochism, and Not-So-Benign Violations." *Leviathan: Interdisciplinary Journal in English*, no. 2 (2018): 13–31.

Irigaray, Luce. "When our lips speak together." Translated by Carolyn Burke. *Signs: Journal of Women in Culture and Society* vol. 6, no. 1 (1980): 69–79.

Jameson, Fredric. *The Political Unconscious: Narrative as a Socially Symbolic Act*. New York: Routledge, 2002.

Johnson, Peter. "Pornography Drives Technology: Why Not to Censor the Internet." *Federal Communications Law Journal* vol. 49, no. 1 (1996): 217–226.
Kaite, Berkeley. *Pornography and Difference*. Bloomington: Indiana University Press, 1995.
Kannas, Alexia. "All the colours of the dark: Film genre and the Italian giallo." *Journal of Italian Cinema & Media Studies* vol. 5, no. 2 (2017): 173–90.
Kannas, Alexia. *Deep Red*. New York: Columbia University Press, 2018.
Kannas, Alexia. *Giallo!: Genre, Modernity, and Detection in Italian Horror Cinema*. New York: SUNY Press, 2020.
Kant, Immanuel. *Critique of Pure Reason*. Translated and edited by Paul Guyer and Allen Wood. Cambridge: Cambridge University Press, 1998.
Kant, Immanuel. *The Critique of Judgement*. Translated by James Creed Meredith. New York: Oxford University Press, 2007.
Keating, Shannon. "The Spectacle of Lesbian Sex in Prestige Cinema." *BuzzFeed*, Nov 25, 2016. https://www.buzzfeed.com/shannonkeating/the-handmaiden-and-lesbian-sex-scenes.
Kemal, Salim. *Kant's Aesthetic Theory: An Introduction*. London: Macmillan, 1992.
Kerner, Aaron. "Sadistic Laughter: A Case for 'Non-Ethical' Viewing." In *The Palgrave Handbook of Violence in Film and Media*, edited by Steve Choe. Cham: Palgrave Macmillan, 2022.
Kerner, Aaron, and Julian Hoxter. *Theorizing Stupid Media: De-naturalizing Story Structures in the Cinematic, Televisual, and Videogames*. Cham: Palgrave Macmillan, 2019.
Kerner, Aaron, and Jonathan Knapp. *Extreme Cinema: Affective Strategies in Transnational Media*. Edinburgh: Edinburgh University Press, 2016.
"Killed by a temper tantrum: Wheelchair man plunges to his death down elevator shaft after ramming lift doors." *Daily Mail*, October 8, 2010. https://www.dailymail.co.uk/news/article-1318802/Korean-man-wheelchair-falls-death-missing-lift.html.
King, Mike. *The American Cinema of Excess: Extremes of the National Mind on Film*. Jefferson, NC: McFarland & Company, 2009.
Kipnis, Laura. *Bound and Gagged: Pornography and the Politics of Fantasy in America*. Durham, NC: Duke University Press, 1999.
Kiss, Erika A. "Between Mimesis and Technē: Cinematic Image as a Site for Critical Thinking." *Journal of Aesthetic Education* vol. 51, no. 3 (2017): 42–57.
Kolnai, Aurel. *On Disgust*. Edited by Barry Smith and Carolyn Korsmeyer. Chicago: Open Court, 2004.
Komiya, Megumi, and Barry Litman. "The Economics of the Prerecorded Videocassette Industry." In *Social and Cultural Aspects of VCR Use*, edited by Julia R. Dobrow, 25–44. Hillsdale, NJ: Lawrence Erlbaum Associates, 1990.
Korsgaard, Mathias Bonde. "Creation and erasure: music video as a signaletic form of practice." *Journal of Aesthetics & Culture* vol. 4, no. 1 (2012): no pagination. https://doi.org/10.3402/jac.v4i0.18151.
Kotsko, Adam. *Awkwardness*. Washington: Zero Books, 2010.
Kovacevich, Alexsandra, and David Huron. "Two studies of autonomous sensory meridian response (ASMR): The relationship between ASMR and music-induced frisson." *Empirical Musicology Review* vol. 13, nos. 1–2 (2019): 39–63.
Koven, Mikel J. *La Dolce Morte: Vernacular Cinema and the Italian Giallo Film*. Lanham, MD: Scarecrow Press, 2006.

Kozel, Susan. *Closer: Performance, Technologies, Phenomenology*. Cambridge, MA: MIT Press, 2007.
Kracauer, Siegfried. *Theory of Film: The Redemption of Physical Reality*. Princeton: Princeton University Press, 1997.
Kristeva, Julia. *Black Sun: Depression and Melancholia*. Translated by Leon S. Roudiez. New York: Columbia University Press, 1989.
Kristeva, Julia. *Intimate Revolt: The Powers and Limits of Psychoanalysis*. Translated by Jeanine Herman. New York: Columbia University, 2002.
Kristeva, Julia. *Powers of Horror: An Essay on Abjection*. Translated by Leon S. Roudiez. New York: Columbia University Press, 1982.
Kristeva, Julia. *Revolution in Poetic Language*. Translated by Margaret Waller. New York: Columbia University Press, 1984.
Kristeva, Julia. *Strangers to Ourselves*. Translated by Leon S. Roudiez. New York: Columbia University Press, 1991.
Kristof, Nicholas. "The Children of Pornhub: Why does Canada allow this company to profit off videos of exploitation and assault?" *The New York Times*, December 4, 2020. https://www.nytimes.com/2020/12/04/opinion/sunday/pornhub-rape-trafficking.html.
Laine, Tarja. "Imprisoned in Disgust: Roman Polanski's *Repulsion*." *Film-Philosophy* vol. 15, no. 2 (2011): 36–50.
Lane, Anthony. "*The Handmaiden*." *The New Yorker*, October 17, 2016. https://www.newyorker.com/magazine/2016/10/24/the-handmaiden-and-christine.
"Laughter," *RadioLab*, NPR, February 25, 2008. https://www.wnycstudios.org/podcasts/radiolab/episodes/91588-laughter.
Laukkanen, Anu. "Hips Don't Lie? Affective and Kinaesthetic Dance Ethnography." In *Working with Affect in Feminist Readings: Disturbing Differences*, edited by Marianne Liljeström and Susanna Paasonen, 126–39. London: Routledge, 2010.
Lauzen, Martha M. "The Celluloid Ceiling: Behind-the-Scenes Employment of Women on the Top 100, 250, and 500 Films of 2015." *Center for the Study of Women in Television and Film*. San Diego: San Diego State University, 2016.
Leggott, James. "Come to daddy? Claiming Chris Cunningham for British art cinema." *Journal of British Cinema and Television* vol. 13, no. 2 (2016): 243–61.
Lehman, Peter. *Pornography Film and Culture*. New Brunswick, NJ: Rutgers University Press, 2006.
Levinas, Emmanuel. *Totality and Infinity: An Essay on Exteriority*. Translated by Alphonso Lingis. Boston: Kluwer Academic Publishers, 1991.
Leys, Ruth. "II Affect and Intention: A reply to William E. Connolly." *Critical Inquiry* vol. 37, no. 4 (2011): 799–805.
Leys, Ruth. "The turn to affect: A critique." *Critical inquiry* vol. 37, no. 3 (2011): 434–72.
Lichtenstein, Jacqueline. *The Eloquence of Color: Rhetoric and Painting in the French Classical Age*. Translated by Emily McVarish. Berkeley: University of California Press, 1993.
Lockwood, Dean. "Blackened Puppets: Chris Cunningham's Weird Anatomies." In *Music/Video: Histories, Aesthetics, Media*, eds. Gina Arnold et al., 195–207. New York: Bloomsbury, 2017.
Lyotard, Jean-François. *The Inhuman: Reflections on Time*. Translated by Geoffrey Bennington and Rachel Bowlby. Stanford: Stanford University Press, 1991.

Mackenzie, J. Lachlan. "The syntax of an emotional expletive in English." In *Emotion in Discourse*, edited by J. Lachlan Mackenzie and Laura Alba-Juez, 55–86. Amsterdam: John Benjamins Publishing Company, 2019.
Mandau, Morten Birk Hansen. "'Directly in your face': a qualitative study on the sending and receiving of unsolicited 'dick pics' among young adults." *Sexuality & Culture* vol. 24, no. 1 (2020): 72–93.
Manning, Erin. *Politics of Touch: Sense, Movement, Sovereignty*. Minneapolis: University of Minnesota Press, 2007.
Marks, Laura U. *The Skin of the Film: Intercultural Cinema, Embodiment, and the Senses*. Durham, NC: Duke University Press, 2000.
Marks, Laura U. *Touch: Sensuous Theory and Multisensory Media*. Minneapolis: University of Minnesota Press, 2002.
Marso, Lori. "Feminist Cringe Comedy: Dear Dick, The Joke Is on You." *Politics & Gender* vol. 15, no. 1 (2019): 107–29.
Massumi, Brian. *Parables for the Virtual: Movement, Affect, Sensation*. Durham, NC: Duke University Press, 2002.
Matherne, Samantha. "Kant's Expressive Theory of Music." *The Journal of Aesthetics and Art Criticism* vol. 72, no. 2 (Spring 2014): 129–45.
Matherne, Samantha. "Kant on Aesthetic Autonomy and Common Sense." *Philosopher's Imprint* vol. 19, no 24 (June 2019): 1–22.
McCormack, Mark, and Liam Wignall. "Enjoyment, exploration and education: Understanding the consumption of pornography among young men with non-exclusive sexual orientations." *Sociology* vol. 51, no. 5 (2017): 975–91.
McDonald, Paul. *The Philosophy of Humour*. Penrith UK: Humanities-Ebooks, 2012.
McMahon, Melissa. "Beauty: Machinic repetition in the age of art." In *A Shock to Thought: Expression after Deleuze and Guattari*, edited by Brian Massumi, 43–8. New York: Routledge, 2002.
McNair, Brian. *Striptease Culture: Sex, Media and the Democratization of Desire*. London: Routledge, 2002.
McNary, Dave. "Sacha Baron Cohen *Klown* Remake Sells Out all Foreign Markets." *Variety*, November 17, 2016. https://variety.com/2016/film/markets-festivals/sacha-baron-cohen-klown-remake-sells-1201921177/.
Menninghaus, Winfried. *Disgust: The Theory and History of a Strong Sensation*. Translated by Howard Eiland and Joel Golb. New York: State University of New York Press, 2003.
Merleau-Ponty, Maurice. *Phenomenology of Perception*. Translated by Donald A. Landes. New York: Routledge, 2012.
Middleton, Jason. *Documentary's Awkward Turn: Cringe Comedy and Media Spectatorship*. New York: Routledge, 2013.
Miller, Laura. "*The Handmaiden* Park Chan-wook takes on Sarah Water's brilliant, intricate novel *Fingersmith*." *Slate*, October 20, 2016. https://slate.com/culture/2016/10/park-chan-wooks-the-handmaiden-based-on-sarah-waters-fingersmith-reviewed.html.
Mohan, Megha. "'I was raped at 14, and the video ended up on a porn site.'" *BBC NEWS*, February 10, 2020. https://www.bbc.com/news/stories-51391981.
Morrissey, Steve. "Review: Klown aka Klovn: The Movie." *Movie Steve*, September 27, 2013. https://www.moviesteve.com/klown-2010/.

Mosher, Donald L., and Barbara B. White. "Effects of committed or casual erotic guided imagery on females' subjective sexual arousal and emotional response." *Journal of Sex Research* vol. 16, no. 4 (1980): 273–99.

Moss, Joshua Louis. "Defining transcomedy: Humor, tricksterism, and postcolonial affect from Gerald Vizenor to Sacha Baron Cohen." *International Journal of Cultural Studies* vol. 19, no. 5 (2016): 487–500.

Mulvey, Laura. *Visual and Other Pleasures*. Bloomington: Indiana University Press, 1989.

Münsterberg, Hugo. *Hugo Münsterberg on Film: The Photoplay: A Psychological Study and Other Writings*. Edited by Allan Langdale. New York: Routledge, 2001.

Nancy, Jean-Luc. *Listening*. Translated by Charlotte Mandell. New York: Fordham University Press, 2007.

Nancy, Jean-Luc. *The Ground of the Image*. Translated by Jeff Fort. New York: Fordham University Press, 2005.

Needham, Gary. "Japanese Cinema and Orientalism." In *Asian Cinemas: A Reader and Guide*, edited by Dimitris Eleftheriotis and Gary Needham, 8–16. Honolulu: University of Hawai'i Press, 2006.

Neidlinger, Kristin, et al. "AWElectric: that gave me goosebumps, did you feel it too?" In *Proceedings of the Eleventh International Conference on Tangible, Embedded, and Embodied Interaction*. (2017): 315–24. https://doi.org/10.1145/3024969.3025004.

Neville, Lucy. *Girls Who Like Boys Who Like Boys: Women and Gay Male Pornography and Erotica*. Cham: Springer, 2018.

Newstrom, Nicholas P., and Steven M. Harris. "Pornography and Couples: What Does the Research Tell Us?" *Contemporary Family Therapy* vol. 38, no. 4 (2016): 412–23.

Nichols, Bill, Christian Hansen, and Catherine Needham. "Pornography, Ethnography, and the Discourses of Power." In *Representing Reality: Issues and Concepts in Documentary*, 201–28. Bloomington: Indiana University Press, 1991.

Norelli, Clare Nina. "Scores on Screen. Piano Lessons: Death and Desire in Park Chan-wook's 'Stoker.'" *Notebook Column* (blog), MUBI, September 4, 2018. https://mubi.com/notebook/posts/scores-on-screen-piano-lessons-death-and-desire-in-park-chan-wook-s-stoker.

O'Brien, Ita. "Intimacy on Set Guidelines: Best Practice When Working with Intimacy, Simulated Sex Scenes, and Nudity." Accessed 09/04/2020. https://www.itaobrien.com/intimacy-on-set-guidelines.html.

Paasonen, Susanna. *Carnal Resonance: Affect and Online Pornography*. Cambridge, MA: MIT Press, 2011.

Paasonen, Susanna. "Grains of Resonance: Affect, Pornography and Visual Sensation." *Somatechnics* vol. 3, no. 2 (2013): 351–68.

Paasonen, Susanna. "'We watch porn for the fucking, not for romantic tiptoeing': extremity, fantasy and women's porn use." *Porn Studies* (2021): 1–14. https://doi.org/10.1177/13634607145509 11.

Paasonen, Susanna, Ben Light, and Kylie Jarrett. "The dick pic: Harassment, curation, and desire." *Social Media+ Society* vol. 5, no. 2 (2019): 1–10.

Paasonen, Susanna, et al. "'We hid porn magazines in the woods': Memory-work and porn consumption in Finland." *Sexualities* vol. 18, no. 4 (2015): 394–412.

Pally, Marcia. *Sex and Sensibility: Reflections on Forbidden Mirrors and the Will to Censor*. New Jersey: Ecco Press, 1994.

Palumbo-Liu, David. "Rational and Irrational Choices: Form, Affect, and Ethics." In *Minor Transnationalism*, edited by Françoise Lionnet and Shu-mei Shih, 41–72. Durham, NC: Duke University Press, 2005.

Park, Chan-wook. "Park Chan-wook on relocating Sarah Waters' *Fingersmith* to Korea." Interviewed by Henry Barnes. *The Guardian*, May 17, 2016. https://www.theguardian.com/film/2016/may/17/park-chan-wook-on-relocating-sarah-waters-fingersmith-to-korea.

Park, Chan-wook. "Park Chan-wook's Films Push the Boundaries of Sex and Violence—But That's Not His Intention." Interviewed by Simon Abrams. *Esquire*, October 18, 2016. https://www.esquire.com/entertainment/q-and-a/a49691/park-chan-wook-interview-the-handmaiden/.

Park, Chan-wook. "*The Handmaiden* Director Park Chan-wook on His Masterful New Thriller and the Universal Language of Filmmaking." Interviewed by Britt Hayes. *ScreenCrush*, October 21, 2016. https://screencrush.com/park-chan-wook-handmaiden-interview/.

Patterson, Zabet. "Going On-line: Consuming Pornography in the Digital Era." In *Porn Studies*, edited by Linda Williams, 104–23. Durham, NC: Duke University Press,. 2004.

Peakall, Rod. "Responses of male Zaspilothynnus trilobatus Turner wasps to females and the sexually deceptive orchid it pollinates." *Functional Ecology* vol. 4 (1990): 159–67.

Pefanis, Julian. *Heterology and the Postmodern: Bataille, Baudrillard, and Lyotard*. Durham, NC: Duke University Press, 1991.

Pérez, Raúl, and Viveca S. Greene. "Debating rape jokes vs. rape culture: framing and counter-framing misogynistic comedy." *Social Semiotics* vol. 26, no. 3 (2016): 265–82.

Plantinga, Carl R. "Art Moods and Human Moods in Narrative Cinema." *New Literary History* vol. 43, no. 3 (Summer 2012): 455–75.

Plantinga, Carl R. "Emotion and Affect." In *The Routledge Companion to Philosophy and Film*, edited by Paisley Livingston and Carl Plantinga, 86–96. New York: Routledge, 2008.

Plantinga, Carl R. *Moving Viewers: American Film and the Spectator's Experience*. Berkeley: University of California Press, 2009.

Pollock, Griselda. *Vision and Difference: Femininity, Feminism and the Histories of Art*. New York: Routledge, 1990.

Popova, Milena. "'Slight Dub-Con but They Both Wanted It Hardcore': Erotic Fanfiction as a Form of Cultural activism Around Sexual Consent." PhD diss., University of the West of England, 2017.

"Pornhub removes all user-uploaded videos amid legality row." *BBC NEWS*, December 14, 2020. https://www.bbc.com/news/technology-55304115.

Provine, Robert R. *Laughter: A Scientific Investigation*. New York: Viking, 2000.

Quandt, James. "Flesh and Blood: Sex and Violence in Recent French Cinema." *Artforum International* vol. 42, no. 6 (February 2004): 126–32.

Radway, Janice A. *Reading the Romance: Women, Patriarchy, and Popular Literature*. Chapel Hill: University of North Carolina Press, 1991.

Rhee, Suk Koo. "The Erotic-Grotesque versus Female Agency in Colonial Korea in Park Chan-wook's *The Handmaiden*." *Canadian Journal of Film Studies* vol. 29, no. 2 (2020): 115–38.

Ricoeur, Paul. "Wonder, eroticism, and enigma." *CrossCurrents* vol. 14, no. 2 (1964): 133–66.
Ringrose, Jessica, and Emilie Lawrence. "Remixing misandry, manspreading, and dick pics: Networked feminist humour on Tumblr." *Feminist Media Studies* vol. 18, no. 4 (2018): 686–704.
Riviere, Joan. "Womanliness as Masquerade." *Female Sexuality: Contemporary Engagements* 8 (1999): 127–38.
Robinson, Bradley, and Mel Kutner. "Spinoza and the affective turn: A return to the philosophical origins of affect." *Qualitative Inquiry* vol. 25, no. 2 (2019): 111–17.
Rodowick, D. N. "The Force of Small Gestures." In *Indefinite Visions: Cinema and the Attractions of Uncertainty*, edited by Martine Beugnet, Allan Cameron, and Arild Fetveit, 209–22. Edinburgh: Edinburgh University Press, 2017.
Rosen, Philip, ed. *Narrative, Apparatus, Ideology: A Film Theory Reader*. New York: Columbia University Press, 1986.
Røssaak, Eivind. "Figures of Sensation: Between Still and Moving Images Chapter." In *The Cinema of Attractions Reloaded Book*, edited by Wanda Strauven, 321–36. Amsterdam: Amsterdam University Press, 2006.
Sade, Marquis de. *The 120 Days of Sodom and Other Writings*. Translated by Austryn Wainhouse and Richard Seaver. New York: Grove Weidenfeld, 1987.
Sade, Marquis de. *Justine, Philosophy in the Bedroom, and Other Writing*. London: Arrow Books Limited, 1991.
Schaefer, Claudia. *Bored to Distraction: Cinema of Excess in End-of-the-Century Mexico and Spain*. New York: SUNY Press, 2014.
Scott, Sophie. "Why we laugh," TED video, filmed May 2015. https://www.ted.com/talks/sophie_scott_why_we_laugh?language=en.
Scruton, Roger, and Peter Jones. "Laughter." *Proceedings of the Aristotelian Society, Supplementary Volumes* vol. 56 (1982): 197–228.
Sedgwick, Eve Kosofsky, Adam Frank, and Irving E. Alexander. *Shame and Its Sisters: a Silvan Tomkins Reader*. Durham, NC: Duke University Press, 1995.
Seigworth, Gregory J., and Gregg, Melissa. "An Inventory of Shimmers." In *The Affect Theory Reader*, edited by Melissa Gregg, Gregory J. Seigworth, and Sara Ahmed, 1–25. Durham, NC: Duke University Press, 2010.
Senft, Theresa M. *Camgirls: Celebrity and Community in the Age of Social Networks*. New York: Lang, 2008.
Shaftesbury, Anthony, Ashley Cooper, and Lawrence Eliot Klein. *Characteristics of Men, Manners, Opinions, Times*. New York: Cambridge University Press, 1999.
Shamoon, Deborah. "Office Sluts and Rebel Flowers: The pleasures of Japanese pornographic comics for women." In *Porn Studies*, edited by Linda Williams, 77–103. Durham, NC: Duke University Press, 2004.
Shaviro, Steven. "Beauty Lies in the Eye." *Symplokē* vol. 6, no. 1/2 (1998): 96–108.
Shaviro, Steven. "The Erotic Life of Machines." *Parallax* vol. 8, no. 4 (2002): 21–31.
Shaviro, Steven. "Post-Cinematic Affect: On Grace Jones, *Boarding Gate* and *Southland Tales*." *Film-Philosophy* vol. 14, no. 1 (2010): 1–102.
Shaviro, Steven. *Post-Cinematic Affect*. Washington: Zero Books, 2010.
Shaviro, Steven. *The Cinematic Body*. Minneapolis: University of Minnesota Press, 1993.

Shaviro, Steven. *Without Criteria: Kant, Whitehead, Deleuze, and Aesthetics.* Cambridge, MA: MIT Press, 2009.
Shimizu, Celine Parreñas. *The Proximity of Other Skins: Ethical Intimacy in Global Cinema.* New York: Oxford University Press, 2019.
Shouse, Eric. "Feeling, Emotion, Affect." *M/C Journal* vol. 8, no. 6 (2005): no pagination. https://doi.org/10.5204/mcj.2443.
Silver, Curtis. "Pornhub 2019 Year in Review Report: More Porn, More Often." *Forbes*, December 11, 2019. https://www.forbes.com/sites/curtissilver/2019/12/11/pornhub-2019-year-in-review-report-more-porn-more-often/#1aa7270f4671.
Sobchack, Vivian. *The Address of the Eye: A Phenomenology of Film Experience.* Princeton: Princeton University Press, 1992.
Sobchack, Vivian. *Carnal Thoughts: Embodiment and Moving Image Culture.* Berkeley: University of California Press, 2004.
Sobchack, Vivian. "What My Fingers Knew: The Cinesthetic Subject, or Vision in the Flesh." *Senses of Cinema*, no. 5 (April 2000): no pagination. http://sensesofcinema.com/2000/conference-special-effects-special-affects/fingers/.
Spencer, Herbert. *Essays on Education and Kindred Subjects.* Auckland: Floating Press, 1911.
Spinks, Lee. "Thinking the Post-Human: Literature, Affect, and the Politics of Style." *Textual Practice* vol. 15, no. 1 (2001): 23–46.
Spinoza, Bededictus de. *Ethics.* Translated by R. H. M. Elwes. Auckland: The Floating Press, 2009.
Stacey, Jackie. "'If You Don't Play, You Can't Win' *Desert Hearts* and the Lesbian Romance Film." In *Immortal, Invisible: Lesbians and the Moving Image*, edited by Tamsin Wilton, 67–87. New York: Routledge, 1995.
Stam, Robert. *Subversive Pleasures: Bakhtin, Cultural Criticism, and Film.* Baltimore: Johns Hopkins University Press, 1989.
Stanyon, Miranda. "Serpentine Sighs: De Quincey's *Suspiria De Profundis* and the Serpentine Line." *Studies in Romanticism* vol. 53, no. 1 (2014): 31–58.
Sulimma, Maria. "Lena Dunham: Cringe Comedy and Body Politics." In *Hysterical!: Women in American Comedy*, edited by Sturtevant Mizejewski et al., 379–401. Austin: Texas University Press, 2017.
Sullivan, Kevin. "*The Handmaiden*: How a Victorian-set novel became the Korea-set film." *Entertainment Weekly*, November 9, 2016. https://ew.com/article/2016/11/09/handmaiden-sarah-waters-fingersmith/.
Tan, Ed S. *Emotion and the Structure of Narrative Film: Film as an Emotion Machine.* Mahwah, N.J: Erlbaum, 1996.
Taormino, Tristan. "Calling the Shots: Feminist Porn in Theory and Practice." In *The Feminist Porn Book: The Politics of Producing Pleasure*, edited by Tristan Taormino, et al., 255–64. New York: The Feminist Press at CUNY, 2013.
Thaler, Lore, et al. "Neural correlates of motion processing through echolocation, source hearing, and vision in blind echolocation experts and sighted echolocation novices." *Journal of Neurophysiology* vol. 111, no. 1 (2014): 112–27.
Thomson, Clive. "Bakhtin and Feminist Projects: Judith Butler's *Gender Trouble*." In "Bakhtin: Carnival and Other Subjects," edited by Myriam Díaz-Diocaretz. Special issue, *Critical Studies* vol. 3, nos. 1–4 (1993): 210–28.

Thompson, Kristin. "The Concept of Cinematic Excess." In *Narrative, Apparatus, Ideology: A Film Theory Reader*, edited by Philip Rosen, 130–42. New York: Columbia University Press, 1986.

Thrift, Nigel. "Intensities of Feeling: Towards a Spatial Politics of Affect." *Geografiska Annaler* vol. 86, no. 1 (2004): 57–78.

Thrift, Nigel. *Non-representational Theory: Space / Politics / Affect*. London: Routledge, 2008.

Tolentino, Jia. "*The Handmaiden* and the Freedom Women Find Only with One Another." *The New Yorker*, October 29, 2016. https://www.newyorker.com/culture/jia-tolentino/the-handmaiden-and-the-freedom-women-find-only-with-one-another.

Turvey, Malcolm. "Mirror Neurons and Film Studies A Cautionary Tale from a Serious Pessimist." *Projections* vol. 14, no. 3 (Winter 2020): 21–46.

Ullén, Magnus. "Pornography and its Critical Reception: Toward a Theory of Masturbation." *Jump Cut: A Review of Contemporary Media* no. 51 (Spring 2009): no pagination. http://www.ejumpcut.org/archive/jc51.2009/UllenPorn/text.html.

Vedantam, Shankar, Laura Kwerel, and Tara Boyle. "Laughter: The Best Medicine." *Hidden Brain*, NPR, September 28, 2020. https://www.npr.org/2020/09/25/916997530/laughter-the-best-medicine.

Vernallis, Carol. *Experiencing music video: Aesthetics and cultural context*. New York: Columbia University Press, 2004.

Vernallis, Carol. *Unruly Media: YouTube, Music Video, and the New Digital Cinema*. Oxford: Oxford University Press, 2013.

Vitis, Laura, and Fairleigh Gilmour. "Dick pics on blast: A woman's resistance to online sexual harassment using humour, art and Instagram." *Crime, media, culture* vol. 13, no. 3 (2017): 335–55.

Vozick-Levinson, Simon. "Song You Need to Know: Thom Yorke, 'Suspirium' First taste of the Radiohead singer's horror-flick score is a chilly, gorgeous treat." *Rolling Stone*, September 6, 2018. https://www.rollingstone.com/music/music-features/thom-yorke-suspirium-suspiria-score-717706/.

Waling, Andrea, and Tinonee Pym. "'C'mon, No One Wants a Dick Pic': exploring the cultural framings of the 'Dick Pic' in contemporary online publics." *Journal of Gender Studies* vol. 28, no. 1 (2019): 70–85.

Wanzo, Rebecca. "Precarious-Girl Comedy: Issa Rae, Lena Dunham, and Abjection Aesthetics." *Abjection Incorporated: Mediating the Politics of Pleasure and Violence*, edited by Maggie Hennefeld and Nicholas Sammond, 64–85. Durham, NC: University Press,. 2020.

Ward, Jane. "Queer Feminist Pigs: A Spectator's Manifesta." In *The Feminist Porn Book: The Politics of Producing Pleasure*, edited by Tristan Taormino, et al., 130–9. New York: The Feminist Press at CUNY, 2013.

Whitehead, Alfred North. *Adventures of Ideas*. New York: The Free Press, 1967.

Whitehead, Alfred North. *Process and Reality*. New York: The Free Press, 1978.

Whitehouse, Matthew. "How *Suspiria* Became One of the Best Horror Movie Soundtracks of All Time." *i-D Vice*, August 10, 2018. https://i-d.vice.com/en_us/article/kzyxgz/how-suspiria-became-one-of-the-best-horror-movie-soundtracks-of-all-time.

Williams, Kevin. *Why I [Still] Want My MTV*. New Jersey: Hampton Press, 2003.

Williams, Linda. "Discipline and Fun: Psycho and Postmodern Cinema." In *Reinventing Film Studies*, edited by Christine Gledhill and Linda Williams, 351–78. London: Arnold, 2000.

Williams, Linda. "Film Bodies: Gender, Genre, and Excess." *Film Quarterly* vol. 44, no. 4 (Summer 1991): 2–13.

Williams, Linda. *Hard Core: Power, Pleasure, and "The Frenzy of the Visible."* Berkeley: University of California Press, 1989.

Williams, Linda. "Motion and e-motion: lust and the 'frenzy of the visible.'" *Journal of Visual Culture* vol. 18, no. 1 (April 2019): 97–129.

Williams, Nathan. *The Eye: How the World's Most Influential Creative Directors Develop Their Vision.* New York: Artisan, 2018.

Wojciehowski, Hannah C., and Vittorio Gallese. "Introduction," in *Costellazioni: Rivista di lingue e letterature* 5 (2018): 9–22.

Yoo, Noah. "Thom Yorke 'Suspirium.'" *Pitchfork*, September 4, 2018. https://pitchfork.com/reviews/tracks/thom-yorke-suspirium/.

Yorke, Thom. "Thom Yorke on Scoring the New *Suspiria*." Interviewed by Tim Greiving. NPR, November 3, 2018. https://www.npr.org/2018/11/03/663408956/radiohead-thom-yorke-suspiria-score.

Zagala, Stephen. "Aesthetics: A place I've never seen." In *A Shock to Thought: Expression after Deleuze and Guattari*, edited by Brian Massumi, 60–84. New York: Routledge, 2005.

Zahlten, Alexander. *The End of Japanese Cinema: Industrial Genres, National Times, and Media Ecologies.* Durham, NC: Duke University Press, 2017.

Zarzycka, Marta, and Bettina Papenburg. "Motion pictures: Politics of perception." *Discourse* vol. 35, no. 2 (2014): 163–76.

Zarzycka, Marta, and Bettina Papenburg, eds. *Carnal aesthetics: transgressive imagery and feminist politics.* New York: Bloomsbury, 2012.

Žižek, Slavoj. "Kant with (or against) Sade." *The Žižek Reader*, edited by Elizabeth Wright and Edmond Wright, 283–301. Oxford: Blackwell, 1999.

Media-ography

2 Girls 1 Cup, Marco Antonio Fiorito, 2007, 1 min.
"3-Way (The Golden Rule)," Don Roy, Akiva Schaffer, and Jorma Taccone, *Saturday Night Live*, Season 36, Episode 22, May 24, 2011, 3 minutes.
"8 Simple Rules for Buying My Teenage Daughter," Greg Colton, *Family Guy*, Season 4, Episode 8, July 10, 2005, 22 mins.
9 Songs, Michael Winterbottom, 2004, 71 mins.
25th Hour, Spike Lee, 2002, 135 mins.
A Bigger Splash, Luca Guadagnino, 2015, 125 mins.
"Abused in Bus," Pornhub, 2017, 26 mins.
America's Funniest Home Videos, ABC, 1989–.
American Pie, Paul and Chris Weitz, 1999, 95 mins.
"A Very Crappy Christmas," Adrien Beard, *South Park*, Season 4, Episode 17, December 20, 2000, 22 mins.
Alien^3, David Fincher, 1992, 104 mins.
Amer, Hélène Cattet and Bruno Forzani, 2009, 90 mins.
Antichrist, Lars von Trier, 2009, 108 mins.
Aphex Twin: Come to Daddy, Chris Cunningham, 1997, 6 mins.
Aphex Twin: Windowlicker, Chris Cunningham, 1999, 11 mins.
Assassination Nation, Sam Levinson, 2018, 108 mins.
Autechre: Second Bad Vilbel, Chris Cunningham, 1996, 5 mins.
Bad Trip, Kitao Sakurai, 2020, 86 mins.
Bad Grandpa, Johnny Knoxville, 2013, 92 mins.
Be A Lady They Said, Paul McLean, 2020, 3 mins.
"Bed Intruder," Scott Zabielski, *Tosh.0*, Comedy Central, Season 3, Episode 1, January 11, 2011, 22 mins.
Belladonna of Sadness, Eiichi Yamamoto, 1973, 86 mins.
Berberian Sound Studio, Peter Strickland, 2012, 92 mins.
Björk: All Is Full of Love, Chris Cunningham, 1999, 4 mins.
Bocca bacciata, Dante Gabriel Rossetti, oil on canvas, 1859.
Crash Pad series, Shine Louise Houston, 2006–2008.
The Burial of the Count of Orgaz, El Greco, 1586, oil on canvas, 480 × 360 cm.
Call Me By Your Name, Luca Guadagnino, 2017, 132 mins.
Crimson Girls: Chikan Shihai, Hiroshi Kimura, 2012–2015.
Curb Your Enthusiasm, HBO, 2000–.

Daniel Tosh: Happy Thoughts, Daniel Tosh, 2011, 60 mins.
"Despacito," Luis Fonsi ft. Daddy Yankee, track 9 on Luis Fonsi, *Vida*. Universal Latin, 2019.
Devo: Mongoloid, Bruce Conner, 1978, 4 mins.
Desert Hearts, Donna Deitch, 1985, 91 mins.
Devs, Alex Garland, FX on Hulu, 2020.
Dumplings, Fruit Chan, 2004, 91 mins.
Get Out, Jordan Peele, 2017, 104 mins.
Flex, Chris Cunningham, 2000, 17 mins.
Friday the 13th, Sean Cunningham, 1980, 95 mins.
"Friday the 13th: the Game—Interview with Harry Manfredini and Wes Keltner," Gun, YouTube video, October 29, 2015, 11 mins. https://www.youtube.com/watch?v=dJG_ZiuAoJo.
"FORTNITE ON WHEELS," Ricky Berwick, YouTube video, May 13, 2018, 4 mins. https://www.youtube.com/watch?v=8XDJLMCSY4Q.
"F**k," Christopher D'Elia, *History of Swear Words*, Netflix, Season 1, Episode 1, 2021, 21 mins.
The Giverny Document (Single Channel), Ja'Tovia M. Gary, 2019, 40 mins.
The Handmaiden, Chan-wook Park, 2016, 145 mins.
"How to Become Batman," *Invisibilia*, NPR, January 23, 2015, https://www.npr.org/programs/invisibilia/378577902/how-to-become-batman.
"How To Have an Orgasm," Bob Suarez, *Big Mouth*, Netflix, Season 3, Episode 6, October 4, 2019, 28 mins.
The Hunger, Tony Scott, 1983, 97 mins.
Hungry Bitches, Marco Antonio Fiorito, 2007, 62 mins.
I Am Love, Luca Guadagnino, 2009, 120 mins.
I Love Dick, Amazon series, 2016–2017.
Imitation of Life, Douglas Sirk, 1959, 125 mins.
In Fabric, Peter Strickland, 2018, 118 mins.
"In My Dreams," ANOHNI, track 1 on ANOHNI, *Paradise*. Secretly Canadian, 2017.
"The Inevitable Pull," Thom Yorke, track 9 on Thom Yorke, *Suspiria: Music for the Luca Guadagnino Film*. XL Recordings, 2018.
Irreversible, Gaspar Noé, 2002, 97 mins.
Klown, Mikkel Nørgaard, 2010, 93 mins.
Kustom Kar Kommandos, Kenneth Anger, 1965, 3 mins.
"Lacrimosa," Zbigniew Preisner, track 8 on Zbigniew Preisner, *Requiem for My Friend*. Preisner Productions, 1998.
Let the Corpses Tan, Hélène Cattet and Bruno Forzani, 2017, 92 mins.
"LOVE HOTEL: JAPANESE TRAIN," Sam in Tokyo, YouTube video, September 1, 2018, 8 mins. https://www.youtube.com/watch?v=uQ89EbzXKuw.
"Made You Look," Sam Levinson, *Euphoria*, Season 1, Episode 3, June 30, 2019, 56 mins.
Madonna: Frozen, Chris Cunningham, 1998, 6 mins.
"Man Drinks Ipecac," nikmueller12, YouTube video, January 28, 2009, 5 mins. https://www.youtube.com/watch?v=M4vS4UWZ0nQ.
"Man Sells Dignity to Asshole for $1000," *eBaum's World*, January 26, 2014, 5 mins. http://www.ebaumsworld.com/videos/man-sells-dignity-to-asshole-for-1000/83833293/.
Margaret Cho: CHO Revolution, 2004, 85 mins.

Married Teacher Molester Train, Kanie, 2015, 94 mins.
"Massage Chair," Douglas Goldstein, *Robot Chicken*, Season 2, Episode 9, May 28, 2006, 11 mins.
Melissa P., Luca Guadagnino, 2005, 100 mins.
Monty Python's The Meaning of Life, Terry Jones and Terry Gilliam, 1983, 107 mins.
Mishima: A Life in Four Chapters, Paul Schrader, 1985, 120 mins.
Naqoyqatsi, Godfrey Reggio, 2022, 89 mins.
The Naked Director, Netflix, 2019–.
Nightbreed, Clive Barker, 1990, 102 mins.
The Office, American series, NBC, 2005–2013.
The Office, British original series, BBC, 2001–2003.
"Open Again," Thom Yorke, track 7 on Thom Yorke, *Suspiria: Music for the Luca Guadagnino Film*. XL Recordings, 2018.
Portishead: Only You, Chris Cunningham, 1998, 4 mins.
"Results of the Memorabilia Dump," Scott Zabielski, *Tosh.0*, Comedy Central, Season 4, Episode 10, April 3, 2012, 22 mins.
Romance, Catherine Breillat, 1999, 99 mins.
"Roof Jump," Scott Zabielski, *Tosh.0*, Comedy Central, Season 6, Episode 10, April 22, 2014, 22 min.
"Ricky Berwick," John Elerick and James Patton, *Tosh.0*, Comedy Central, Season 9, Episode 11, June 6, 2017, 21 mins.
Rubber Johnny, Chris Cunningham, 2005, 6 mins.
"Saint Matthew Passion," Johann Sebastian Bach, 1727, 150 min.
Salò, or the 120 Days of Sodom, Pier Paolo Pasolini, 1975, 117 mins.
"SARA LUVV EXTREME PASSIONATE ROUGH FUCK, CUMMING ON COCK MULTIPLE TIMES AND CUM SWALLOW," James Deen, Pornhub, 2021, 11mins.
Shrimp Warp: Aphrodisiac Massage Akiho Yoshizawa, Dera 3, 2016, 123 mins.
Snatch, Guy Ritchie, 2000, 102 mins.
Sombre, Philippe Grandrieux, 1998, 112 mins.
"Sound as Touch," *Radiolab*, NPR, September 24, 2007. https://www.wnycstudios.org/podcasts/radiolab/segments/91514-sound-as-touch.
Stand by Me, Rob Reiner, 1986, 99 mins.
"Stars / Feelings (Medley / Live at Montreux, 1976)," Nina Simone, YouTube video, Jul 23, 2020, 17 mins. https://youtu.be/Mf_5l1yTKNY.
Star Wars IV: A New Hope, George Lucas, 1977, 121 mins.
The Stepford Wives, Bryan Forbes, 1975, 115 mins.
Stoker, Chan-wook Park, 2013, 99 mins.
"Stone Phillips," *The Colbert Report*, Comedy Central, Season 1, Episode 1, October 17, 2005, 21 minutes.
Strange Circus, Sion Sono, 2005, 108 mins.
The Summer of Soul (. . . Or, When the Revolution Could Not Be Televised), Questlove, 2021, 118 mins.
Suspiria, Dario Argento, 1977, 92 mins.
Suspiria, Luca Guadagnino, 2018, 152 mins.
Suspiria 25th Anniversary, Gary Hertz, 2011, 58 mins, DVD.

"Suspirium," Thom Yorke, track 3 on Thom Yorke, *Suspiria: Music for the Luca Guadagnino Film*. XL Recordings, 2018.
The Strange Color of Your Body's Tears, Hélène Cattet and Bruno Forzani, 2013, 102 mins.
Taxidermia, György Pálfi, 2006, 91 mins.
Teorema, Pier Paolo Pasolini, 1968, 98 mins.
There's Something About Mary, Bobby and Peter Farrelly, 1998, 119 mins.
The Tree of Life, Terrence Malick, 2011, 139 mins.
Tosh.0, Daniel Tosh, Comedy Central, 2009–2020.
Trouble Every Day, Claire Denis, 2001, 101 mins.
"Trouble of the World," Mahalia Jackson, 1959, 3 mins.
"Unmade," Thom Yorke, track 13 on Thom Yorke, *Suspiria: Music for the Luca Guadagnino Film*. XL Recordings, 2018.
"You Are My Baby Miss," track 7 in *The Handmaiden (Original Motion Picture Soundtrack)*. CJ E&M Music, 2016.
Youth, Paolo Sorrentino, 2015, 124 mins.
"The Yung and the Restless," *Mike Tyson Mysteries*, Season 4, Episode 9, July 28, 2019, 11 mins.
"Watashi no ichiban etchi na yoru," Motomi Kado, manga, *Fizz* (February 1999): 107–50.
The Wayward Cloud, Ming-liang Tsai, 2005, 112 mins.
Wetlands, David Wnendt, 2013, 109 mins.
"What if men harassed women IRL like they do online?" Miranda King, produced by Bye Felipe, YouTube video, June 7, 2016, 3 mins. https://www.youtube.com/watch?v=y-pNFCcIxow.

Index

2 Girls 1 Cup, 28
25th Hour (Lee), 17, 26, 31, 42, 76, 77–8, 83–6, 88, 99, 177, 185n34, 214, 236, 240, 257n14

abjection (abject), 17, 24, 31, 36n74, 65, 80–7, 99
Adorno, Theodor, 41–2, 53n10
Ahmed, Sara, 3, 32n4
Amer (Cattet and Forzani), 58, 66, 67
Antichrist (von Trier), 67
Aphex Twin: Come to Daddy (Cunningham), 89, 101n27
Aphex Twin: Windowlicker (Cunningham), 89–91
Argento, Dario, 30, 58–63, 69, 72n1
Aristotle, 189, 203n1
ASMR, 186n39

Bach, Johann Sebastian, 49
Bacon, Francis, 13, 64, 65, 92–3, 95, 97, 127n37
Bae, Keungyoon, 165, 183n8
Bakhtin, Mikhail, 13, 18, 30, 32, 193, 196–200, 204n32, 218, 223–5, 232n43, 233n64, 242–4, 253–4
Balsom, Erika, 64, 94
Barthes, Roland, 144, 159n69, 177
Bataille, Georges, 211
Baudelaire, Charles, 202, 204n38
Bay, Michael, 64
BDSM, 136, 155n30
Be A Lady They Said (McLean), 101n19
Beals-Hecht syndrome, 32, 222, 225
Belladonna of Sadness (Yamamoto), 67
Belodubrovskaya, Maria, vii, 9, 33n23
Berberian Sound Studio (Strickland), 58, 98
Bergson, Henri, 195, 207, 211, 221

Berwick, Ricky, 32, 218, 222–9, 233n54, 233n55
Beugnet, Martine, viii, 15–18, 65, 74n22, 98, 102n57, 227
Big Mouth (Netflix series), 211
Björk, 31, 76–7, 88–100, 101n29, 124, 167
Björk: All Is Full of Love (Cunningham), 31, 76–7, 88–100, 101n29, 124, 167
Black Sun: Depression and Melancholia (Kristeva), 54n18
Blanchard, Terence, 78, 87, 88
blur (blurriness), 16, 64–6, 71, 93, 98, 142
body without organs (Deleuze), 12, 66, 98, 121, 242
Bordwell, David, 19–20, 22, 35n62, 150, 159n64
Brinkema, Eugenie, 23–5, 36n74, 47, 145–6, 184n14, 251
Buck-Morss, Susan, 53n5
Burgin, Victor, 114, 126n26

Carnal Resonance (Paasonen), 6, 33n9, 34n35, 54n31, 126n17, 154n18, 159n69, 257n10, 257n15
Carnivalesque, 32, 193, 197–203, 205–6, 208, 217–19, 222–9, 232n43, 233n55, 244
Carroll, Noël, 12, 20, 34, 35n60
Carvalho, Joana, 116, 127n34
Cattet, Hélène, 58, 66
Céline, Louis-Ferdinand, 77, 80–6, 99, 100n13, 240
Champion, Jared N., 221, 232n48, 233n50
Chikan, 31, 97, 119, 124, 130, 136, 137–50, 156n36, 157n49, 158n50, 168, 180, 202, 233n50, 239
Choe, Steve, 183n9
cine-fist, vii, 9

Index **281**

cinema of attractions, 9
Coulthard, Lisa, 103n58, 253, 259n33
Creed, Barbara, 24, 25, 186n41, 197
cringe comedy, 32, 205–18, 229, 245
Critique of Judgment (Kant) 39–41, 74n33, 236
Cruz, Ariane, 136–7, 155n30, 155n31
Cunningham, Chris, 31, 76–7, 88–100, 101n28, 101n29, 102n37, 102n39, 124, 167
cycle of life, 199, 200, 204n32, 224, 228, 244

Daskalopoulou, Athanasia, 133–4, 152, 155n19, 155n20
Davis, Murray, 158n52, 211–13, 231n28, 231n32
De Quincey, Thomas, 60–3, 68–70
Deleuze, Gilles, viii, 242, 4, 12–14, 35n43, 43, 64–6, 91–2, 95, 127n37, 242
Dennis, Kelly, 134, 144
dick pics, 32, 205–18, 229, 231n33, 231n37, 244
disgust, 2, 5, 17, 24, 25, 28, 30, 32, 36n74, 47, 67, 119, 151, 155n29, 177, 191–2, 197–8, 201, 213–15, 218, 224, 227, 229, 235, 242–4, 247, 253–5, 259n33
Doyle, Christopher, 11
Dracula (Bram Stoker), 246
Duncan, Pansy, 207
Dyer, Richard, 132, 257n15

Eisenstein, Sergei, 9, 33n23
embodied simulation, 17, 20–2, 36n67, 117–23, 136, 147, 149, 151–2, 159n62, 175, 178–9, 241–2
emotion, 19–22, 31, 33n23, 34n35, 42–4, 54n19, 61–2, 64, 66, 72, 77, 80, 82, 86–7, 99, 114–15, 117–22, 132, 146–7, 149–50, 152–3, 160–1, 167, 175, 179–82, 186n37, 186n40, 190, 192, 198, 206, 208, 212, 217, 242, 248, 250, 255
Euphoria (HBO series), 208–11, 229
Extreme Cinema (Kerner and Knapp), 16, 25–8, 99
Extreme Cinema, 98–9, 102n57

Family Guy, 206
Fenech, Edwige, 57
fetish (fetishism), 5, 21, 24, 26–7, 30–1, 96–7, 100, 111, 112–17, 122–5, 136, 141, 146, 147–53, 167–82, 185n28, 185n36, 238–41, 244

Fetveit, Arild, 94
Figure/figure (Deleuze), 13–14, 64–6, 92, 127n37, 242
filone, 72n1
Fingersmith (Waters), 161–2, 184n17
Forzani, Bruno 58, 66
Foucault, Michel, 41, 153n2
Freud, Sigmund, 23, 113, 192–3, 197, 203n11
Friday the 13th (Sean Cunningham), 62, 73n18

Gallese, Vittorio viii, 18–22, 31, 117–22, 127n38, 127n43, 128n46, 130, 147–51, 241–2
Galt, Rosalind 7, 27, 110, 115, 125n16, 126n22, 256
giallo (neo-giallo) 30, 52, 57–9, 61–2, 66, 72n1, 73n3, 73n6
Glass, Philips 45, 47, 51, 72, 255
Goblin, 60–2
Goldstein, Avram, 19
goosebumps, x, 2–5, 18, 22, 24, 34, 52, 72, 76, 99, 182, 186n39, 236–7, 244, 247, 253–5
grotesque realism, 13, 30, 32, 198, 243, 253
Guadagnino, Luca, 17, 30, 51, 57–60, 62–3, 65, 67, 69–70, 72n1, 88, 237–8
Guattari, Félix, viii, 4, 12–14, 95
Guerra, Michele, 18–21, 118–20, 122, 128n46, 150, 151

Hallam, Lindsay, 57–8, 66–7, 72n1
Hanich, Julian, viii, 11, 118, 153n2, 190–2, 204n39, 214–15, 243
Haptic, 120
Hard Core (Williams), 134, 174, 33n9
Harman, Graham, 19, 53n16, 107–9, 111, 115, 122, 125n5, 175, 221
Hobbes, Thomas, 195–6
Hogarth, William, 68–9

Imitation of Life (Sirk), 43, 49, 52, 217
Irigaray, Luce, 169, 184n18

Jackass (franchise), 191, 205
Jackson, Mahalia, 43–4, 52, 95, 217

Kannas, Alexia, vii–viii, 72n1
Kant, Immanuel, x, 30, 39–51, 53n7, 68, 70, 74n33, 78, 107, 109–10, 116, 123, 193–4, 202, 235–6, 238, 254
Kierkegaard, Søren, 194

King, Martin Luther, Jr., 44
Kipnis, Laura, 240
Kish, Daniel, 21, 35n64
Klown (film; Danish TV series), 215, 217, 231n38
Kracauer, Siegfried, 10
Kristeva, Julia, 17, 24–5, 35n51, 36n74, 44, 48, 54n18, 77, 80–3, 85–7, 99, 135, 197, 242

laughter, 2–4,11, 26, 28, 30–2, 78, 121, 146, 189–203, 203n6, 204n39, 205–8, 211, 214, 216–22, 227–9, 229n3, 235, 240, 242–7, 253, 256
Lee, Spike, 17, 26, 31, 42, 77–8, 80, 85–6, 88, 99, 214, 236, 240
lekton (lektonic), ix, 43, 52, 59, 61–2, 65, 70, 72, 87, 91, 99, 135–6, 175, 180, 237, 255
lesbian romance (film), 161, 167, 182
Levinson, Sam, 83, 208–9, 230n11
Leys, Ruth, 26
Lockwood, Dean, 92–4, 96

Madonna: Frozen (Cunningham), 89–91
Malick, Terrence, 39
Marks, Laura U., 11, 17, 34n31, 66, 118
Massumi, Brian, 2–4
Menninghaus, Winfried, 191–2
Merleau-Ponty, Maurice, 7, 54n16
Middleton, Jason, 207, 229
Miller, Laura, 167–8, 170, 175, 184n17, 184n23
mirror neurons, vii, 9, 19–20, 31, 117–21, 123–4, 128n46, 128n54, 147, 149, 179, 241
Mr. Hankey, 199–200, 244
Mulvey, Laura, 112, 114, 126n22, 163, 239, 255–6
Münsterberg, Hugo, 10

Naked Director (Netflix series), 138
Nancy, Jean-Luc, 27
"New French Extremity," 16, 98–9
Nichols, Bill, 148
Nicolodi, Daria, 60, 73n11

"Open Again" (Yorke), 66, 69–72

Paasonen, Susanna, viii, 6, 14–15, 31, 33n9, 34n35, 34n37, 48, 110–13, 115, 126n17, 130–2, 134, 137, 142, 151, 154n5, 155n25, 155n29, 155n31, 156n32, 157n47, 159n69, 159n72, 169, 208, 215, 217, 232n37, 235, 239–40, 251, 256, 257n10, 257n15
Park, Chan-wook, 31, 96, 119, 124, 152, 160–2, 164–8, 170–3, 178, 181, 183n4, 186n43, 207, 214, 236–7, 240–1, 244–6, 248, 253, 255
Plantinga, Carl, 6–7, 12
Pollock, Griselda, 172
Pornhub, 6, 136–7, 140–1, 146, 157
pornography (porn), vii, 1, 5–6, 26, 32, 33n9, 96, 100, 110–11, 117, 119–24, 130–59, 161, 167–9, 171, 179, 183n9, 184n23, 202, 212, 216, 228–9, 235, 239–42, 251, 256, 256n3, 258n27
potlatch 210–11
Powers of Horror (Kristeva), 36n74, 77, 80, 99, 100n5, 100n6, 100n12
prehension, 2, 8, 12, 22, 47–8, 54n31, 115, 119, 151, 227
Provine, Robert R., 189–90

reality effect, 144
Revolution in Poetic Language (Kristeva), 17
Rhee, Suk Koo, 62, 164–5, 167
Rubber Johnny (Cunningham), 89–90, 92–3

Sade, Donatien Alphonse François Marquis de, 125, 160, 163–7, 175–7, 182, 183n11
"Saint Matthew Passion" (Bach), 49
Scott, Sophie, 190, 219–20
Shamoon, Deborah, 139
Sharpton, Al, Rev., 44
Shaviro, Steven, 6, 8, 14–15, 29, 33n20, 39–41, 48–9, 52, 78, 89–91, 102n39, 107–9, 131
Shimizu, Celine Parreñas, viii, 6, 154, 169, 182, 184n12
Shouse, Eric, 4, 76
Simone, Nina, 54n19
Sobchack, Vivian, 6, 11, 34n32, 41, 62, 118, 120, 128n49, 227
South Park, 199
Spencer, Herbert, 193
Stacey, Jackie, 160–1, 182
Stoker (Park), 119, 207, 236–7, 244–6, 248, 251 5, 250n26
Suspiria (Argento), 30, 58–60, 62–3, 69, 72n1, 73n11, 74n19

Suspiria (Guadagnino), vii, 30, 51, 57–72, 74n32, 88, 237–8, 255
Suspiria de Profundis (De Quincey), 60–3, 68–70, 74n33
"Suspirium" (Yorke), 66, 69–70
Swinton, Tilda, 30, 59, 63
Synaesthesia, 11

Taormino, Tristan, 1, 131, 140
The Colbert Report, 36n79
The Handmaiden (Park), 31, 96, 124–5, 152–3, 160–82, 183n8, 185n28, 240–1, 246
The Hunger (Scott), 169–73
"The Inevitable Pull" (Yorke), 66
The Tree of Life (Malick), 39, 49, 52
Tosh.0, 26, 32, 191, 218–29, 232n46

"Trouble of the World" (Yorke), 43, 217
Turvey, Malcolm, vii, 19–22

von Trier, Lars 67

Waters, Sarah, 161–2, 1833n4, 183n9, 184n17
Whitehead, Alfred North, 8, 14, 41, 48, 53n7, 115, 227, 236, 239
Williams, Linda, 6, 21, 31, 33n9, 120–2, 128n54, 132, 134, 144, 149–50, 153n2, 154n12, 159n62, 174, 229, 257n15
Wojciehowski, Hannah, 118, 121, 127n38, 127n43

Yorke, Thom, vii, 30, 51, 60, 65–6, 68–72, 88, 95, 237–8, 255